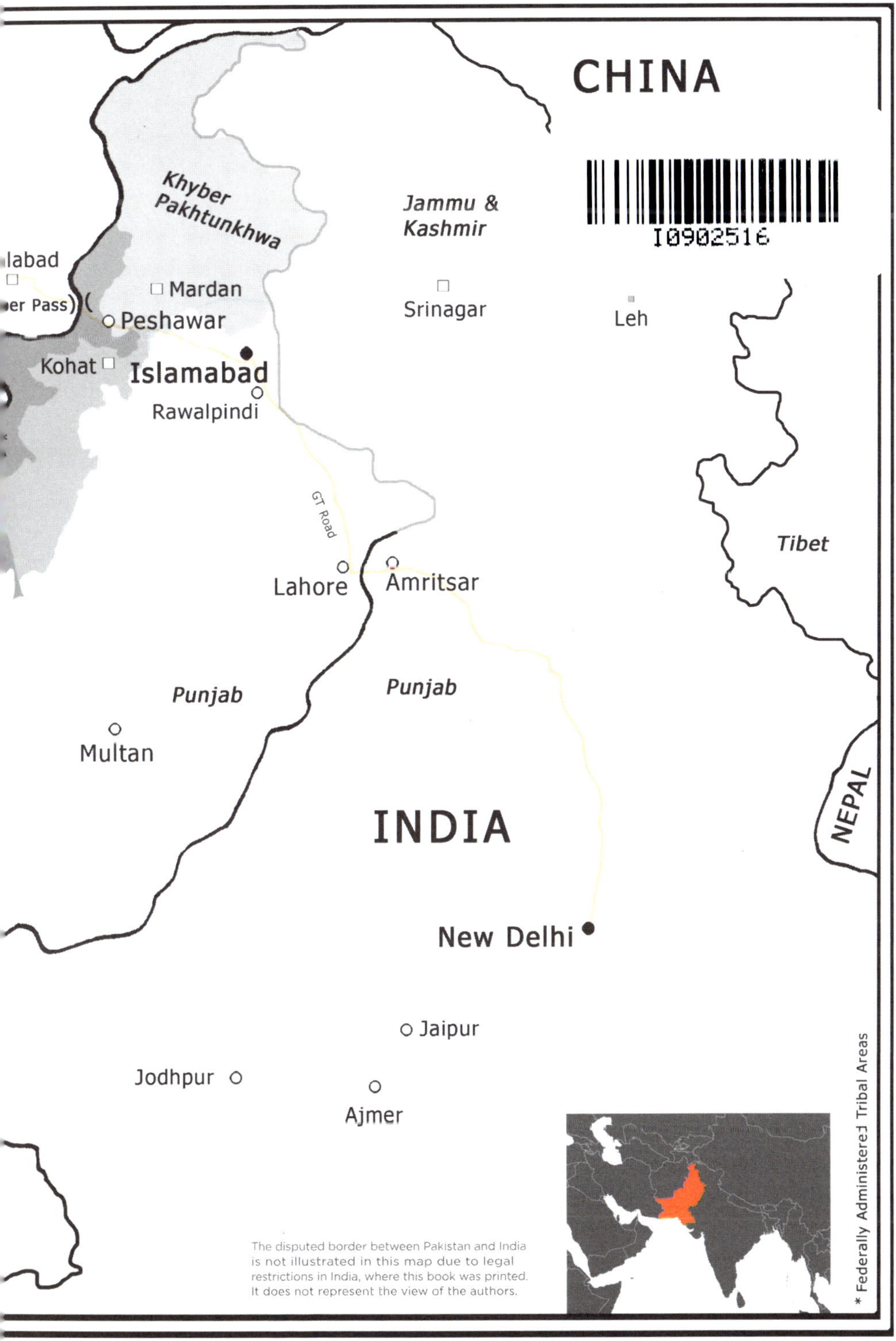
CHINA
Khyber Pakhtunkhwa
Jammu & Kashmir
Mardan
Peshawar
Srinagar
Leh
Kohat
Islamabad
Rawalpindi
GT Road
Tibet
Lahore
Amritsar
Punjab
Punjab
Multan
INDIA
NEPAL
New Delhi
Jaipur
Jodhpur
Ajmer
The disputed border between Pakistan and India is not illustrated in this map due to legal restrictions in India, where this book was printed. It does not represent the view of the authors.
* Federally Administered Tribal Areas

پشاور کے فوٹوگرافر

PHOTO PESHAWAR

To our teachers,
Zindagi rahi to phir milenge, Inshallah
If life gives the chance, we'll meet again, Inshallah

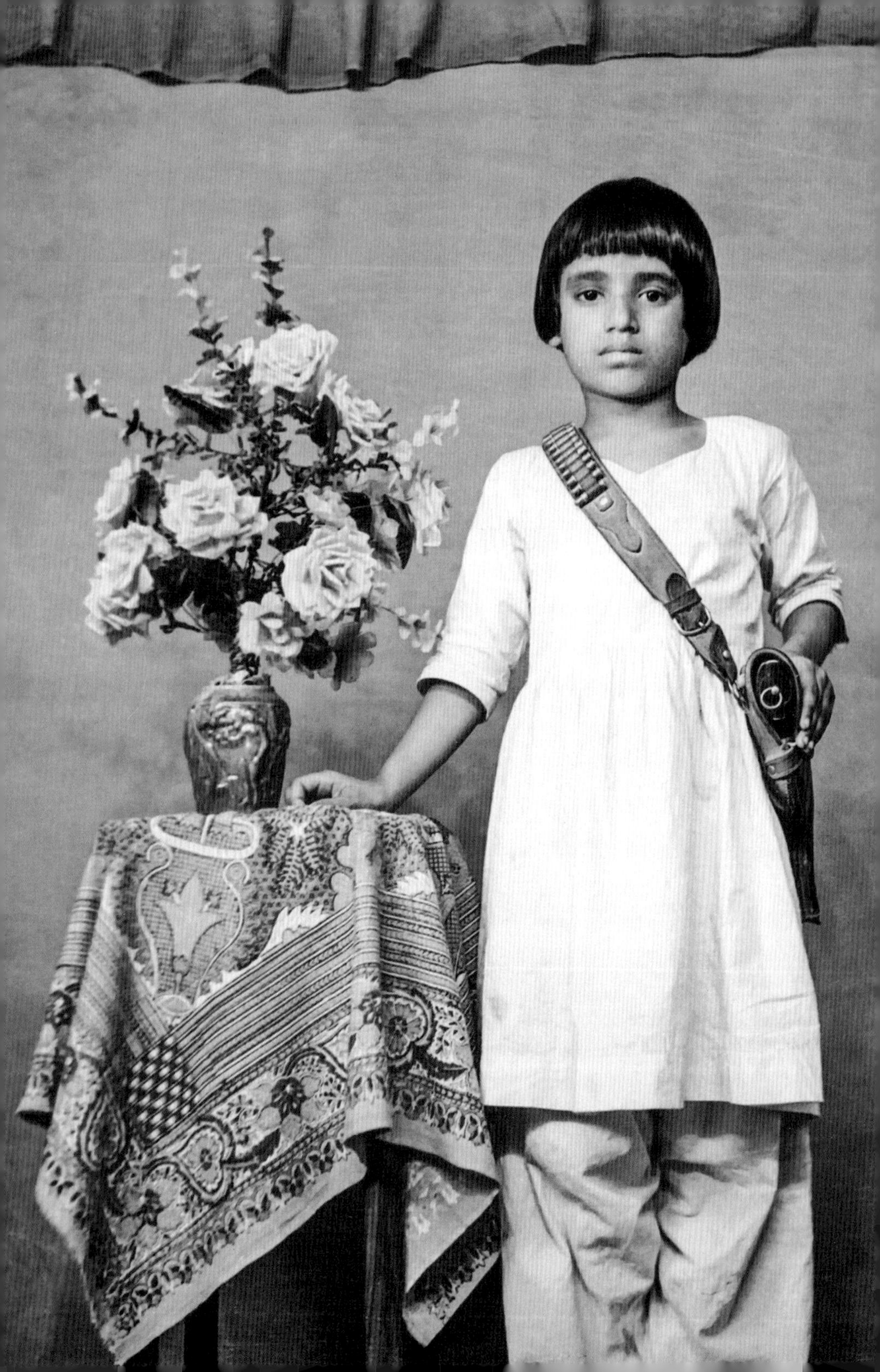

پشاور کے فوٹو گرافر

PHOTO PESHAWAR

SEAN FOLEY / LUKAS BIRK

Foreword by OMAR KHAN

MAPIN Publishing | PIX PUBLISHING

foreword

Photography as *craft* is what this splendid volume examines – photography at the living, bleeding intersection of culture, war, frontier and fantasy, the sheer human inventiveness that results from a magnificent and tragic brew of technology and history. Sean Foley and Lukas Birk look directly at the practising photographers, the various kinds of *craftsmen* that have sprung up to define self-representation for generations of Peshawaris. Passion, persistence, good luck and the ability to bond and understand their human subjects are what give this incisive book its heft. The fine details distinguishing studios on Saddar Road from those on Cinema Road, the curation of great photographs that uplift a people's history stretching back seventy years make every page-turn a pleasure. I was particularly taken with the *minute cameramen*, or manual Polaroid-*wallah*s (if I may call them that) roaming the bazaars, manipulating chemicals in wooden box cameras through old jacket sleeves as images condense in the stopgap darkness. Rarely has photography seemed so vibrant and consequential.

As has been pointed out many times, the camera and gun arrived hand-in-hand on the 'Frontier' – the border area between British India and Afghanistan – in the 19th century. Both were taken up with relish by locals, who built their own rifle and camera-making shops, the latter despite the supposed Islamic edict against human depiction. This taboo has been re-affirmed by the Taliban and other religious conservatives today; but even then it has not stamped out the 'scourge' of photography – so powerful is the desire among most of the population to see their reflection. I'm not so sure it is only religious feelings that drive some to disapprove of photography; its very potency is also unsettling. My grandmother, a Kakazai who came by way of Jalalabad village in Hoshiarpur district to Lahore in 1947, believed that taking a photograph risked snatching away your soul.

And can photography not itself be a religious undertaking? “A man can only meet God through work in which he has lost himself,” says master photographer Tahir Usman, an artist and probable Sufi whose self-portraits are the most remarkable in this book.

Christopher Pinney’s *Camera Indica* (1997) was the first in-depth exploration of living photography in the subcontinent. *Photo Peshawar* is a worthy sequel, a concise ethnography of photographers. It reveals in part how the ancient *ustaad/talib*, or teacher/student tradition, fit like a glove to absorb refugees and technologies to create distinct representational practices and forms. The minute camera mechanics are different in Afghanistan and Peshawar, suggesting that a single inventor or craftsman could influence generations of practitioners. The ability to adapt to an ever-changing political landscape is also remarkable. After the 1979 invasion of Afghanistan, men were literally posing like Rambo to fight the Russians; today, they are more likely to be fighting erstwhile allies who fire at them from invisible drones high up in the sky. Yes, there are many guns and defenders and vanquishers here, but it is heartening to see that images of great Pathan pacifists like Bacha Khan are also still current.

Foley and Birk’s selections emphasise the self-reflective sophistication of the photographers and their customers. Indeed, photography and identity are latched together in Peshawar. This is a book worth lingering over, in order to absorb the way trends in iconography have been taken up and uniquely adapted in a dusty border town buffeted by decisions made thousands of miles away. Somewhere between Hollywood and Bollywood, Peshawar grew from a hundred thousand to two million souls in two decades. The pictures that fell by the wayside, or were hoisted on placards, or made it into people’s drawing rooms and into lockets, were made by gifted and committed artisans. They show themselves able to balance a constellation of forces to their customers’ delight. Photographers – the true *filmi* heroes of *Photo Peshawar*.

Omar Khan
January 2018

Page 2: Large format portrait, Jamalistan Studio, c.1960s.

authors' foreword

PHOTO PESHAWAR explores the culture of photography in the Pakistani frontier city of Peshawar from the late 1940s to the present day. Our own relationship to the city goes back to 2005 when we interviewed foreign tourists there, en route from Afghanistan via the tribal areas and Khyber Pass. Afghanistan was, the tourists confided, a troubled and magical land: a place that will change your life – and the light! they always mentioned, had this special quality.

So we decided we had to go.

Unsure, however, of where to find more tourists to 'study' on the follow-up trip in Afghanistan, we meandered at will and stumbled across all types of photographic wonders: studios still using large format film cameras, hand-colourists of black-and -white portraits, and – imagine! – paper-negative box cameras on the streets, so we happily digressed from our original purpose. And although we had separately been travelling to the region since the early nineties, this particular episode of the heart was our first – however tangential and cursory – dip of the toes into its photographic culture, and so planted the seed for our return to Afghanistan in 2011 for the *Afghan Box Camera Project*. Researching the culture of Afghan photography led us back over the Khyber Pass to Peshawar as we traced the stories of the Afghan photographers who fled there as refugees during the war years, and back in the sweltering summer heat of Peshawar in 2012, again in 2013, and in the cooler winter months of 2014, what we found inside those photographic studios, in between stories and images and samovars of sweet green tea, was the inspiration for this book.

Sean Foley & Lukas Birk
March 2018

Opposite: Numerical shorthand, 786, for the Islamic blessing *Bismillah ir-rahmani ir-rahim*, found hanging in many Peshawari photo studios, as well as being written in customer account books. It means, 'By the will of Allah, the most merciful and gracious' and is a common Muslim invocation to bless endeavours.

۷۸۶

introduction

Photography in Peshawar has historically and culturally found itself wedged between the multi-denominational Indian subcontinent and predominantly Muslim Afghanistan; and artistically it is caught between the creative and conservative forces of both. The result is a rich and largely unexplored photographic tradition, variously borne of British rule, the Partition of India, war in neighbouring Afghanistan, the rise of the Taliban, local tribal law, a historical prohibition on image-making in Islam, the practice of *purdah* (the veiling of females in public), and the regional movie industry: a historically infused mixture in which there is a tangible stress between the practice of photography as it is pursued and the culture in which it is lived.

The particular focus of this book is on photographers who work in two areas of Peshawar:[1] Saddar Road, the relatively genteel and elite new city area, and Cinema Road, representing a more *chowk*-like energetic old city culture. There are also references to smaller enclaves which house studios such as those around Randaz Bazaar, close to the 'ladies' market' – which, as the name implies, sells women's cosmetics, jewellery and fabrics – and Sikandar Pura (meaning, 'the town of Alexander', as in 'the Great' who passed through in 327 B.C.). Smaller establishments on the edge of the old city, including those in Kohat, a garrison town south of Peshawar, also make their way into the narrative of this book. Between them, the photographers who work in these studios hold decades of experience, where expertise with both camera and paintbrush can overlap to stunning visual effect.

The primary service provided by Peshawari studios, on the whole, is portrait photography, in both official as well as personal and familial spheres, though on

Cinema Road photomontages are the forte (a factor contingent on its location). Other popular image-making areas include function photography – wedding photography, and the videography that often accompanies it, is particularly lucrative in all areas of the city. Newspaper photographers are also at large, capturing spontaneous newsworthy moments, as well as the set pose. More scarce, however, are the itinerant 'taxi' photographers, studio-less 'travelling' photographers who traverse the highways and byways of the tribal areas bordering Afghanistan, and pass through the old city to develop their customers' photographs. While this photographic landscape is overwhelmingly male dominated, in recent years, female or 'lady' photographers have increasingly appeared. Working away from male-run studios, they often operate inside female-only beauty parlours – another form of purdah, or veiling, which secures their identity, as well as those of their female customers. Arguably, women are the most marginalised of all photographers in Peshawar.

Peshawar

A one-time trading post along the Silk Route, known in later centuries by the byname, *City of Flowers*, Peshawar clings to the autonomous tribal north-west of Pakistan directly bordering Afghanistan, and is the provincial capital of Khyber Pakhtunkhwa, previously the North-West Frontier Province. A large portion of western Pakistan, sweeping across the colonially-imposed Durand Line into Afghanistan, including Khyber Pakhtunkhwa, is dominated by the Pashtun tribal group, making this one of the largest tribal territories on earth; and shared cultural and familial ties stretching across the border make the international boundary in many ways irrelevant. Following the Soviet invasion of Afghanistan in 1979, and the civil war that followed, Peshawar became home to hundreds of thousands of Afghan refugees, and it was the main Afghan resistance (or *Mujahedin*) base. Transforming into a den of international intrigue, 1980s Peshawar was home to a melange of foreign spies, journalists and aid-workers – Noor Muhammad Khan, a resident American writer and musician, even called it the 'Casablanca of Pakistan'.[7] Nowadays, although most of the Afghan refugees have been repatriated, the city still has a strong Afghan feel to it; and there is constant photographic traffic between Peshawar and its neighbour through the porous border.[٣]

The tightly snaking road that leads over the Khyber Pass into eastern Afghanistan and on to the Afghan capital passes through the fiercely independent tribal areas (FATA: Federally Administered Tribal Areas). From around 2005, conflict over the autonomy of the tribal areas reached a point of open warfare, in large part due to the territory being a Taliban stronghold, for which it has become the ongoing target of both highly controversial and locally resented US drone attacks, as well as incursive Pakistani military operations.[٤]

While Peshawar is not situated within the bounds of these tribal areas, it does directly border them, and as the provincial capital has suffered frequent and at times drastic levels of extremist violence, including suicide attacks on universities and schools. The photographers of Cinema Road, one of the key areas explored in this book, have witnessed their fair share of violence with a number of cinemas in and around the area being bombed by religious extremists who accuse the cinema proprietors of spreading 'anti-Islamic' values. Photo studios, however, have not been targeted so far.

Photography in Peshawar, late 1870s to 1947

Professional studio photography was firmly established in Peshawar during British rule, particularly in the latter half of the 19th century, at a time when the medium flourished throughout the Indian subcontinent.[٥] It was also a time when the city was located at the frontier of the British Empire, and thus served as a gateway for the British army marching over the Khyber Pass to wage war in Afghanistan. During the Second Anglo–Afghan War (1878–1880) photographers such as Irishman John Burke (c.1843–1900) travelled with British military forces to photograph, and subsequently sell catalogues of the photographs they took of the conflict.[٦] Interestingly, Burke's photographs – or, at least, downloaded copies freely available from the internet – can also be found displayed in some of the vitrines of Peshawar's existing studios. Similarly, alert searching can turn up images taken by Mela Ram & Sons, K.C. Mehra & Sons and Randolph Bezzant Holmes – all well-known practitioners with namesake studios that were based in the city, which together span an era from the late 19th century up to Partition in 1947.

Upmarket studios, like the aforementioned, tended to be located within and around the military cantonment – as with the present-day studios on Saddar Road – and were mostly owned by British, but also reportedly, native Hindu, Sikh and Christian photographers. However, local Muslim-owned photo studios such as Electric Company on Hospital Road, founded in 1937 by Muhammad Sharif Janbaz (1912–1985; p.75), as well as Umar Khan's Studio on Arbab Road could also be found. Catalogues from Umar Khan's backlist, comprising turn-of-the 20th century tribal skirmishes were still being sold in Peshawar in the 1980s[v] – a century after John Burke was, in his own way, photographically chronicling the politics of the area and profiting from it.

The culture of photography in Peshawar – the making and dissemination of images relating to the region and its people for both commercial and non-commercial purposes – remained quite a stable world until 1947. With the Partition of India in that year, however, it would undergo tumultuous change.

The 1947 Partition of India resulted in the birth of the Islamic Republic of Pakistan and its arch (now nuclear) rival, the Republic of India: it provoked one of the greatest migrations of humanity in modern history and resulted in an appalling series of massacres, whose epicentre was in the state of Punjab where communal violence prevailed on an unprecedented scale and, en masse, Sikhs and Hindus murdered Muslims; and Muslims murdered Sikhs and Hindus. It is estimated that up to two million people were killed in the violence and fifteen million uprooted – though the numbers vary wildly. What is certain is that within only a few months of Partition, a new face of photography came into being in Peshawar as an effective photographic partition resonated a broader demographic shift – with mostly Hindu, non-Muslim and non-native photographers leaving the city for India and elsewhere, and a new wave of mostly Muslim photographers and photographers-to-be, running from the gamut of violence in Punjab, arriving from India, and taking up the photographic mantle. Anxious for their, and their families' future in Peshawar, established photographers in the city such as Mela Ram & Sons left for India in the wake of this tragic turn of events, while R.B. Holmes emigrated to New Zealand.

The newly arrived refugee-photographers would train the next generation of photo-takers in Peshawar, shaping the professional landscape of the medium in the city for decades to come; and this history still resonates most keenly, in living memory, in the photo studios of Saddar Road.

Saddar Road & older studios

Neighbouring the military cantonment, photo studios in Saddar Road's comparatively elite surroundings serve a variably middle and upper class clientele; the measure of status often being conditioned by those who pass through the studio's doors – from political and military leaders to the wealthy and influential – with portraits of them adorning the studio walls in order to claim patronage, respect, class and taste.

Historically, too, the area abounds in established photographic pedigree. Pre-Partition practitioners and studios of note, mentioned previously, such as R.B. Holmes and Mela Ram & Sons, were located in the immediate area, as were post-Partition studios of distinction including the Royal, the National, SM Shah's and Wahab Studio on Mall Road. Today, only the Wahab Studio remains open. Further afield, though inside the city, older photo studios that still function include Malik Sons in Sikandar Pura and Gul Sons near Nishtar Abad Chowk, which were both founded in the mid-1960s; as well as Jamalistan Studio on Hospital Road, which was opened at the end of the 1950s by Jamil Ahmad (p.69). The Khyber Photo Studio, in the old town, and in the university area, the Imperial Photo Studio, both of which are now closed, were also part of the same post-Partition stock. And then there is Zaidi's Studio on Arbab Road (which is adjacent to Saddar Road).

Founded shortly after Partition, Zaidi's is one of the most prestigious 'old school' photo studios in Peshawar, whose trainees have risen to become some of its most senior photographers, namely Abdul Rashid (p.71), Haidar Zaidi (p.71) and Muhammad Iqbal (p.71). Ashraf Ali Zaidi (1932–1983; p.61), the studio's founder, was amongst the migrants from India in 1947, opening the studio shortly after becoming a resident. By the early 1960s, Zaidi had established himself as a 'VIP' photographer, and client records titled 'VVIP' (Very Very Important Person) from 1963 include Chief Justices, Home Secretaries, Army Chiefs, First Secretaries, and a Regional Governor – a position of distinction the studio, now run by son-in-law, Abdul 'Gul' Rab, still holds.

Another notable long-time establishment located on Saddar Road is Azeem's, founded in 1949 by Abdul Rashaq (d.2004; p.71). In 1952, following the accidental death by drowning of his son, Azeem, he handed over the studio to his student, Muhammad Mustafa, and it is still run by descendants of the latter. A number of senior photographers, including those mentioned above, who apprenticed with Zaidi also earned spurs at Azeem's, and, like Zaidi, Abdul Rashaq was known to have been a severe task-master.

In the midst of a visibly proactive studio culture, what also distinguishes Saddar Road, based on his sheer personality and artistic merit – is the presence of Uncle Tony (p.194–195), a photographer, who operates very much outside the norms of the usual Peshawari studio network. In fact, in over half a century in the business, he hasn't taken on a single apprentice.

Uncle Tony a.k.a. Fakhar Azam Azer (b.1939) moved to Peshawar with his family from India during Partition in 1947. Initially, picking up the ropes of photography from his hobbyist father, and then on the job as a freelance magazine photographer in the city, in 1960 he earned a diploma in photography from Budapest. Since the 1950s, motivated by his love for travel, Uncle Tony has been circuiting the globe, taking photographs and working in countries ranging from Saudi Arabia (where he used his first Kodak Brownie), to Moscow, Hawaii, Wales (where his brother lives), as well as across the border in India. In this time, he has photographed some notable personalities: a young Colonel Gaddafi, Princess Diana on an official visit to Pakistan, the Duke of Edinburgh, and American archivist of Afghan culture and former Peshawar-resident Nancy Dupree (1927–2017; p.200).^ Photographic inspiration and guidance, throughout his life, he says, has come from his travels and his mentors such as the Indian actor Sajan Jee (1921–2000), as well as master Indian photographer, O.P. Sharma (b.1939) who worked in collaboration with Sajan Jee, as well as a Peshawari local historian and retired police officer, named Aftab Ahmad.

Cinema Road

Gun-toting heroes, villains deliriously drunk on whiskey, 'loosely' attired dancing girls, and (fake) blood: this is the quintessential photographic imagery produced by the photo studios of Cinema Road (p.110–111), who are (in)famous for churning out risqué movie montages of young male customers posing with, embracing, and cuddling up to actresses and female singers in images derived from the Pashtun and regional film industry. Located only a few kilometres from the new city inside the more conservative old walled one (businesses here tend to close on Friday, the Islamic day of prayer; on Saddar Road they close on Sunday), studios on Cinema Road have historically been positioned to cater to the inner city cinema-goers; and in contrast to Saddar Road, customers come here for fun.

On Cinema Road selling photo-montages is the main preoccupation, and rows of small tightly packed studios line both sides of the thoroughfare enthusiastically touting their visual wares out front. The interiors are often choc-a-bloc with even more garish and melodramatic images that lure male customers inside the studios with the promise of emulating their favourite Pashtun movie stars. Customers pose with 'whiskey' bottles in hand (p.83) – the 'whiskey' is tea or diluted cola – or cozy up to a seductive starlet; or brandish a pistol; or combine all for effect. Sometimes the guns are real – Peshawar is awash with them – but the women who are cuddling up to customers are, given the cultural issues surrounding the visual representation of conjugality, usually images of female models sourced from the internet.

Undoubtedly the most popular male Pashtun movie star, whose image is sought-after for montages, is Jahangir Khan (p.113), even more so than the godfather of Pashtun cinema, Badar Munir (1940–2008), after whom Cinema Road was renamed in 2011.[٩] And while some of the older photographers, with a nostalgic soft-spot for the female entertainers of their youth, display portraits of erstwhile performers such as Deeba, Noor Jahan, and Musarrat Shaheen (p.88–89), it is from montaging images of contemporary female stars such as Gul Panra, Nadia Gul and Ghazala Javed (the latter killed in a drive-by shooting in Peshawar in 2012)[١٠] that they make their money. These days, the Pashtun entertainment industry predominates in local cinemas, though formerly Indian films were popular and occasionally Hollywood ones too. The U.S. movie *Rambo III* (1988), in which a lone American hero battles the might of the Soviet Union in Afghanistan, with a little help from the Mujahedin, was, in particular, popular with the resident Afghan refugee population on release, as were the movie montages Cinema Road studios produced based on the movie (p.102–105).

The Pashtu-language cinema industry of post-millenium Peshawar, however, is in trouble[١١] – due, in part, to the rise of home and personal viewing on CDs, DVDs and the internet. Of the three cinemas that Cinema Road was previously home to – the Novelty, Tasveer Mahal and Picture House – only the Picture House remains open. Another reason for the decline in the industry is the perceived vulgarity and immorality of contemporary Pasthun films (in comparison to the family-orientated glory days of the 1970s).[١٢] In recent years, cinemas in Peshawar have actually come under attack by religious extremists who denounce the industry, and by association its patrons, labelling them un-Islamic.[١٣] As a consequence, bomb threats against cinemas in the city are common, and deadly attacks do occur. In 2009 an explosion outside the Tasveer Mahal cinema on Cinema Road, reportedly killed ten bystanders and injured dozens;[١٤] in 2012 a blast outside the Picture House down the street from the Tasveer Mahal injured eight[١٥]; and in 2014, just days before we began one of our own periods of research, a grenade attack inside the Picture House left between four people dead and, once again, dozens of innocent people injured.[16] Eleven days later in the Bacha Khan Chowk area of the city, three explosions in the Shama cinema killed thirteen.[17] Naturally, with such violence at their doorstep, life changes for the photographers: their nerves suffer, some feel ever-conscious of potential threats, they worry about their own safety. Mostly, however, they worry about their families.

Unsurprisingly, customers have been scared off by arbitrary and unsolicited violence, though more so from the cinemas than the road itself. The result has been a boon to CD and DVD shops that sell Pashtu-language and, in general, Pakistani titles, and yet simultaneously a curse, as these shops sell the very movies religious extremists denounce as morally degrading. It's not, however, only the moving image which is targeted, as the same shops sell local music CDs, which are also considered by detractors as un-Islamic, *particularly* those by female singers. Hence, they too have moved into the front-line. Furthermore, rumours that these shops sell adult material under the counter and screen pornography in the backrooms have been enough to incur the ire of extremists, and shops selling DVDs around the area of Nisht Arabad Chowk have come under attack.[18]

The times, likewise, are proving a challenge for Cinema Road photo studios, and the same ailments that trouble cinemas, trouble them:[19] rapidly changing and widely available technologies such as phone-cameras (presently considered the main culprit of image-dissemination), dwindling numbers of cinema-goers (which always fall rapidly after a security alert), and – at least in the eyes of some – association with a commerce of disrepute, because there is no escaping the fact that the photomontages that Cinema Road studios produce and sell – albeit, extremely tame – are considered morally questionable from certain conservative perspectives. Culturally, this seems consistent since the photographers produce photographic versions of the same 'sexualised' themes that come under such voracious attack from Islamic extremists in their moving cinematic dimensions. Cinema Road photographers know this – and while some voice their understanding literally, others do so more obliquely. Daoud (p.138–139), a Cinema Road photographer, originally from Afghanistan, who for years had made his living from selling movie montages, wouldn't even allow himself to be photographed by the authors against a display of his own work, fully aware that physical touch between a man and an 'immodestly' dressed woman, is perceived as unseemly behaviour – even holding her hand – *even* if it is only a photomontage. Instead, Daoud, pulled across a milky blue backdrop inside his studio, and posed in front of that.

Starting out as apprentices

The majority of established Peshawari photographers began their careers as young apprentices, and a shared memory amongst them is, quite literally, starting "on the ground". That is, many photographers began their careers by sweeping the floors of the photo studios they worked in, at times having to do so for years, because long before they were entrusted with a camera, a paint brush (for hand-colouring portraits), or even a sheet of film, apprentices were typically considered house-hold help, charged with washing dishes, shopping for groceries, and serving tea to guests and clients. Only after one or more years, were they slowly introduced to the functioning of a studio, at first observing their teachers at work and by studying their photographs to "get the idea".

Abdul Rashid, who began working in Azeem's on Saddar Road in 1950 when eight years old, took his first practice photos when he was around twelve, and his first commercial photos a few years later. When he started out he couldn't even reach the height of the plate camera in the studio. As he grew up, however, he gradually learnt how to 'finish' a photograph, by retouching negatives, lighting, handling film, developing, and, principally, by clicking legible pictures. This process of photographic education was almost universally the case. Amjad, of Malik Sons in Sikandar Pura, spent close to seven years doing chores for his employer, while at the same time being coached in the dark room techniques of manual printing and developing. On one occasion, he recalls, he was told by his teacher: "This is photo paper, you need to keep it away from light!" Amjad found this new knowledge all rather bewildering. How on earth, he wondered, was he going to cut paper in the dark?

A number of still active senior Peshawari photographers trace their apprenticeship years to Zaidi's on Arbab Road, including Abdul Rashid, Muhammad Iqbal (of Saddar Road) and Haidar Zaidi. These photographers all speak of their time with Zaidi as a formative period, remembering their 'ustad' (meaning, teacher or aficionado in Urdu) as a meticulous and demanding, and, at times, harsh instructor who drilled his pupils in the working craft of the studio, as well as, for him, the sacrosanct rules of business – which were: *always* be on time, and *always* preserve the negatives. Testament to Ustad Zaidi's unwavering edicts are the tens of thousands of hand-filed black-and-white and colour portrait negatives dating back to the early 1960s that still occupy the upper floor of his prestigious studio.

Once apprentices had acquired the necessary skills they moved freely between different studios in the city and beyond, periodically establishing their own spaces. "The lamb leaves the mother," pronounces Abdul Rashid – and so it is expected: a necessary progression to enhance ones' photographic repertoire as different studios would have different specialties. Abdul Rashid, for instance, went on to open the Peshawar Photo Company after Zaidi's, and latterly Jumbo Studio; Muhammad Iqbal opened Naqash Studio, and Haidar Zaidi has the Evernew Studio. In many instances, these studios are father-and-son-run family businesses, such as Malik Sons, Jumbo, Evergreen, Naqash, Famous, Shan Studio and Jamalistan. Zaidi's, however, did briefly veer from the status quo. Now run by Abdul Rab, the son-in-law of the founder, the studio was run by Zaidi's wife for a year after he passed away.

Making studio photographs

For decades the mainstay of Peshawari studios was black-and-white photographs and, as elsewhere, this involved a series of specialised steps, each with its own associated tasks. It began with 'exposing', that is, taking the photograph, which included the intricate arts of lighting and posing and setting backdrops; then, developing the film in a darkroom; after which followed retouching the negative with a sharpened pencil for cosmetic enhancement; this was followed by printing the negative, and so, back into the darkroom; and finally the print would be hand-coloured, if colour was desired (even after the arrival of colour film photography, hand-colouring was in demand, and there are still skilled artisans who offer the service). Lastly the print had to be framed and packed and, as evinced by near-ubiquitous 'NO CREDIT' signs, payment was usually upfront.

An important part of making a studio photograph was retouching the negatives, which involved pencilling over the exposed negative image to increase definition in the positive print, and to eradicate any visible flaws or damage on the negative due to the vagaries of exposure quality. Peshawari photographers recommended using a HB or 2HB pencil, cut first with a knife, and then sharpened. The nib had to be very sharp – and the more delicate the touch of the re-toucher, the more seamlessly lines would blend in with the exposed negative. Many photographers did their own retouching, and according to Muhammad Iqbal of Naqash Studio, "The best way to know who is an expert photographer is by looking at the finger tips." A sharpener of two pencils per day in his retouching prime, Muhammad's own fingertips are still stained with traces of ingrained pencil lead from decades of retouching (p.58–59).

Hand-colouring usually followed retouching and, like retouching, served among other aesthetic purposes, a cosmetic one – which according to author Ben Gilmour, writing on hand-colouring in Kohat, a town south of Peshawar, in 2007, was an art form appreciated by customers, who believed a hand-coloured portrait made a "man more handsome, and a woman more beautiful."[٢٠] In contrast to retouching, however, hand-colouring was considered a specialist tradition, and hand-colourists of merit – as with photographers – could receive the honorary title of 'master' of their art from their peers.

In Peshawar, the hand-colourists and photographers we interviewed were adamant that only watercolours should be used in embellishing photographs as they were reflective surfaces, while oils were strictly for paintings. Across the border, in Afghanistan and Iran, however, oils were also used on photos, at times being applied directly by the finger. The watercolours that were used by Peshawari hand-colourists often came from coloured strips of paper manufactured by companies such as Kodak and Fuji, which they soaked in water to release the paint. Some of the studios on Cinema Road that we encountered also availed of food colouring. The "miracle" of this colour, says old-time Cinema Road photographer Noor Rehman, was that the photo stood out "fresh and bright" for a long time, and the dyes were cheap: only a few paisa for six colours. Food colouring was also edible, and photographers would simply lick their brushes clean! as master hand-colourist Tahir Usman (p.155) of Cinema Road jokingly enacted at the end of a commission by us.

Tahir, a hand-colourist and photographer working on Cinema Road since the 1970s, used to hand-colour over a dozen portraits a day, he recalled, typically, using brown for an adult male face and a purplish tone for children and young women. If the face and garments of the customer matched, he chose another colour for the clothes so that the face would stand in contrast, sometimes encircling the head with a halo for the same purpose. And if the photograph had a section out of focus, he would paint accordingly 'out of focus', with the edges of the image diffused (p.183).

According to Tahir, hand-colouring thrived up until the mid-2000s, and he with it. In fact, customers requested hand-coloured portraits from him subsequently, because they appreciated the finished product more in comparison to a cheaper digital counterpart. But finally, the art succumbed to a new age of image production. Tahir, who painted his last hand-coloured portrait for a local customer in 2011, explains: "I never got sick of this work, the work got sick of me."

Tahir's affliction was, of course, the arrival of digital technology, which forced all Peshawari photographers to adapt and often replace their analogue techniques to survive commercially. One of the most important photographic techniques to be digitally revolutionised in Peshawar, in particular on Cinema Road, was the technique of photomontaging.

Studio photomontage

A photomontage is a type of photographic composite, known in the trade in Peshawar as a 'chain', 'attachment' or 'joining' and is the outcome of cutting and joining two or more photographic images together to make a single print (p.95). Making montages with medium format and 35mm film, as was mostly the case in pre-digital Cinema Road studios, was very much a labour-intensive process.

To start with, the base image had to be photographed. Cinema Road montages were mostly focussed on the regional movie industry so base images would usually be made by shooting negatives from movie posters. Regardless of the movie, this poster inevitably contained a male actor (whether hero or villain) for the male customers to emulate, and, more often than not, an accompanying female object of affection. The process of copying the poster, and making photographic copies, in general, was known as 'copy-to-copy' or 'CTC'.

Next, the head of the male actor on the negative would be carefully tinted red (p.107). This poster negative would then be exposed onto light-sensitive photo paper, and as (theoretically) no light would have gone through the tinted part of the negative, the actor's head would disappear. The photographer would then take a negative of a client's head he had photographed, and expose it on top of the enlarged base image on the same paper – the client's head slotting as precisely as possible into the blank area. Alternatively, the photographer could cut the actor's head out from the base image, and place a cut-out negative of the client's head on the base image negative (without the original head), and then enlarge them at the same time. In either case, hand-colouring followed.

There was much more to analogue photomontaging, however, than just movies and males yearning after songstresses. Haji Muhammad Iqbal of Capri Studio on Cinema Road remembers that his brother had a variety of styles he created himself. A favourite was to get a man to put his finger on his temple, creating a 'V' with his arm, and between his bent arm, standing on the bicep, add a full-length image of the same customer. Once a customer came from the former American consulate in Peshawar, he recalls, a woman, who saw a montage of a man holding his own head, and she requested the picture for herself. When she returned to the U.S., she wrote asking for more, and so he made two more copies and sent them on, so famous had the pose with the man – or now, woman – holding his, or her own head become.

Minute cameras:[٢١] *lustruni wallah*

While classic photographic techniques were refined in studios, one set of photographers always made their livelihoods on the street: the *lustruni wallah* (meaning, 'sleeve guys' in Pashtu). These photographers could be found at designated spots around the city, with what in Indian parlance was commonly called the 'minute' (pronounced: *min't*) camera: a wooden box with lens, housing a makeshift darkroom for developing a paper negative (p.186–187). The sleeve was, in particular, the camera's trademark – a long tube of cloth, perhaps a recycled old trouser or jacket sleeve – projecting out the side or rear of the camera, which stood on a tripod, into which the photographer inserted his arm to adjust the photographic paper inside. Working with natural light, photographers used photographic paper instead of film as a 'negative' and after making an exposure, developed the paper-negative inside the camera where trays of chemicals were placed. Minute camera photographs were an inexpensive and time-saving alternative to studio photographs; the whole process might only take a few minutes, and the photographs were sometimes hand-coloured and montaged on request.[٢٢]

A number of Peshawari studio photographers worked with the minute camera. Kala Khan (d.2013) a.k.a. Safir Aman (meaning, 'Sword of the Merciful') started out as a minute camera photographer in the early 1960s pitching his merchandise outside the old city walls; his nephew Fayaz Ahmad (p.225) now runs Shama Studio on Cinema Road. Aslam Tahir Moghul (p.91), a photographer in his early seventies, who still works on Cinema Road, came into the trade as what he calls a 'standing photographer', using a minute camera outside Kabuli Gate on the northern end of the road. Aslam learnt how to use the minute camera from his father, who, he says, picked it up from a Sikh photographer before Partition. Abdul Latif, the proprietor of Shan Studio in Randaz Bazaar learnt the minute camera as a ten-year-old boy in the 1980s, from his father, Mateen. Together they had a pitch on Cinema Road and also took commissions in the turbulent tribal area of Waziristan to make identity card portraits of locals, as well as Afghan refugees. In the tribal areas they worked within the protective zones of Pakistani military encampments as it was deemed too dangerous to work outside. And lastly, in a temporary swing of fortunes – since he had already completed an apprenticeship at the prestigious Zaidi's Studio on Arbab Road – senior photographer Abdul Rashid spent one year working with the minute camera on Cinema Road in the early 1960s.

Over the years, minute camera photography on Cinema Road, as well as the rest of the city, was to change and grow. Following the 1979 Soviet invasion of Afghanistan, hundreds and thousands of Afghans were forced to seek refuge in Peshawar and the surrounding region – Afghan minute camera photographers were on the move too. Some like Gul Zaman, Shah Wali and Majeed from Jalalabad carried their cameras with them across the border, and on arriving in Peshawar set up pitches on Cinema Road, bolstering the numbers of minute photographers in the area. Relationships with the new arrivals, by all accounts, were harmonious – the Afghans, in any case, didn't pose much competition for established studios and seemed to work in harmony with their Pakistani counterparts. Cinema Road photographers, like Muhammad Iqbal (p.91) of Kamran Studio, even rented space to Afghan photographers outside their own businesses (this is how Muhammad came to learn how to use the camera himself).

A number of differences exist between the minute camera used in Peshawar, which seems to have been the most commonly found model on the Indian sub-continent and the camera which the Afghans brought with them into exile. First was the name: 'min't camera' used on the Indian subcontinent, though the Pashtu and Dari (Afghan Persian) speaking Afghan photographers understand *faoree-kamra* and *kamra-e-faoree*, respectively, meaning: 'urgent' camera. The most obvious physical difference was that the Afghan camera was bigger and heavier, and on closer inspection it used an adjustable rod for focusing while a bellows was often, in addition, used on the minute camera. The Peshawari camera, also, had a drop-down tank at the back for the fixing agent, while the Afghans placed it in a tray inside the body of the camera. And finally, in Peshawari cameras the focus plate, unlike in the Afghan model, wasn't attached to a pole; its position was changed by hand.[٢٣]

The last of the Afghan minute camera photographers left Cinema Road by the turn of the millennium. Some returned home, while others moved to different parts of the city such as the Nasir Bagh Afghan refugee camp. There, during the mass repatriation of Afghan refugees in the mid-2000s, Afghan minute camera photographers prospered due to a huge demand for cheap identity photographs. Within a few years, however, the venerable technology had succumbed – refugee numbers were dwindling dramatically, lessening demand; the Afghan photographers were themselves returning home; and in the broader context, cheap digital photographs were becoming more widely available. In Afghanistan however, where the photography trade had been in stasis due to years of conflict, the camera was still in limited use until 2012.[٢٤]

Taxi photographers

'Taxi' or 'outdoor' photographers, as they are sometimes known, are also studio-less, itinerant photographers who roam the outskirts of Peshawar and the region, on foot or on bicycle, picking up work as they go along. Artistically, they are, arguably, on the same plane as studio photographers in Peshawar, though because of their itinerant condition as well as the social class of the clients they cater to, are considered less accomplished by their peers – the same reaction that minute camera photographers used to receive. What they further share in common with minute camera photographers is that they make themselves very easy to spot. Abdul Wali (p.207), a photographer for almost twenty years and an itinerant photographer for the most part, carries his old 35mm Yashica camera decorated with a multi-coloured tape slung around his neck to heighten his visibility and announce his profession; his tiny digital camera is kept solidly gripped in his hand ready to shoot. Abdul works mostly on the Grand Trunk Road, the main east–west artery out of Peshawar, photographing ordinary people in everyday situations: hotel workers on the job, truck drivers posing with their vehicles and fair-goers enjoying a day off work. In years gone by, he carried stuffed polyester lions and bouquets of plastic flowers as props for his customers but he no longer has the need as his images can be easily manipulated and situations simulated by digital laboratories on Cinema Road.

Besides 'ordinary' photographs, Abdul offers 'trick' photos, such as double exposures where customers can shake their own hands, montages of male clients embracing female entertainers, and, reminiscent of what Haji Iqbal's brother sold in his Cinema Road studio, the famed trick photo of a man holding his own head.

Nowadays, digital studios effortlessly take care of all the trick effects for Abdul, but he used to do all the compositing himself. Multiple exposures of customers in the past were all shot on one negative by covering up parts of the lens with a piece of card, with a quarter or half fraction cut out (p.204–205). The card would be revolved during a second or third exposure, with Abdul rewinding the film after every shot to ensure each exposure landed on the same negative. (The edges of the overlapping exposures appear soft and with a slight transition due to the light that leaks from one exposure onto the other.) Abdul's montages used similarly rudimentary techniques, and involved cutting out images from positive prints, placing them together, and then re-photographing the conjoined pieces to make the final image. His fascinating analogue composites came to an end in 2009 – the same year he went digital.

Another taxi photographer is Aziz Rehman Slonaar (p.219), who works mostly around the village of Chamkani, west of Peshawar. Aziz has worked as a travelling photographer for twenty-five years since the mid-1990s, bicycling his way along village roads with – just like Abdul Wali – a camera slung around his neck to attract customers. Usually he carries an air gun as a prop for photos, but *never* plastic flowers, and most of his photos, like those of Abdul Wali, capture ordinary people: vegetable vendors at work, children at a corner shop. Sometimes his bicycle ends up in the shot, an accidental, but charming trademark. Aziz only went digital in 2013, and every few days, he travels to Shama Digital Studio on Cinema Road to develop his photographs; a big attraction of the studio being that it digitally frames his photographs with colourful floral borders, which is definitely an added selling point for customers.

Making a living from 'taxi photography', however, has become difficult in the last few years. "Everyone", these photographers say, has a camera on their phone, and they complain that their service simply isn't required.[٢٥] Aziz admits to finding it an increasing struggle, while Abdul Wali survives only hand to mouth, and can't afford to send any of his five children to school. Two of his sons are in a *madrassa*, an Islamic religious school, where at least they get fed every day.

The trials of colour film & development

The use of colour film photography, much like the practice of 'taxi photography', is on the edge of obsolescence in Peshawar. And it was slow to root. On making its début in the city in the 1970s, development and back-up services for colour photography were, for the most part, lacking; the process was time-consuming and expensive; and for many years after it was introduced, Pakistani bureaucracy remained content with black-and-white identity photographs, which contained demand – had officialdom required colour images earlier, as they later would, it might have established the practice as standard sooner. Some studios didn't make the move to colour until as late as the mid-1980s, almost thirty years after it was introduced both on the subcontinent and Afghanistan,[٢٦] and with such limited development possibilities there wasn't much motivation to do so.

However, even from the early days, there existed a niche market for colour portraits in Peshawar emanating from the elite customers of Saddar Road. Unsurprisingly, therefore, the pioneer of colour film portraiture in the city was the

VIP Studio, Zaidi's, which began offering the service in 1976. Undeterred by the lack of developing opportunities at the time, Zaidi's manually developed colour film themselves. Abdul Rashid of Jumbo Studio, who learnt the technique directly from Ashraf Ali Zaidi, recalls that producing just two colour photographs could take a whole working day; and, although, by the late 1970s, studios could send colour films to laboratories in Karachi, 1,300 km away, the prints could take up to a week to be returned. It wasn't, actually, until the first half of the 1980s that multicoloured light really appeared on the horizon in the Saddar Road area, when in 1984 one of the first film colour developing machines arrived at Gulf Colour Lab, now DH Digital (although they still developed black-and-white film until 2001).

The trials that colour film faced in Peshawar, however, pale in comparison to those undergone in neighbouring Afghanistan. In the mid-1990s, Afghanistan, under the yoke of the Taliban, had the distinction of being the only country in the world to ban photography (exceptions irregularly being made for identity photographs).[٢٧] To circumvent this, some studios in Kabul worked clandestinely and smuggled their rolls of exposed colour film across the border to Peshawar.[٢٨] In Peshawar, the films were developed in laboratories and the prints smuggled back. Both studios and customers on the Afghan side of the border risked imprisonment, beatings, or worse for their involvement in this activity. But for one Afghan working in the photography business in Peshawar, it was a golden business opportunity.

In 1998, Imad, who works with DH Digital on Saddar Road, became (by his own account) the first person to bring colour processing machines to Afghanistan by smuggling two such machines into Kabul from Dubai, labelled as 'X-ray equipment'. Trained in photographic chemistry in Malaysia and Singapore, Imad understood the technicalities of how to function developing machines, and, coming from Afghanistan, he understood the needs of the local market – hence, business boomed. Imad's employee would collect rolls in the evenings from similar studios dotted around the city. Developing the films through the night, they were delivered the next day. Once a week, Imad collected films from outside Kabul. On the first Eid (marking the end of the fasting period of Ramadan) just one month after the

Taliban were ousted from Kabul in November 2001, Imad received fourteen hundred rolls of film to develop; mostly images of family and friends celebrating the holiday. Seeing the 'Taliban-free' potential for his business, Imad immediately ordered two more machines from Pakistan.

Is photography *haram*?

While there has never been a 'Taliban-like' ban on photography in Peshawar, the production of photographic images is nevertheless controversial, particularly ones that display women in public space. Traditionally within Islam there is a prohibition on the image in human or animal form, pictorially or photographically. This prohibition was, as noted, most infamously executed by the Afghan Taliban's 1996 edict banning photography outright in Afghanistan. But the question of whether photography is *haram* (that is, 'forbidden' or 'sacrilege') under Islamic law is not clear-cut at all, and the ins and outs of if and when it's permitted and in what situations is widely discussed and contested within the world of Islamic theology and generally amongst Muslims. On the ground in Peshawar, it's no different; everyone has a different perspective on speaking to them, and often it's a generational matter with family elders sometimes holding more conservative views on the matter than the younger members of the family.[۲۹]

Photographers, of course, have their own perspective on the issue. Tahir Usman, a photographer and former hand-colourist on Cinema Road, looks at the situation like this: "If a *mullah* thinks it's haram, then it's haram, but I don't. I serve humanity through photography, through food, tea, and hospitality, I make money and spend it on the welfare of others. If a person is dying, I give help to them, so with our thoughts for humanity this 'sin' can be forgiven – that is, if it is a sin. I'm thinking about the welfare of humanity. *Not to breathe the heart of humanity is the greatest sin* – if the heart is satisfied with these things then it's not haram." Pointing to three copies of the Qur'an beneath a cloth on a shelf, Tahir adds: "See those, if I didn't do photography, how could I buy them?" Fayaz Ahmad of Shama Studio, around the corner from Tahir on Cinema Road, is likely to agree. Returning Haj pilgrims who print photographs from their trips to Mecca receive discounts from Fayaz, and he always pops in a verse from the Qur'an on a chit of paper. If they don't have the money, he prints Haj photographs for free.

Women in photography

A fiercely contested and – for the photographers we interviewed – an arguably less nuanced issue than the permissibility of photography in itself, since the pressure not to display, produce or disseminate images of women is far more clear-cut and a daily concern than any type of social pressure not to work in photography *in itself*, is the public display of women in a photograph; and here one should consider that a major influence on the values attributed to photography in Peshawar are not inherently 'Islamic' *per se*, but, in part, an embodiment of the tribal, honour-bound and male-dominated Pashtun culture, predominant in eastern Afghanistan and Pakistan.

Vast numbers of women in the Pashtun areas of both Pakistan and Afghanistan live under purdah, that is public veiling. Breaking purdah is considered shameful, and in a gun-ridden society ruled by patriarchy, and inherently traditional notions of honour and pride, the repercussions are commonly violent. It is therefore widely unthinkable for most men to share private images of any female members of their families, whether wives, sisters or daughters (exceptions are made for the very young, the elderly and the deceased) with other than the closest of relatives. One recent male customer of Zaidi's Studio who brought his wife for a portrait, requested the photographer leave when the lights and camera were set, and took the digital photograph himself. The digitised photographic file was then transferred to a CD, without any employee of the studio viewing the image, and so in this manner his wife's identity had been concealed and the basic edict of purdah maintained. Anecdotes like these are not atypical and underline even more the seriousness of the trust placed on photographers commissioned to photograph the female members of families.

It should further be noted that many of the Peshawari photographers we met were not ethnically Pashtun. Some were Hindko-speaking (Hindko is a dialect of

Punjabi spoken by native city-dwellers, that is 'Peshawaris') as well as native Urdu-speaking non-Pashtun Partition-time migrants from India. But whether they share these views or not, they have to be highly conscious of them with regard to their customers, and sometimes, their own families. While photographers were eager to share baby-shots of daughters, and proudly tell stories of their daughters' painting and photographic artistic abilities, they also scratched out faces of females on photographs, awkwardly positioned hands to hide women's faces, and in one instance, disposing of a wife's image to present only the husband, cut a forty-year-old large format negative in two (p.173).

While photographing women is a sensitive subject in Peshawar, so are women who take photographs. Occasionally, studios are commissioned for female-only functions such as womens' celebrations at weddings. (Whether male and female guests mix or are segregated at wedding celebrations, or whether women guests are invited at all, is usually a matter mandated by social class). Occasionally, young male photographers, preferably boys, are permitted to photograph these events. One Peshawari photographer still squirms, twenty years after the fact, when remembering that, because he was too old to photograph women at a particular wedding function, he had to shave his beard off to appear suitably under-age.

In recent years, however, customers have begun requesting women to photograph the events and a number of women photographers, mostly based in beauty parlours with closed exteriors, now cater to a female-only clientele in the city. After getting married, however, they may have to stop since it is at the discretion of the husband whether his wife continues to work. (Some of the daughters of the male photographers we interviewed, who had been trained by their fathers to photograph weddings, met with precisely this fate following their own marriages.) Added to that, male photographers often don't hold female photographers in high esteem. The phenomenon of increased numbers of woman photographers in the city came about with the digital age. Perceived as lacking knowledge in traditional analogue photographic skills, further combined with a perceived dearth of knowledge of the new, due, it is believed, to lack of training and experience, women photographers simply aren't counted, we were told, as 'real' photographers.

Digital change & the fate of the old

Besides bringing more women into the business, the digital age brought hard-drives, computer screens and countless pirated copies of Photoshop – all of which were first discovered by the more upmarket studios in the cantonment area in Peshawar from the early to mid-2000s, before spreading to other parts of the city; the studios on Cinema Road had all more or less converted by 2009. Digital photography also brought with it unaccustomed demands: photographers had to learn new technological skills, it required money for new equipment, and, suddenly, there were a lot of words to read on cameras and computer screens, so ideally photographers had to be literate. *Ideally*, they had to read English. Unsurprisingly, there were older photographers who found it difficult or impossible to keep up; and to exacerbate the situation, the Pakistani government, taking advantage of cheaper and easy-to-manage photo technology, began to employ its own in-office staff to take identity photographs for official documents, so the profitable identity photo business that Peshawari studios had relied on for so long – now steadily declined.

Digitisation, furthermore, heralded the threat of social irrelevance – one might even say professional insecurity. Formerly, it took years to become a trained studio photographer in a Peshawari studio, now it was seemingly instant. As Mumtaz Ahmad (p.133) of Gul Sons Studio says: "In the old days a client didn't know how I made a photograph and it had more value –'here is an ustad' they thought, 'making my photo.' It had more magic, it was more special. Nowadays, even a small child can take a photo digitally." Mumtaz's looking back to the good old days is echoed on Cinema Road. When Mansoor visits his friend Zubi in Capri Studio, retouching and hand-colouring are favoured subjects. "And now the printer has come," says Zubi dismissively, "but it doesn't last like watercolour." So nostalgia has bitten – but at least for some it's reversible. Uncle Tony of Saddar Road actually gave up on digital photography after he had adopted the technology, even experimenting with the creative possibilities of embellishing his images with Photoshop filters. But it had "no quality" he says, so he returned to using film.

Yet digital *did* triumph and decisions had to be made. Studios that had thousands of negatives from decades in the analogue business now had to decide what to do with them. In Zaidi's and Malik Sons, two of the more established studios in Peshawar, with generation-long relationships to clientele, they have reservoirs of tens of thousands of film negatives dating from the 1960s, all of which are systematically filed and numbered. Customers still return to have photographs printed digitally from negatives produced forty or fifty years ago – leading one to believe, therefore, that still, as of 2017, the most common sign found in Peshawari photo studios – 'Negatives are not given to customers' – has not *quite* seen its day.

But for other studios these old exposures were using up space and becoming an unprofitable burden. Up until about a decade ago, Mumtaz Ahmad of Gul Sons Studio was, like Zaidi's and Malik Sons, still storing thousands of negatives in his studio; some of the negatives dating back to the mid-1960s when his father first opened the business. But after he went digital in the mid-2000s, Mumtaz didn't want to hold on to them any more, and posted an announcement in a local newspaper: customers would have to claim their negatives before a certain date, after which they would no longer be available. When the deadline passed, Mumtaz burnt them all. Daoud of Cinema Road did likewise, because: "Now, I need this," he says, indicating the digital montages lining the walls of his studio. Jamalistan Studio have threatened to do the same, but so far have been lent a reprieve.

photo peshawar

Large format portrait, Jamalistan Studio, c.1960s.

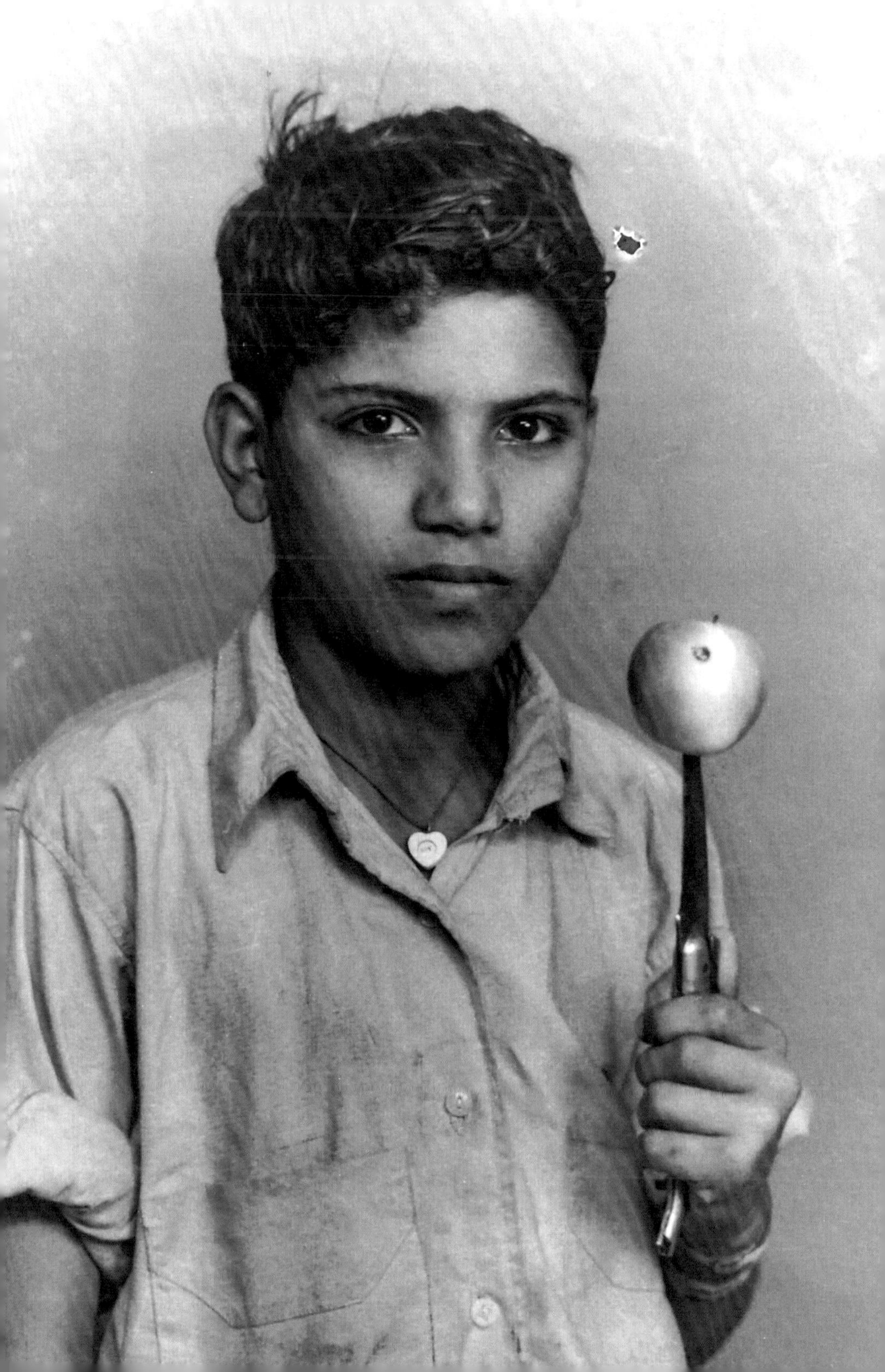

Large format portrait, Jamalistan Studio, c.1960s.

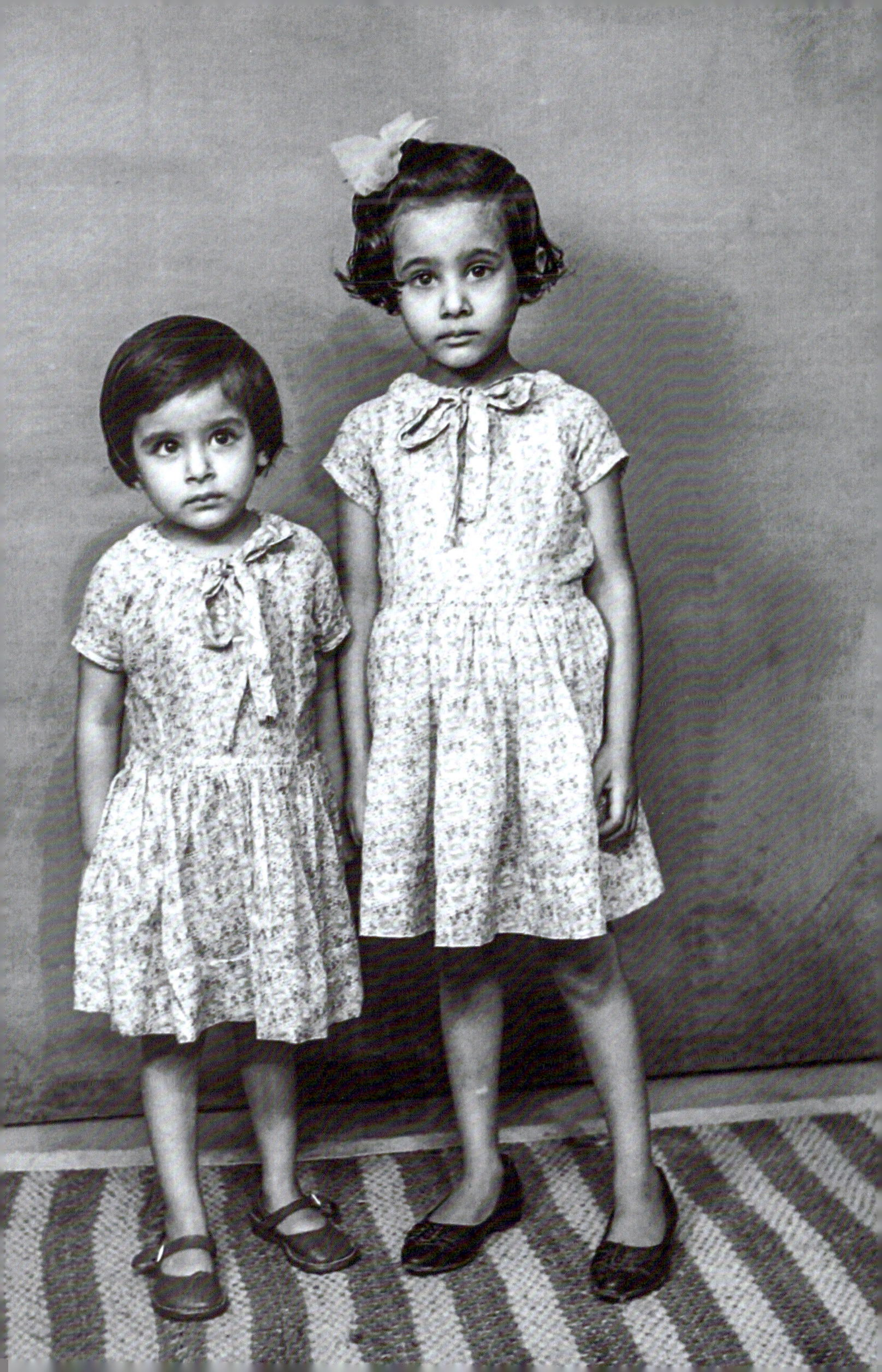

Large format portrait, Jamalistan Studio, c.1960s.

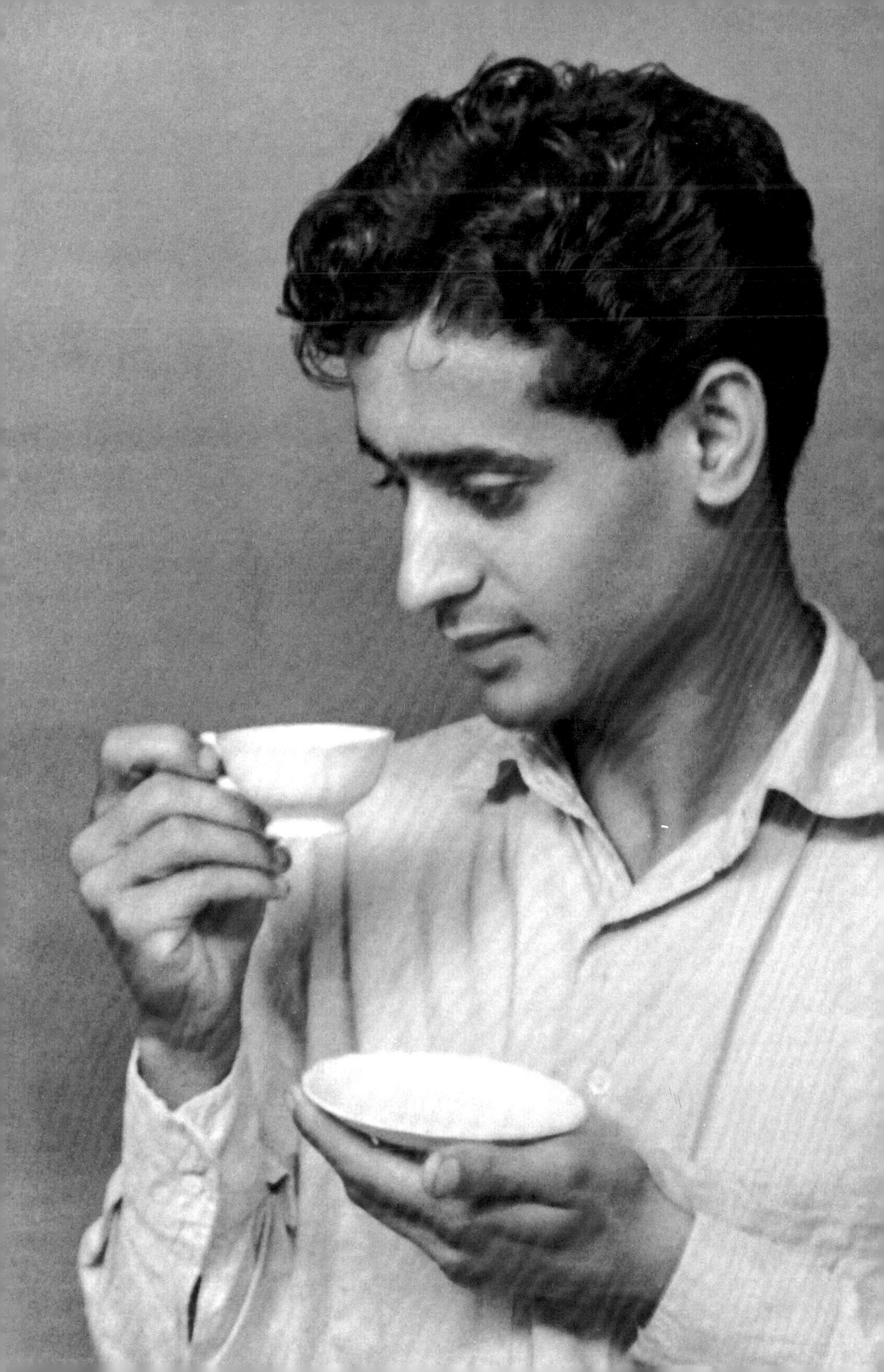

Large format portrait, Jamalistan Studio, c.1960s.

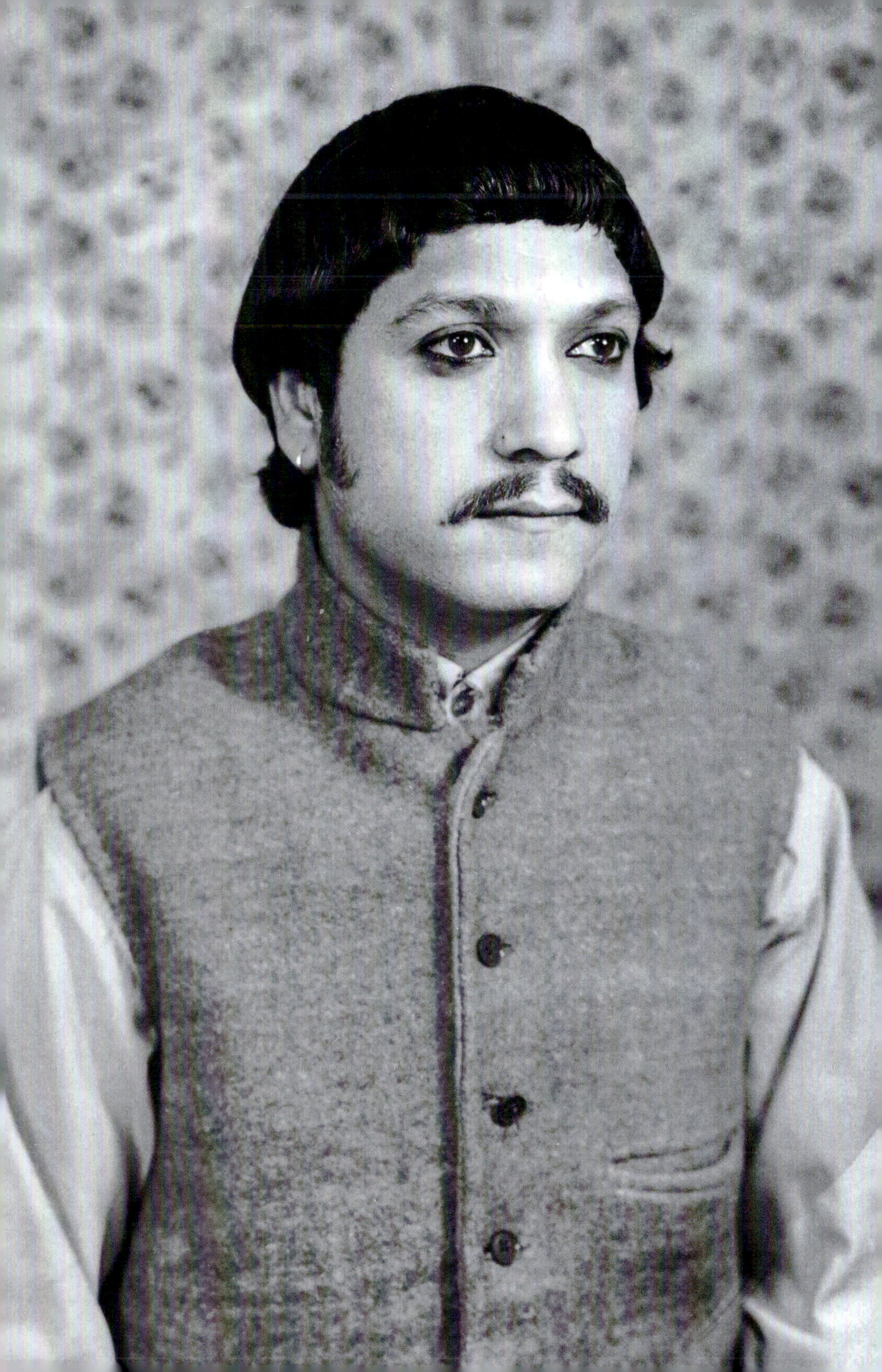

Opposite: Large format portrait, Jamalistan Studio, c.1960s.

Pages 48 & 49: Large format portraits, Jamalistan Studio, c.1960s.
Hats, blazers and other props were kept by studio to dress customers for their portraits.

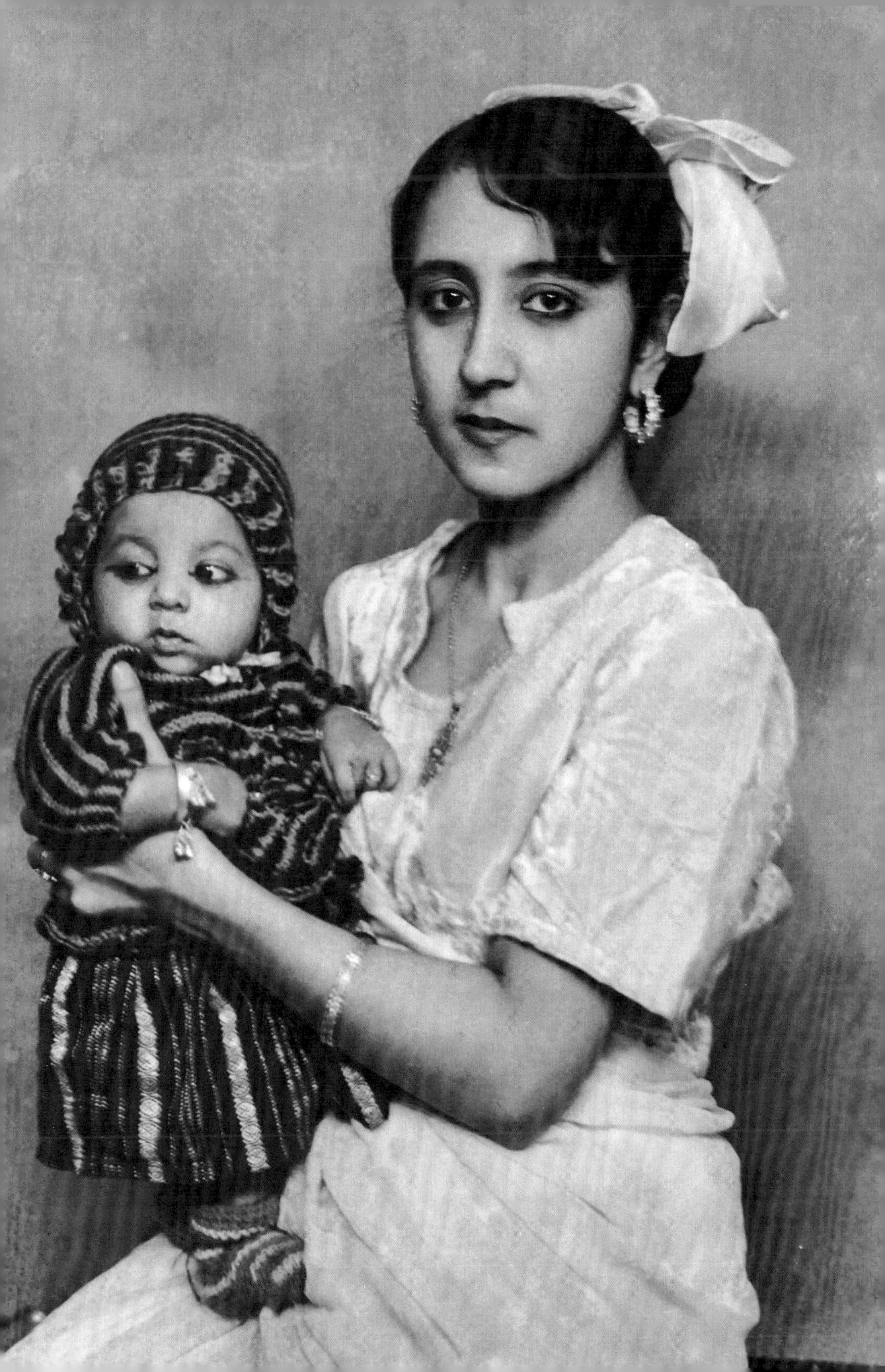

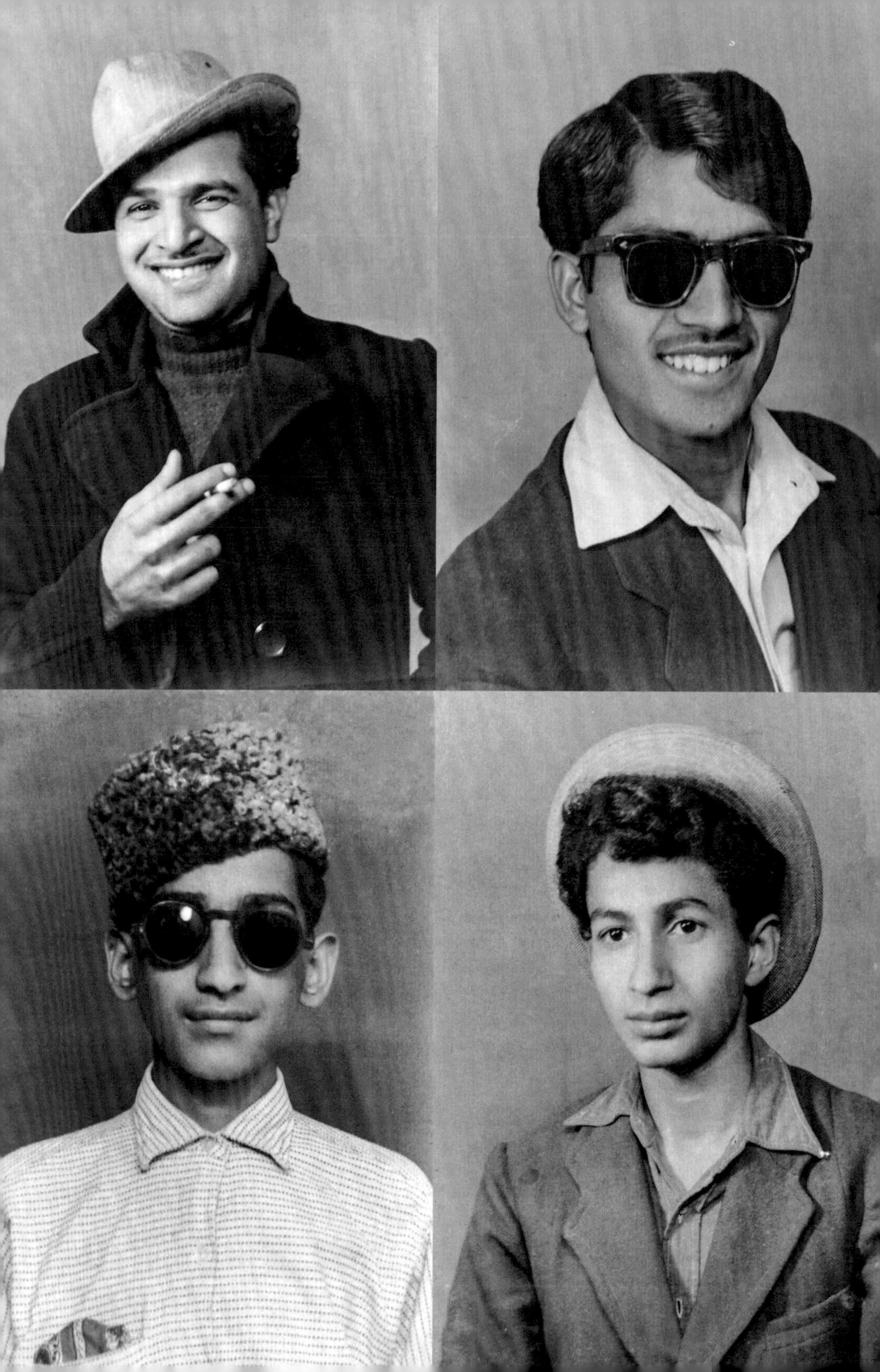

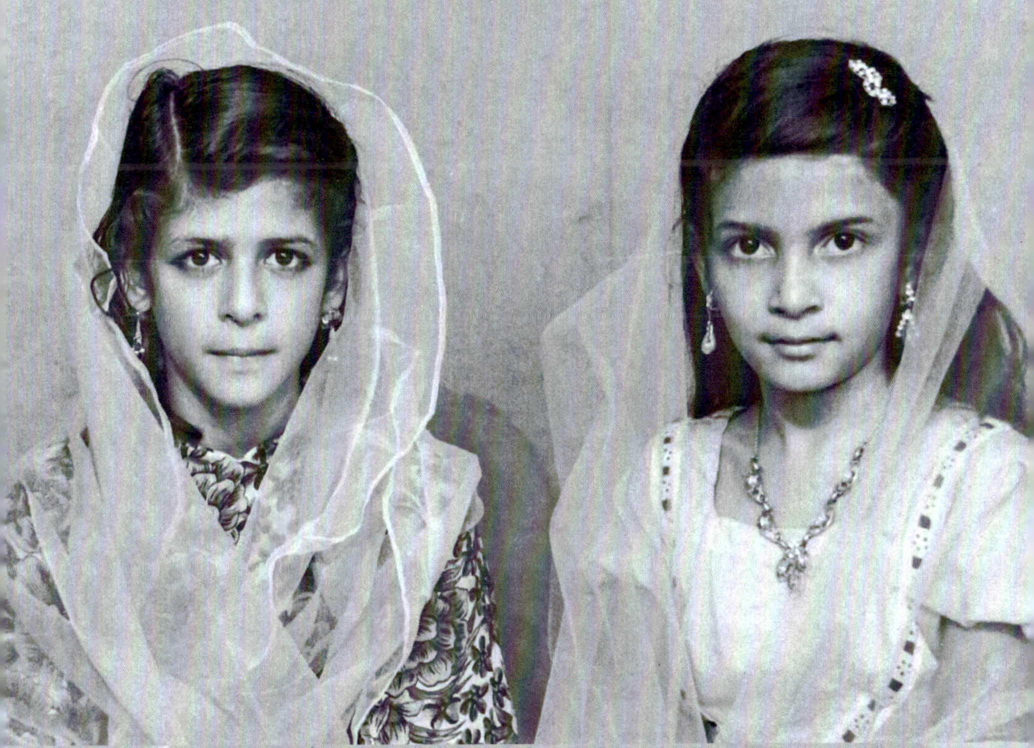

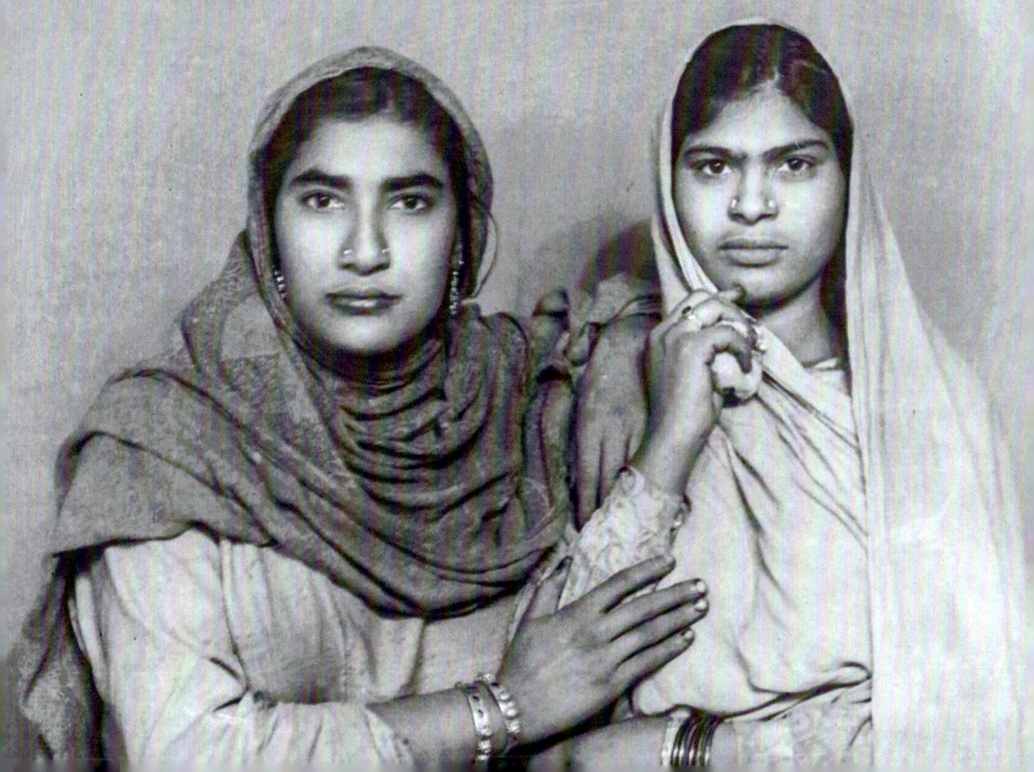

Opposite: Double-exposed large format portrait. Jamalistan Studio, c.1960s.

Pages 52 & 53: Large format portraits, Jamalistan Studio, c.1960s; *Pages* 54–55: Accidental double-exposure. Large format portrait, Jamalistan Studio, c.1960s; *Pages* 56–57: Funeral photograph. Occasionally, families requested images of their deceased relatives as memorabilia. Studios were also commissioned by the authorities to do postmortem photography in cases of suspicious deaths. Jamalistan Studio, c.1960s.

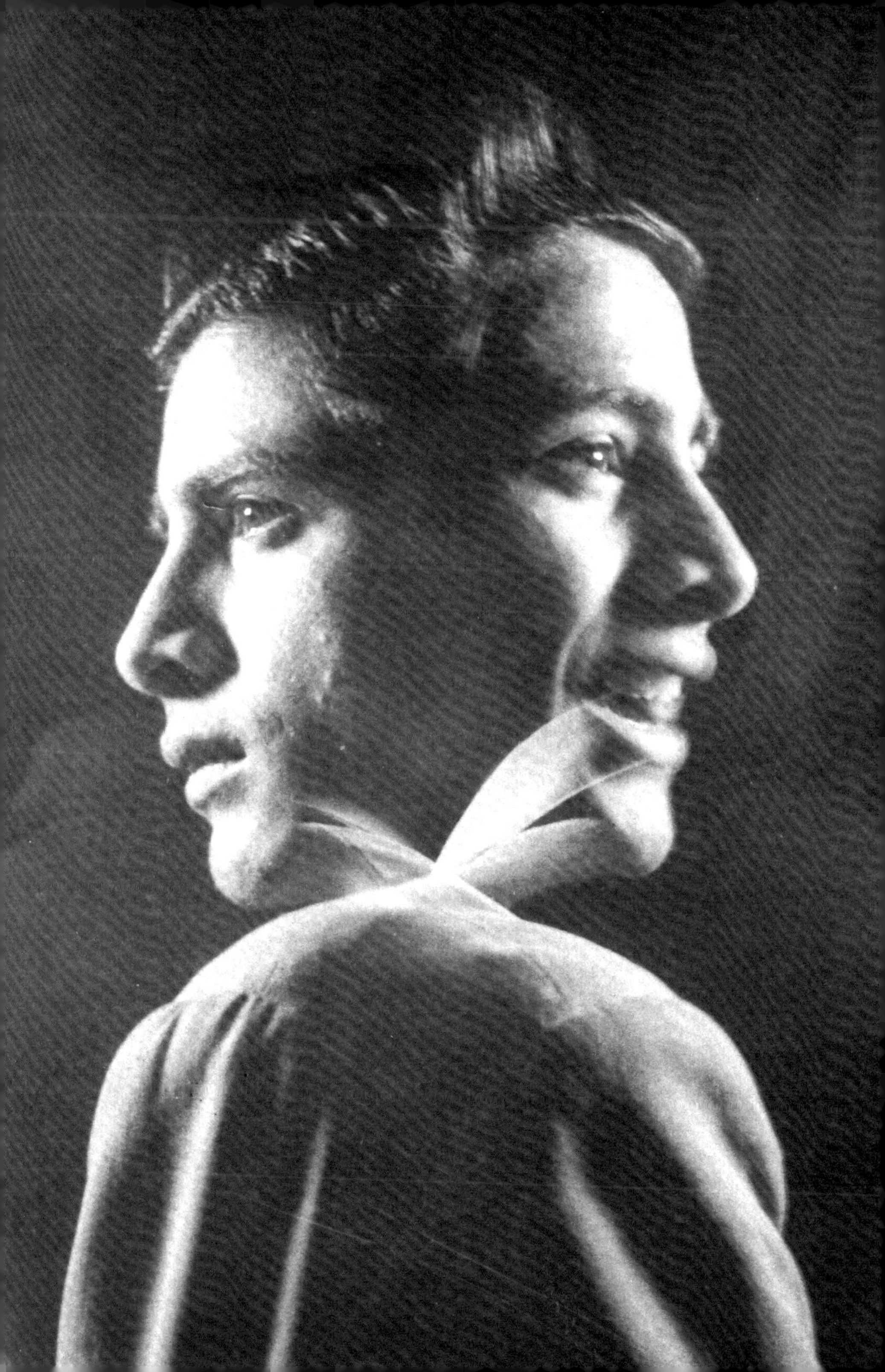

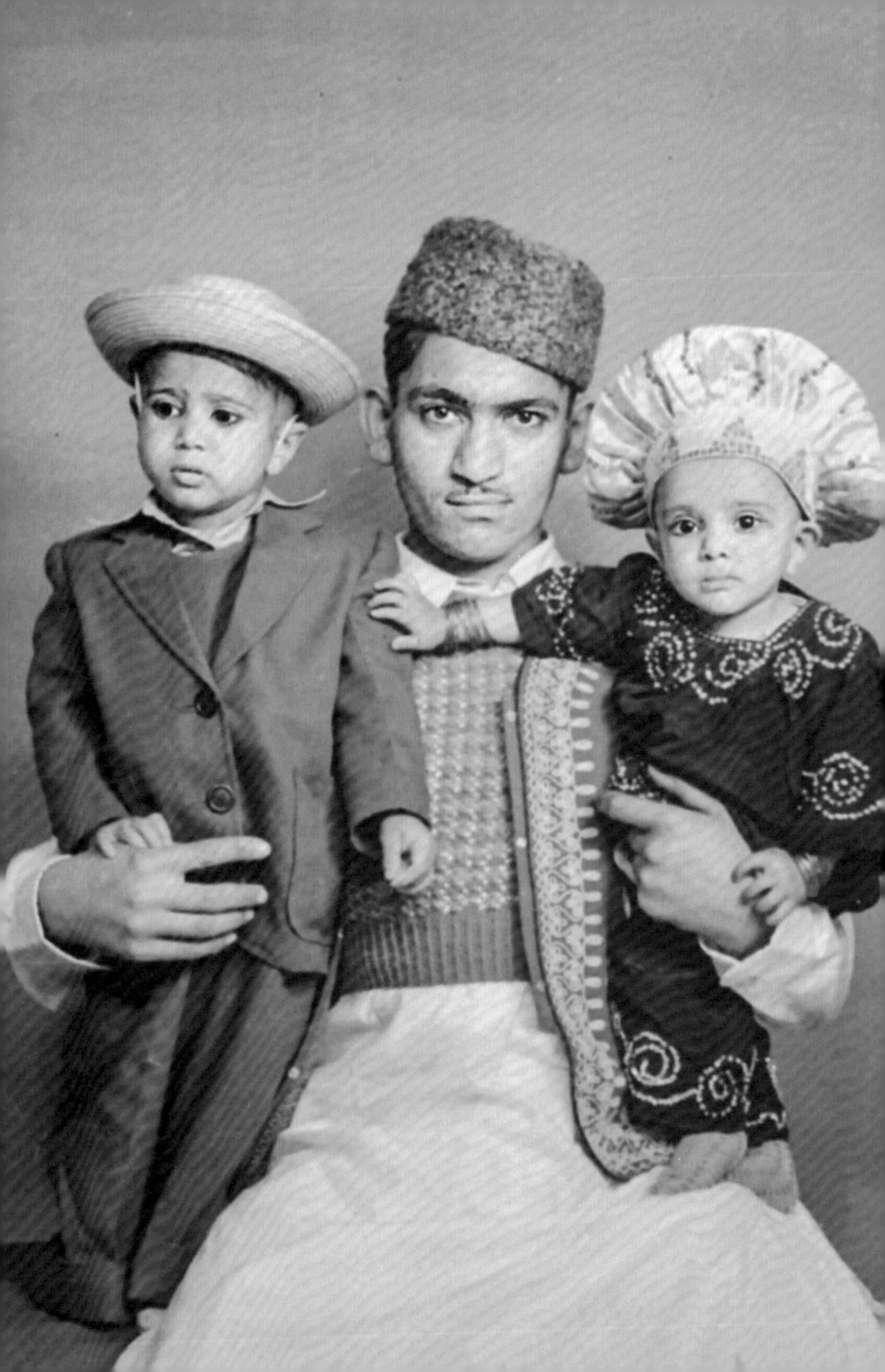

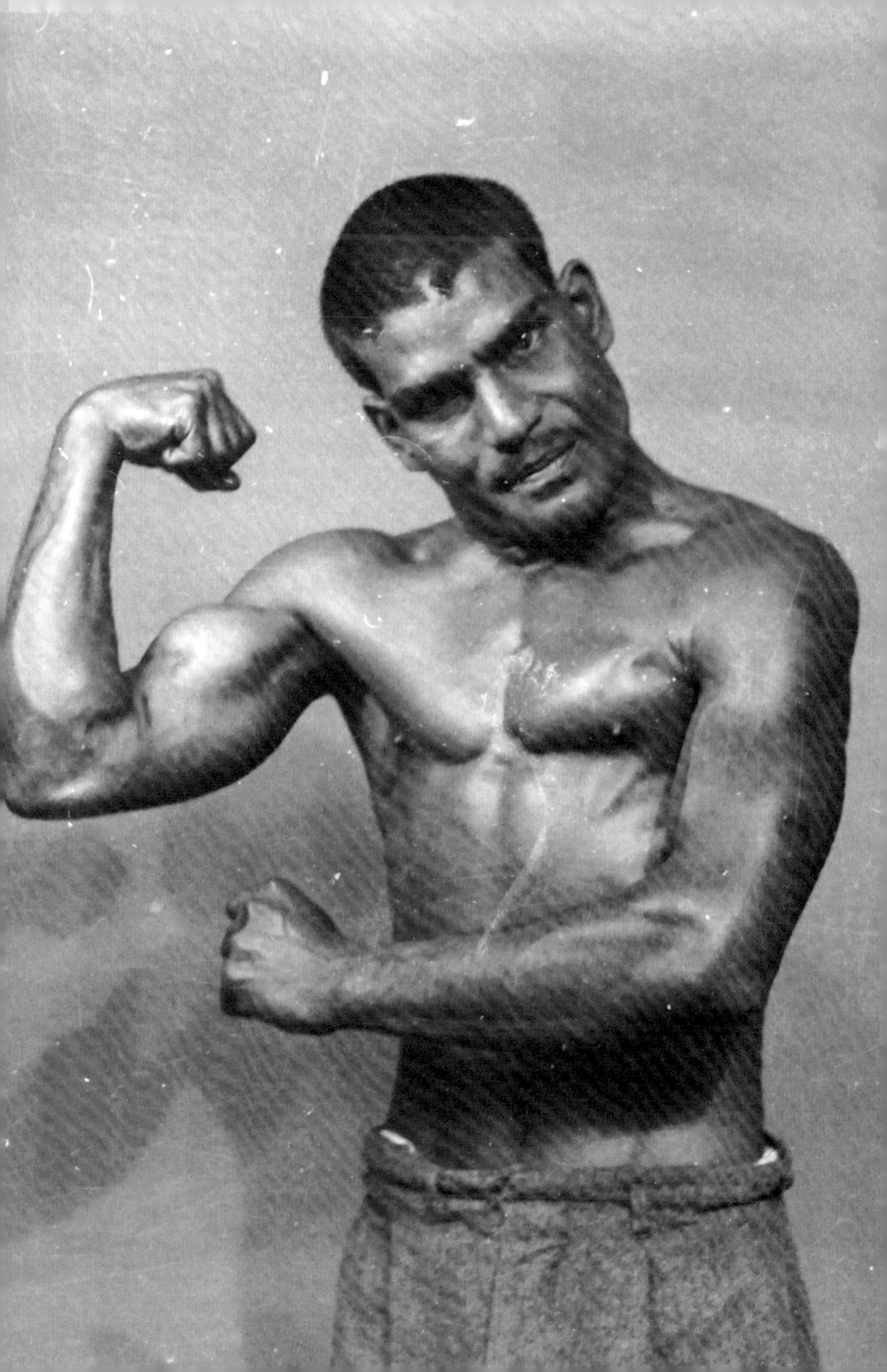

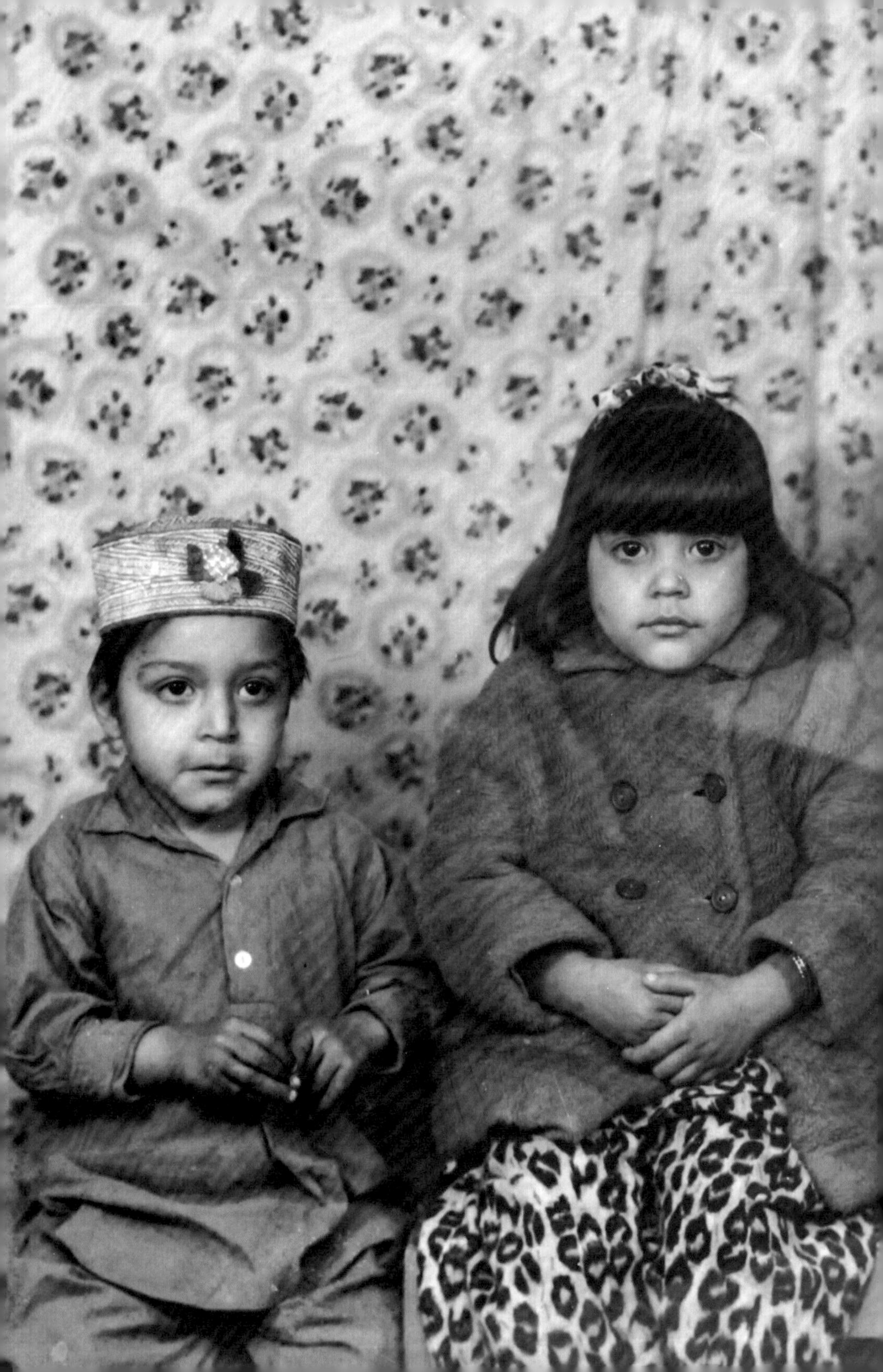

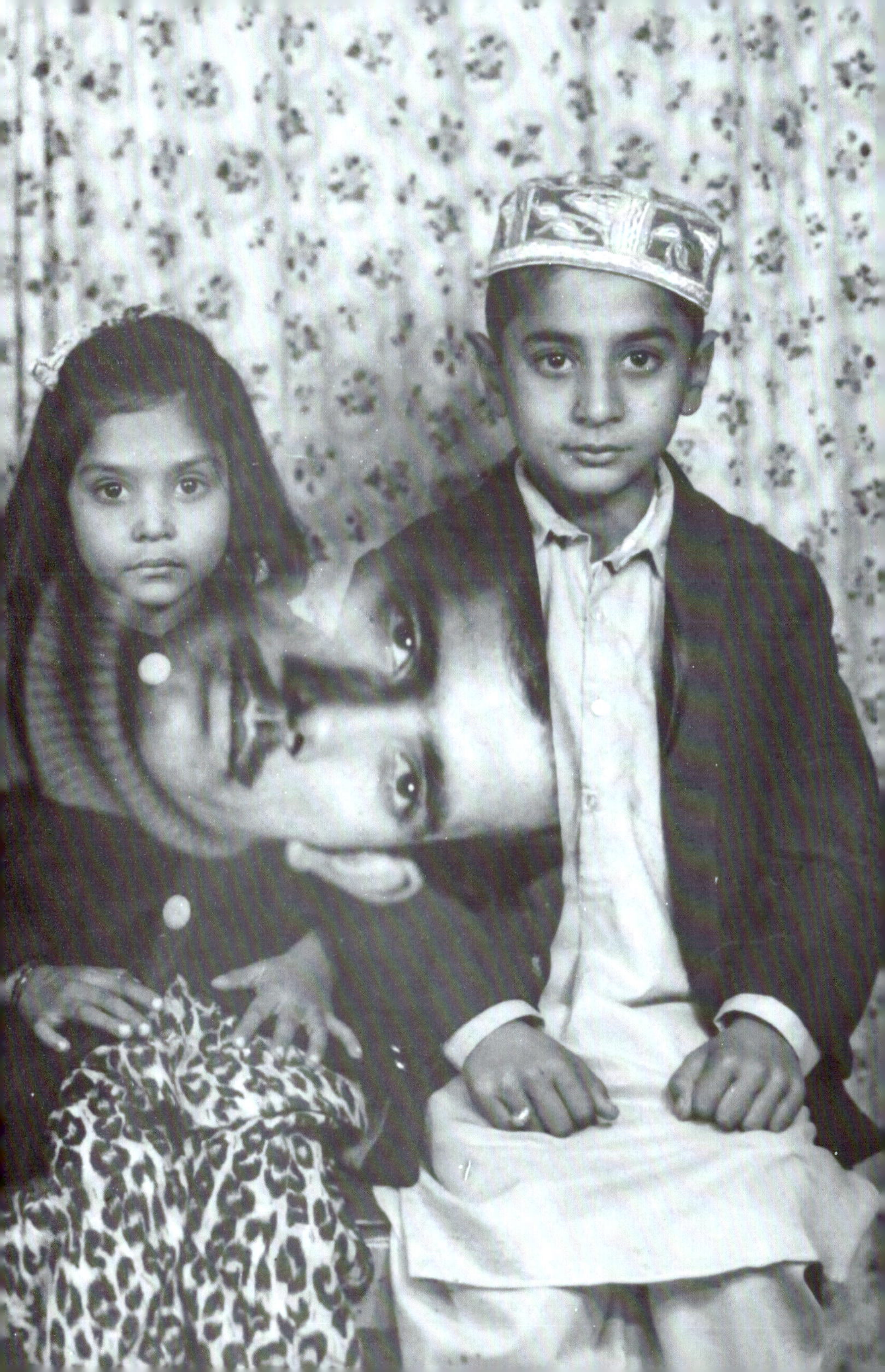

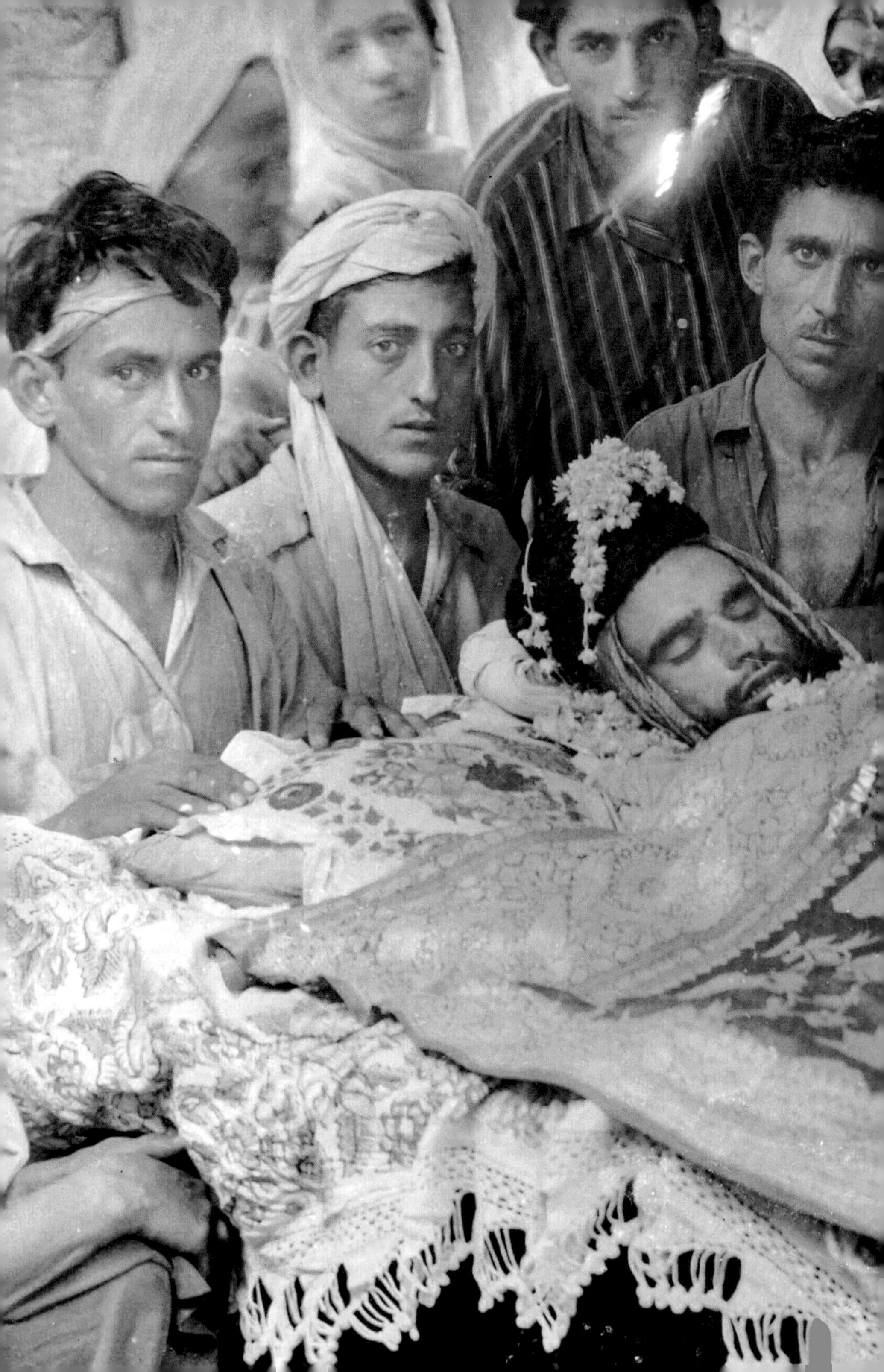

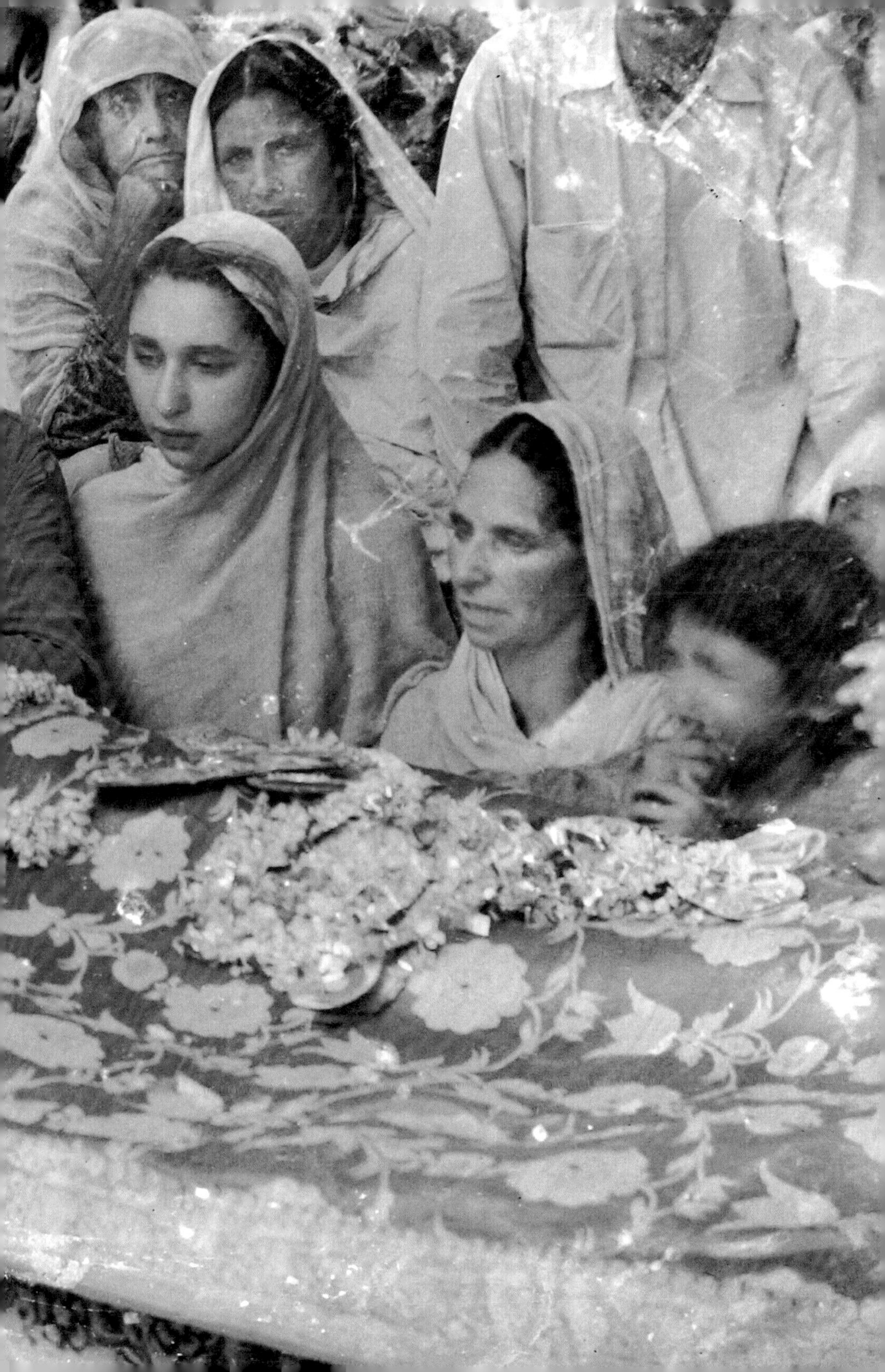

Muhammad Iqbal of Naqash Studio proudly displaying his pencil-lead stained fingertips—evidence of his years of retouching negatives.

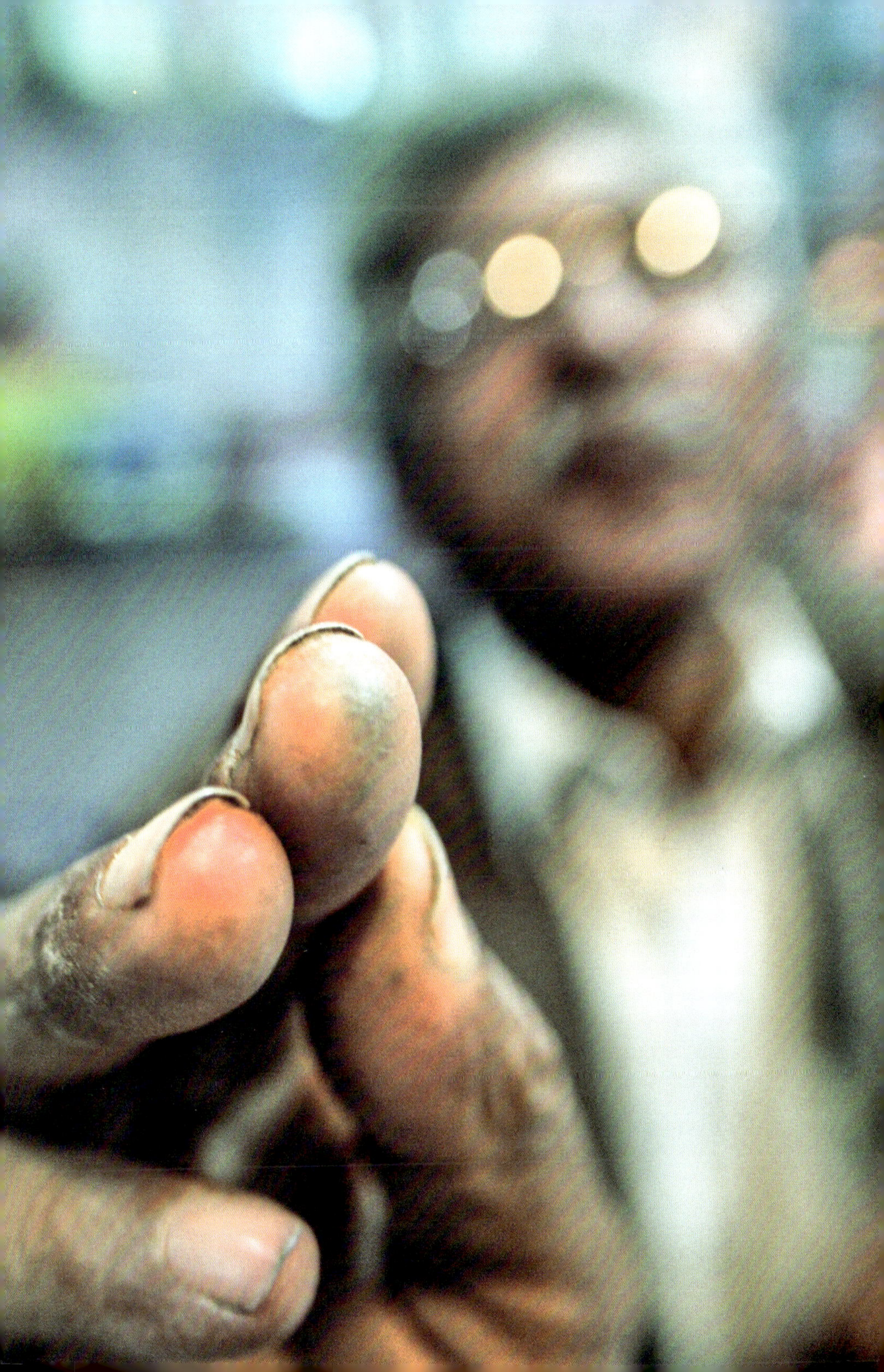

Opposite: Hand-coloured portrait of Ashraf Ali Zaidi (1932–1983), a senior photographer in Peshawar. Originally coming to Peshawar from India during the Partition of 1947, Zaidi gradually became the chosen VIP photographer in the city. The photograph was hand-coloured by Zaidi himself.

Pages 62–63: Fatima Jinnah exits an aircraft ahead of her brother, Muhammad Ali Jinnah, founder of Pakistan, in Lahore, two months after Independence and the founding of the state of Pakistan. Photo by Ashraf Ali Zaidi,1947.

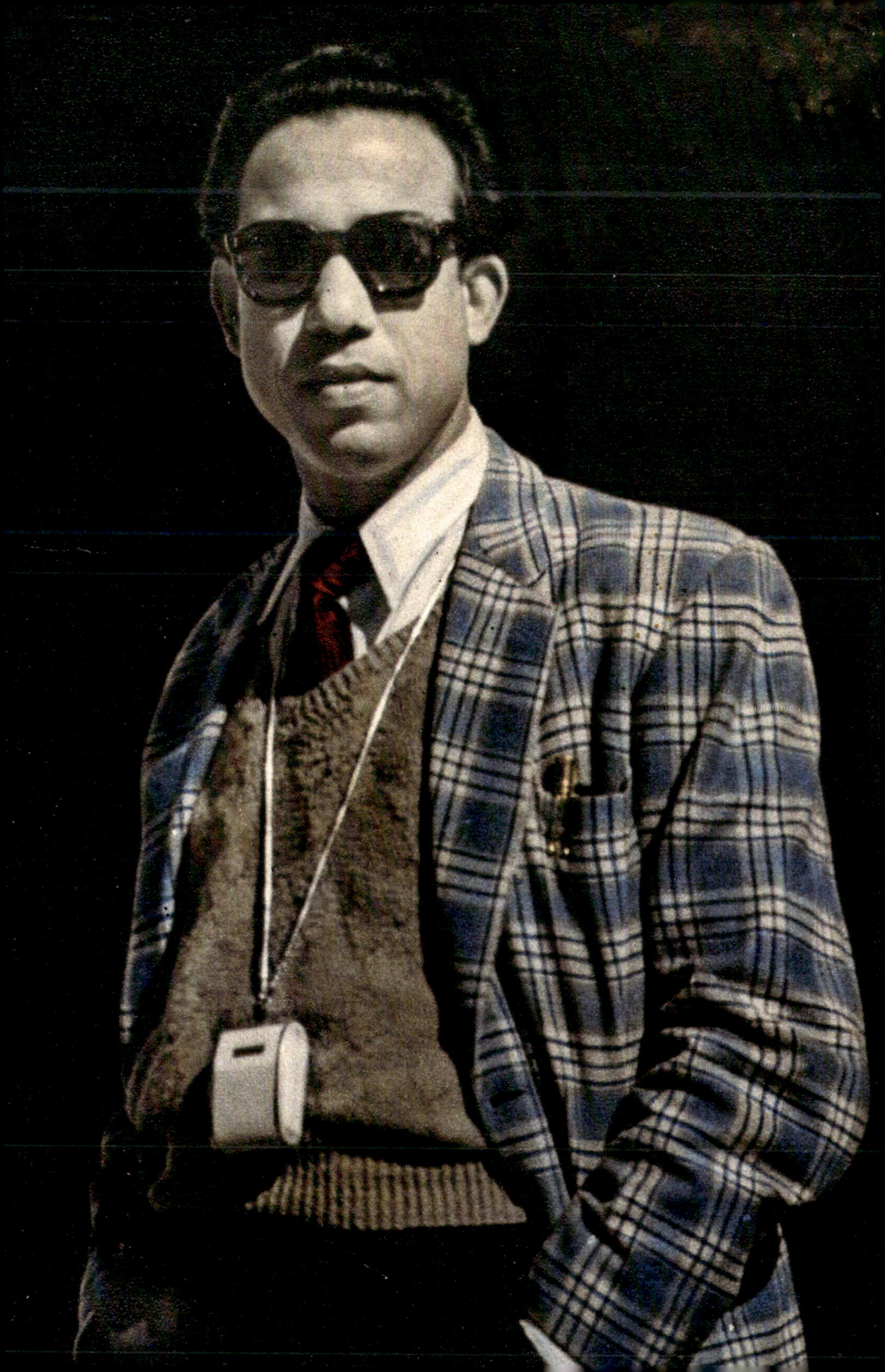

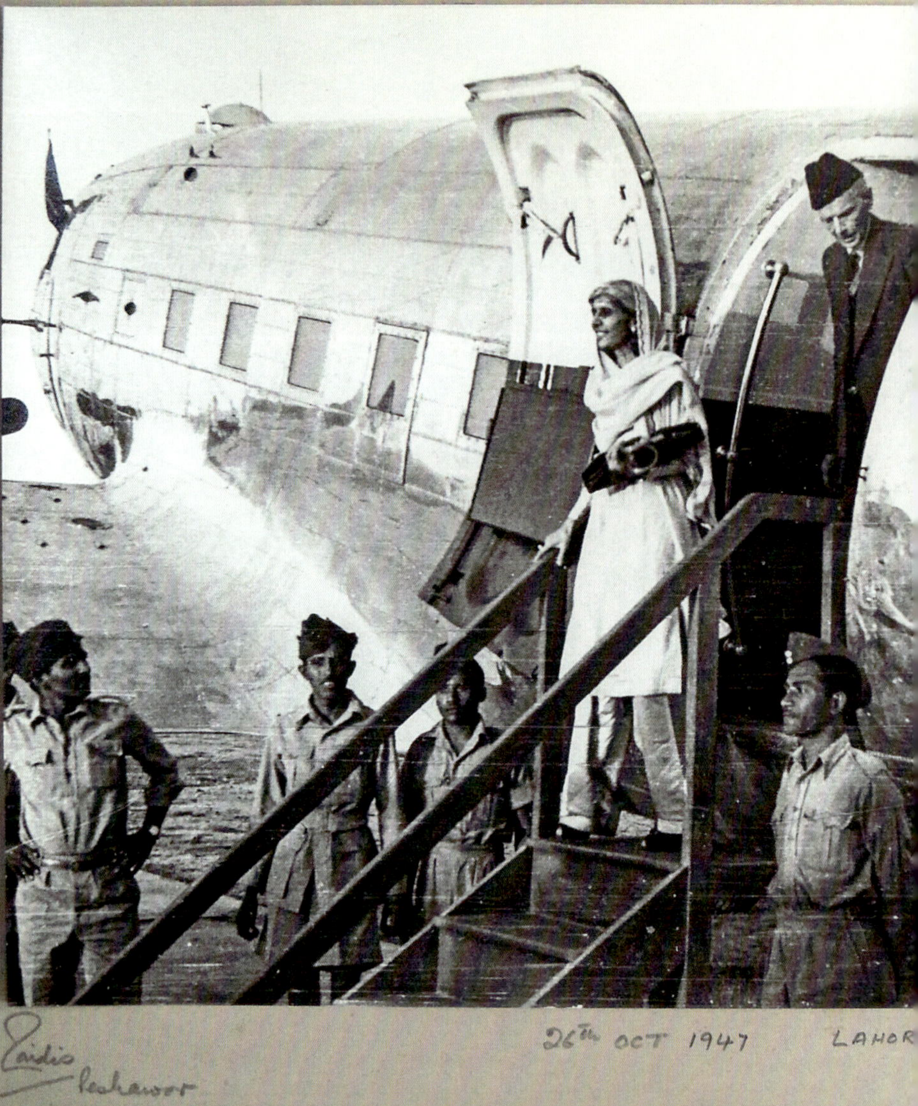

Zaidis
Peshawar

26th OCT 1947 LAHOR

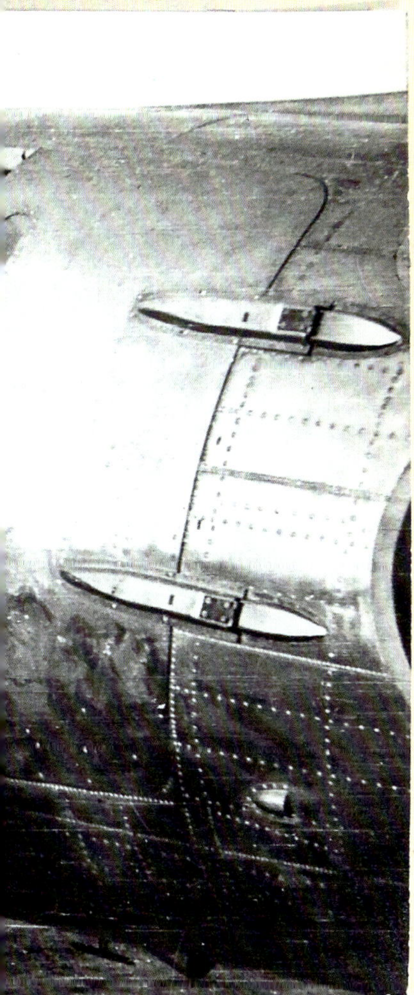

RPORT

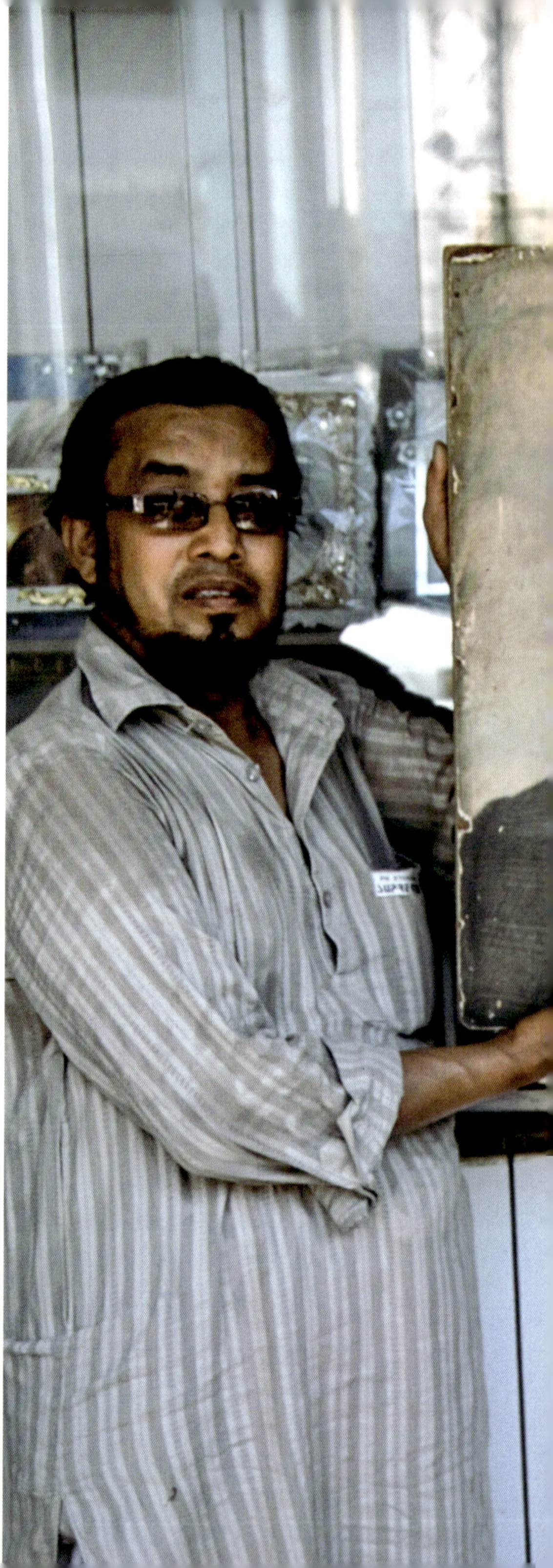

Opposite: Jamalistan Studio proprietor, Muhammad Wakeel (right) and younger brother, Muhammad Aqeel (left), pose with a late 1950s hand-coloured portrait of their father, Jamil Ahmad (p.69), who founded the studio in the 1950s. The brothers took over the studio, located opposite Naz Cinema, after their father's death in 1970.

Pages 66–67: A postmortem family montage. Jamil Ahmad (right) and his son, Aqeel (left) of Jamalistan Studio. Following Jamil Ahmad's death, Aqeel, who had never been photographed with his father during his lifetime, had this montage made, c.1975.

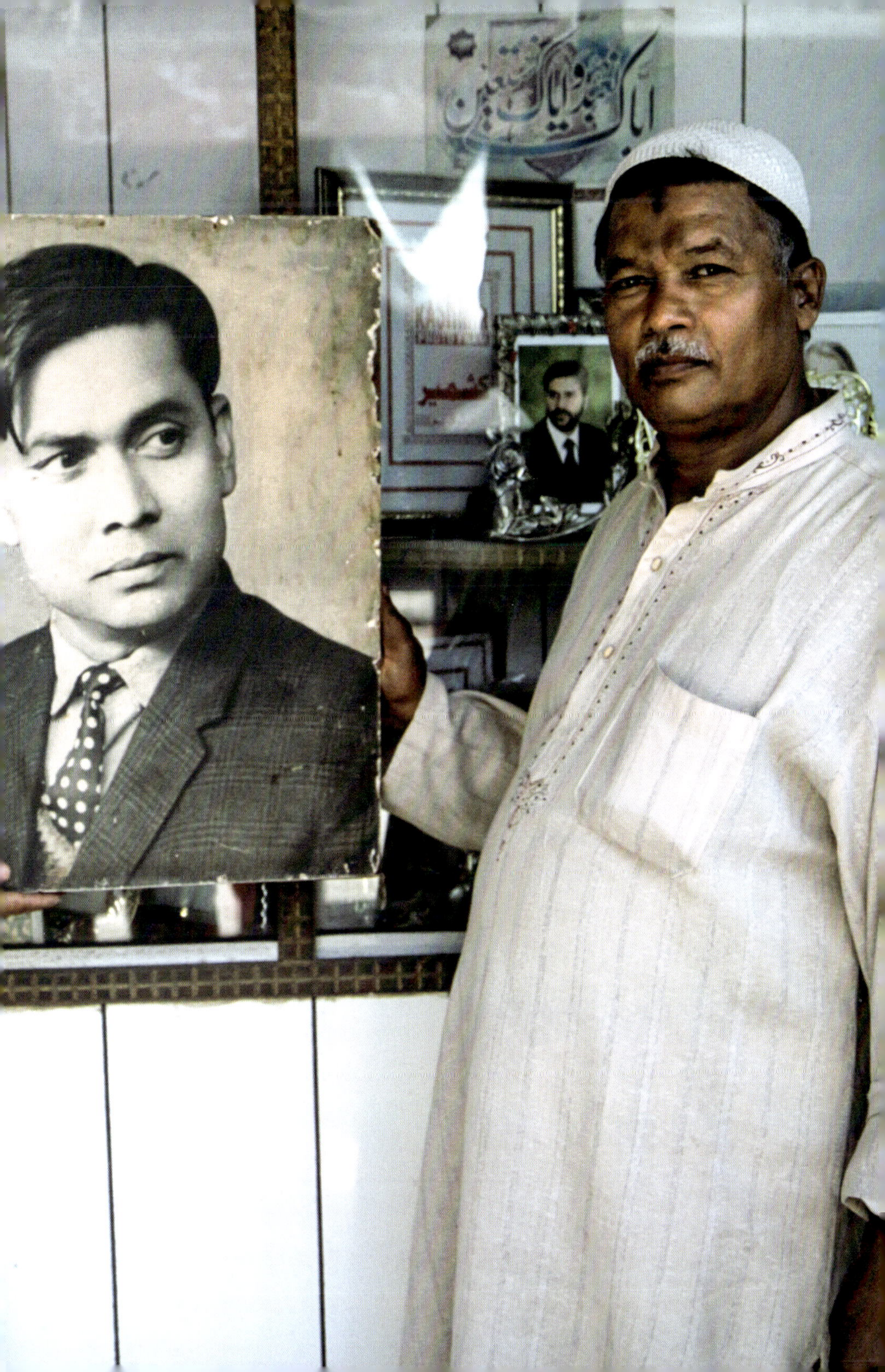

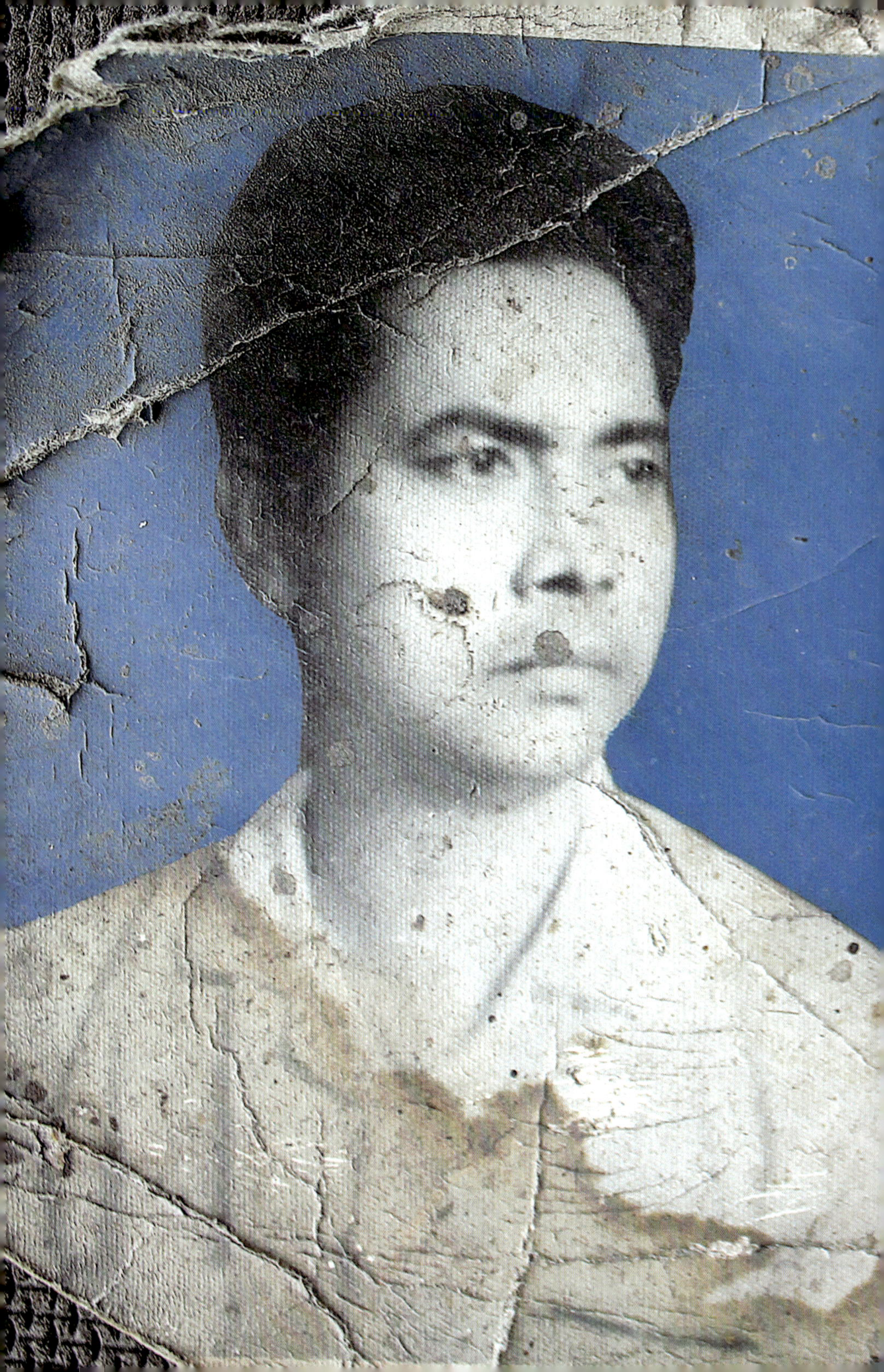

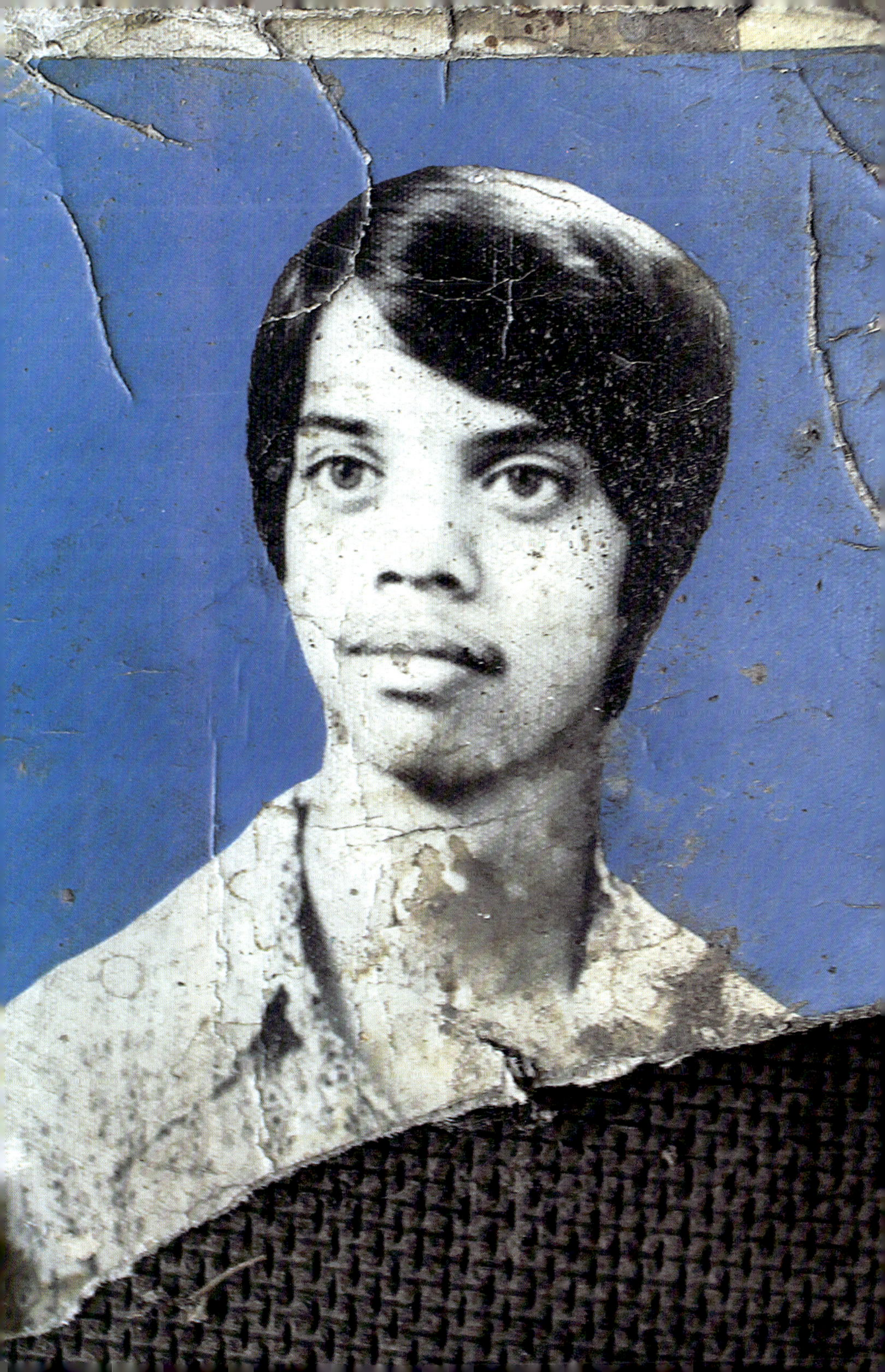

Jamil Ahmad opened Jamalistan Studio in the 1950s after training in National Studio in the Saddar Road area. His teacher was a Partition-time immigrant from India. Donning fashionable attire for portraits, Jamil Ahmad wore a traditional *shalwar qamiz* (a long loose shirt and trousers) to work.

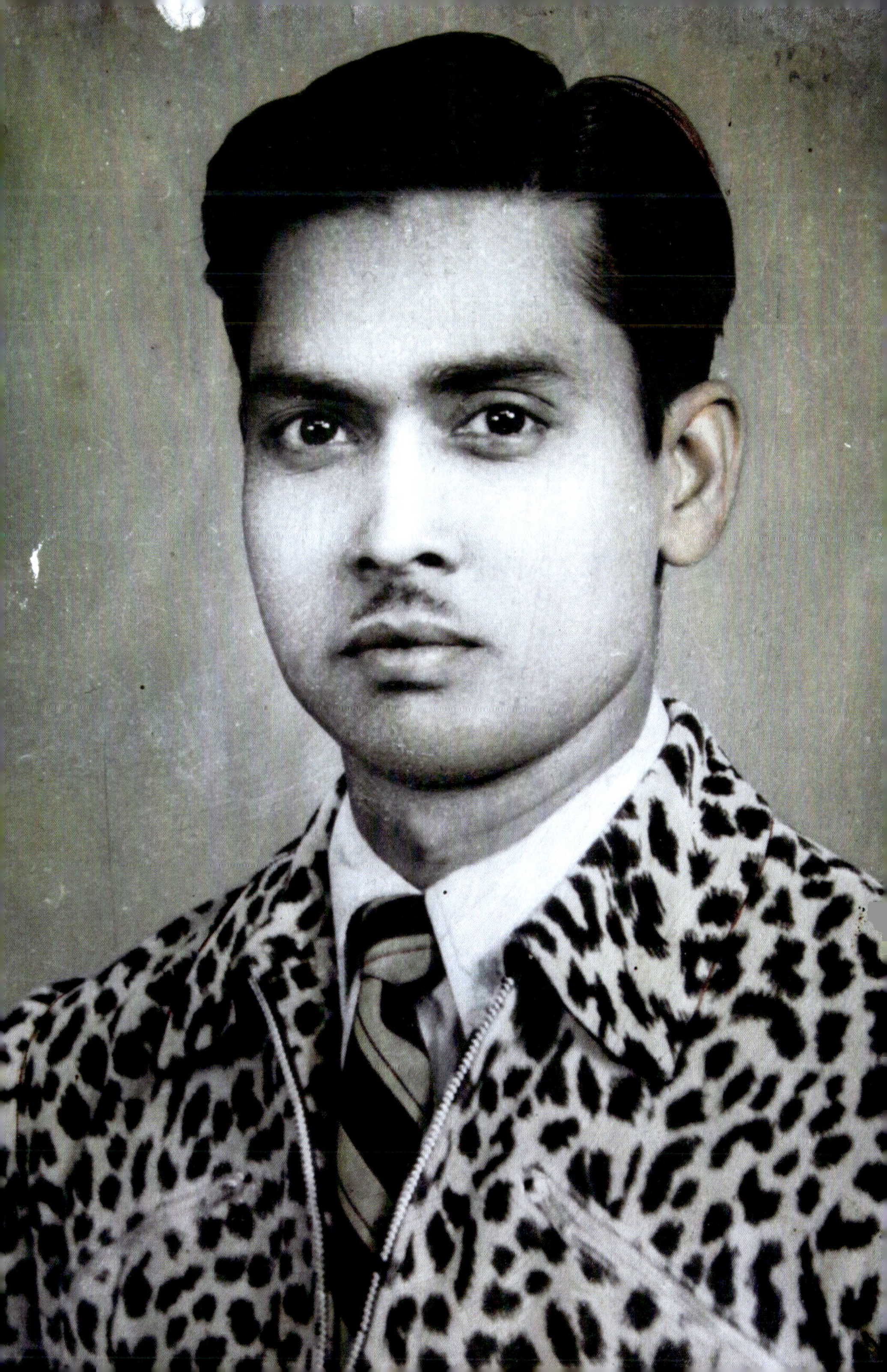

Top right: Abdul Rashaq, founder of Azeem Studio on Saddar Road. Prior to 1952, he was mentor to Abdul Rashid (top left) and Haidar Zaidi (bottom left). The photograph was taken in 2003, a year before he died.

Top left: Abdul Rashid (b.1942) owner of the now-closed Peshawar Photo Company, and latterly Jumbo Studio, was an apprentice to both Abdul Rashaq (top right) and Ashraf Ali Zaidi (p.61).

Bottom right: Muhammad Iqbal, owner of Naqash Studio, photographed by his mentor Abdul Rashid (top left) in the Peshawar Photo Studio in 1974. He also worked for Haidar Zaidi (bottom left) in the Evernew Studio and Ashraf Ali Zaidi (p.61).

Bottom left: Haidar Zaidi owner of the Evernew Studio, who as well as being an apprentice of Abdul Rashaq (top right) and Ashraf Ali Zaidi (p.61) worked in Jamalistan Studio after the founder, Jamil Ahmad (p.69) passed away. Pictured here at around seven years old, Haidar was brought by his uncle from his hometown of Delhi to Lahore in Pakistan, shortly after Partition in 1947.

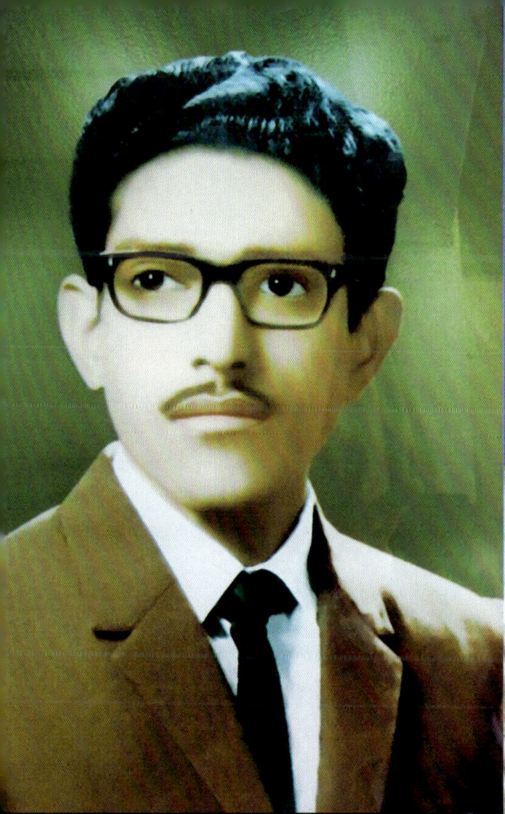
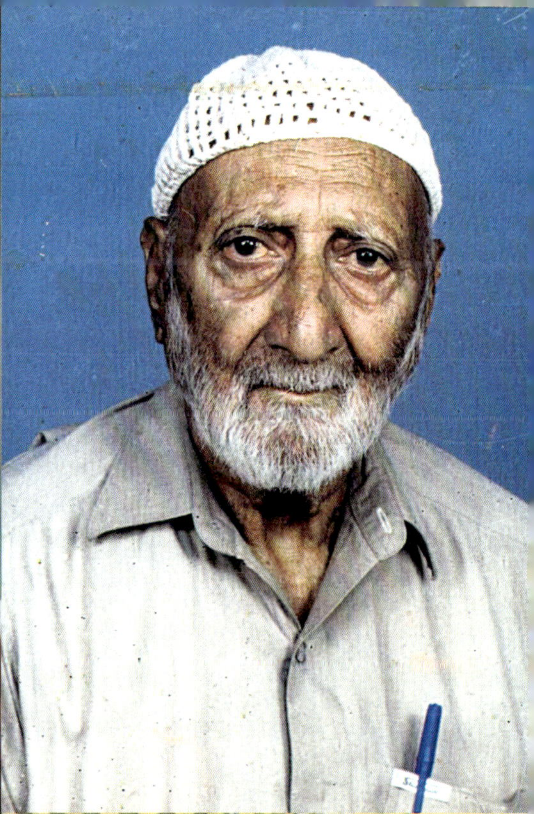
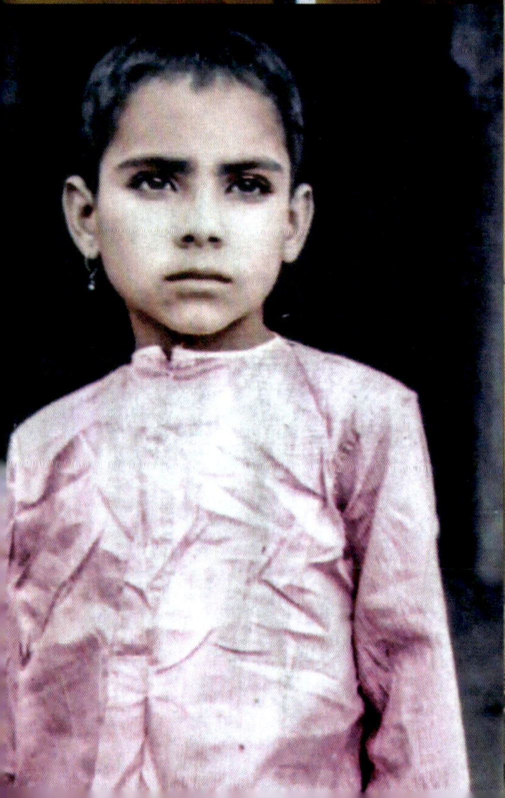
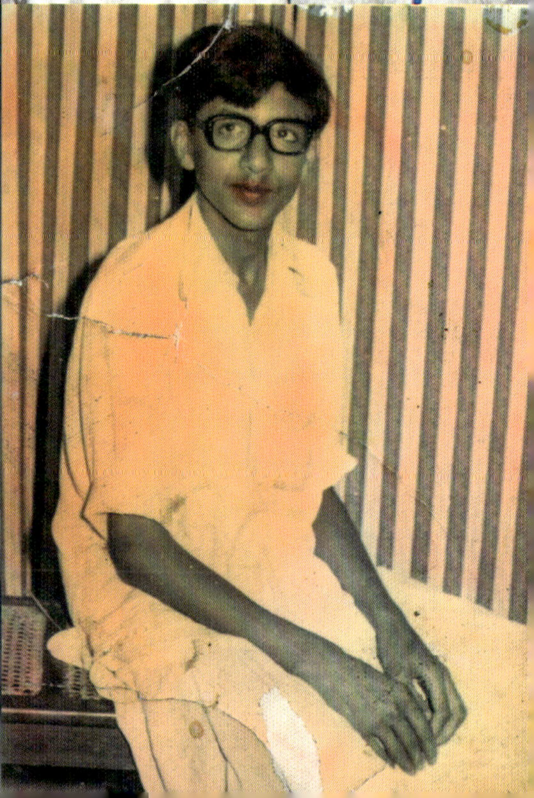

Hand-coloured black and white portrait of a businessman from Kabul, commissioned during the Afghan Civil War (1992–1996), but never collected by the customer. Jamalistan Studio, early 1990s.

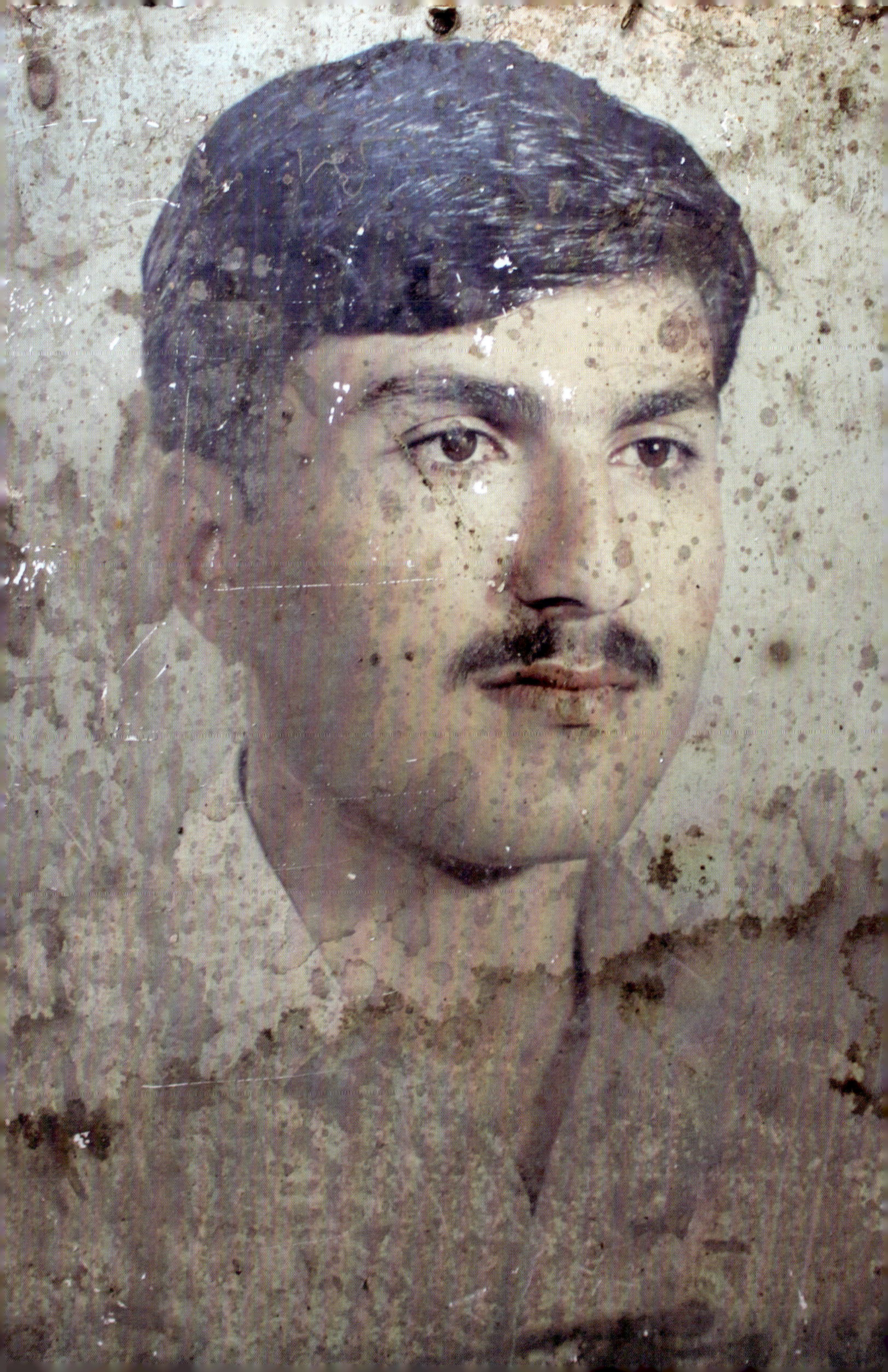

Muhammad Sharif Janbaz (centre) with friends in Mumbai. Trained as a calligrapher and sign-painter, he studied photography in Lahore, Delhi and Mumbai before opening his studio, the Pakistan Photo Electric Company in 1937 in Peshawar; it closed in 1950. Hand-coloured photograph, c.1920s.

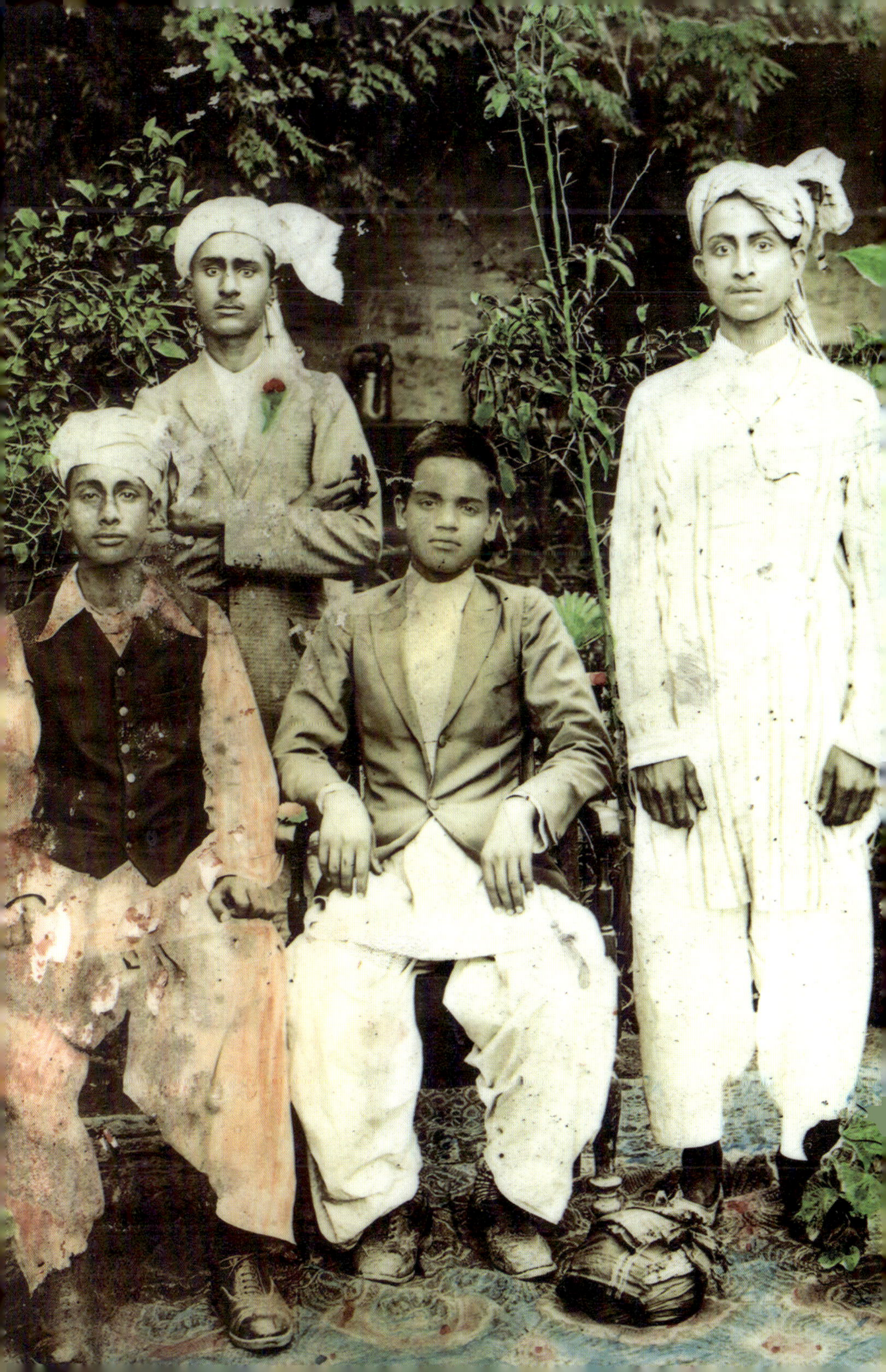

Opposite: Young Kalasha women dance during Springtime festivities. The Kalasha, a non-Muslim minority who live in remote north-western Pakistan, worship multiple deities and claim descent from the fourth century empire builder, Alexander the Great. On the back of the photograph is written 'Kafiristan', meaning: place of non-believers (non-Muslims). The image is part of a childhood collection of photographs belonging to local historian Muhammad Ibrahim Zia, son of calligrapher and photographer Muhammad Sharif Janbaz (preceding page), c.1940s.

Pages 78–79: Picture House cinema on Cinema Road, a target of a grenade attack by religious extremists in early 2014, killing five cinema-goers; a number of photo studios are clustered around the cinema. 2012.

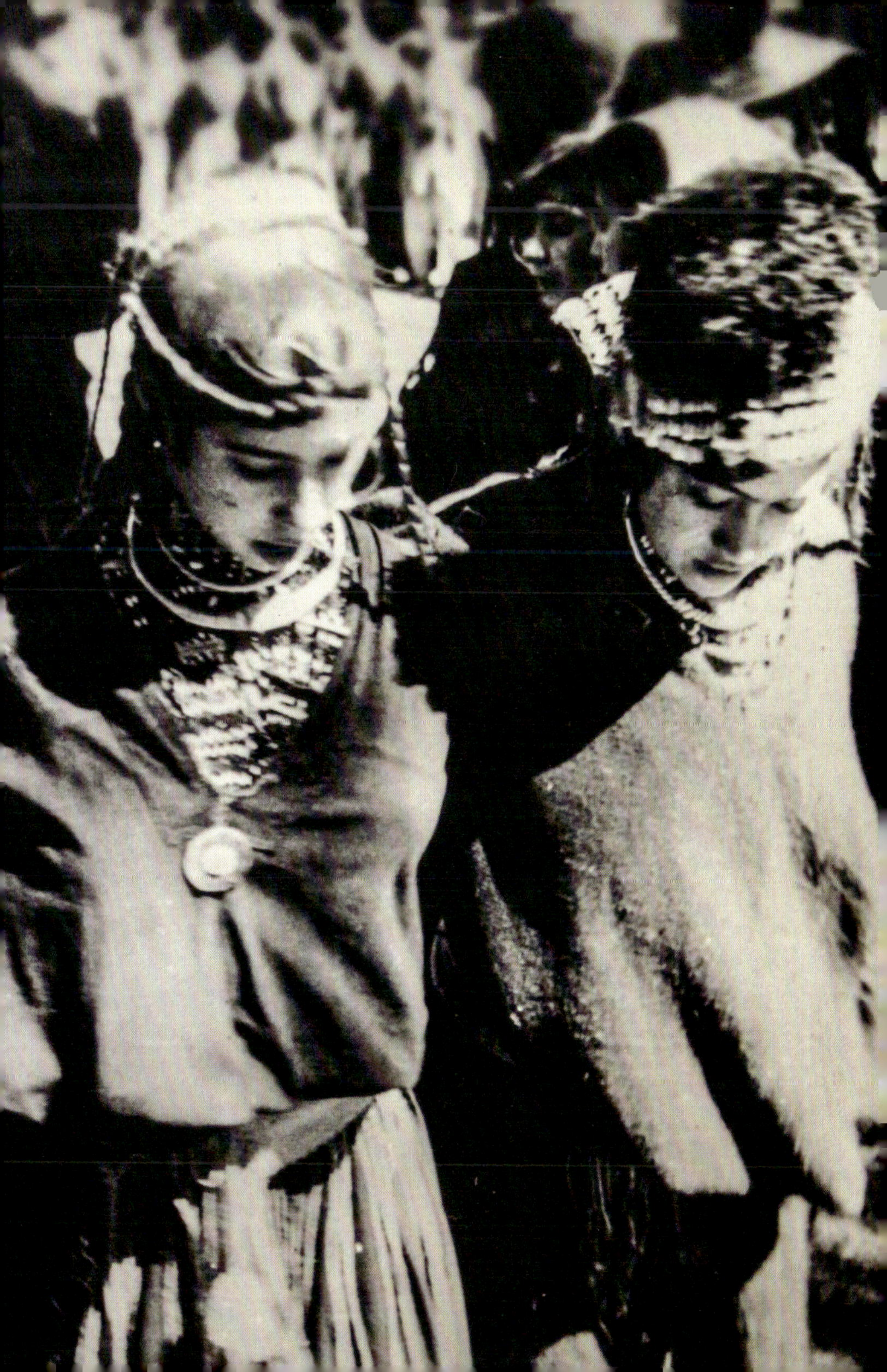

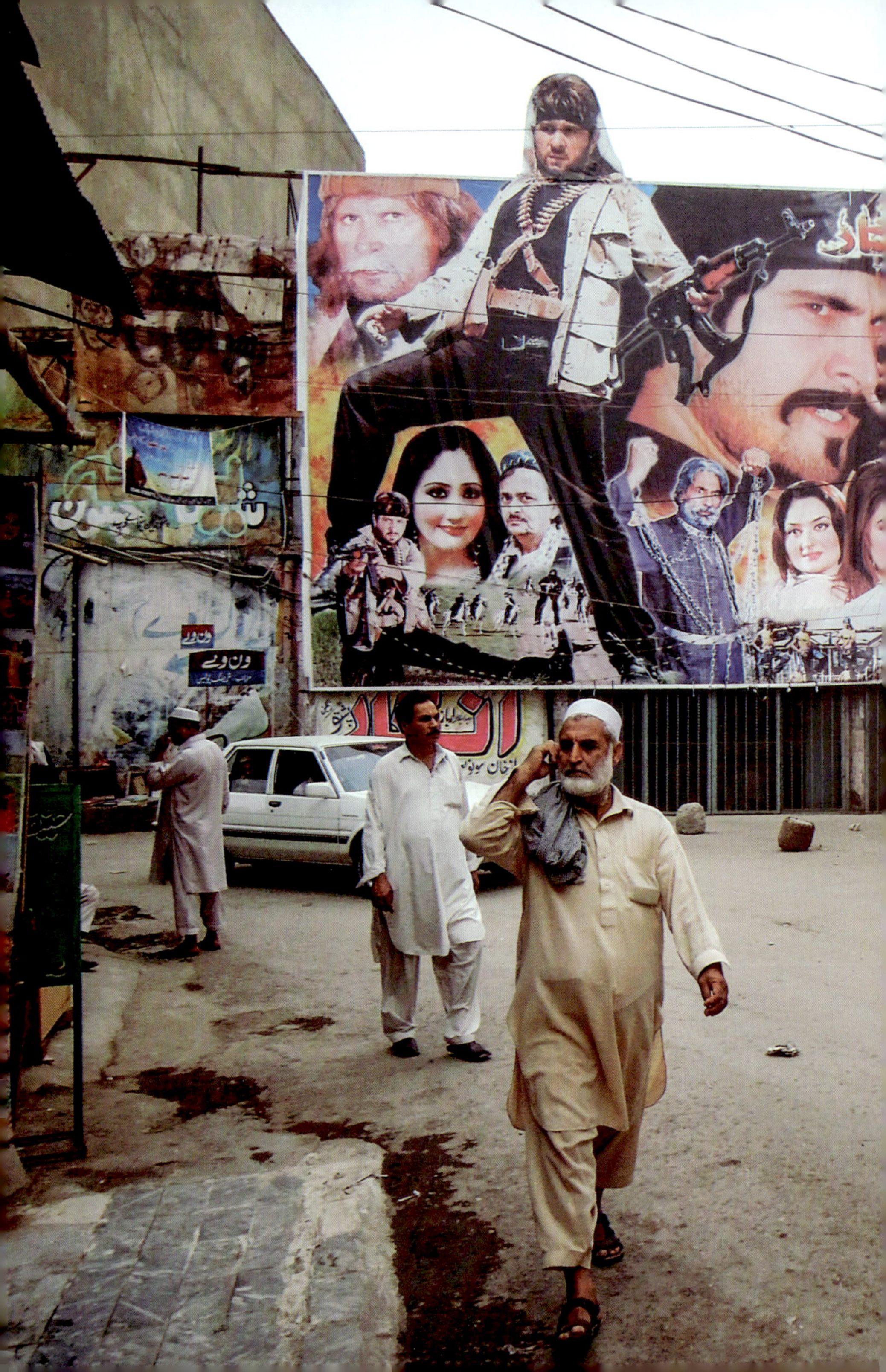
ون وے
ون وے

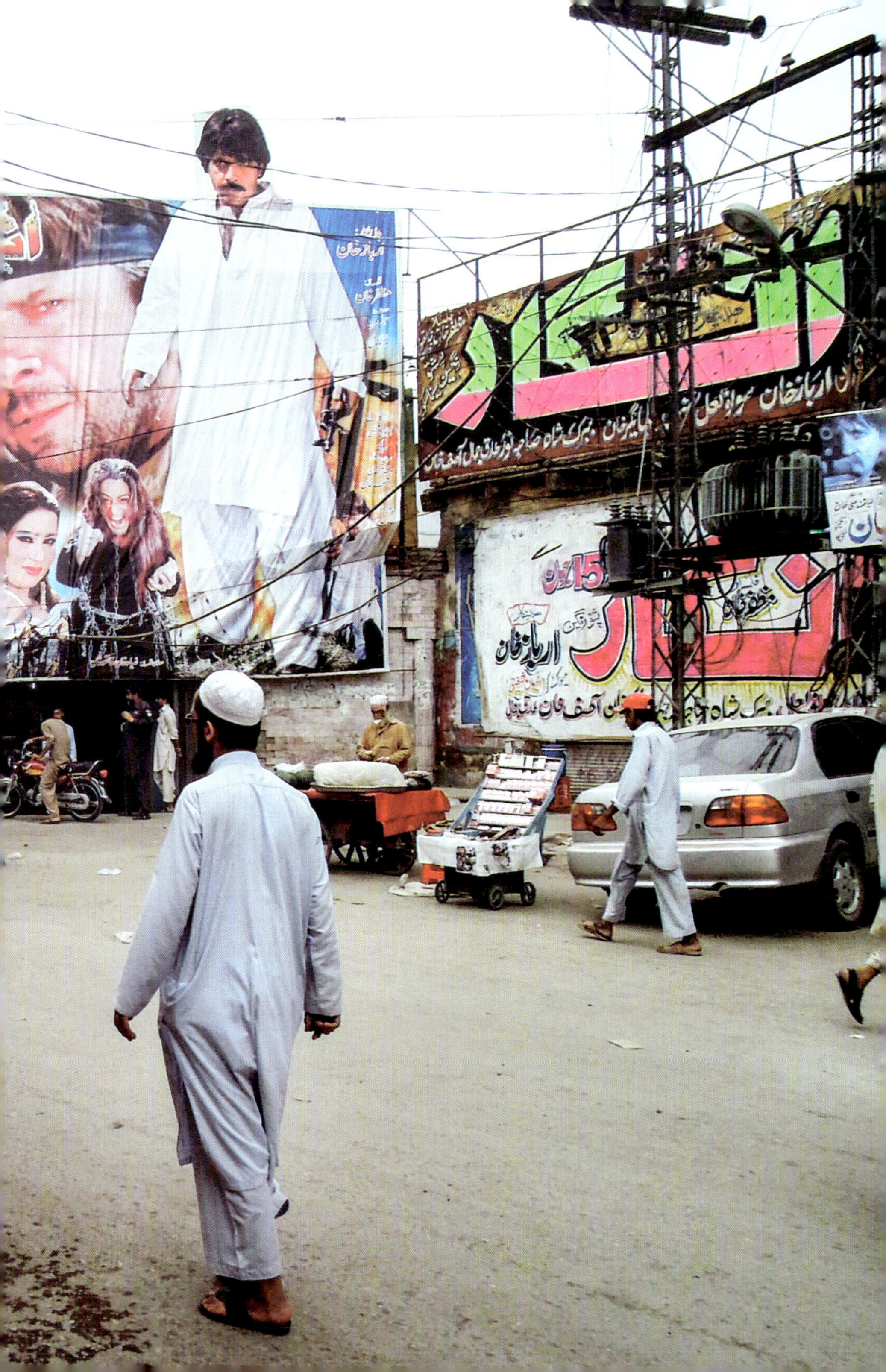
ارباز خان

Opposite and pages 82 & 83: Colour photographs from Javed Studio on Cinema Road, printed from single 35mm negatives. Studios in Peshawar started using colour film around 1976, in some cases developing them by hand. Hand-painted backdrops and props were commonly used before digital manipulation. Whiskey bottles were filled with tea or soft drinks, but the guns were often real. The portrait of the woman is taken from a movie, c.1990s.

Pages 84–85: Paintings advertising the Hollywood movie, *Snow White and the Huntsman*, outside Naz Cinema, also known as English Cinema, opposite Jamalistan Studio on Hospital Road. In contrast to the Naz Cinema, the cinemas on Cinema Road only show regional films, 2012.

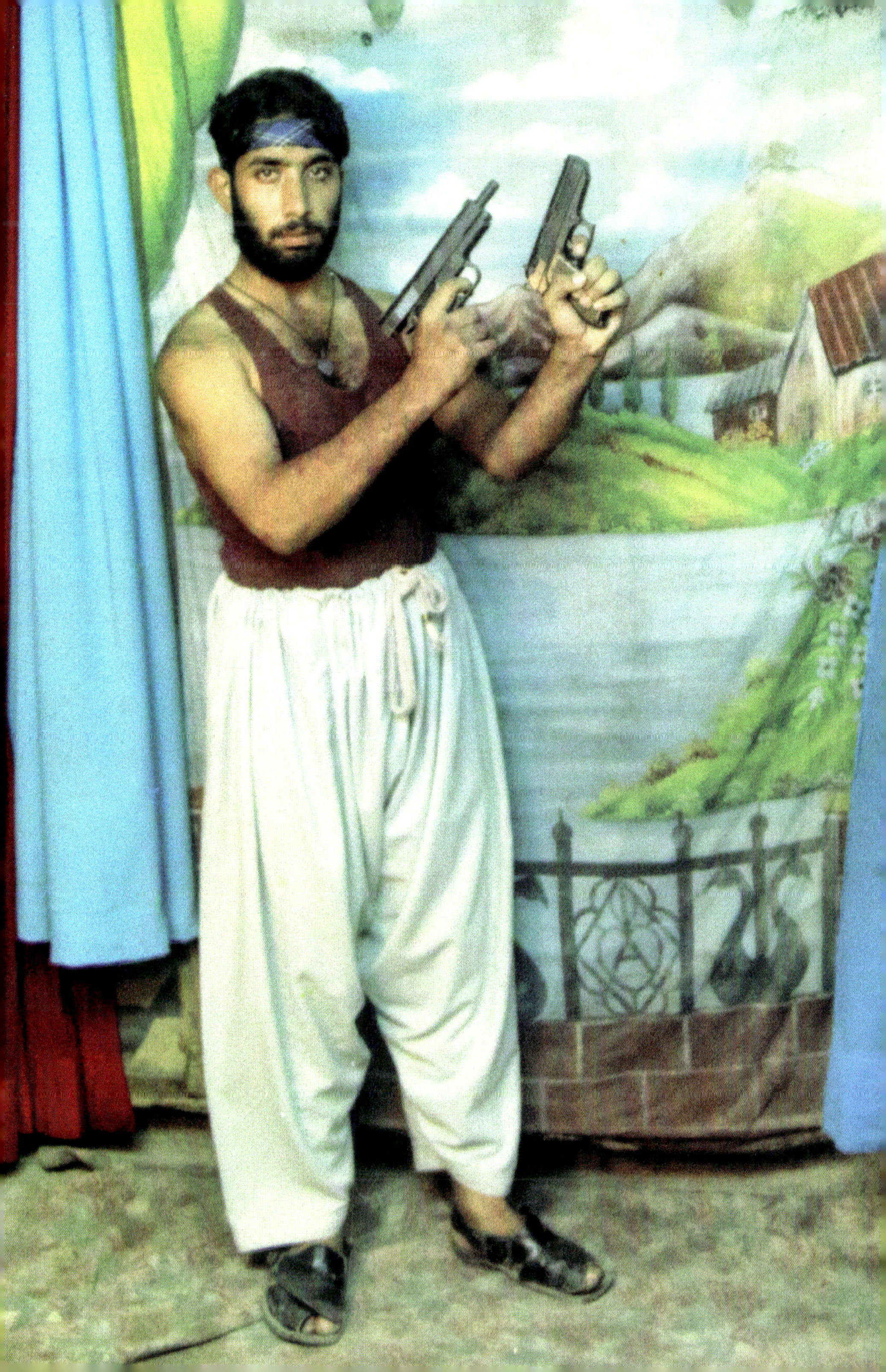

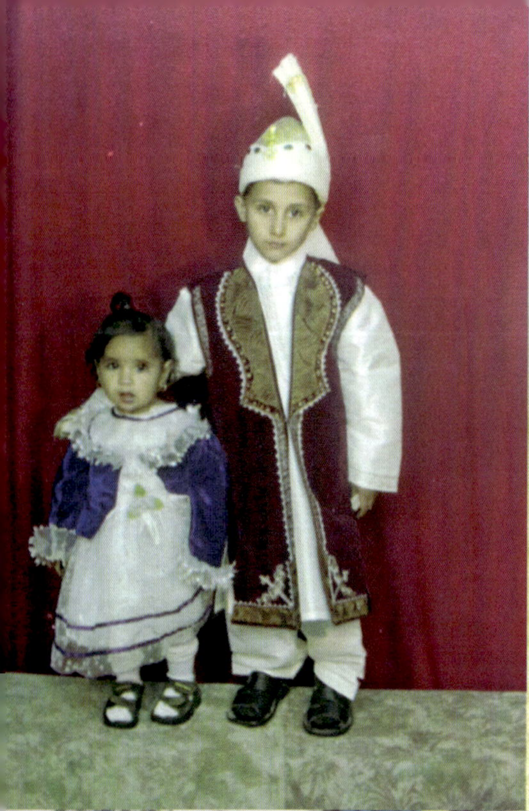
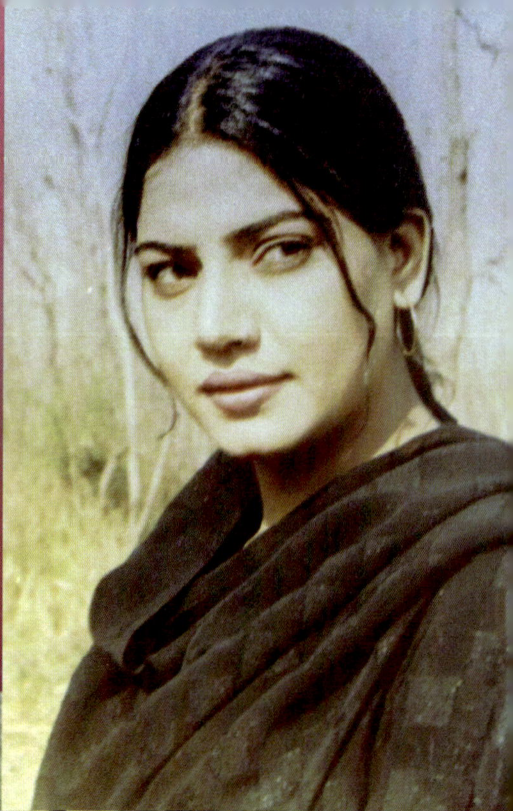
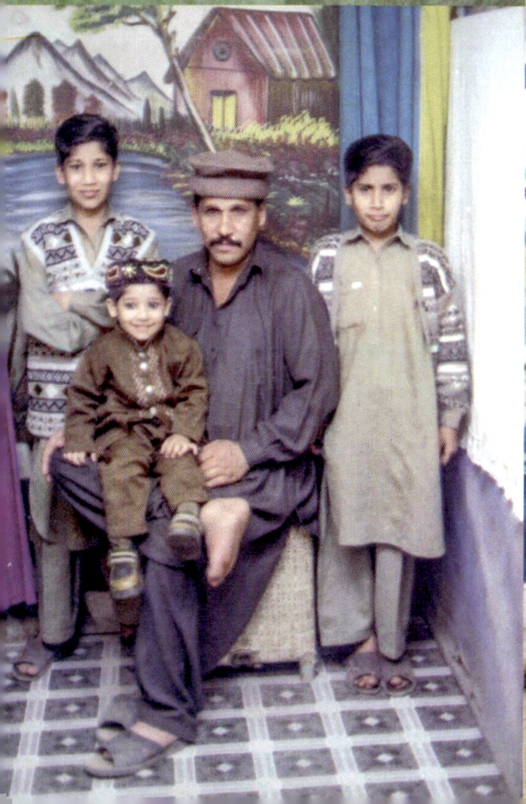
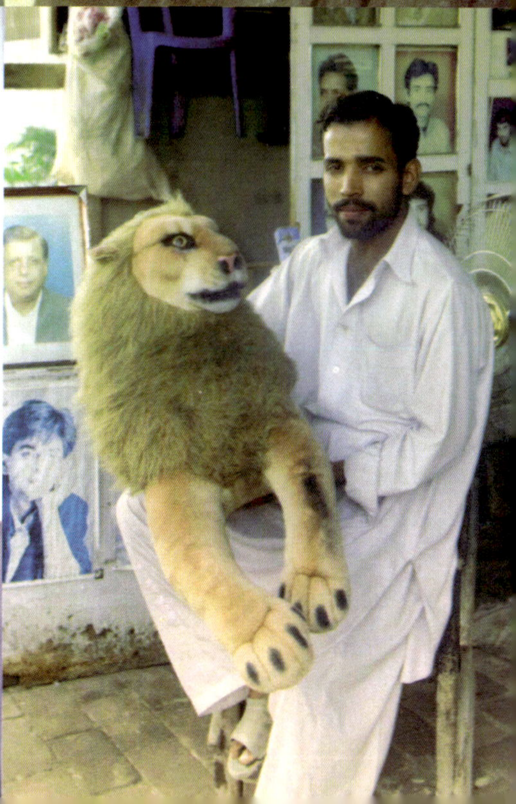

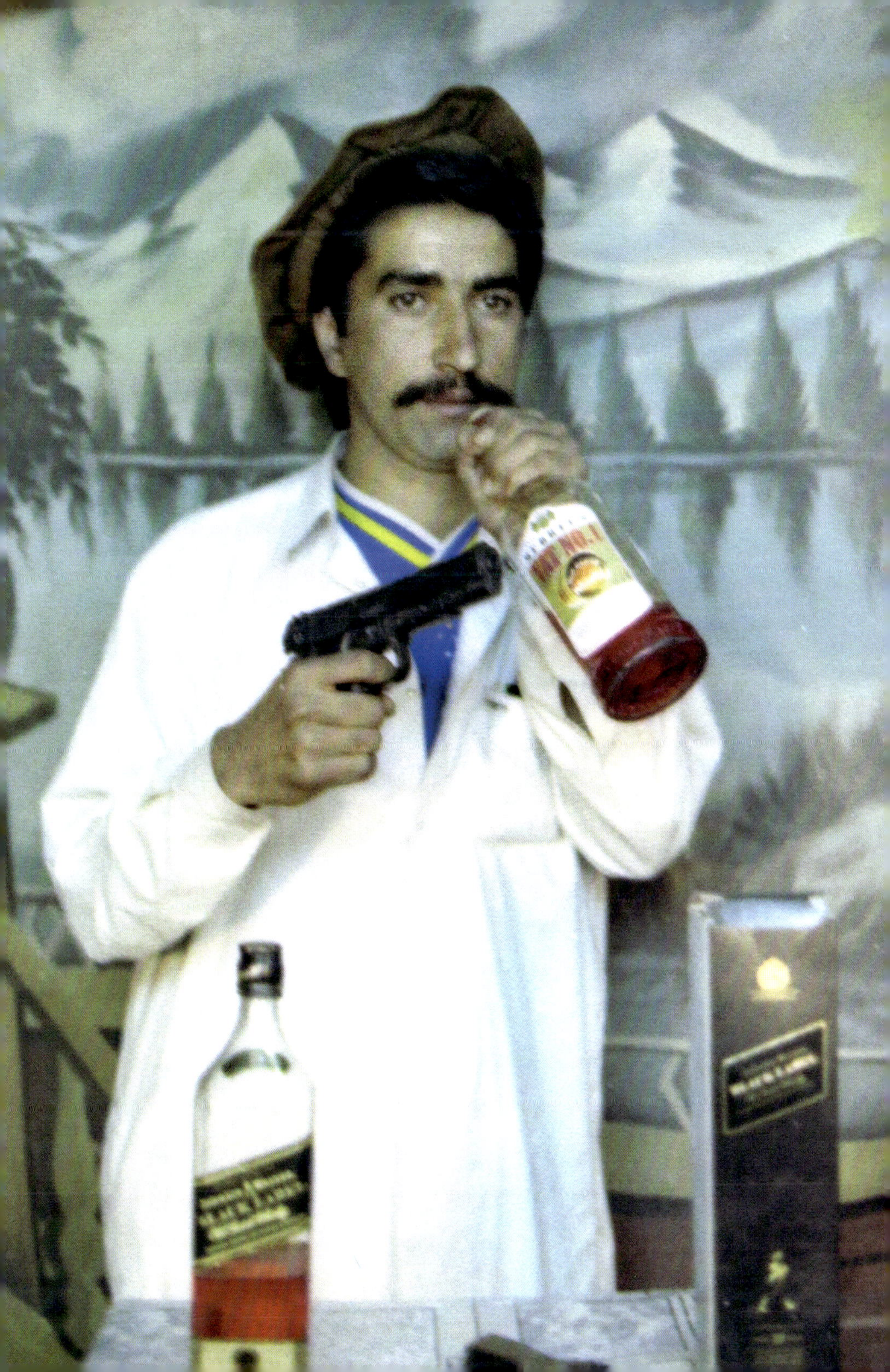

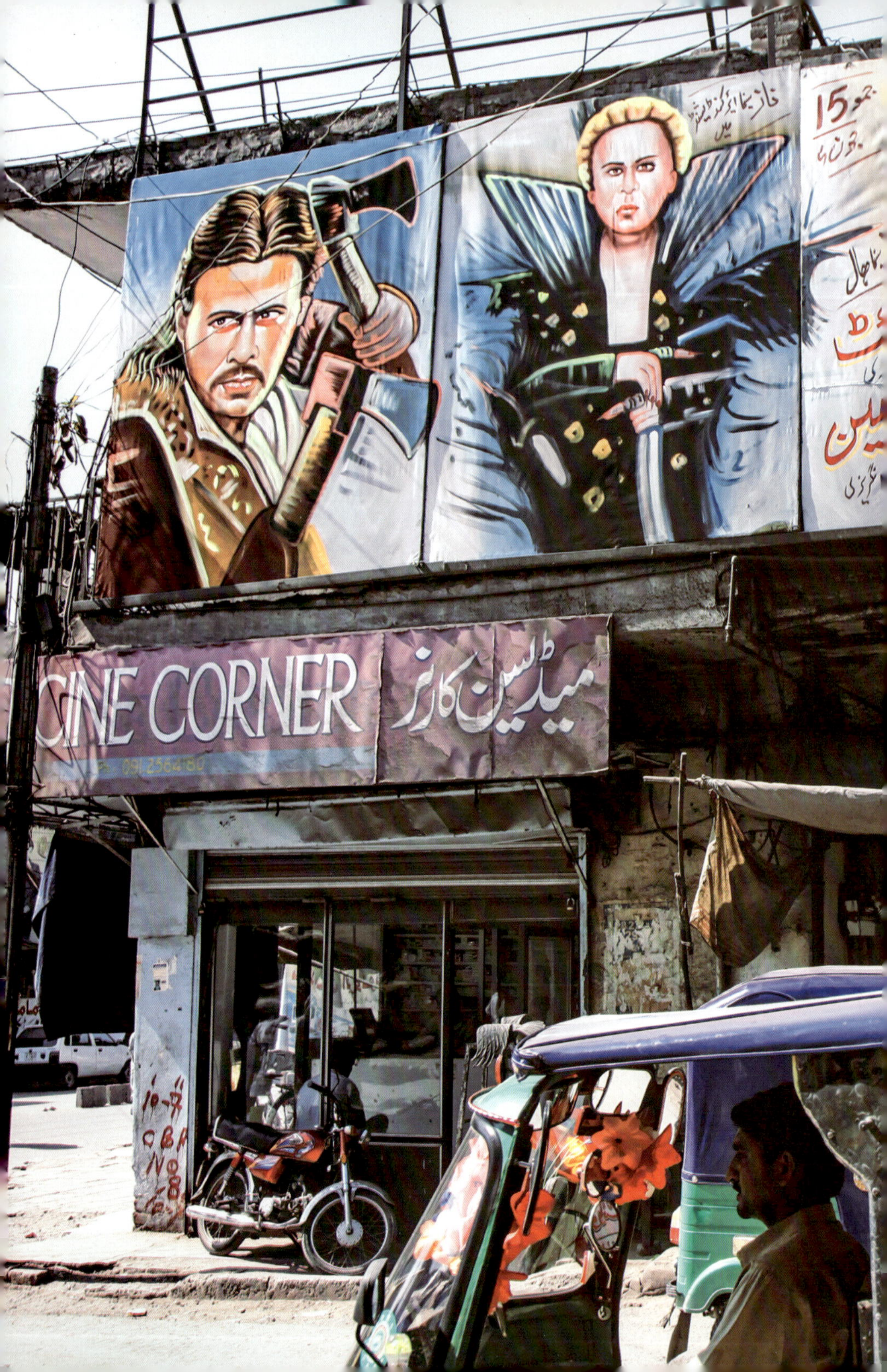
CINE CORNER
میڈیسن کارنر

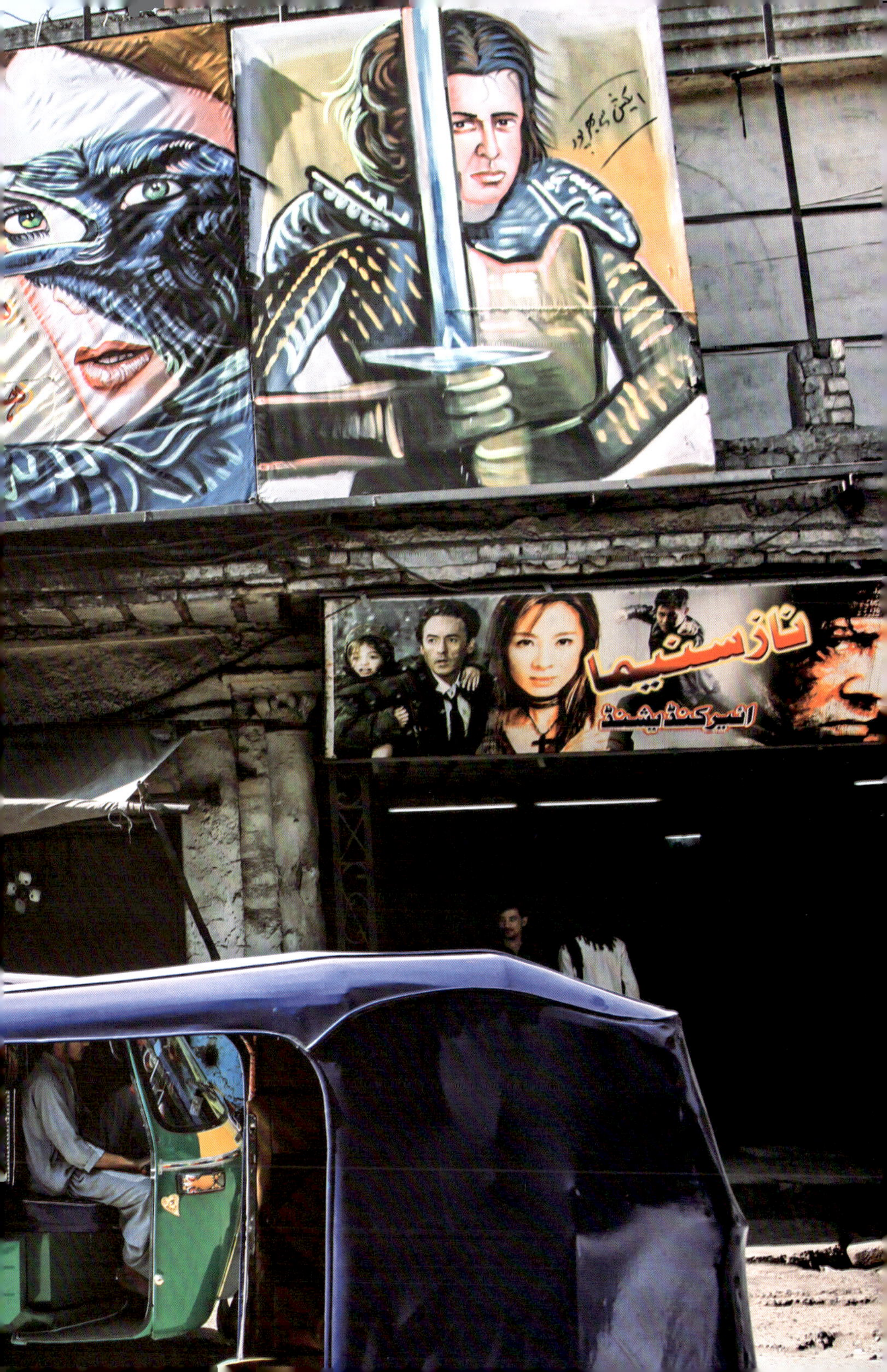
ناز سنیما
ائیرکنڈیشنڈ

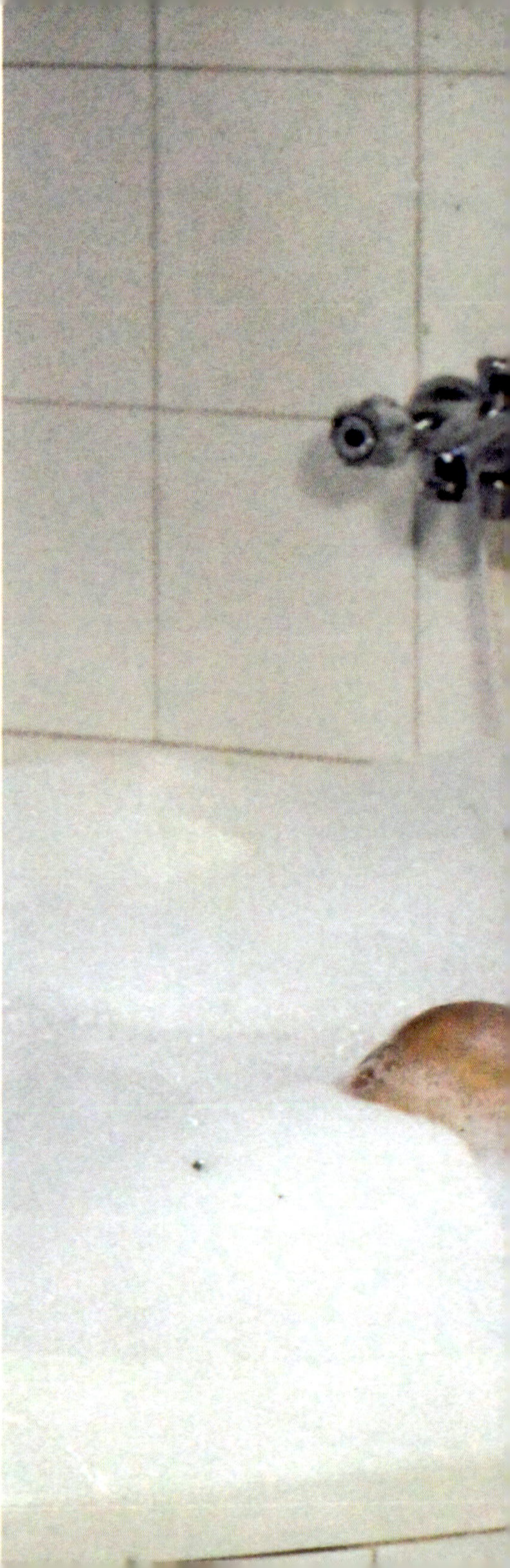

Opposite: Cinema poster from Capital Cinema on Saddar Road. In recent years, cinemas in Peshawar have been bombed by religious extremists who consider cinematic entertainment immoral.

Pages 88–89: Musarrat Shaheen dances far right in a second Capital Cinema poster. The former Pashtun actress unsuccessfully ran for political office in Khyber Pakhtunkhwa in 2013.

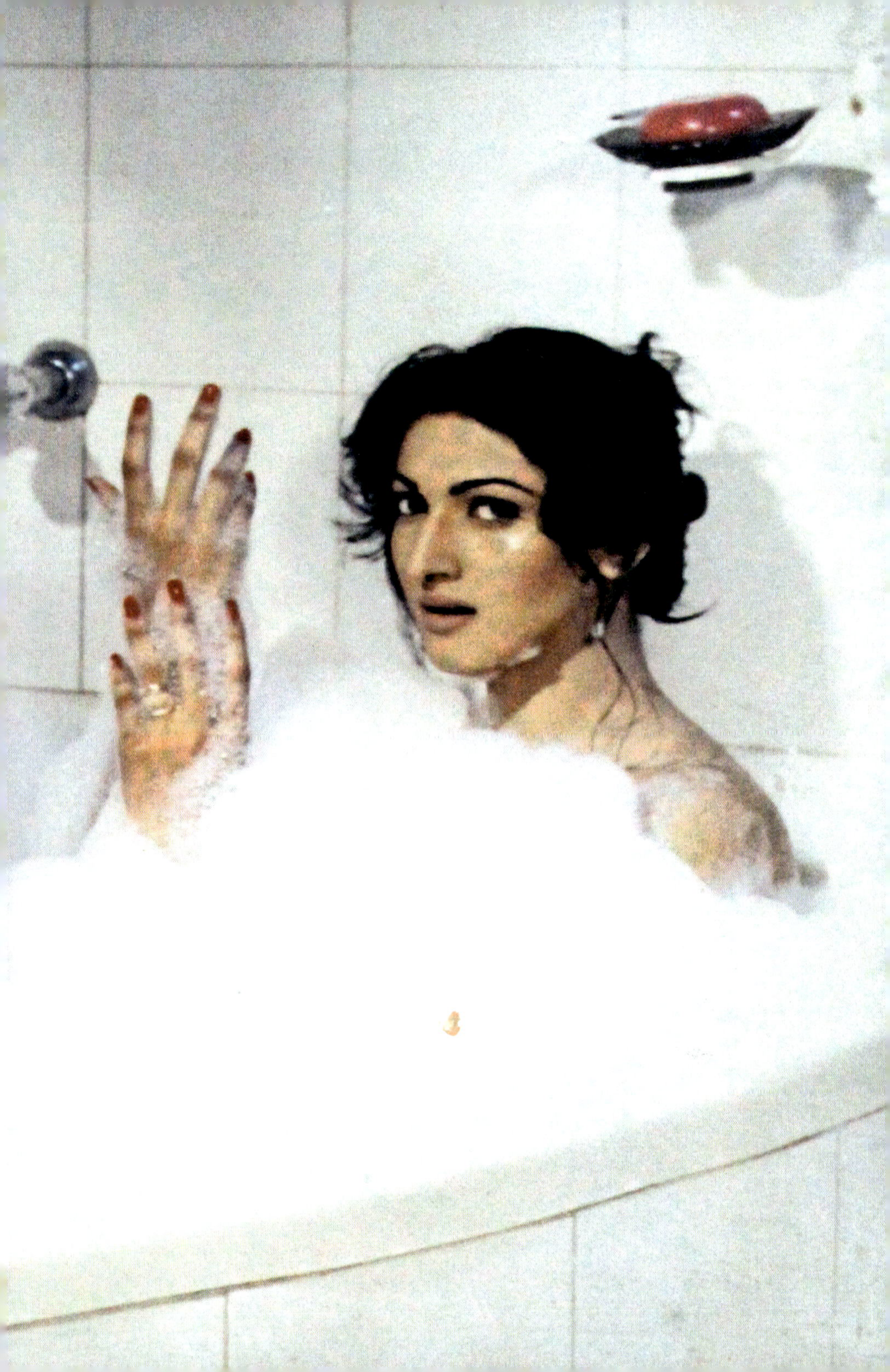

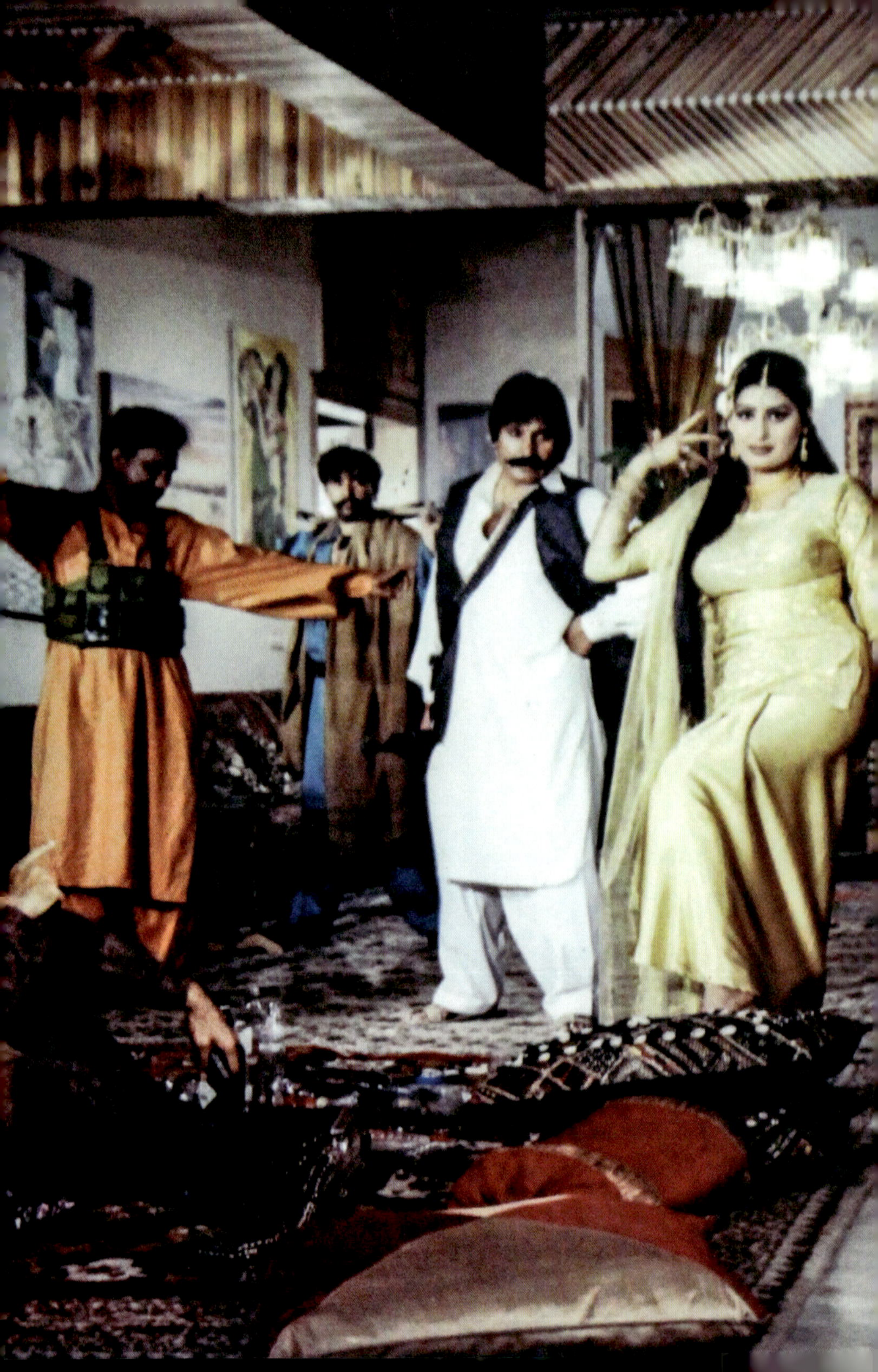

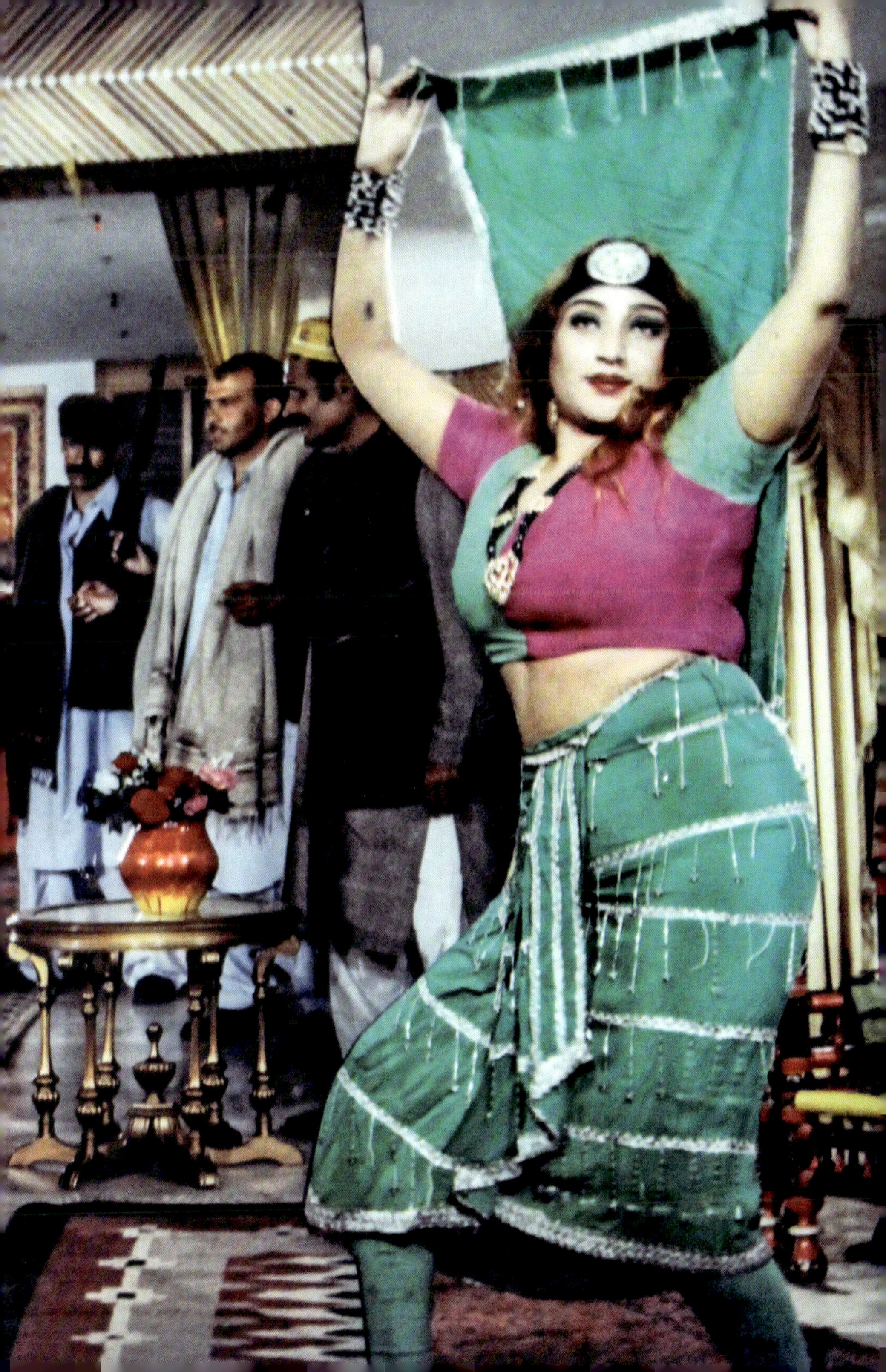

Muhammad Iqbal (standing), owner of Kamran Studio on Cinema Road, with his friend and fellow photographer, Aslam. Taught by his father, as a young boy, Aslam began his photographic career on the paper-negative minute camera.

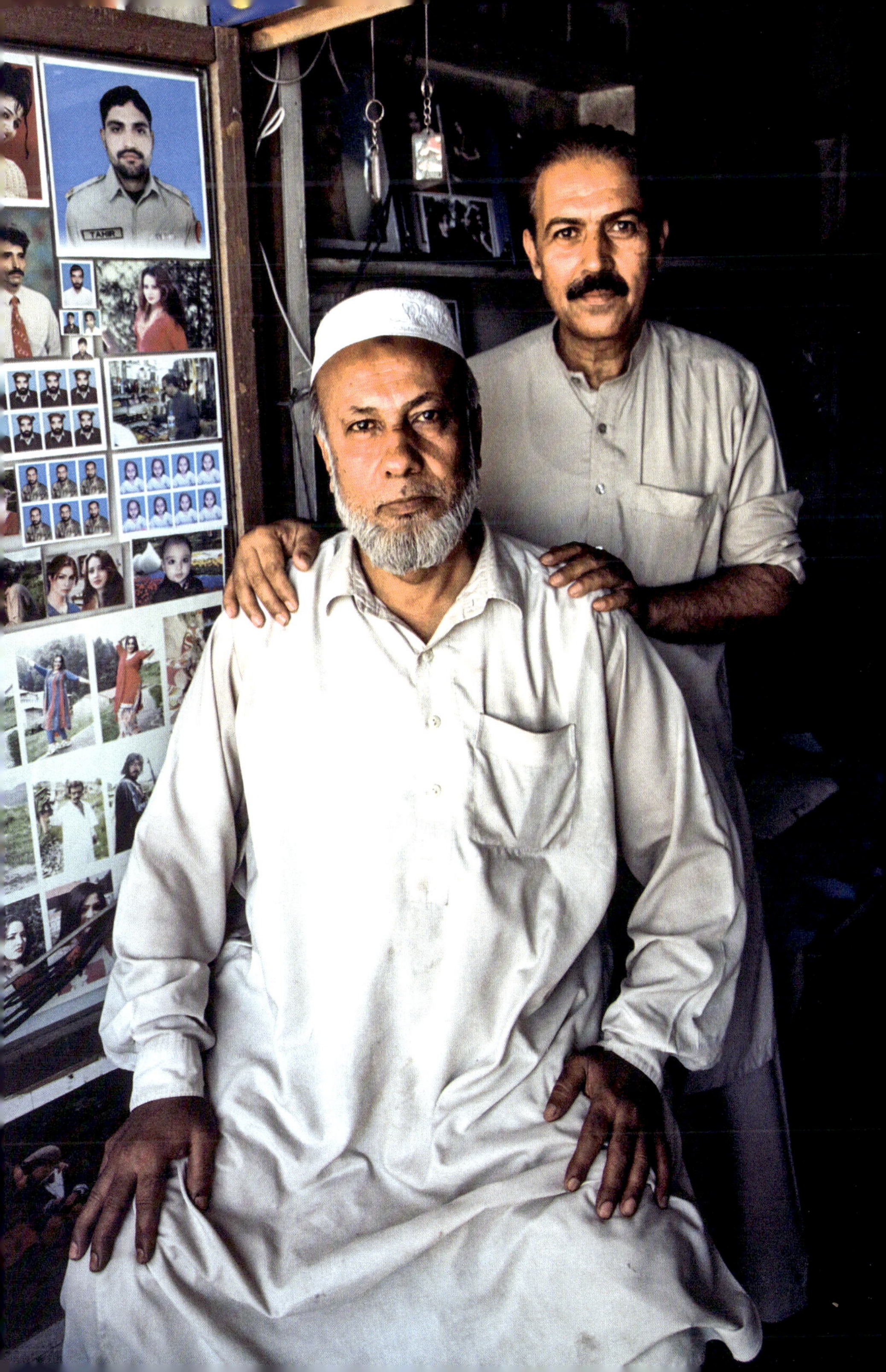
TAHIR

A hand-coloured montage with a customer's face inset, based on the Pashtu-language film *Bangles & Cuffs*. The helicopter, which does not appear in this scene of the movie, is the photographer's addition, possibly influenced by the neighbouring war in Afghanistan between the Afghan Mujahedin and Russians, Kamran Studio, 1980s–1990s.

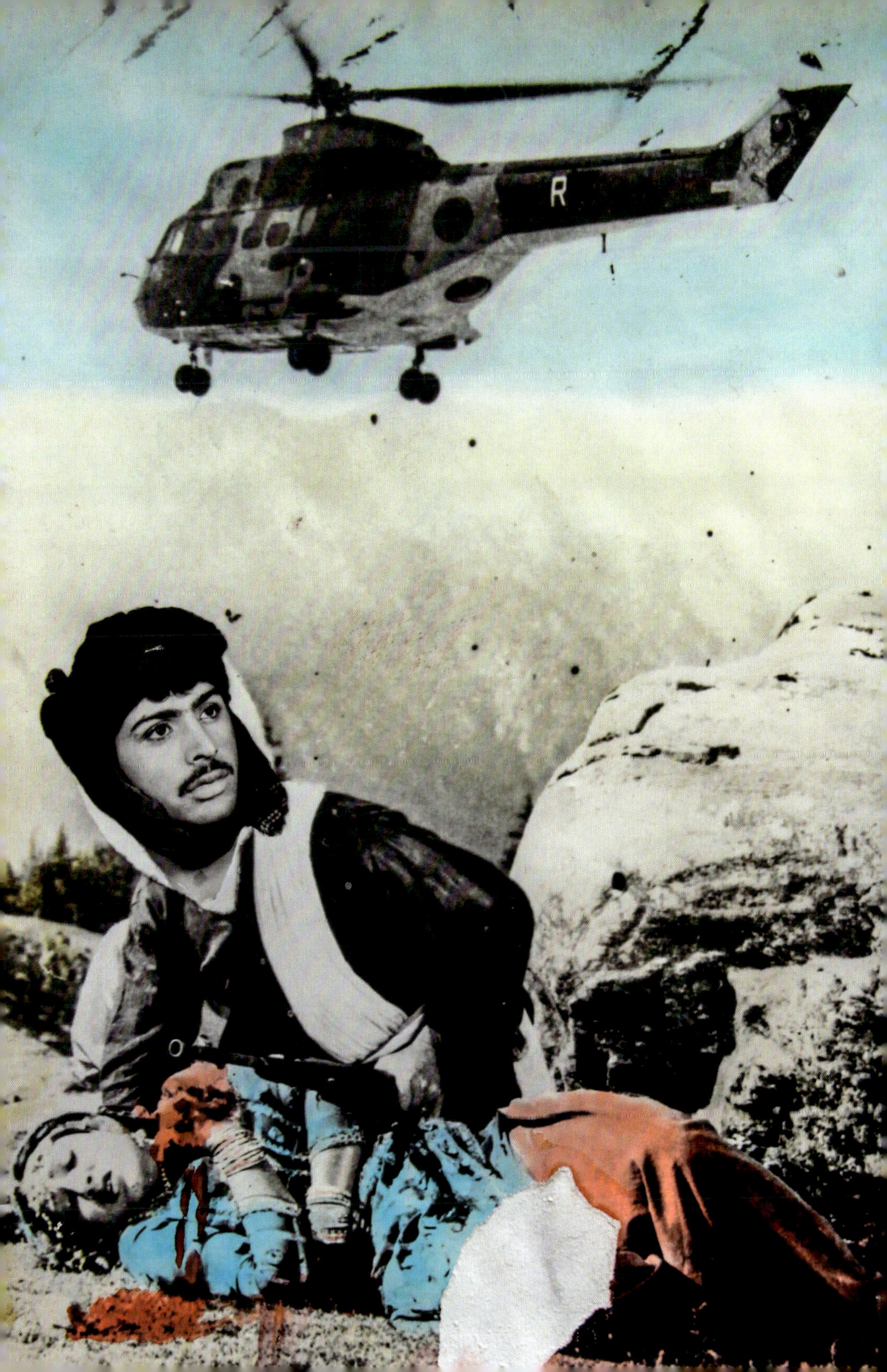
R

Opposite & pages 96 & 97: Hand-coloured montages based on Indian movie posters; male customers have their faces inset to pose alongside actresses. Kamran Studio, 1990s.

Pages 98–101: Hand-coloured portraits of foreign tourists, Kamran Studio, 1990s; *Pages* 102–105: Hand-coloured montages based on a *Rambo Part III* movie poster. The 1988-released movie struck a chord amongst the Afghan population in the city as the main character fought against the Russian invaders in Afghanistan alongside local Mujahedin. Peshawar was a major Mujahedin base in the 1980s and 1990s, and was home to hundreds of thousands of Afghan refugees. Kamran Studio, 1990s.

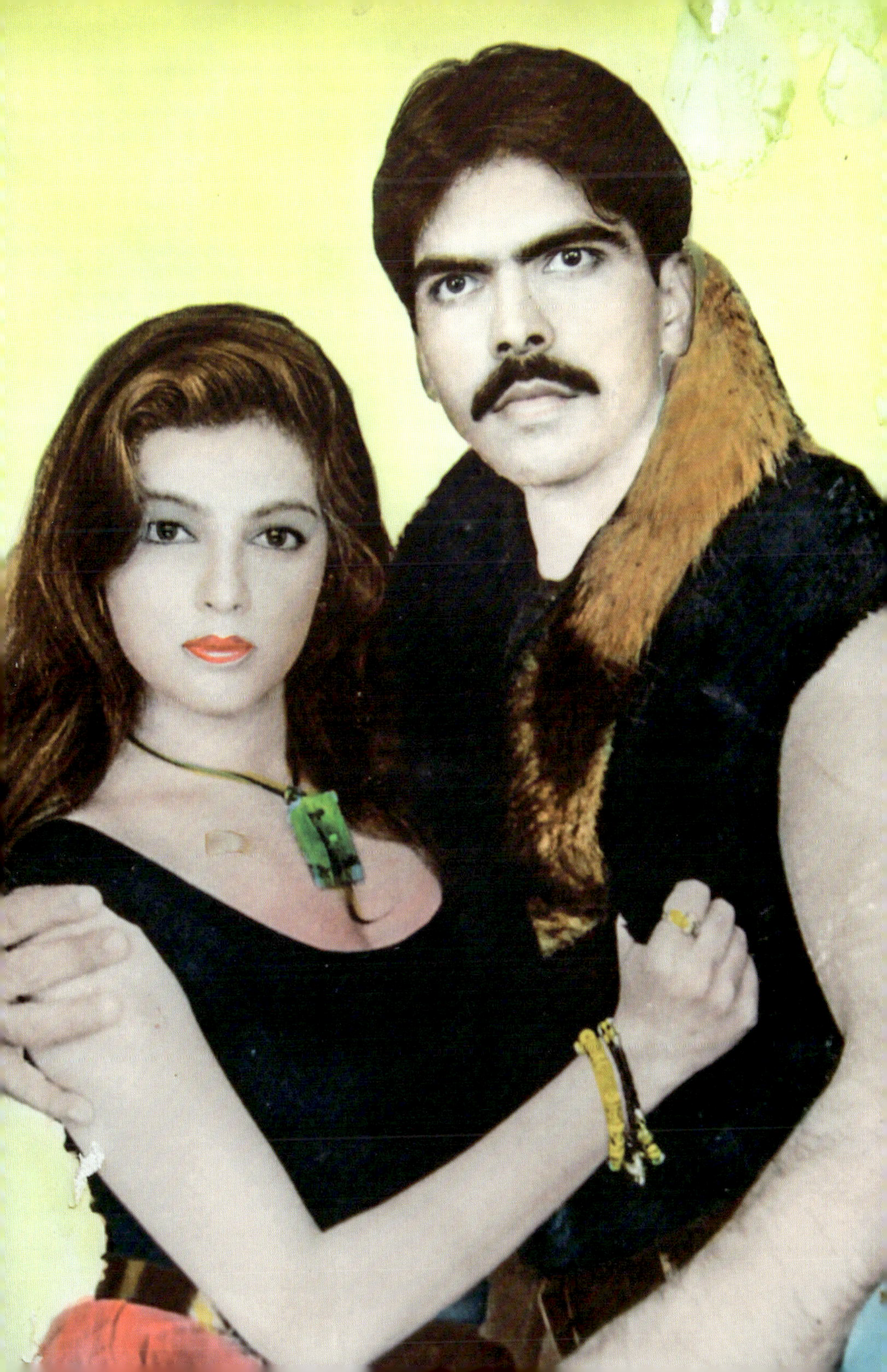

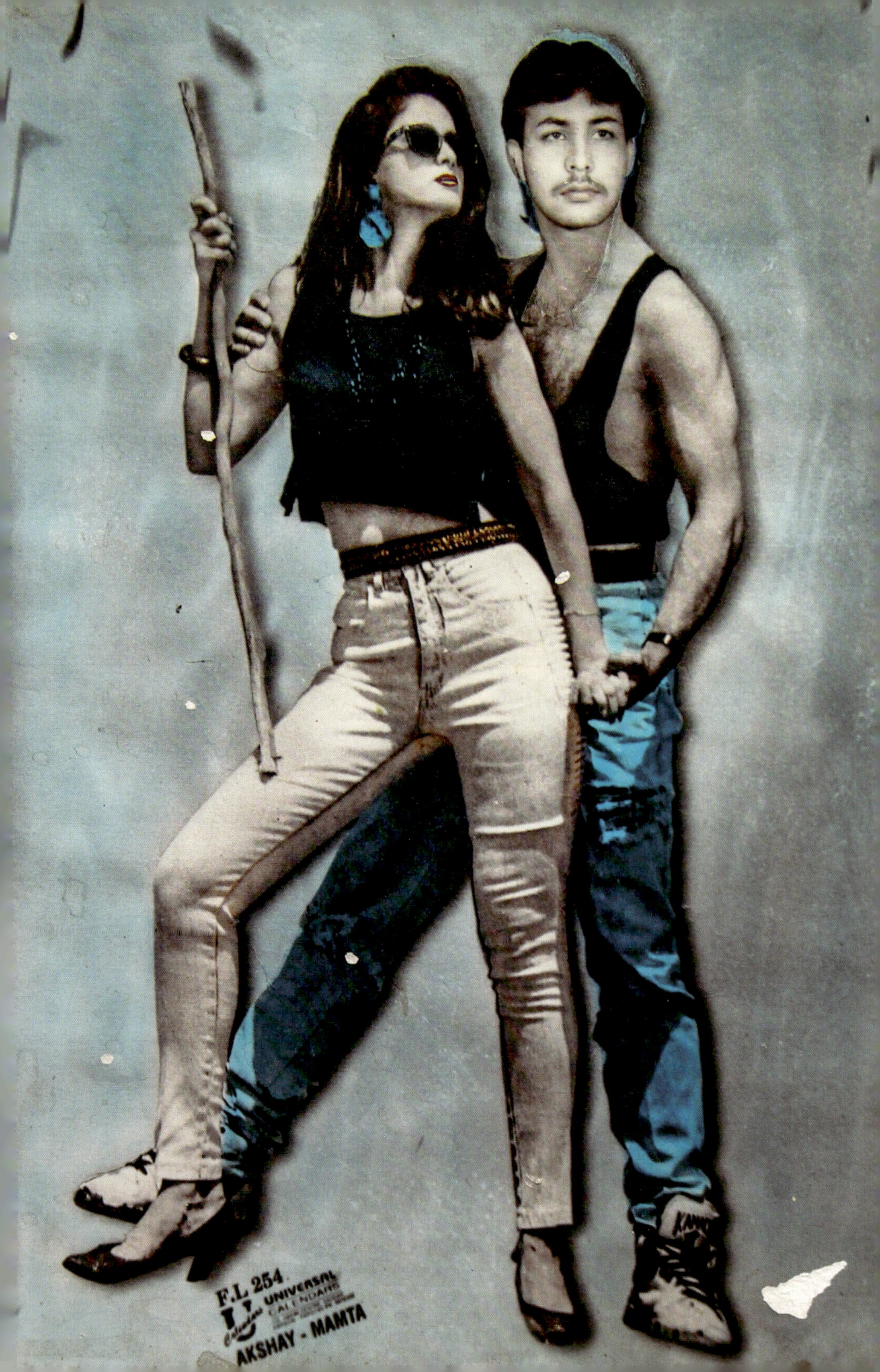
F.L 254
UNIVERSAL
CALENDARS
AKSHAY - MAMTA

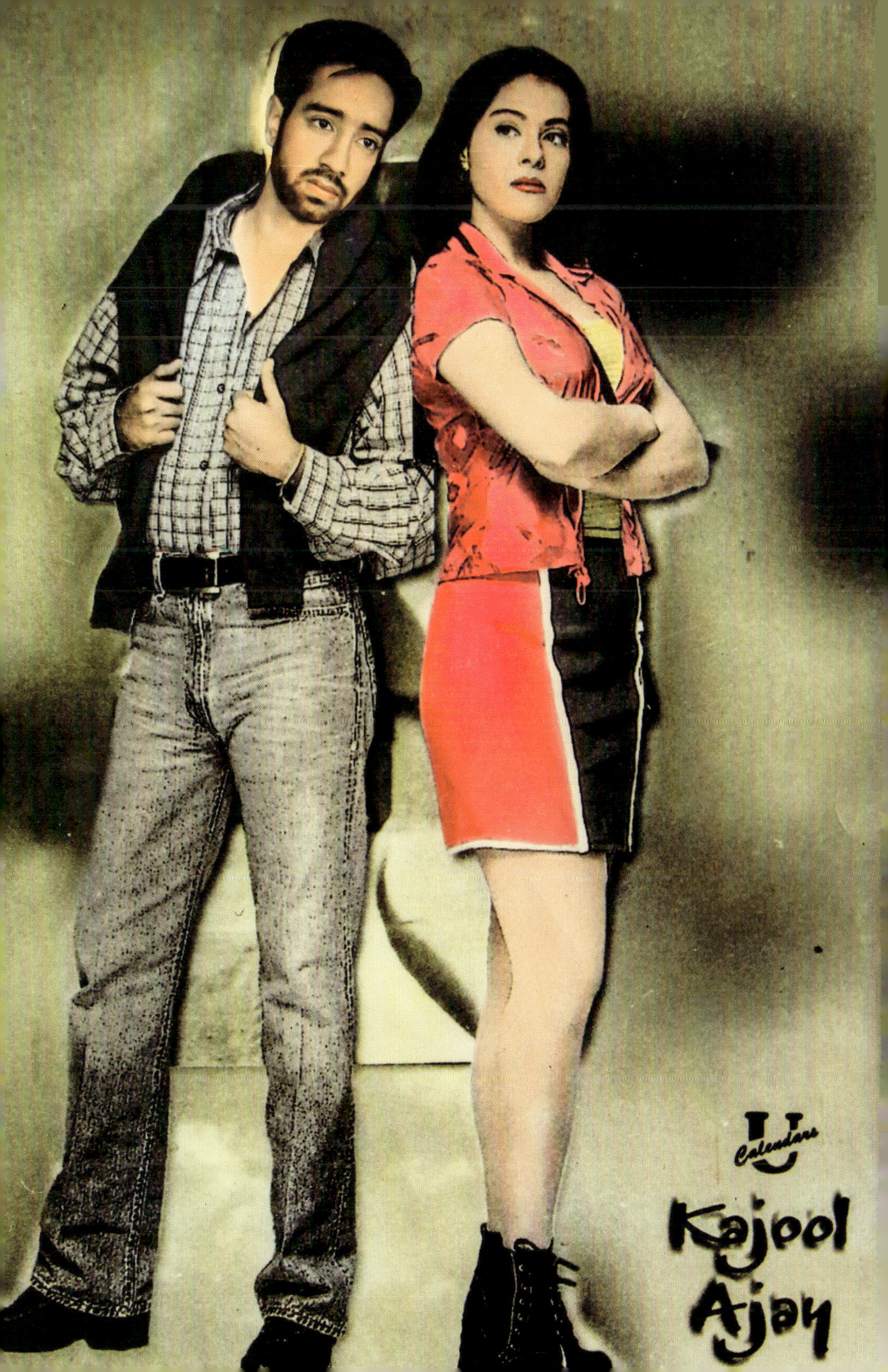
U Calendars
Kajool
Ajay

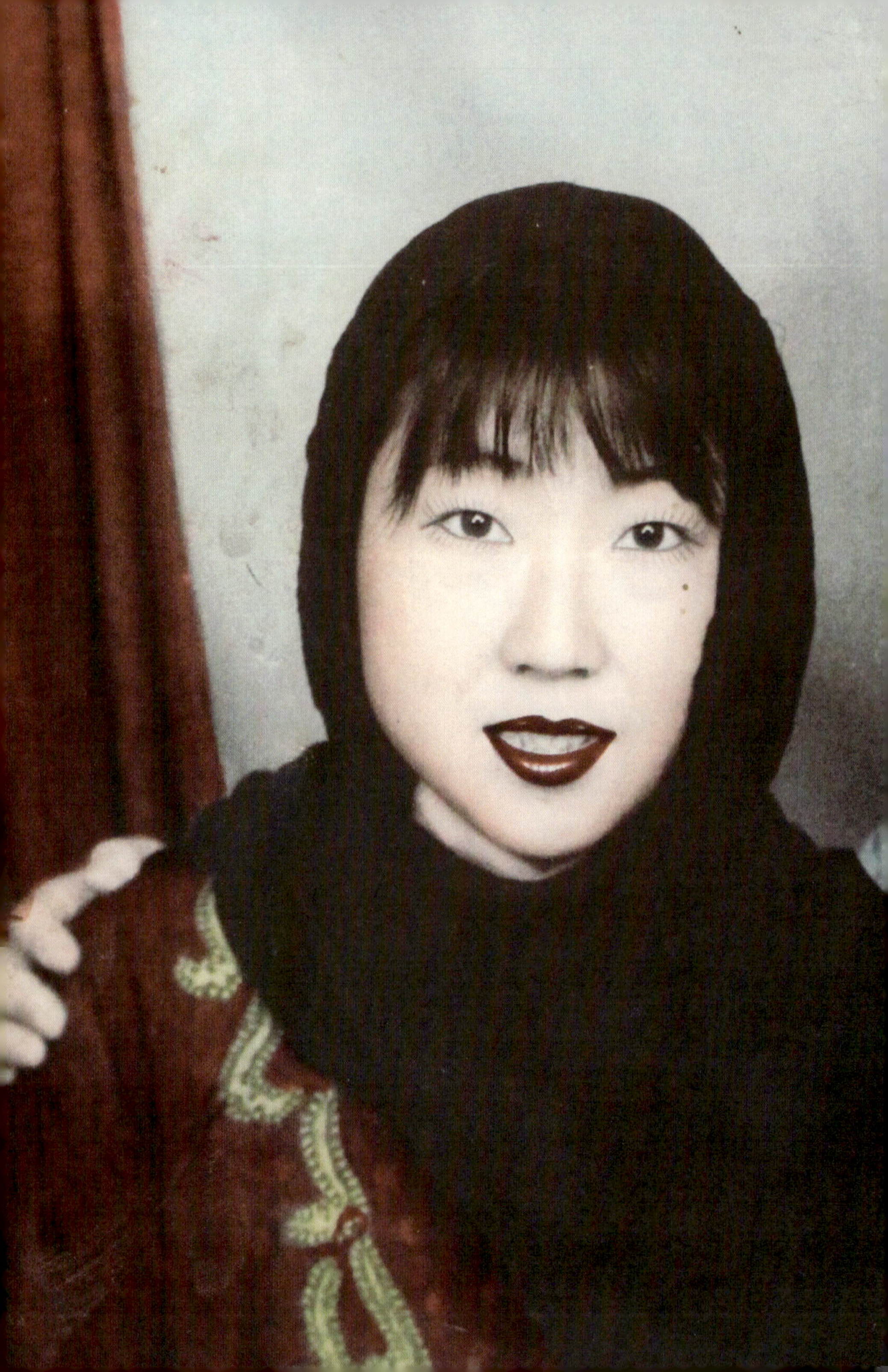

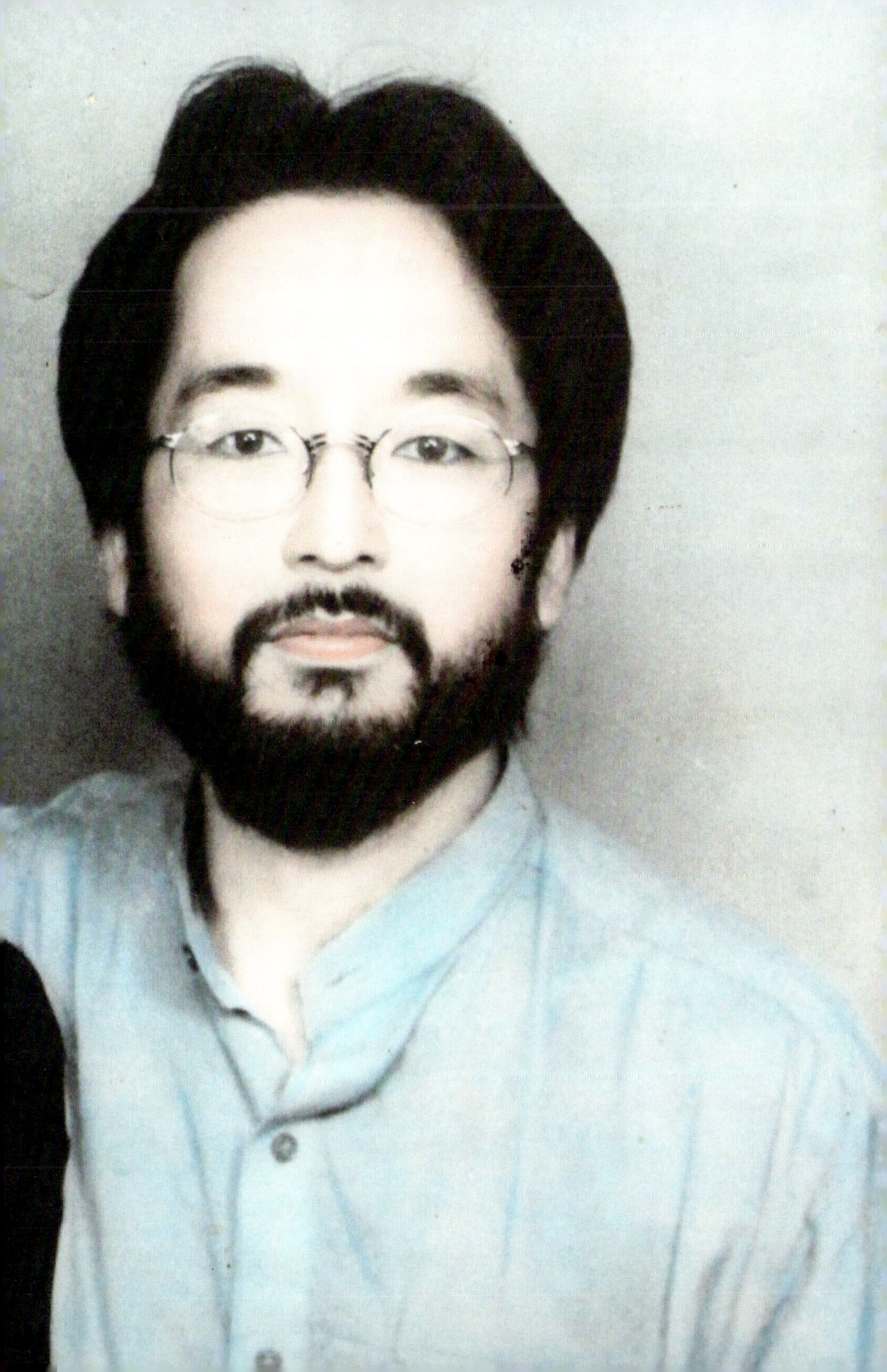

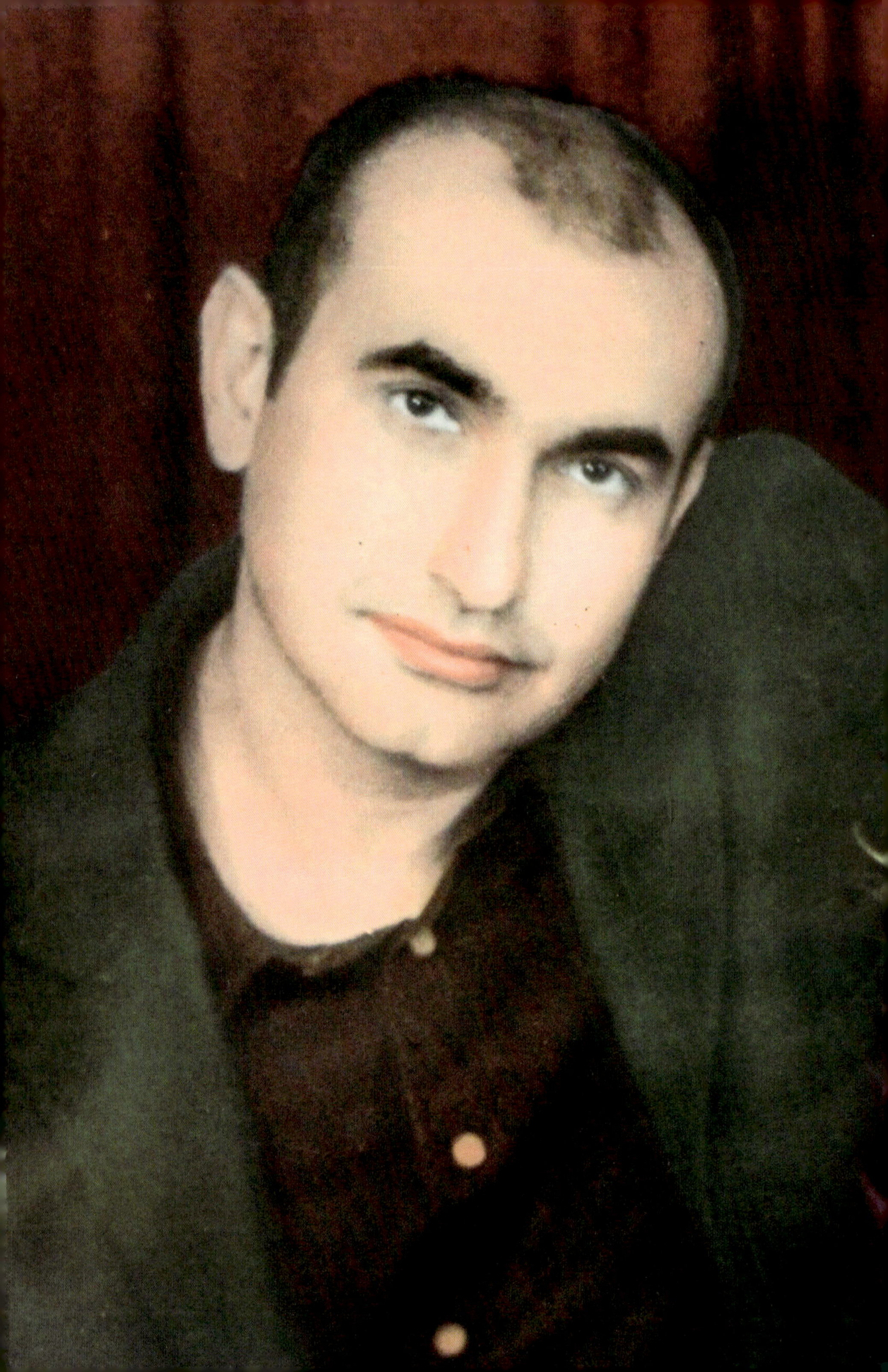

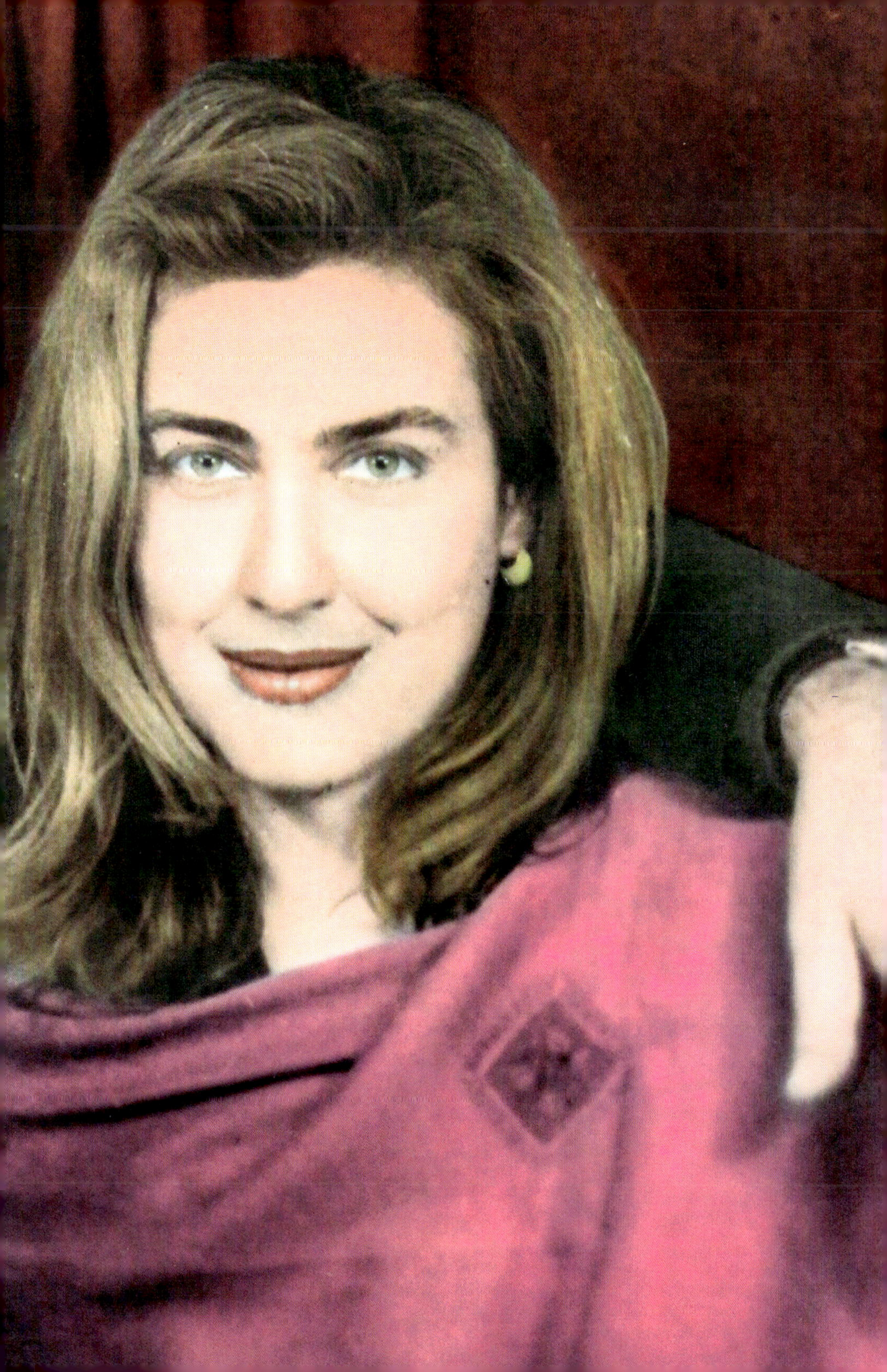

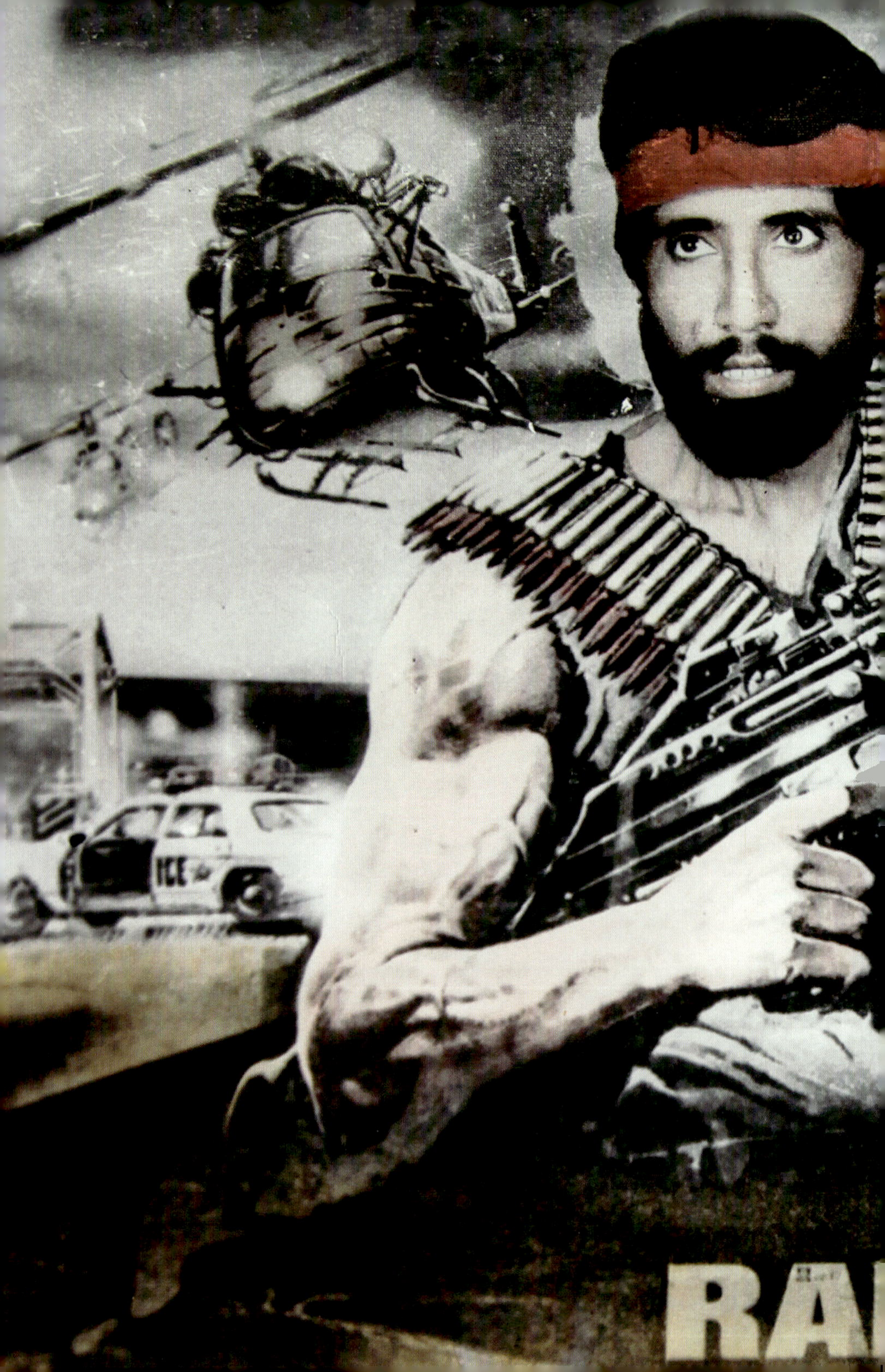

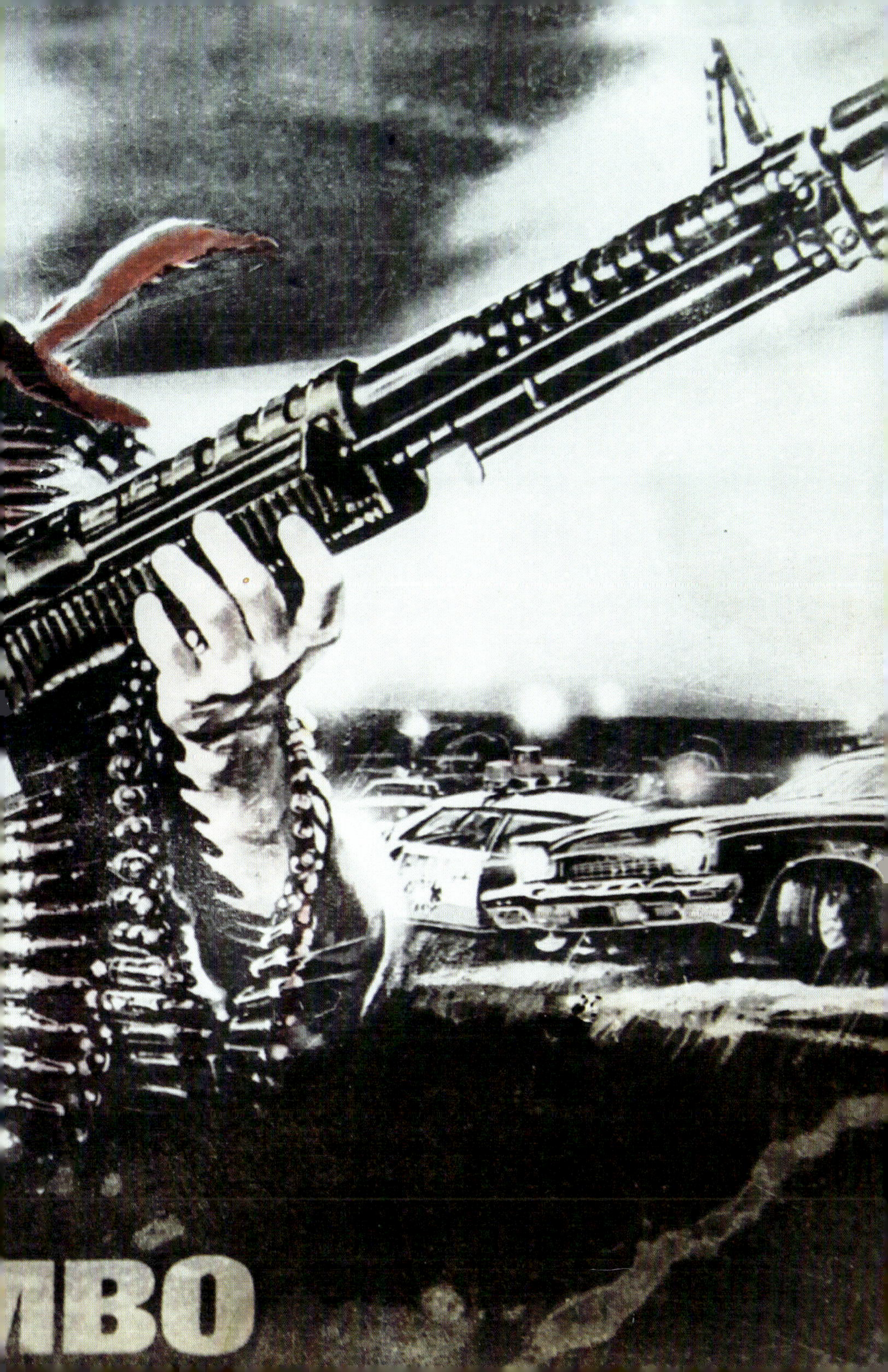
MBO

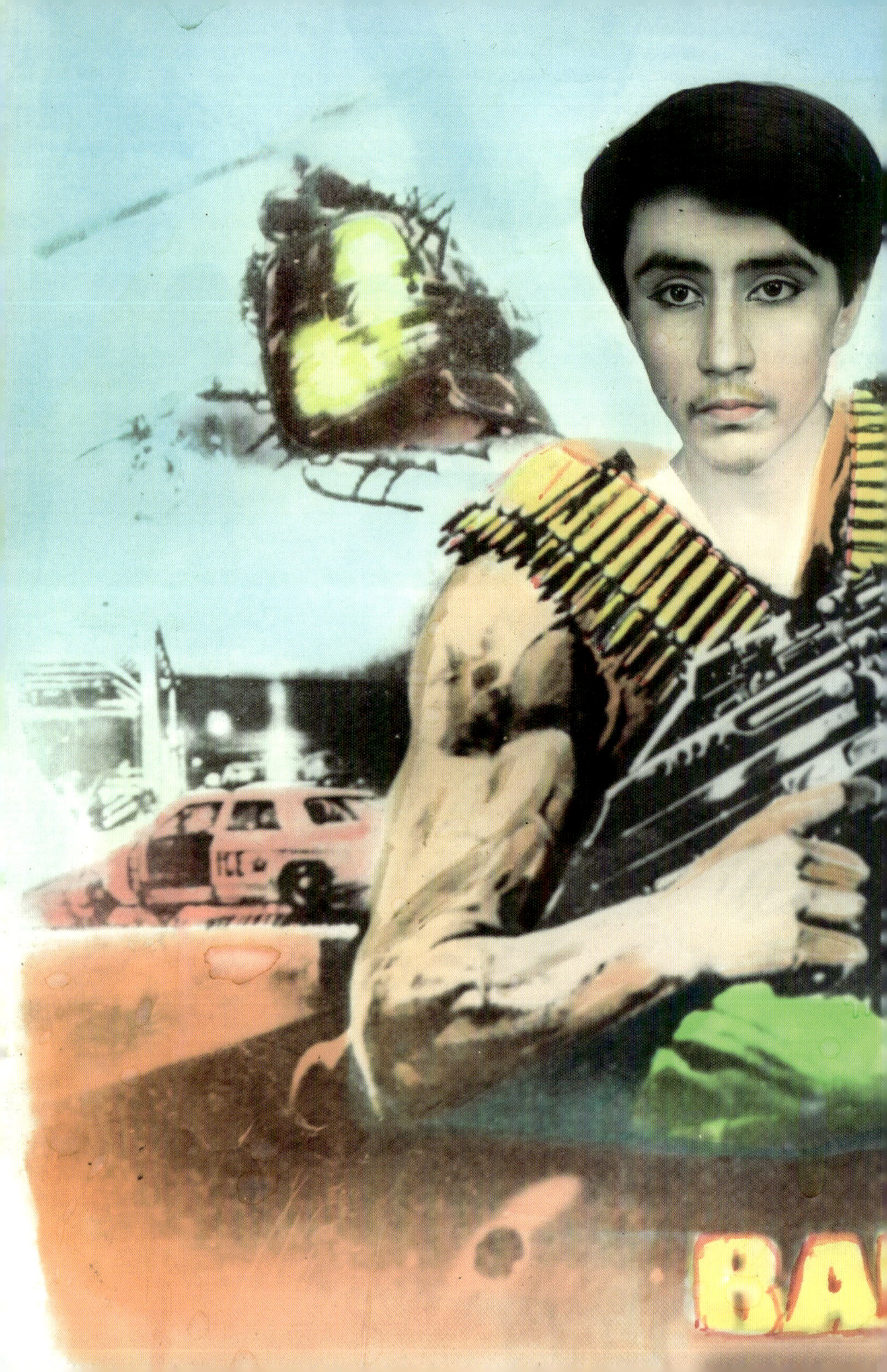
BA

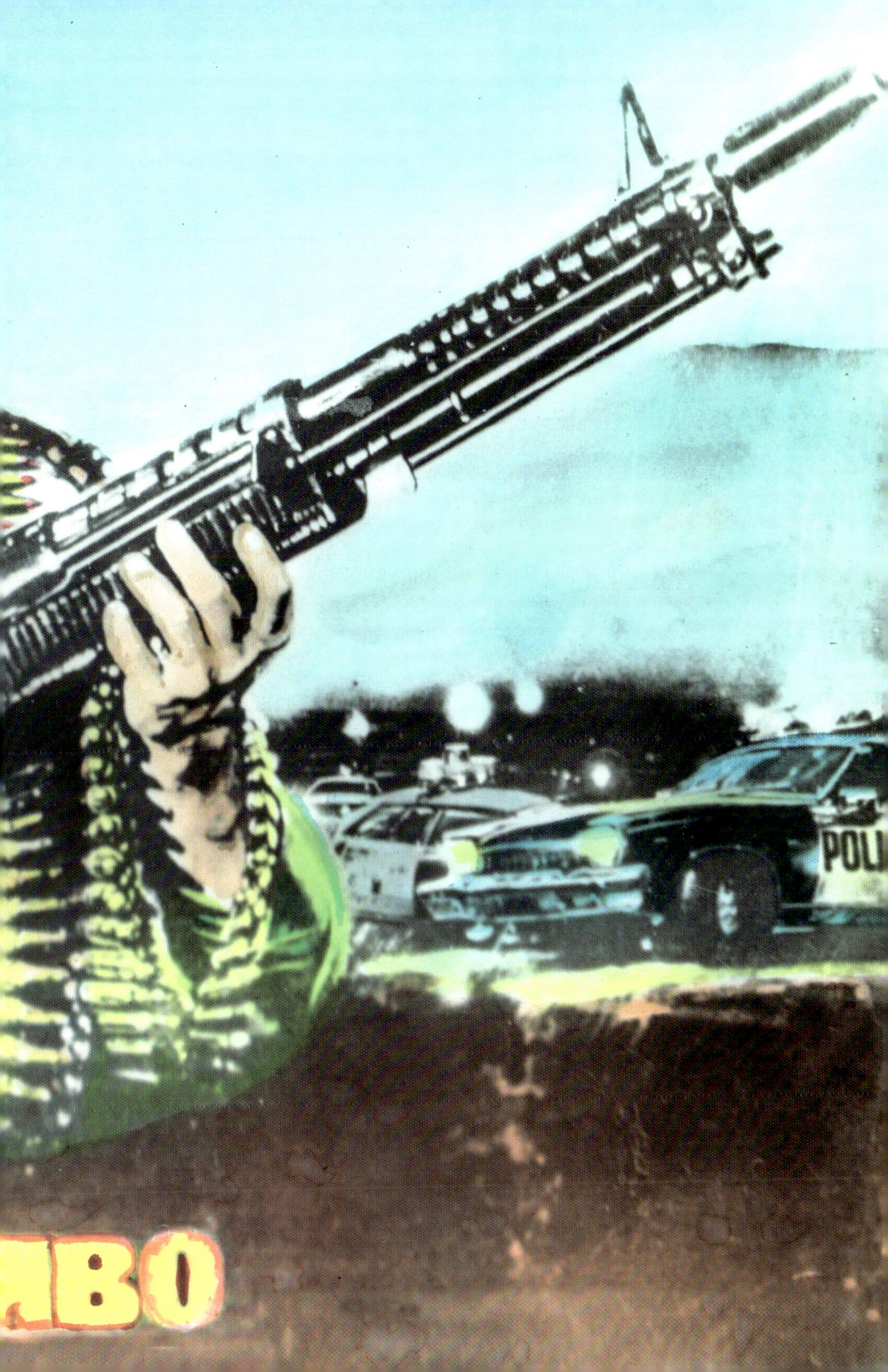

A medium format negative of a film scene, prepared for montaging. The head of the male actor was tinted red to block exposure on enlarging; a client's heads was then printed on top.

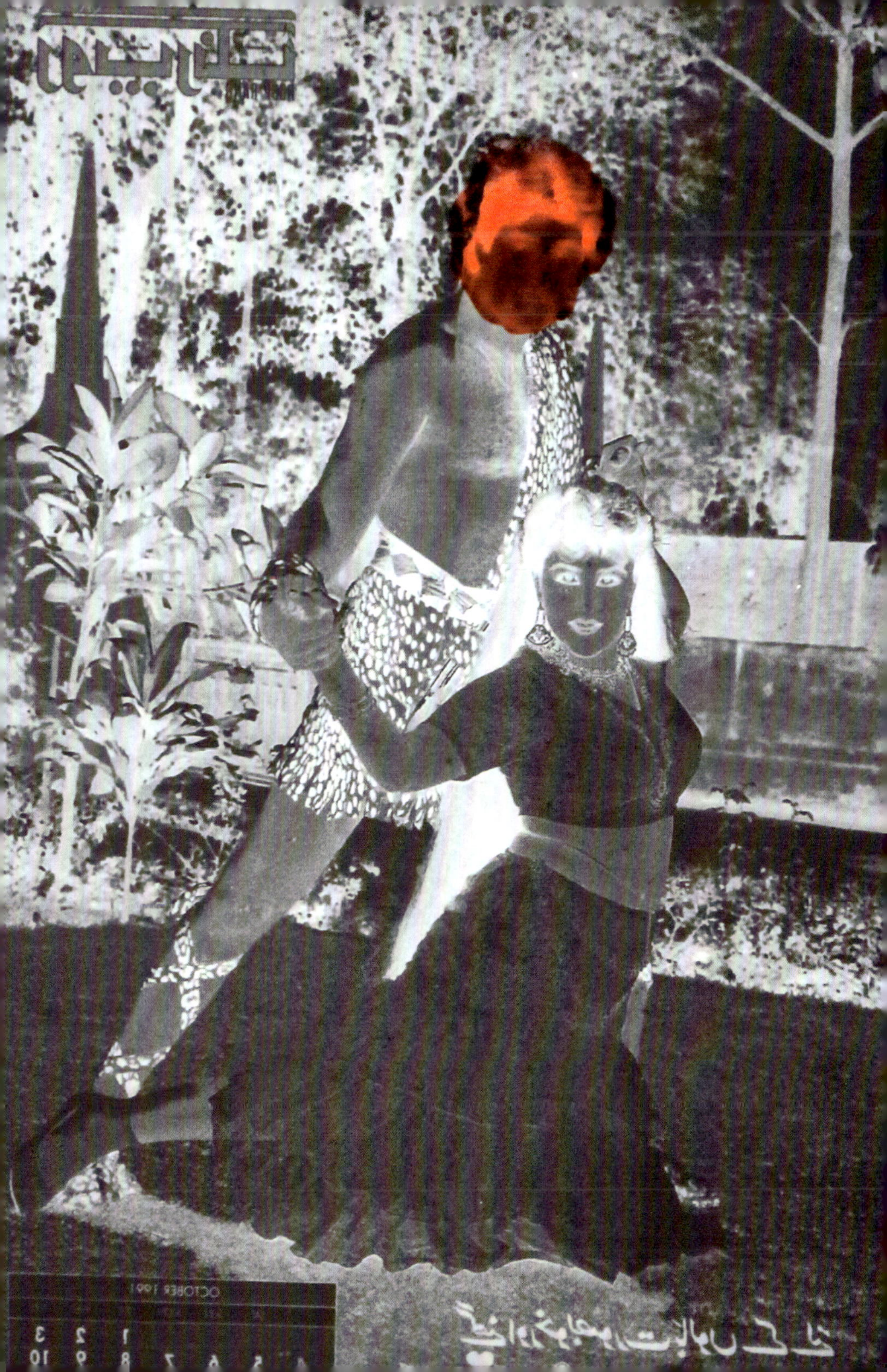
OCTOBER 1991

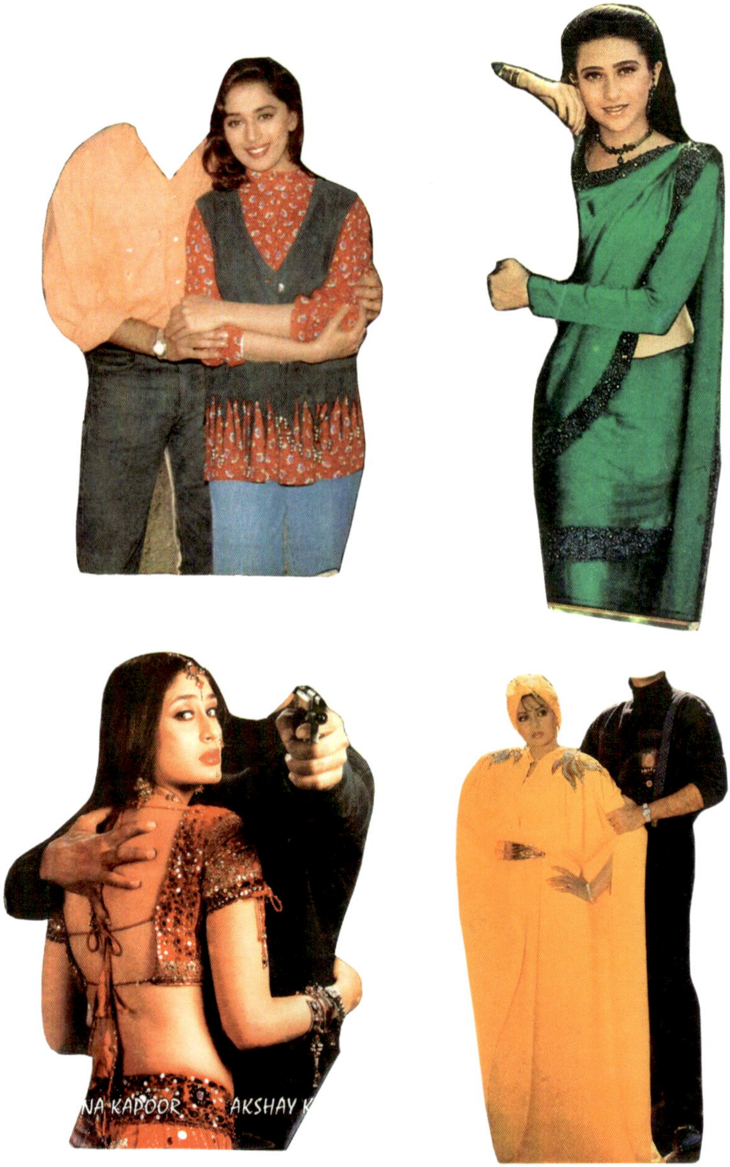

Magazine cut-outs of actresses, actor couples, and singers used in making montages with customers by the travelling photographer Abdul Wali (p.207), c.2000.

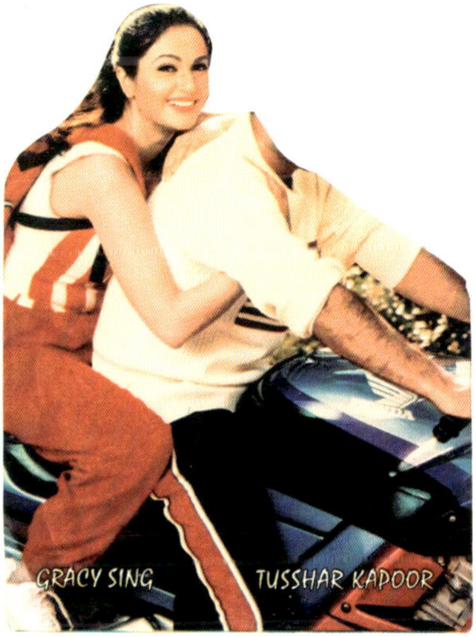
GRACY SING
TUSSHAR KAPOOR
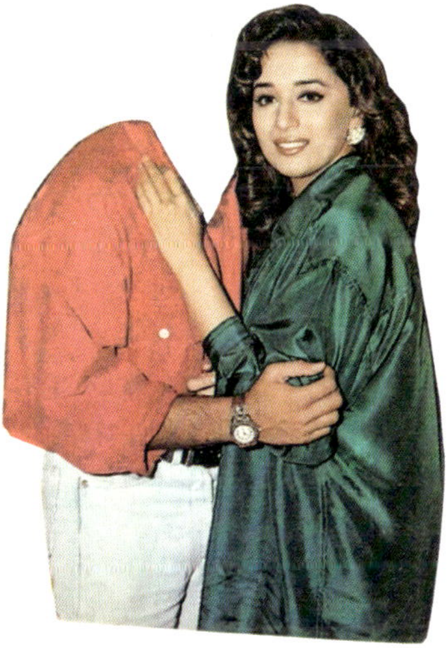
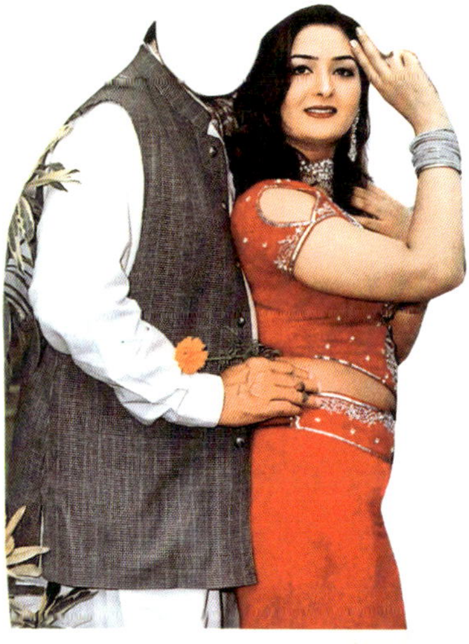
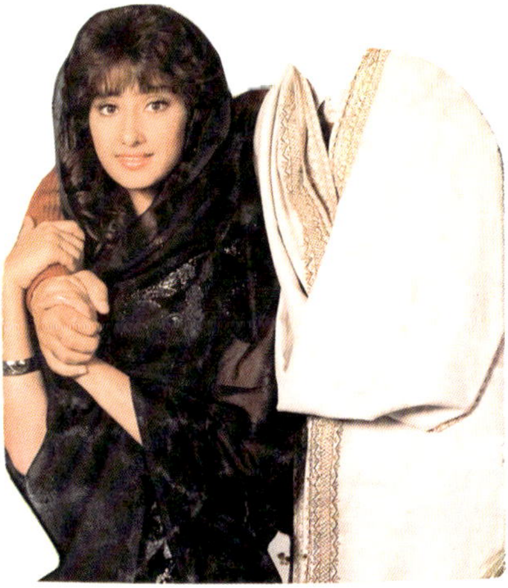

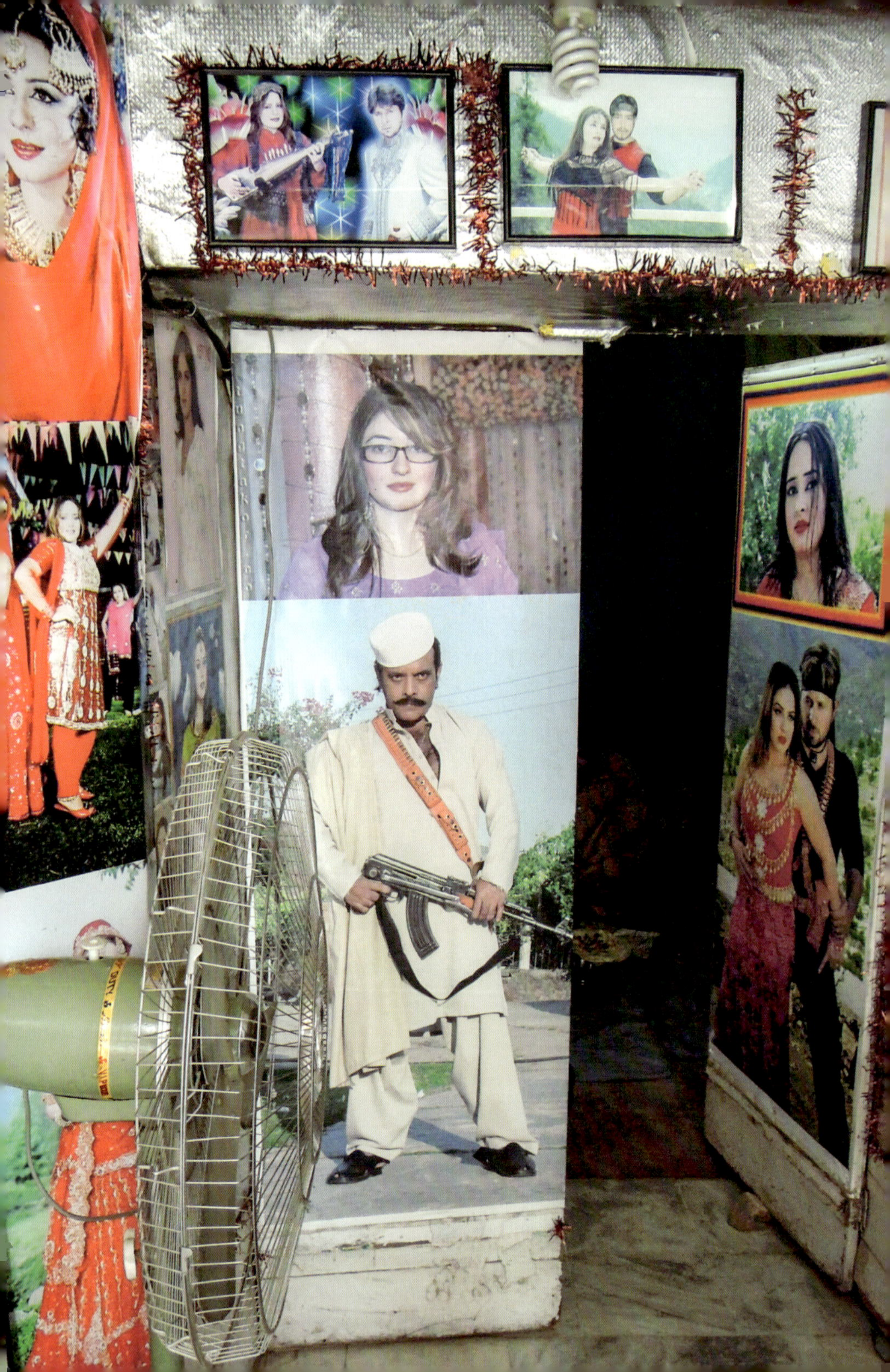

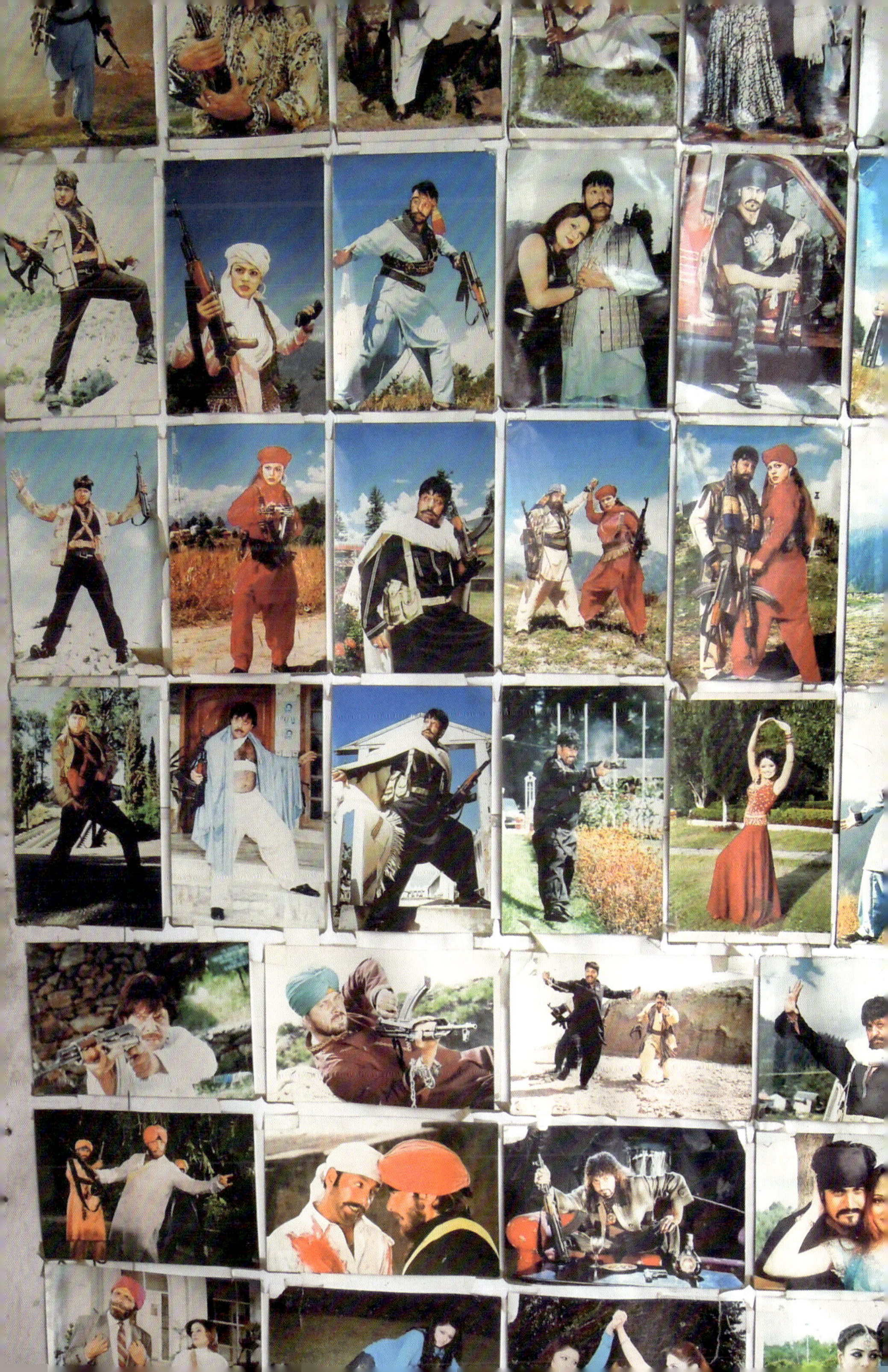

Preceding pages 110 & 111: Entrance to Khyber Studio on Cinema Road covered with images of Pashtun entertainers and film scenes.

Opposite: Jahangir Khan, a major star of Pashtu-language film, and the most popular actor used in movie montages on Cinema Road.

Pages 114–115: Ghulam Farooq outside of Famous Studio on Cinema Road, established in 1978 by his father, Farooq Hussain Quereshi; *Pages* 116–117: Ghulam Farooq photographs a customer for a montage.

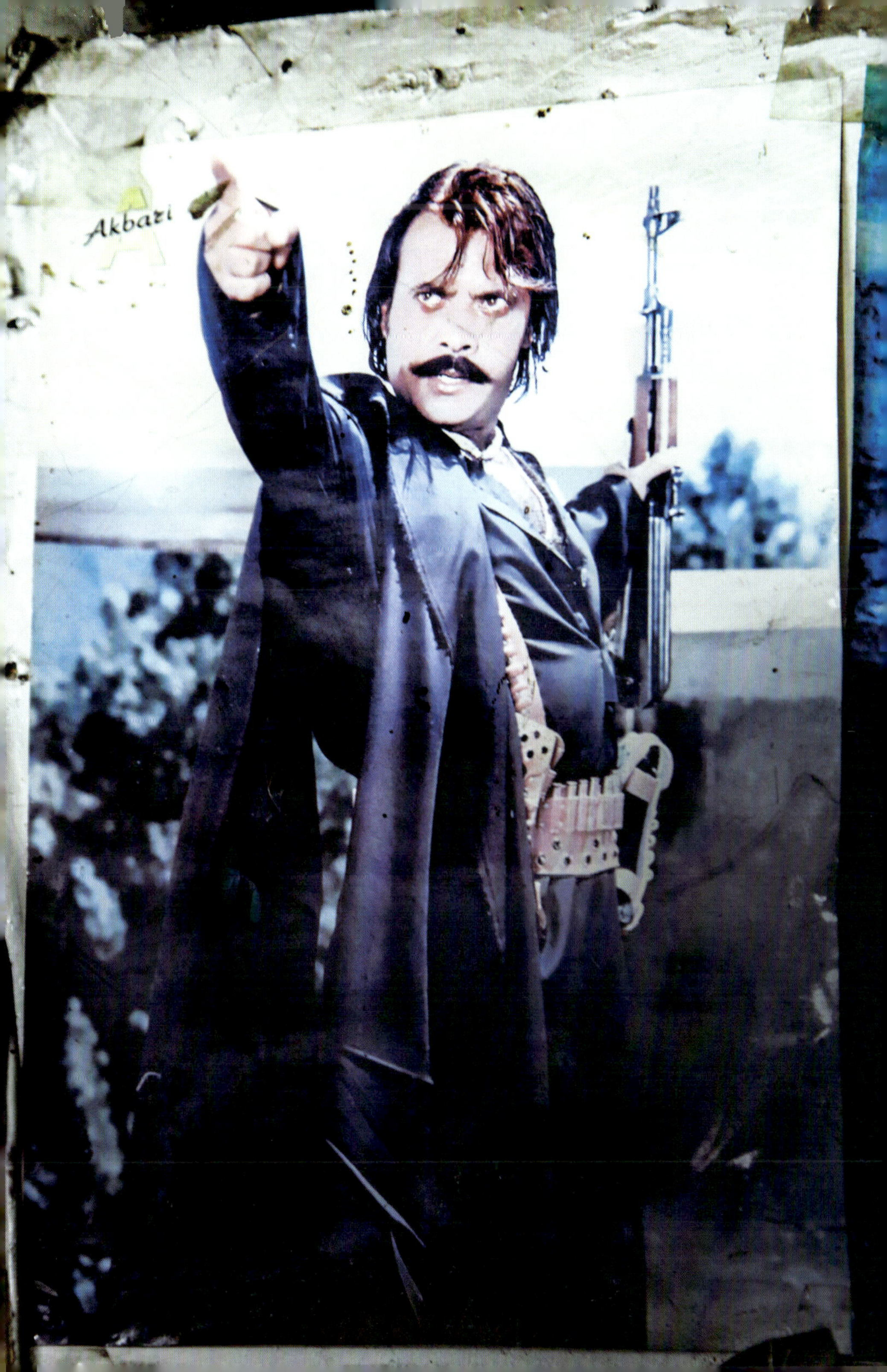
Akbari

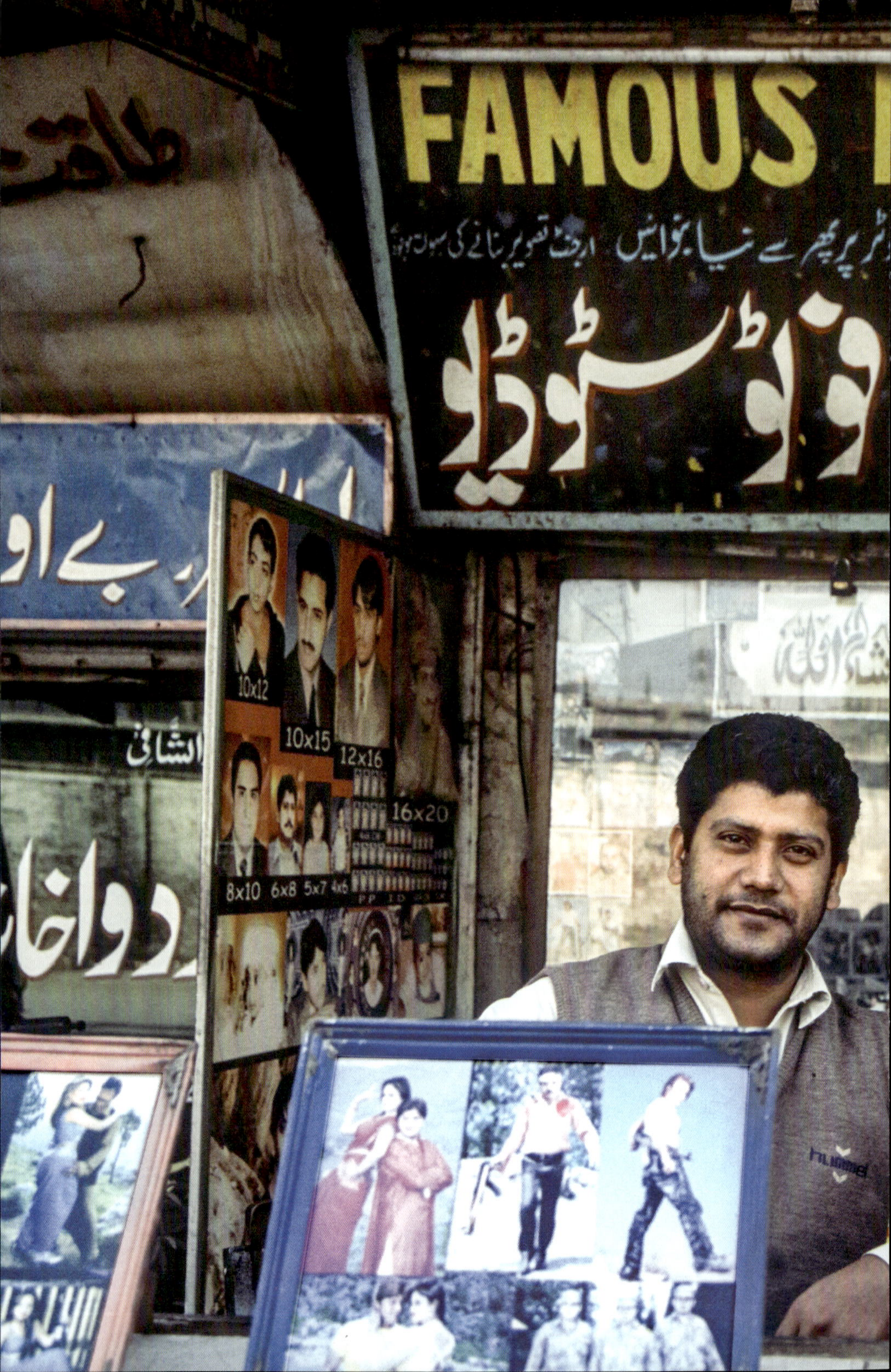
FAMOUS
10x12
10x15
12x16
16x20
8x10
6x8
5x7
4x6

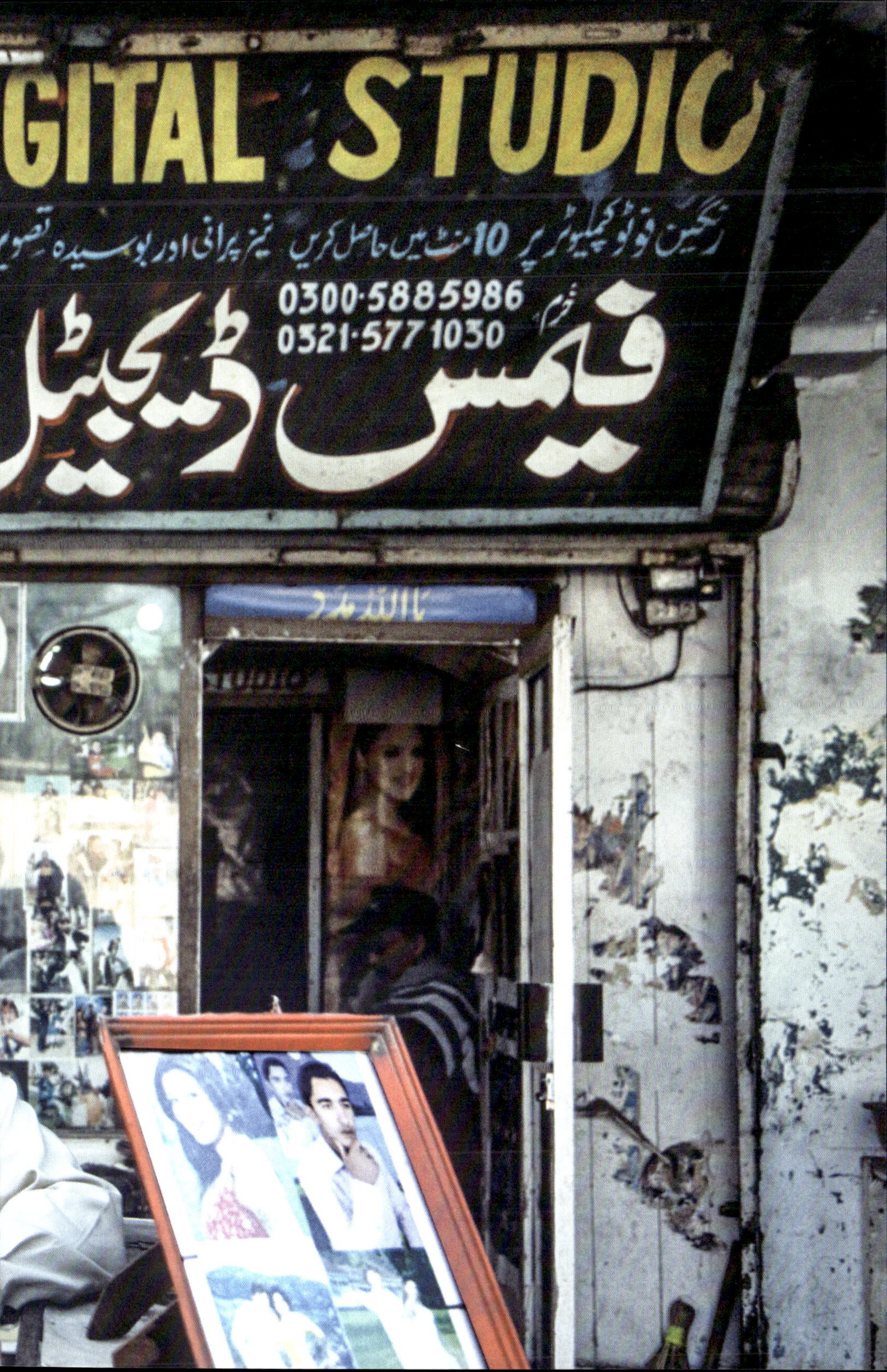
GITAL STUDIO
رنگین فوٹو کمپیوٹر پر 10 منٹ میں حاصل کریں نیز پرانی اور بوسیدہ
0300-5885986
0321-5771030
فیمس ڈیجیٹل
یا اللہ مدد

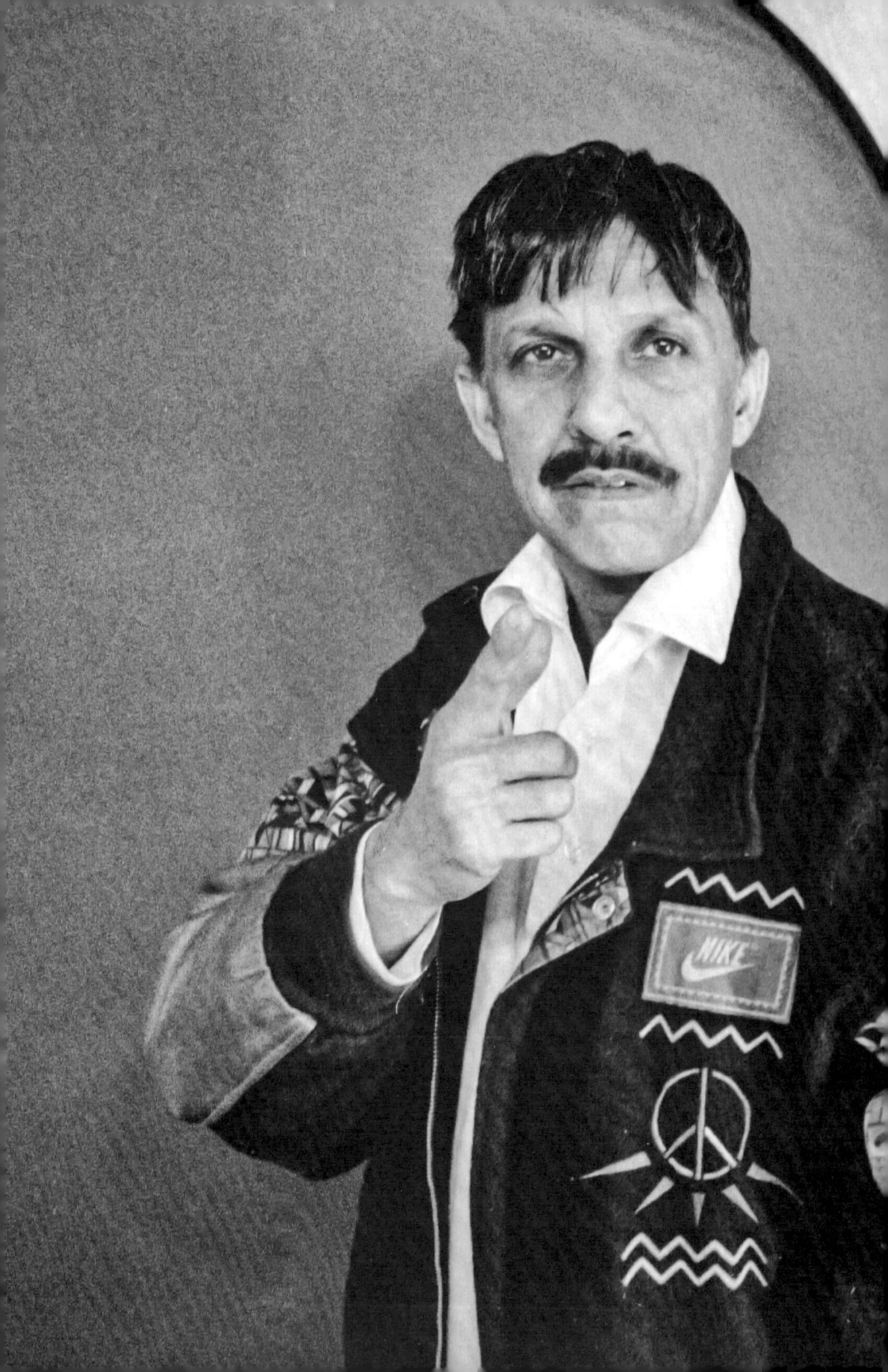
NIKE

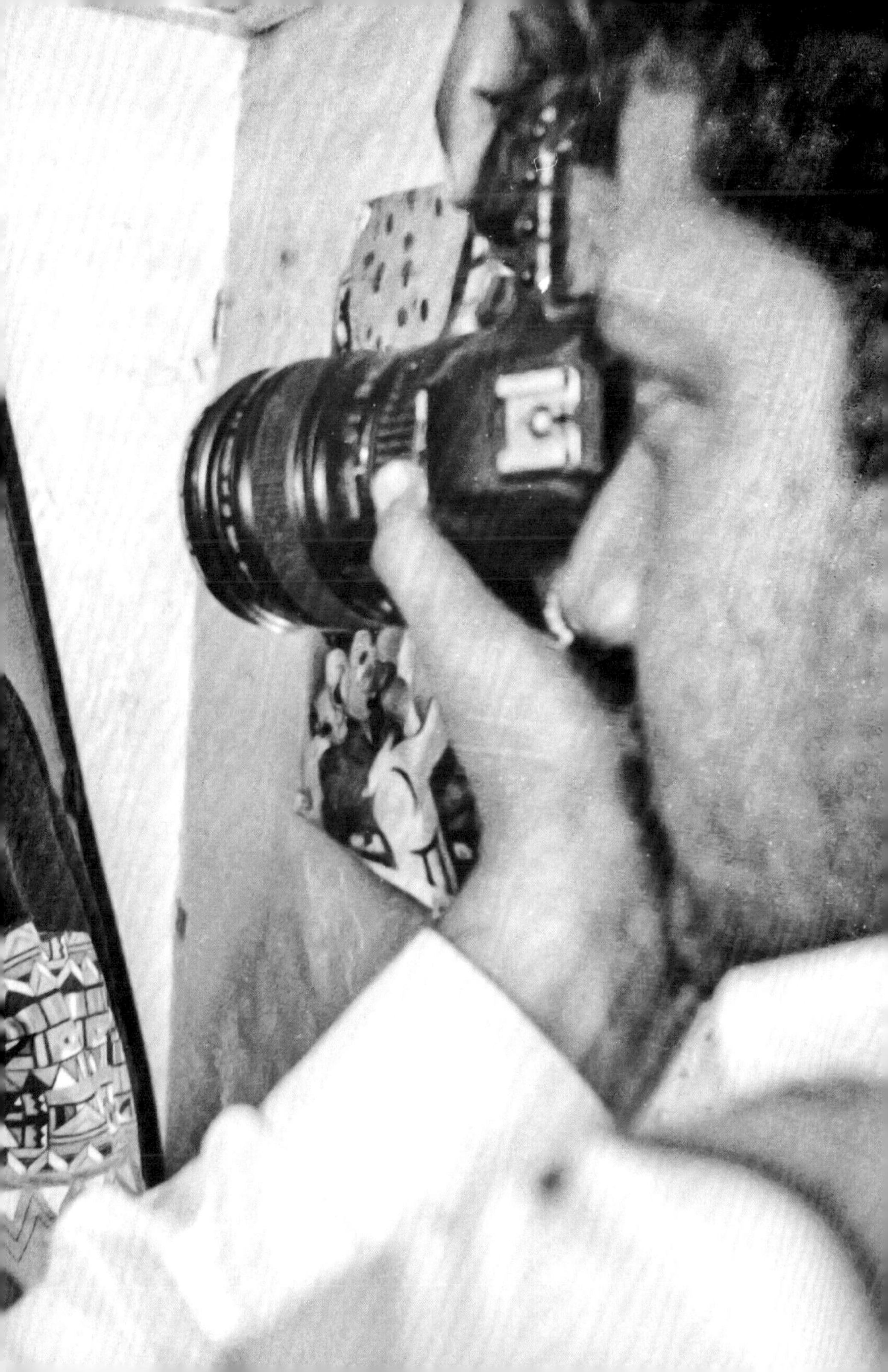

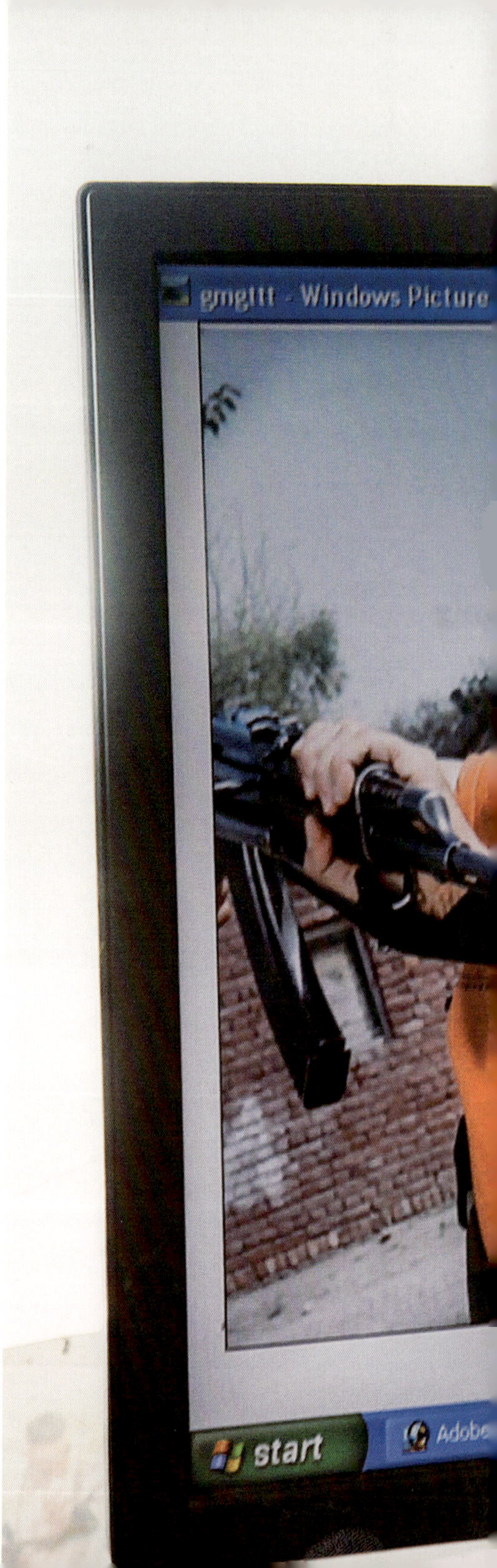

Opposite: A digital movie montage by Ghulam Farooq of Famous Studio. Not fond of analogue montaging, which he found laborious, Farooq's primary work nowadays is digital montaging, which he calls 'photo-change'.

Pages 120–121: Picture House cinema on Cinema Road, photographed a few weeks after the February 2014 grenade attack by religious extremists which killed five cinema-goers. "It was like watching a movie," said one Cinema Road photographer, adding, "it is real and not real–it just happens."

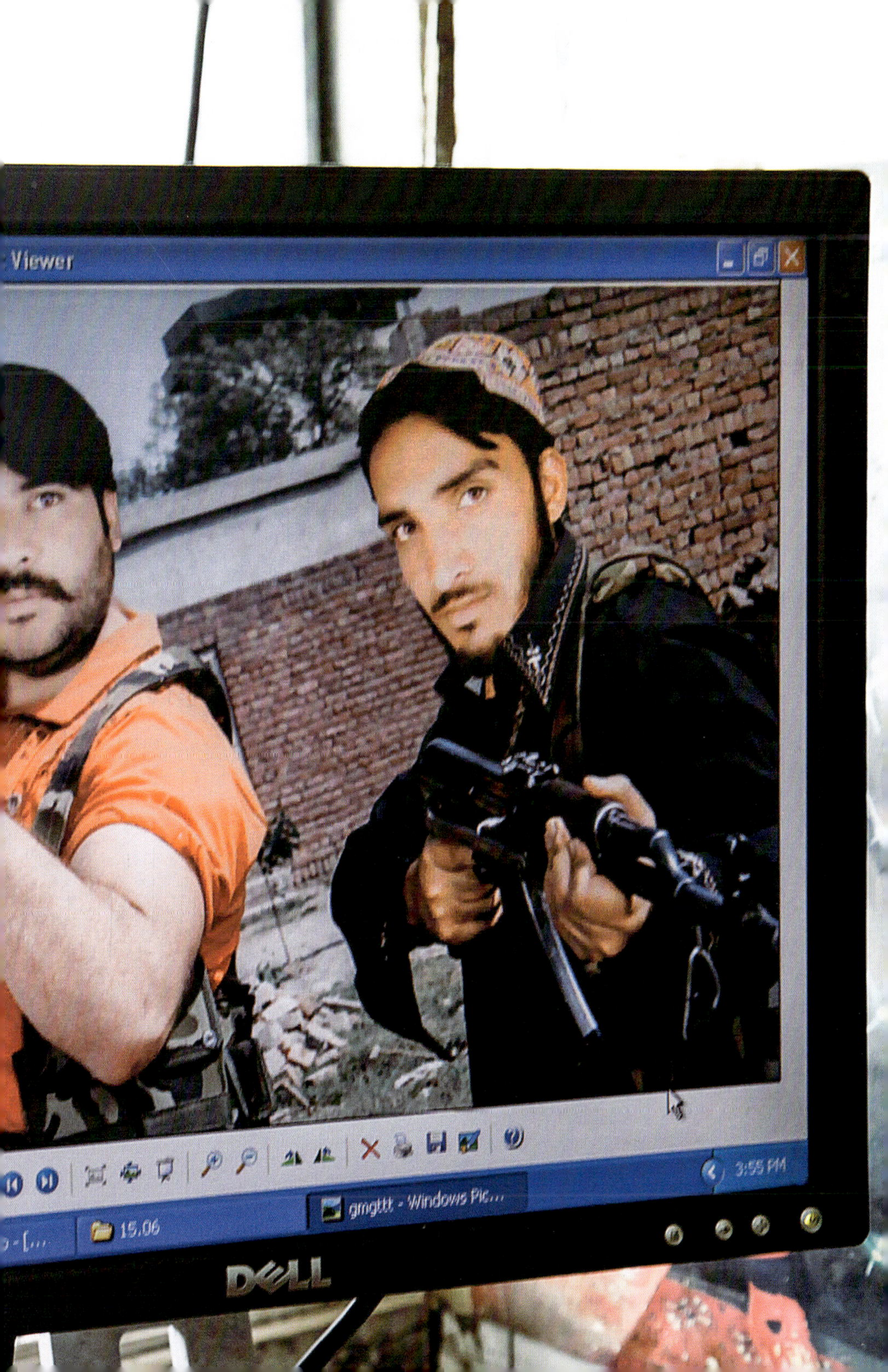
Viewer
3:55 PM
gmgttt - Windows Pic...
15.06
DELL

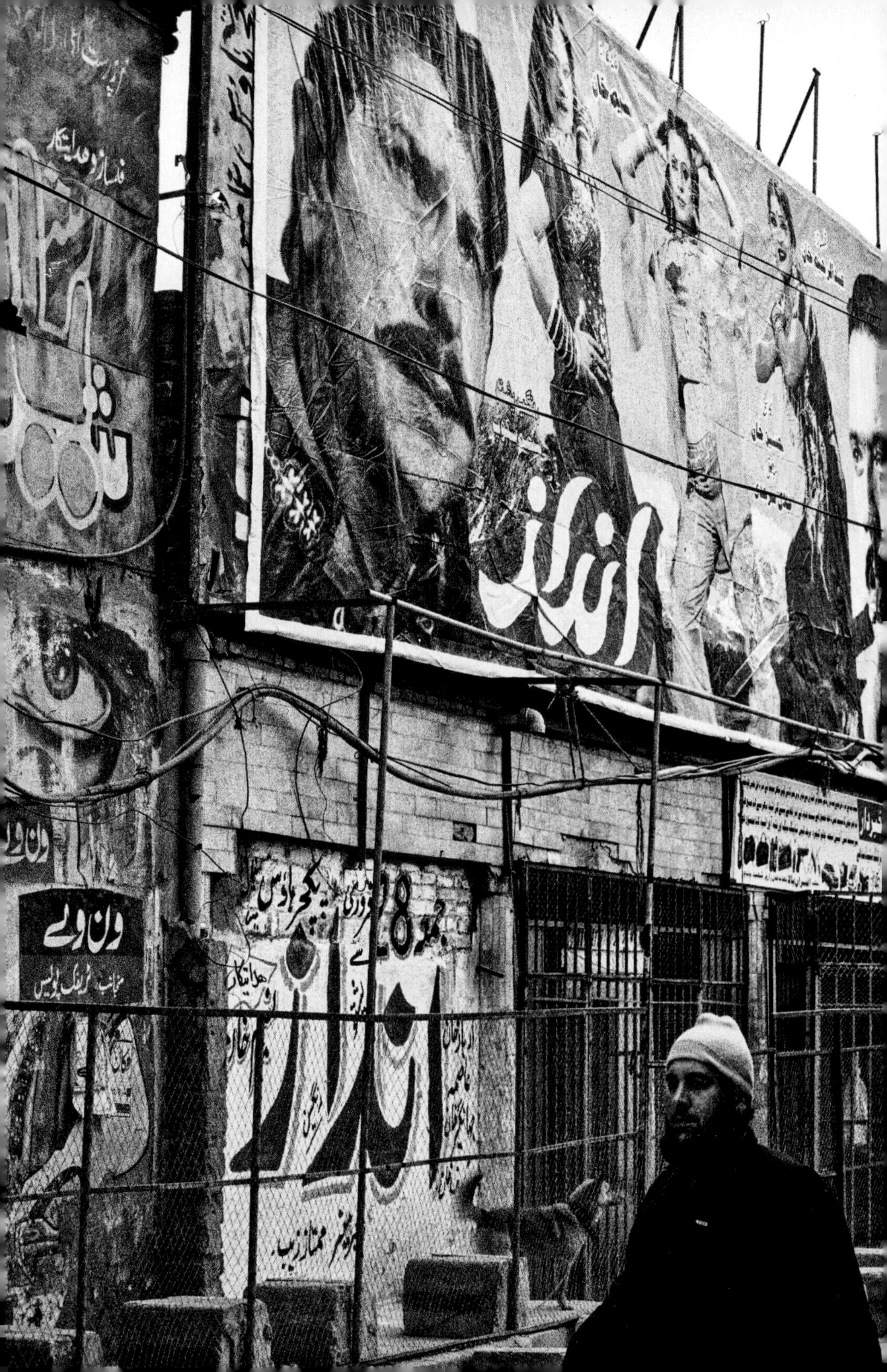
ون وے
منجانب ٹریفک پولیس

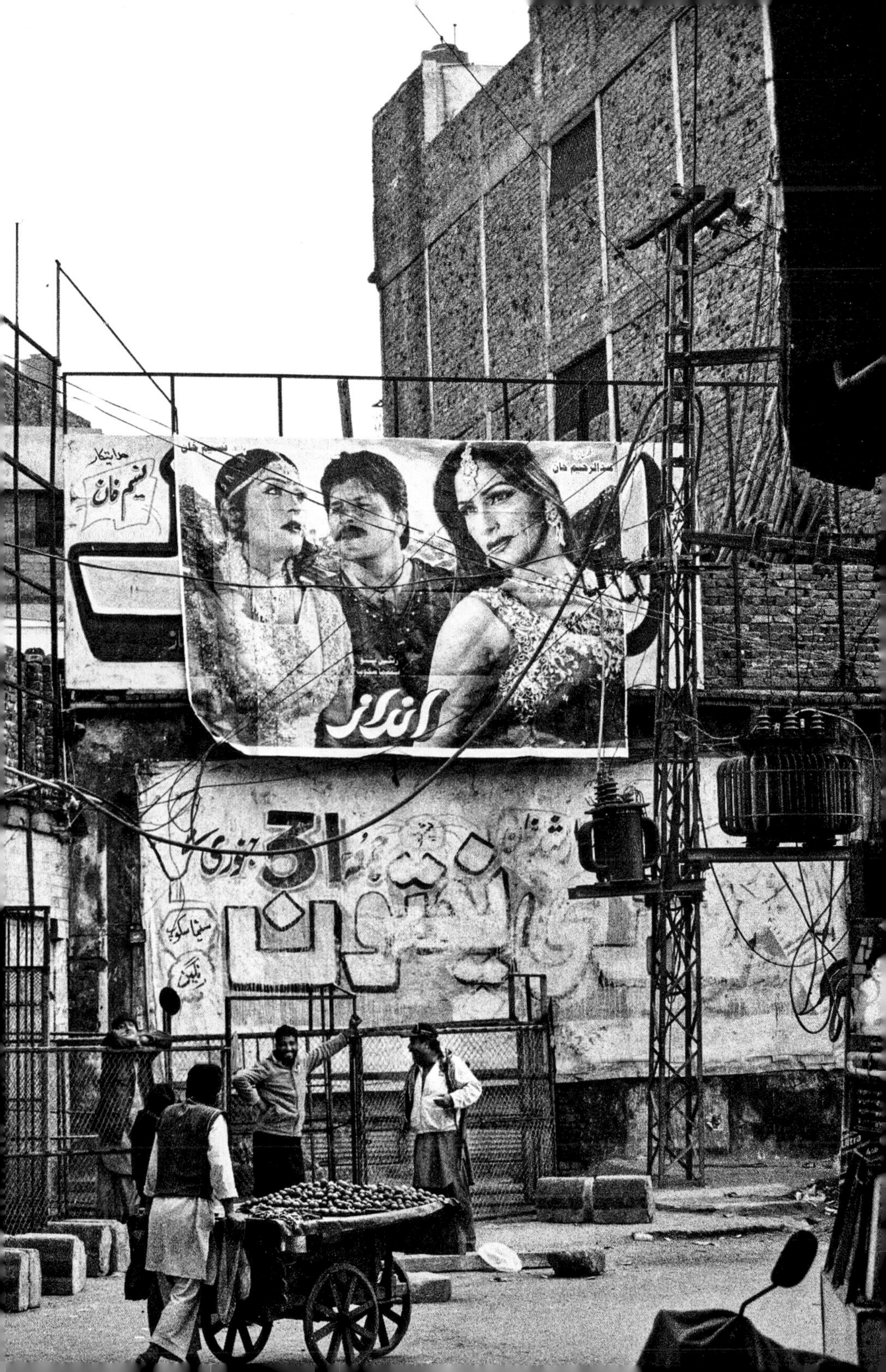
نسیم خان
انداز
31 جنوری

Opposite: Khan Abdul Gaffir Khan (1890–1988), known as 'Bacha Khan' or King of Chiefs, was a Pashtun independence activist against British Rule. As with his friend, Mahatma Gandhi, he promoted non-violent resistance. Many Peshawari photographers have images of Bacha Khan as well as other freedom fighters from the Independence movement in their private and commercial collections. Hand-coloured photograph, Famous Studio, c.1980s–1990s.

Pages 124 & 125: Hand-coloured photographs from Capri Studio on Cinema Road.

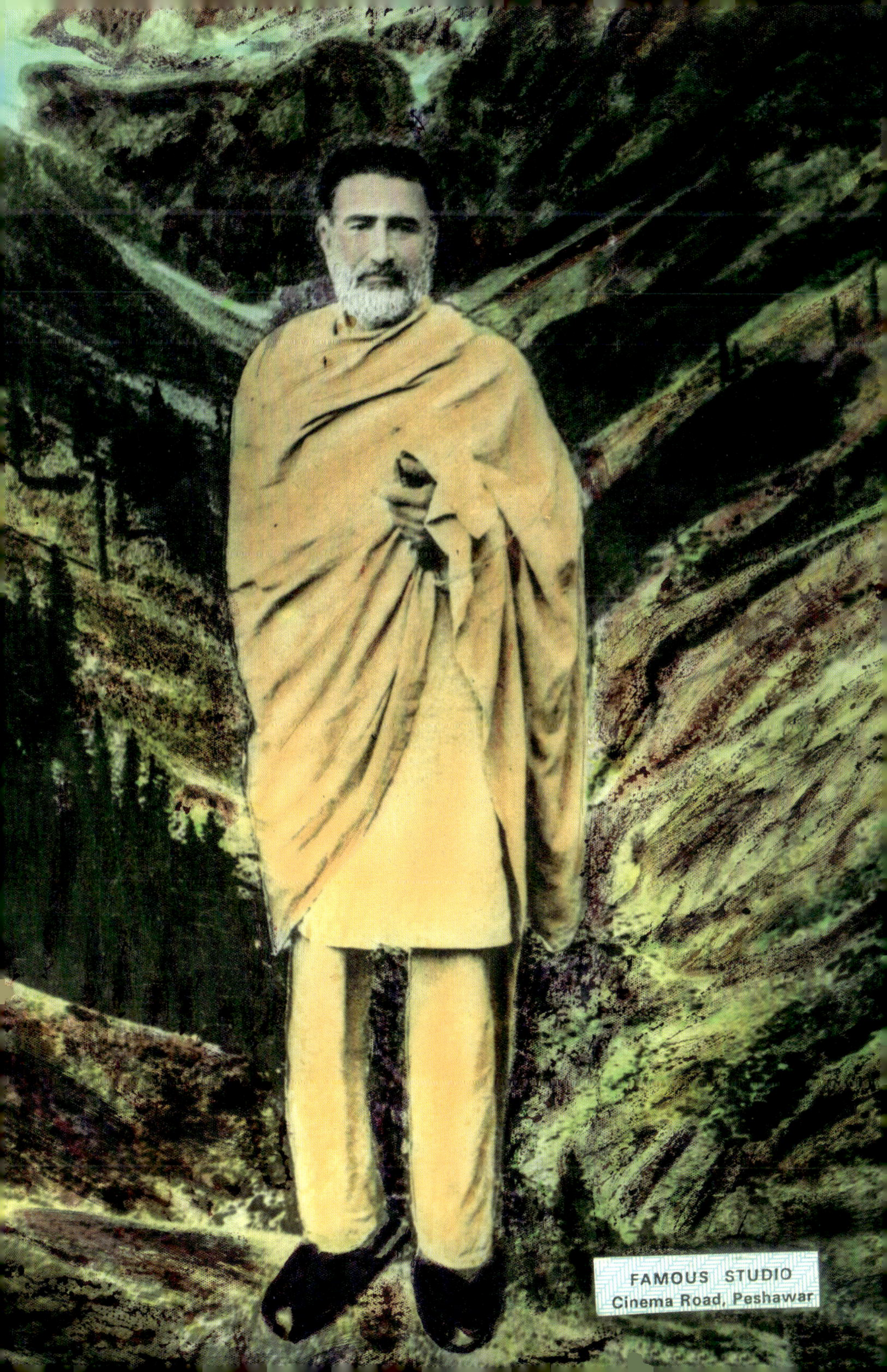
FAMOUS STUDIO
Cinema Road, Peshawar

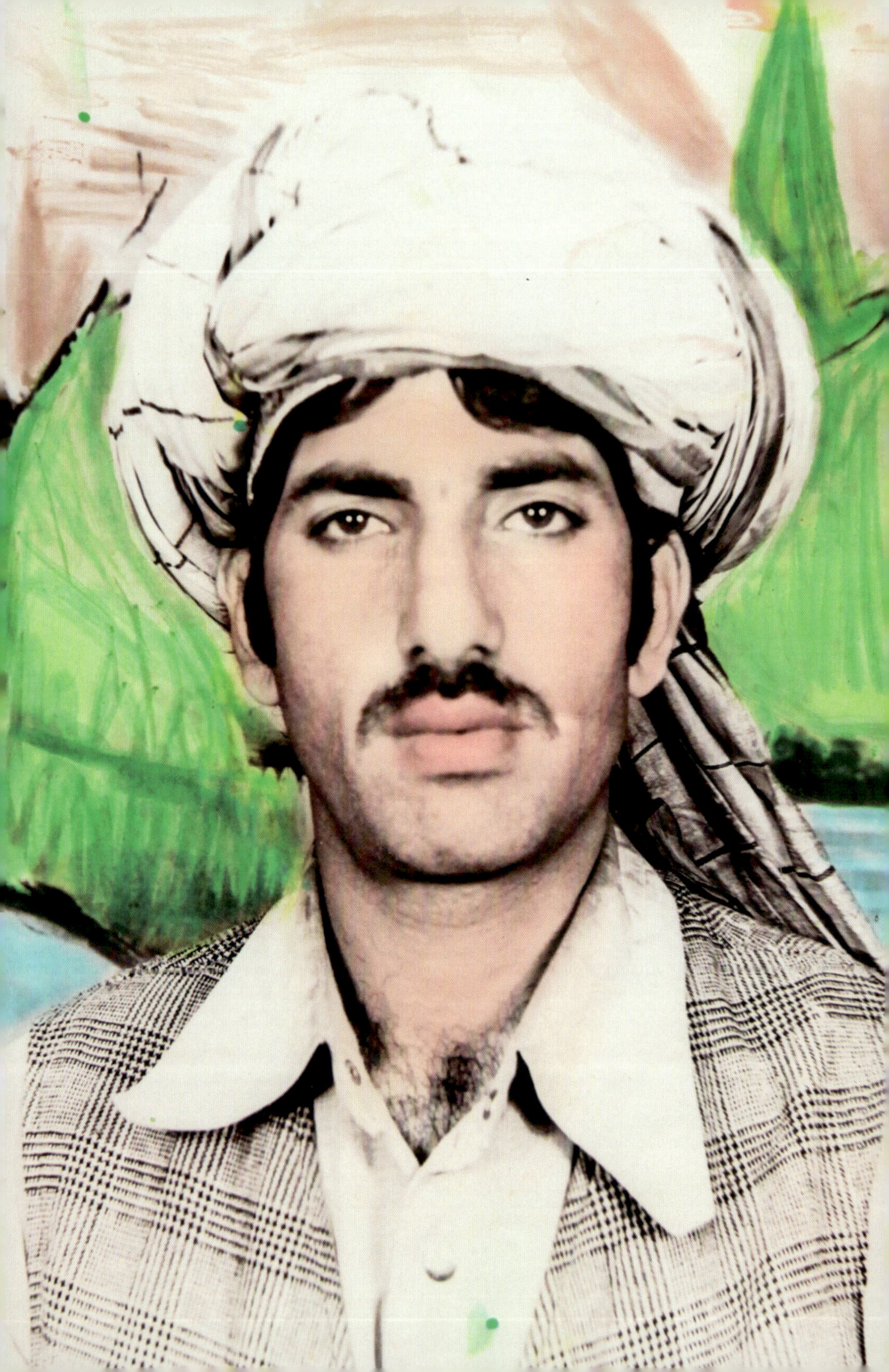

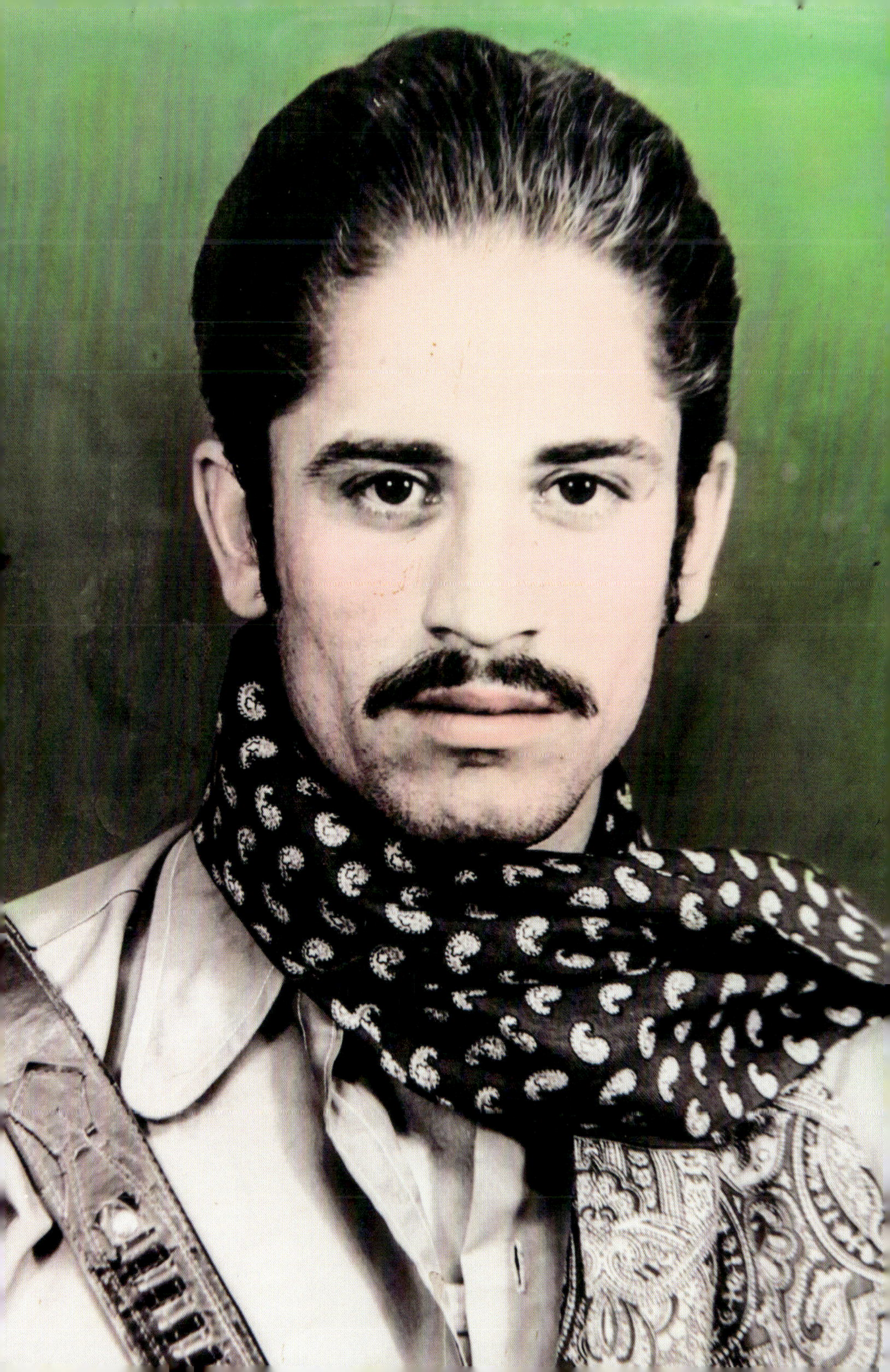

Hand-coloured portrait from Capri Studio on Cinema Road, where Haji Muhammad Iqbal took images of Peshawar's residents for three decades. His son, Muhammad Zubair a.k.a. Zubi, now runs the studio-cum-shop as a wholesale centre, with customers frequently coming across the border from Afghanistan.

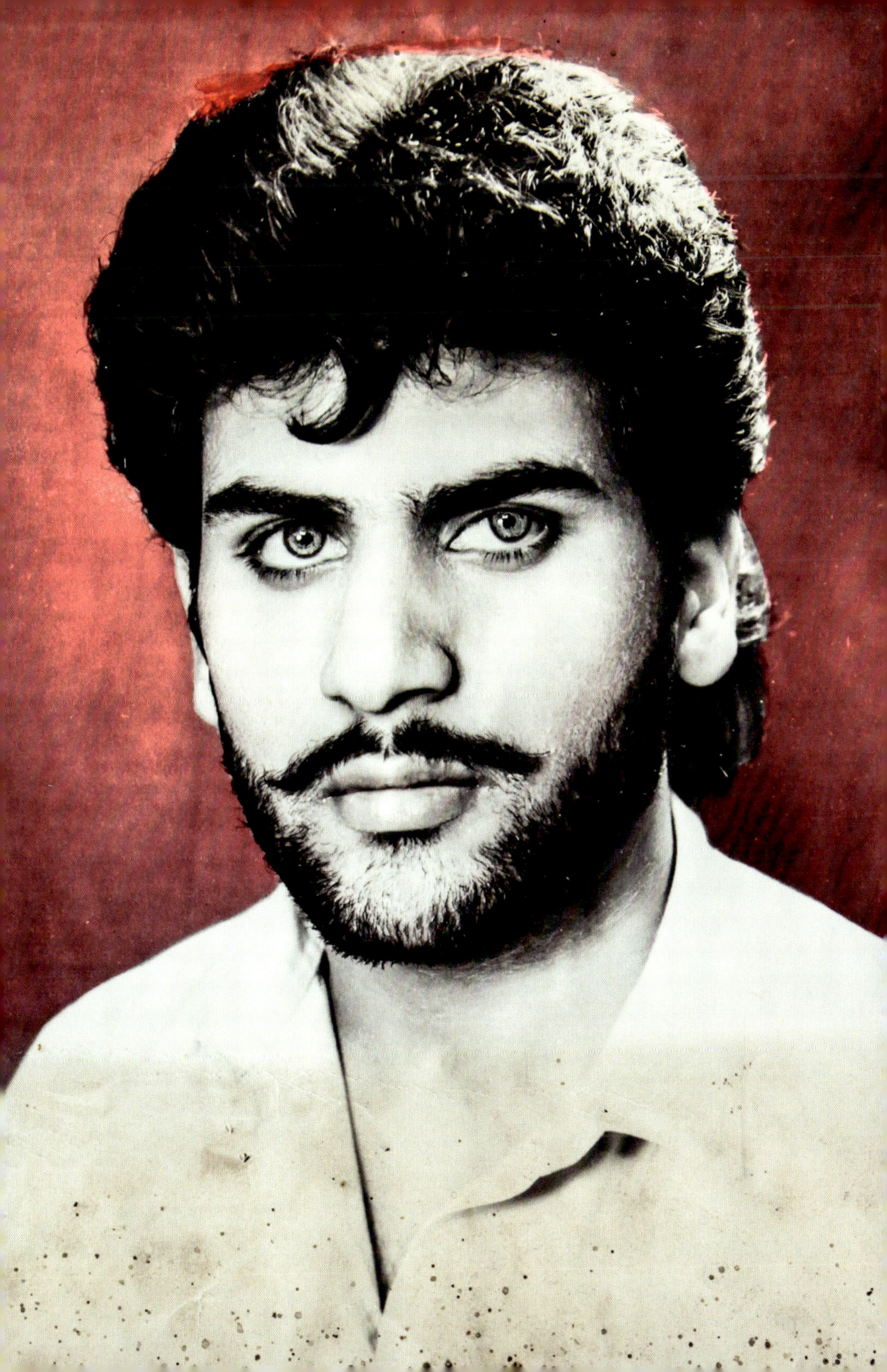

Colour film portrait by Capri Studio, Cinema Road.

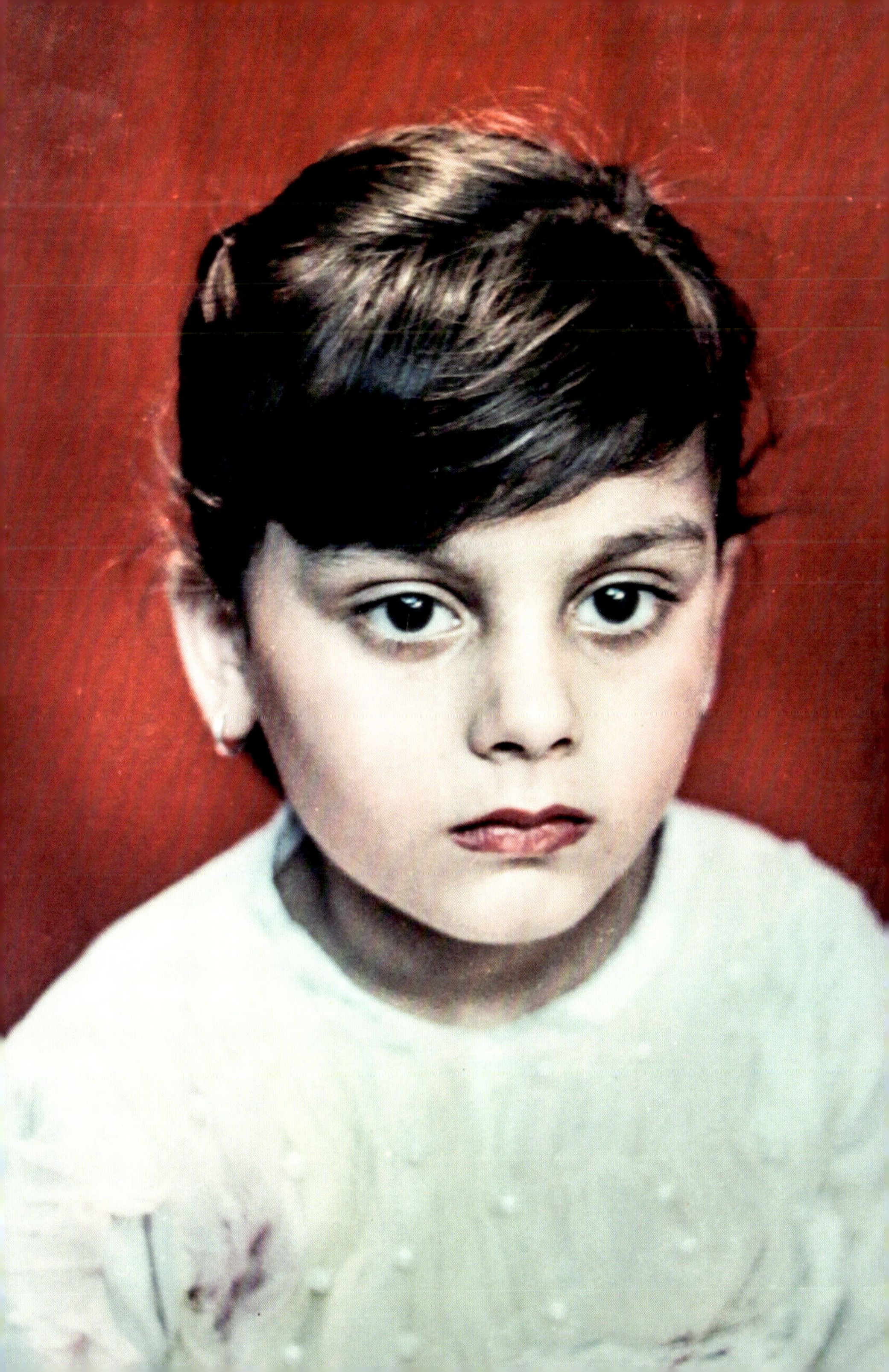

Muhammad Gul, founder of Gul Sons Studio in the mid-1960s. After three decades in photography, Muhammad Gul gave up taking photographs and became a religious scholar. His sons took over his studio in the Sikander Pura area. For this portrait, Muhammad Gul was provided by the studio with a pair of lens-free spectacle frames, so as to avoid the possibility of any reflection or glare obscuring the eyes. Colour film portrait by Wasila Studio.

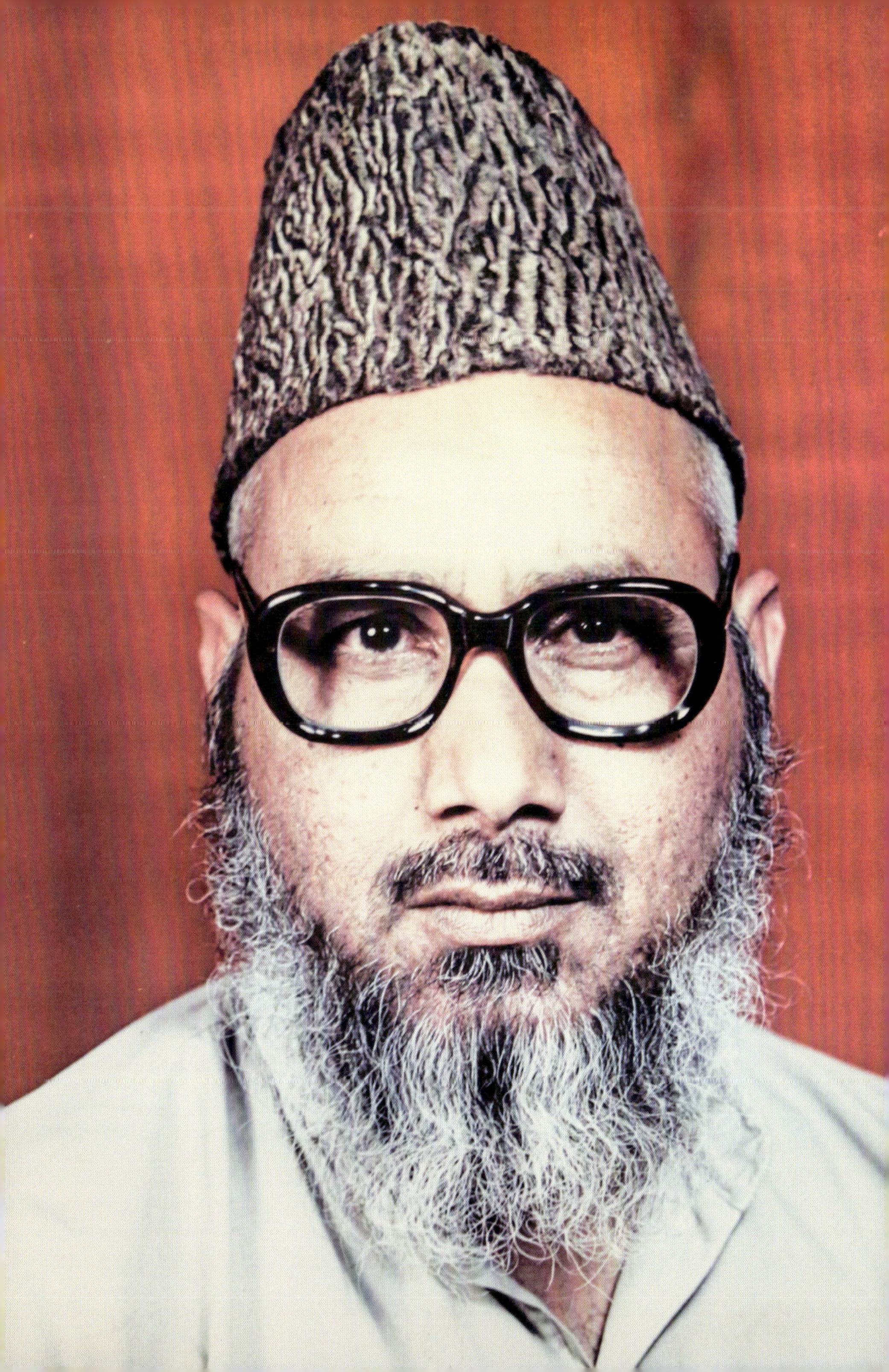

Opposite: Mumtaz Ahmad and son. Mumtaz runs Gul Sons Studio, founded in the 1960s by his father (p.131).

Pages 134 & 135: Rickshaw decorations with scenes from Pashtu-language movies. On the top left is legendary Pashtun film actor Badar Munir, after whom Cinema Road was officially renamed in 2011.

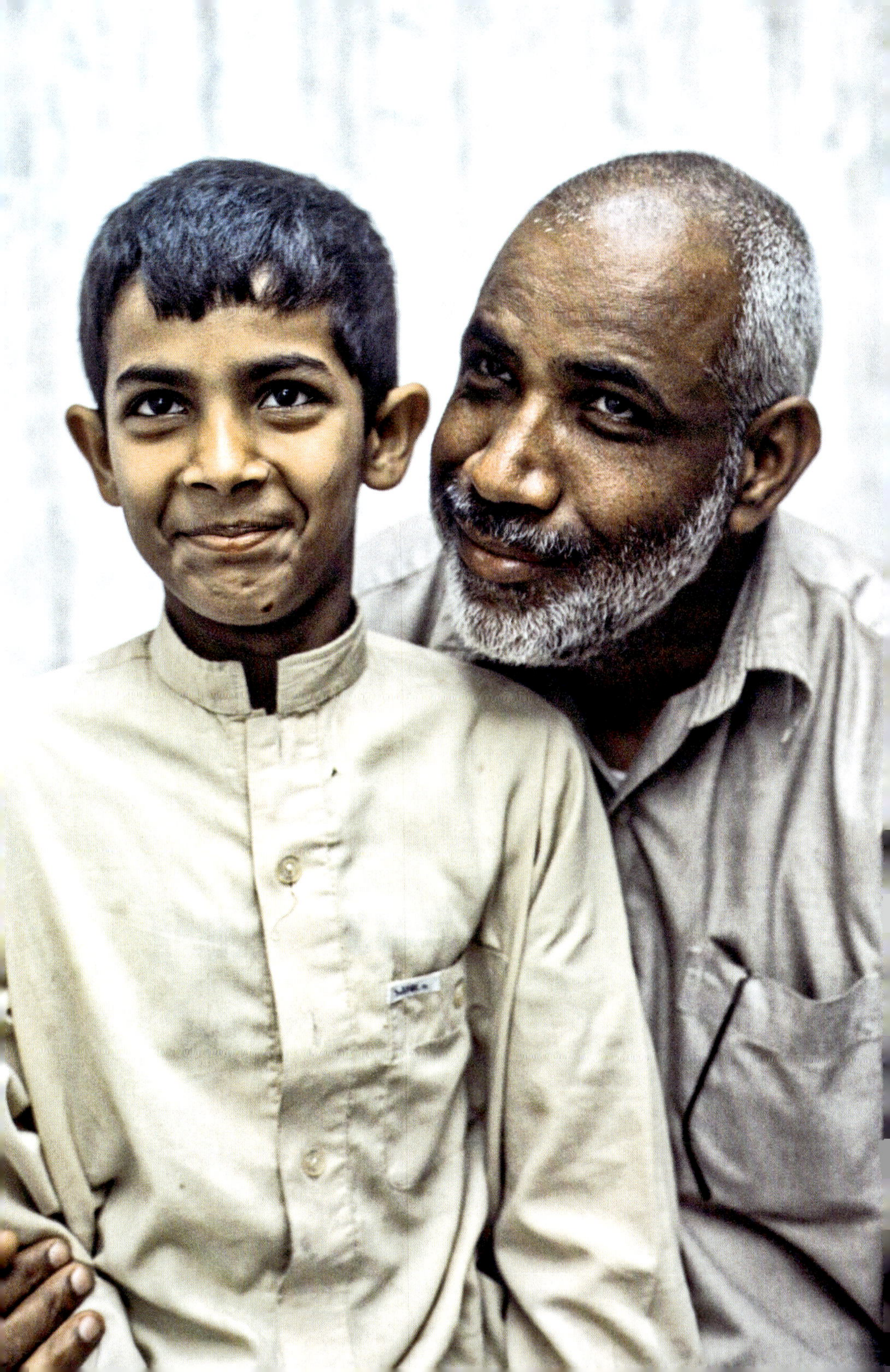

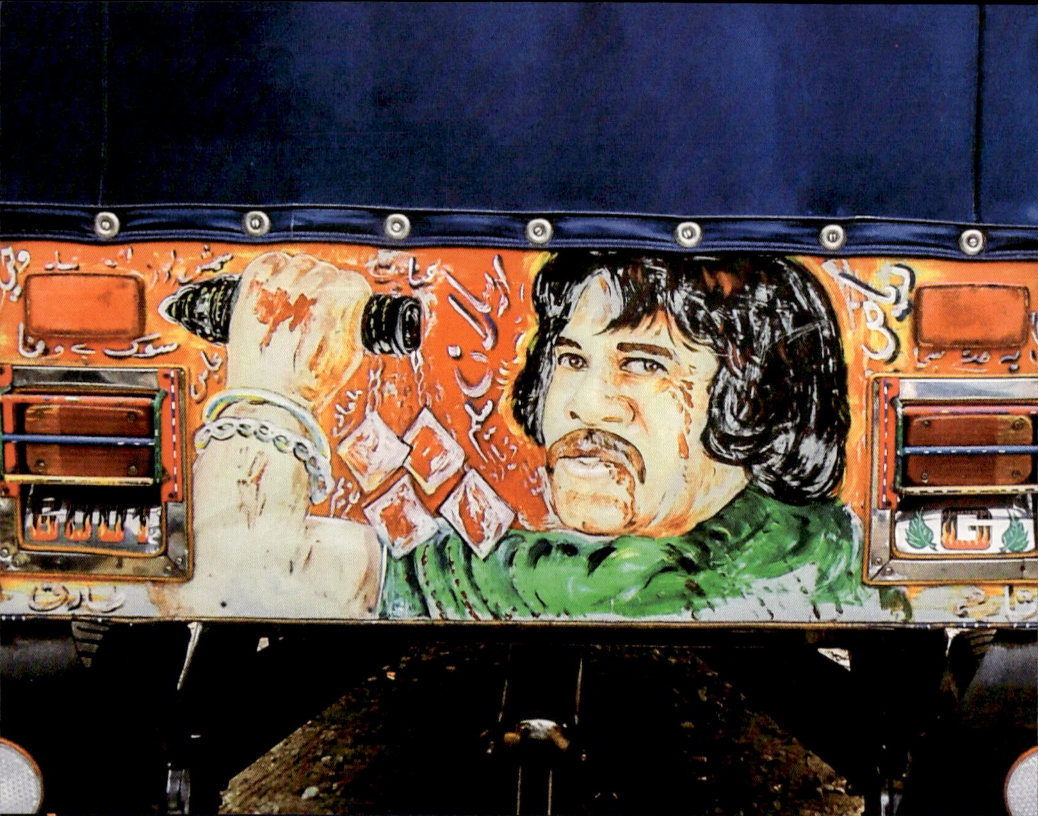

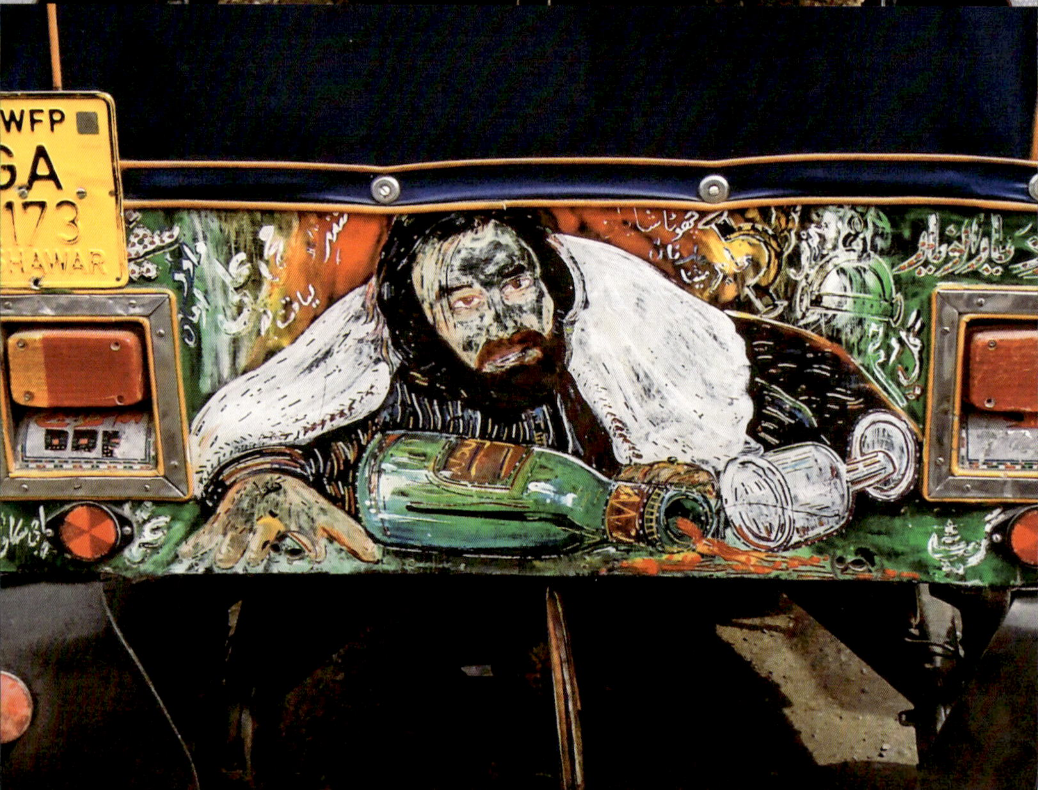
WFP

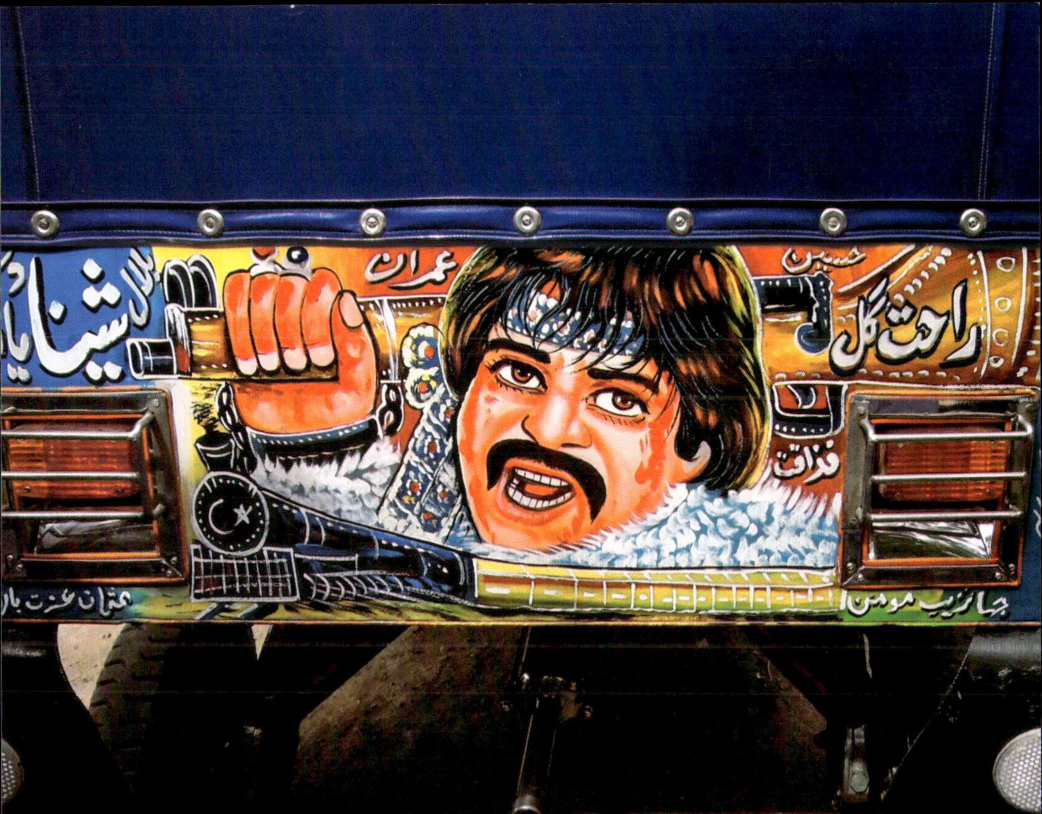
عمران
راحت گل

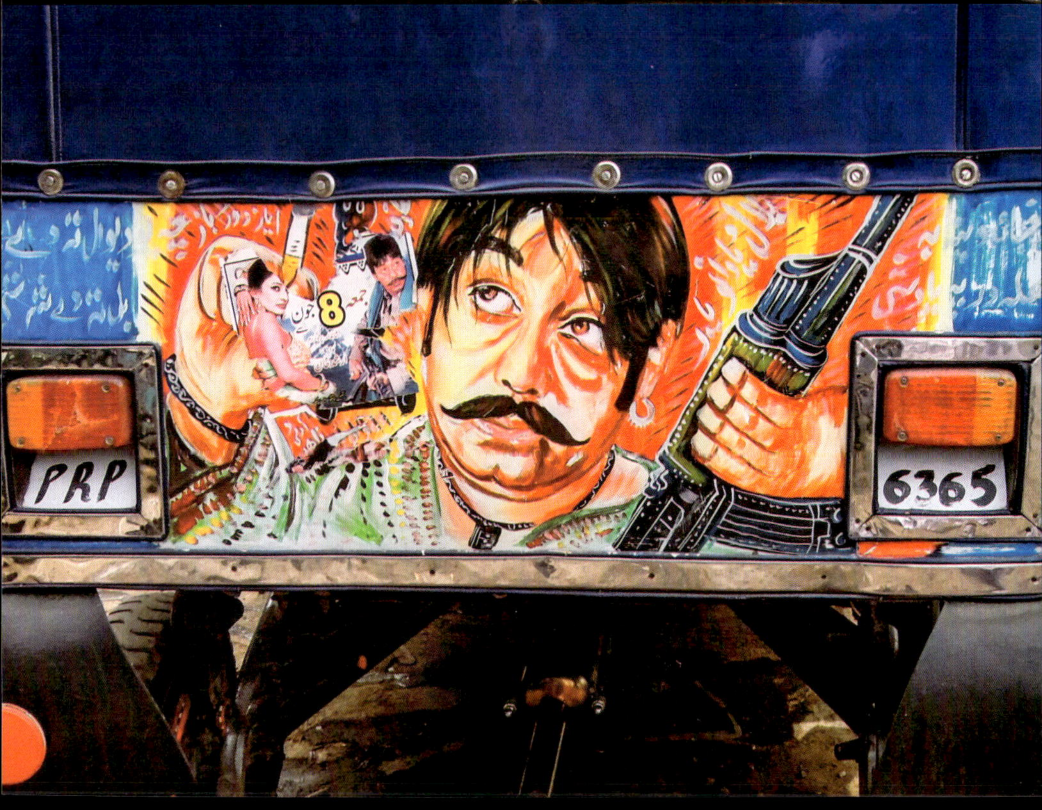
PRP
6365

Opposite: Hand-painted backdrop in Daoud's Welcome Studio on Cinema Road. The blue curtain is for official portraits, while the red and yellow are decorative.

Pages 138–139: Daoud, a native of Jalalabad, Afghanistan, sitting outside of his studio on Cinema Road. Coming to Peshawar in 1980, he was taught photography by his Hindu teacher in Afghanistan. Daoud does not read or write and so does everything pictorially on the computer. Nowadays he also works as a videographer for weddings, and has taught his daughters the skill.

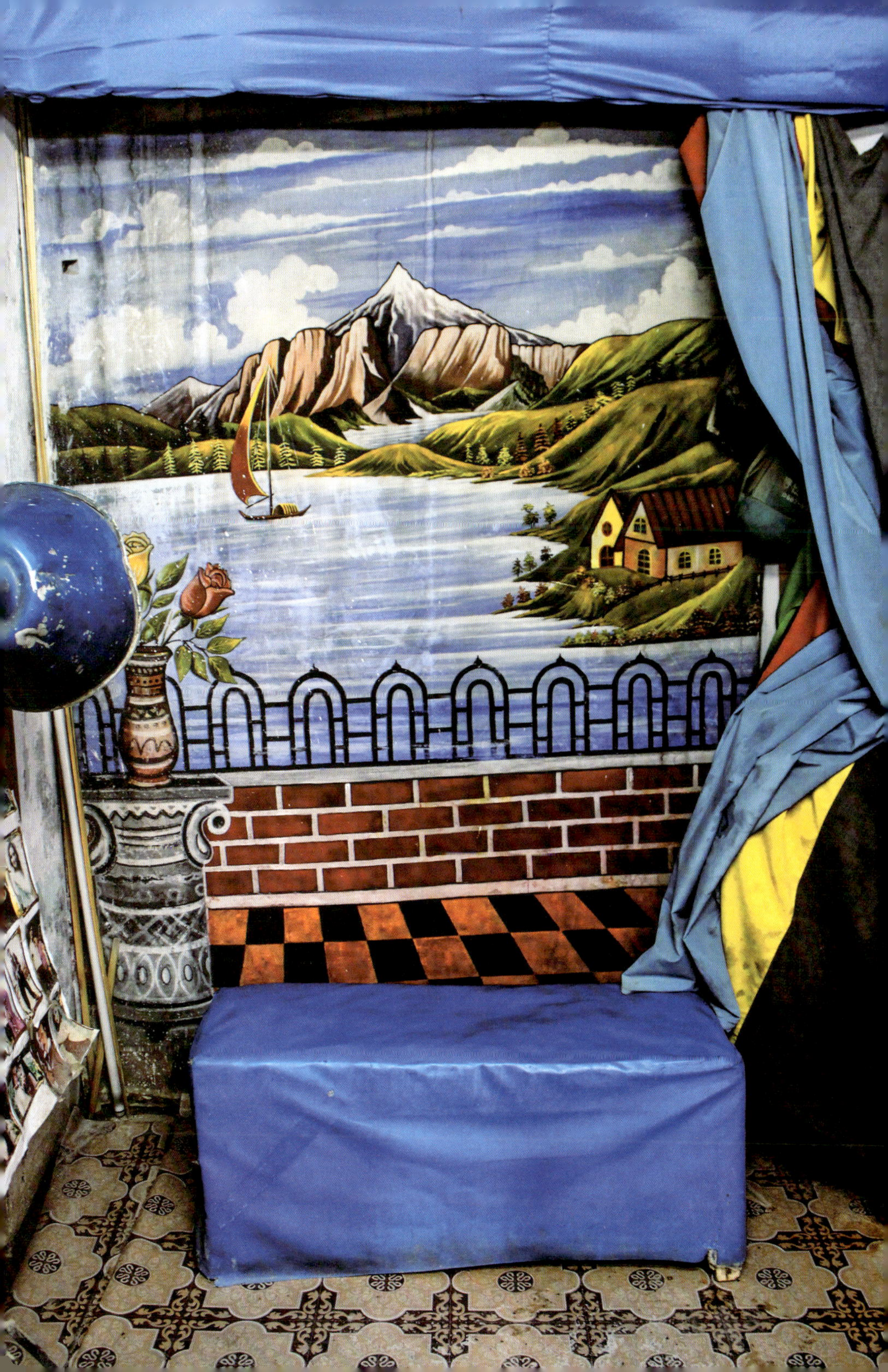

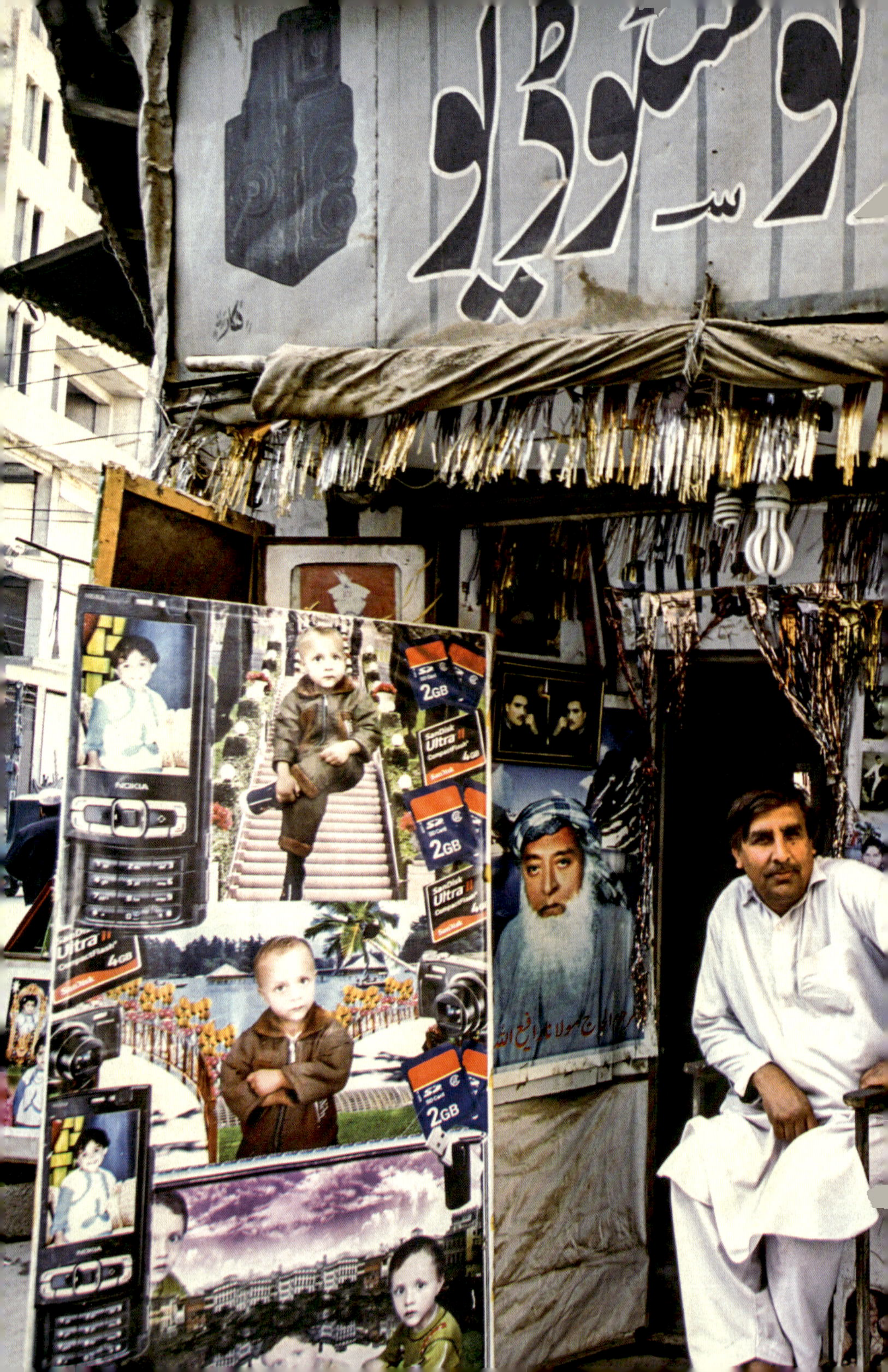
NOKIA
2GB
SanDisk Ultra II
4GB

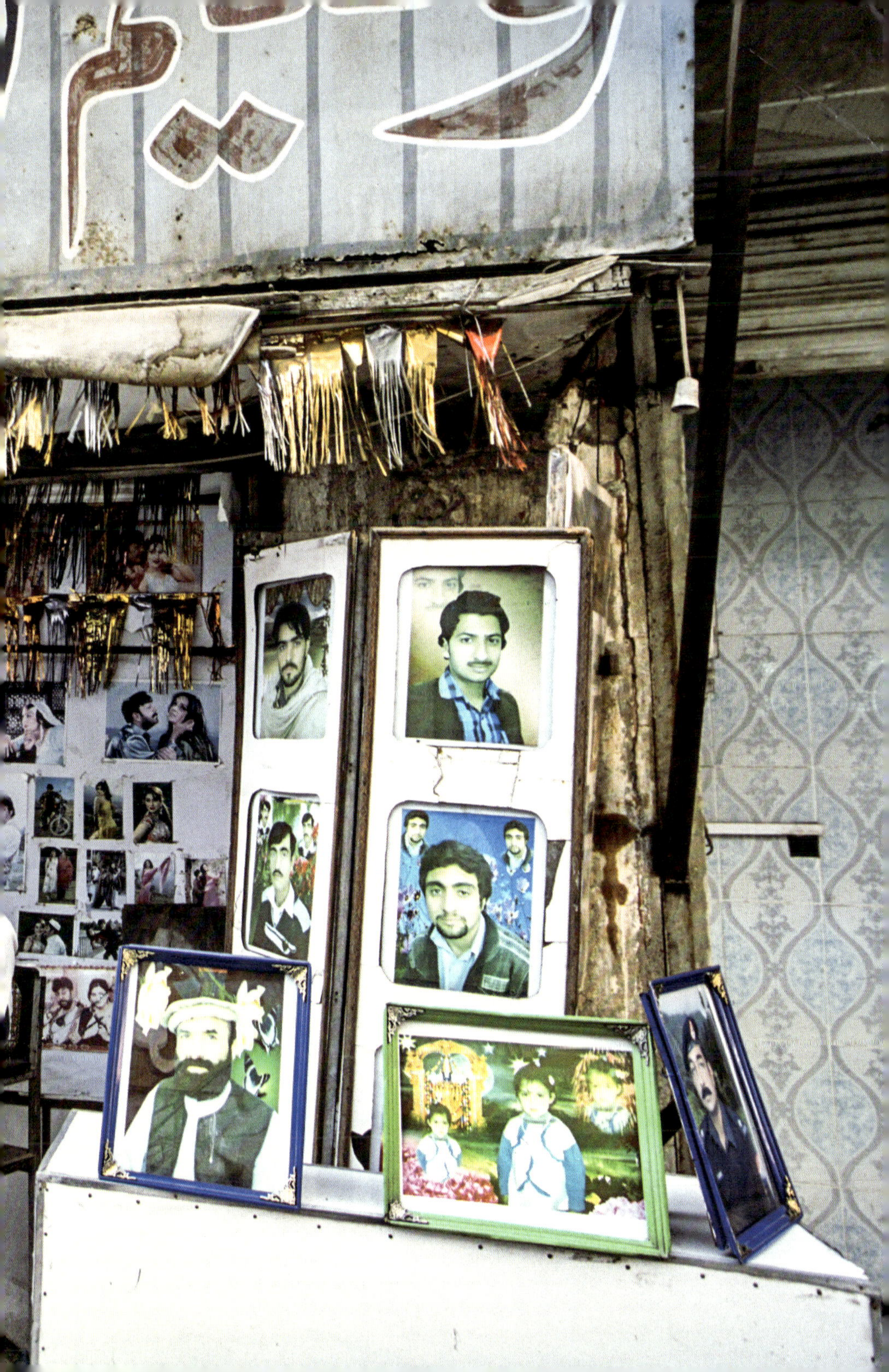

Opposite: Hand-coloured photograph of classic Indian actress and native Pashtu speaker, Madhubala (1933–1969), by Daoud of Cinema Road. Madhubala's father was a painter of cinema billboards from Peshawar.

Pages 142–143: Hand-coloured image of a classic movie scene.

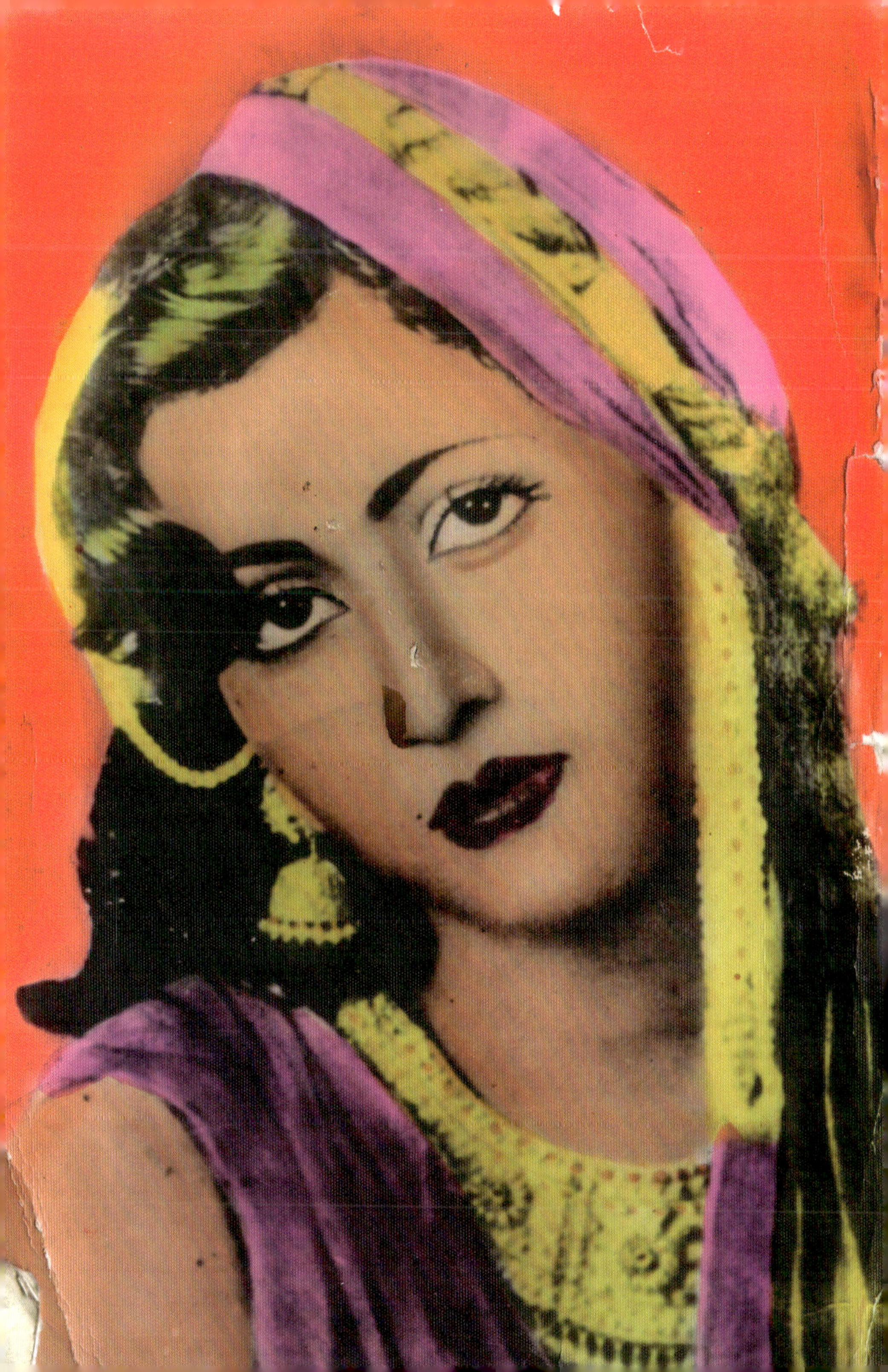

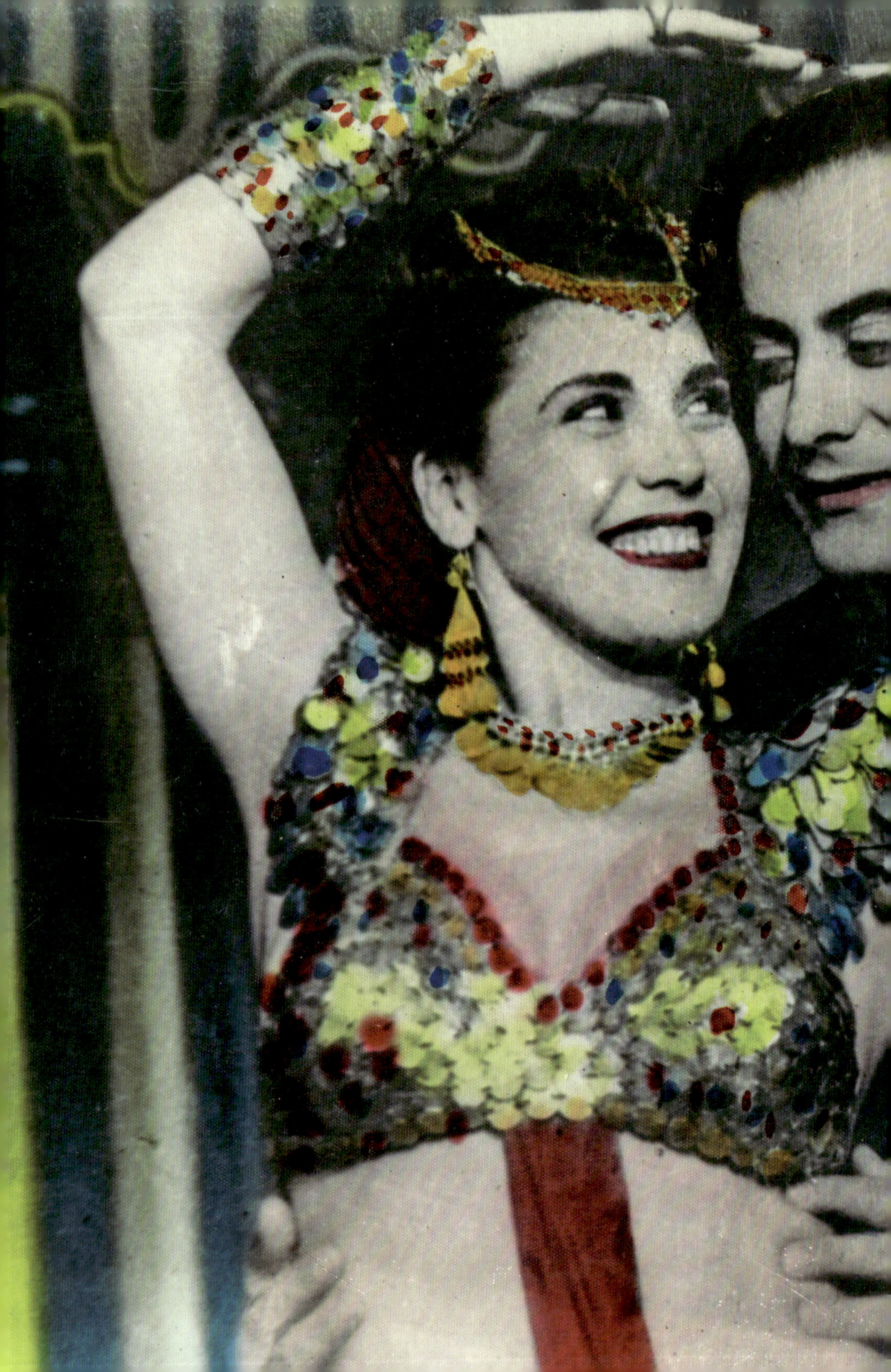

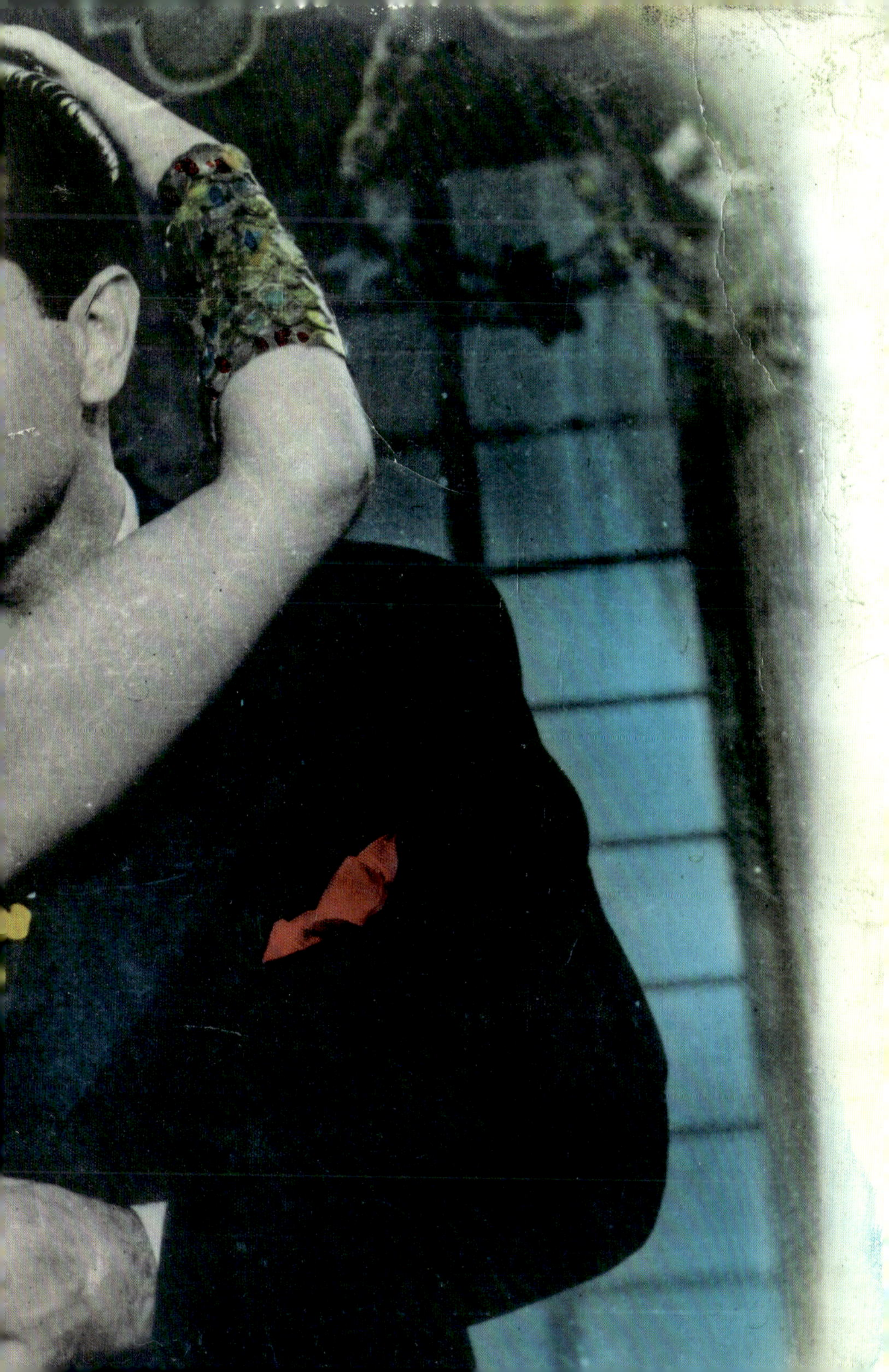

Noor Rehman of Cinema Road explains the difficulty of retouching and painting the eyes on a portrait. Photo by Fida Ustad; hand-colouring by Noor Rehman, early 1990s.

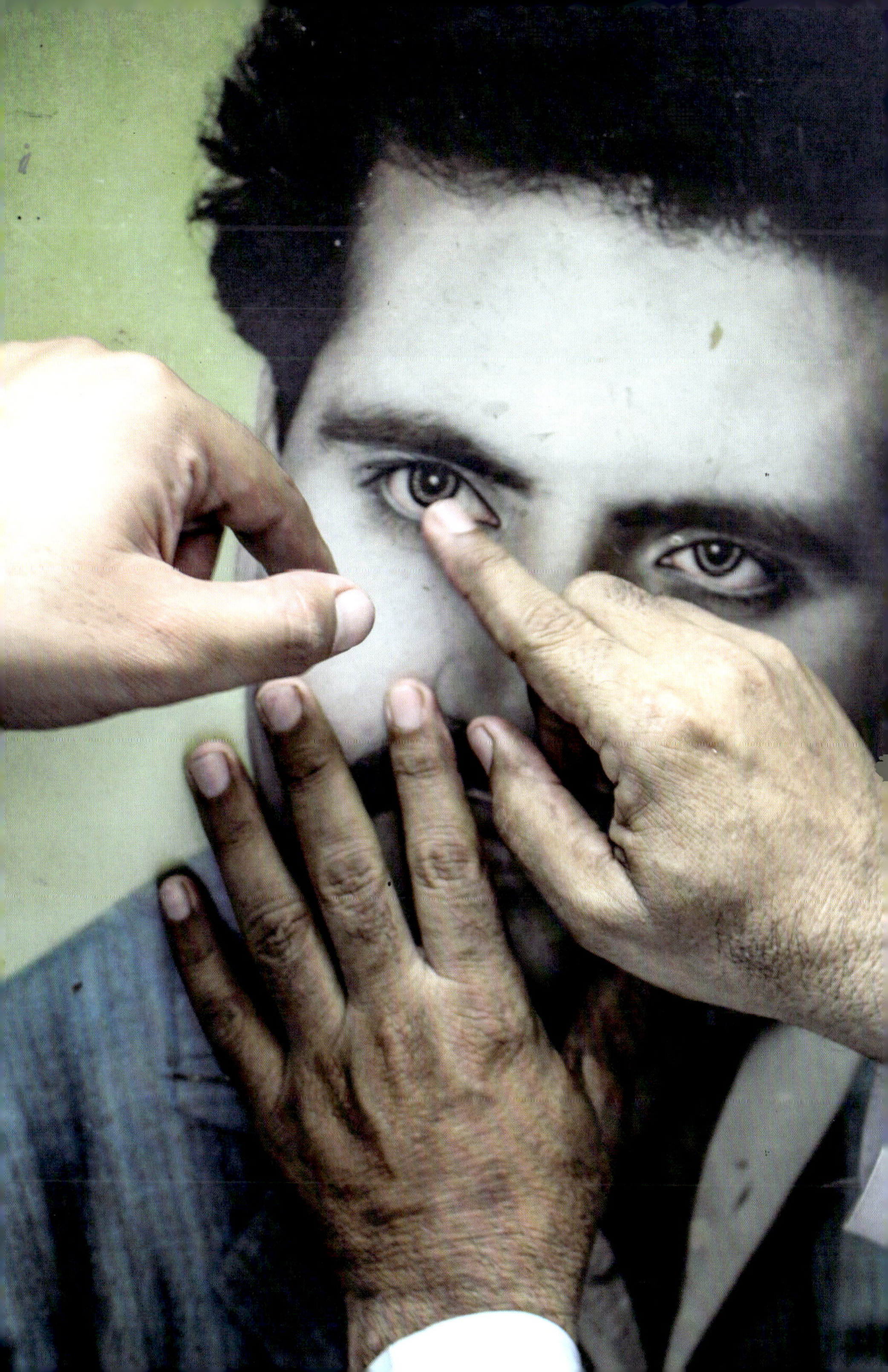

Photo of a newly married Hindu couple, Bishan and Sheela Lal. Bishan comes from a family of *dhobiwallah*s (laundry-washers) who, along with other members of Peshawar's Partition-time Hindu community, decided to remain in the city after 1947. The purse that Bishan's wife, Sheela, a nurse, is holding was used to place money gifts from guests at the wedding, and was a wedding gift from her mother, as was Bishan's suit. Sagheer Photo Studio, 1975.

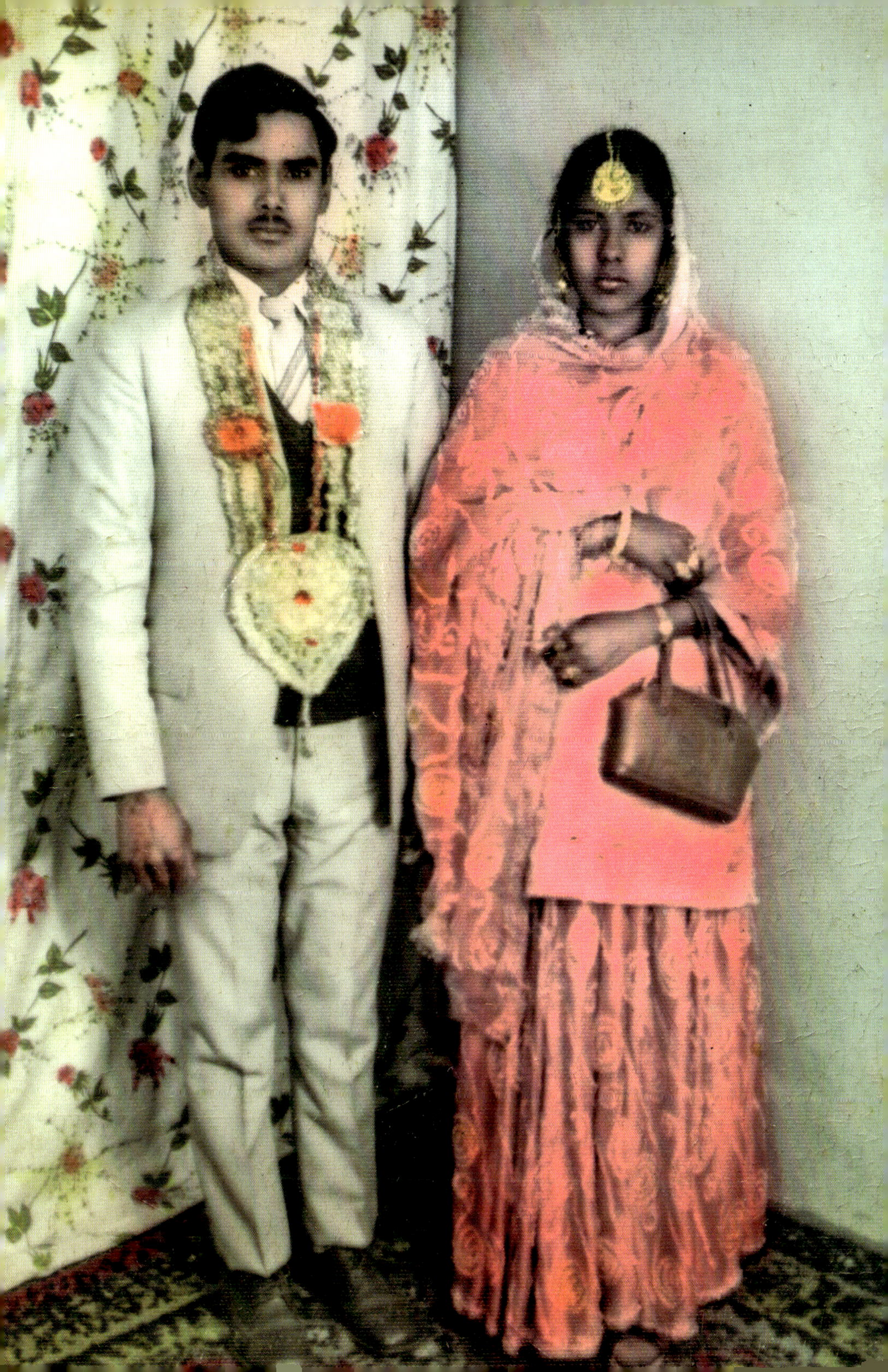

Hand-coloured photograph by Muhammad Iqbal, Kamran Studio, c.1990s.

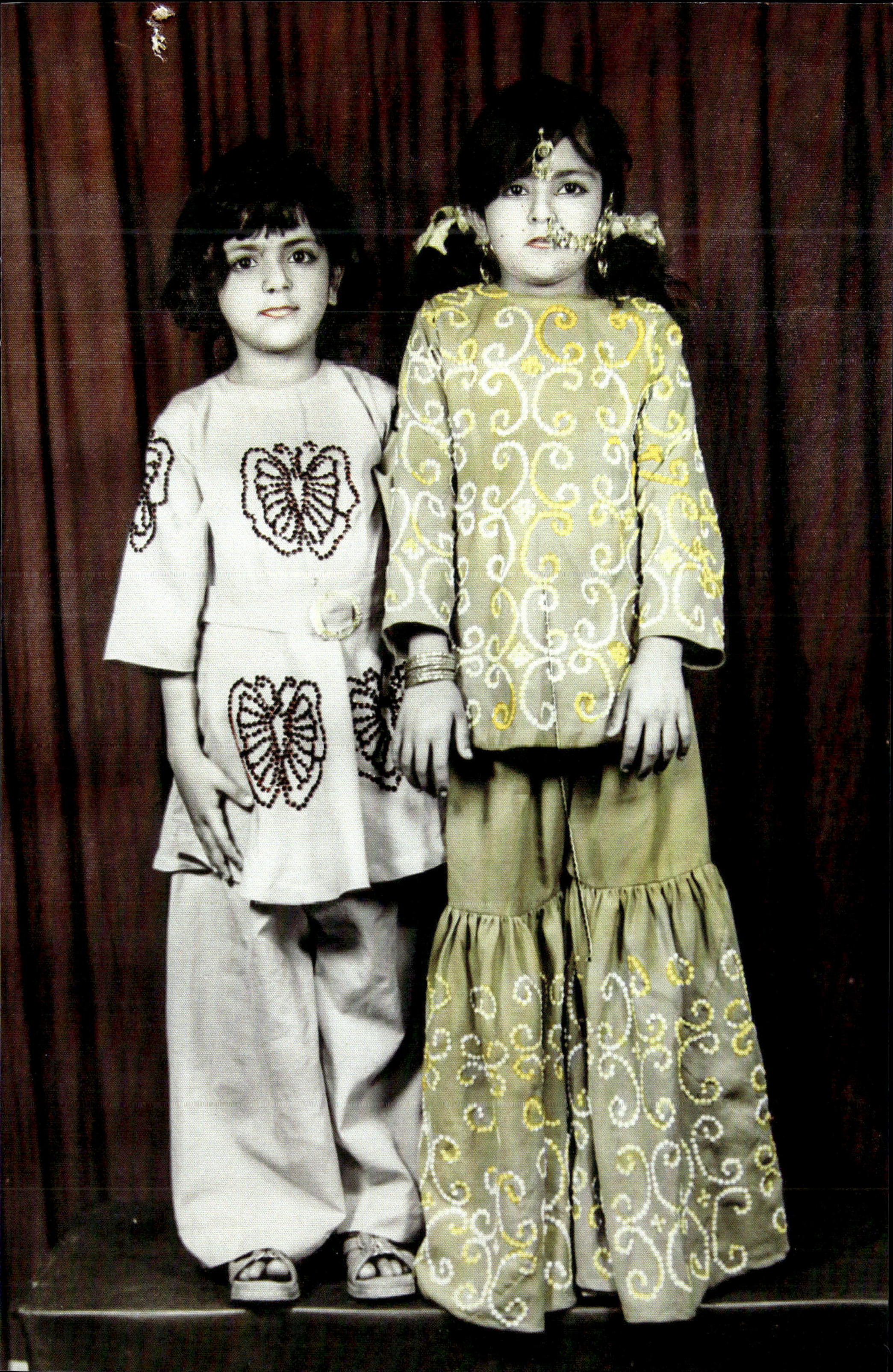

Hand-coloured photograph of a Hindu customer
by Tahir Usman, c.1980–1990s.

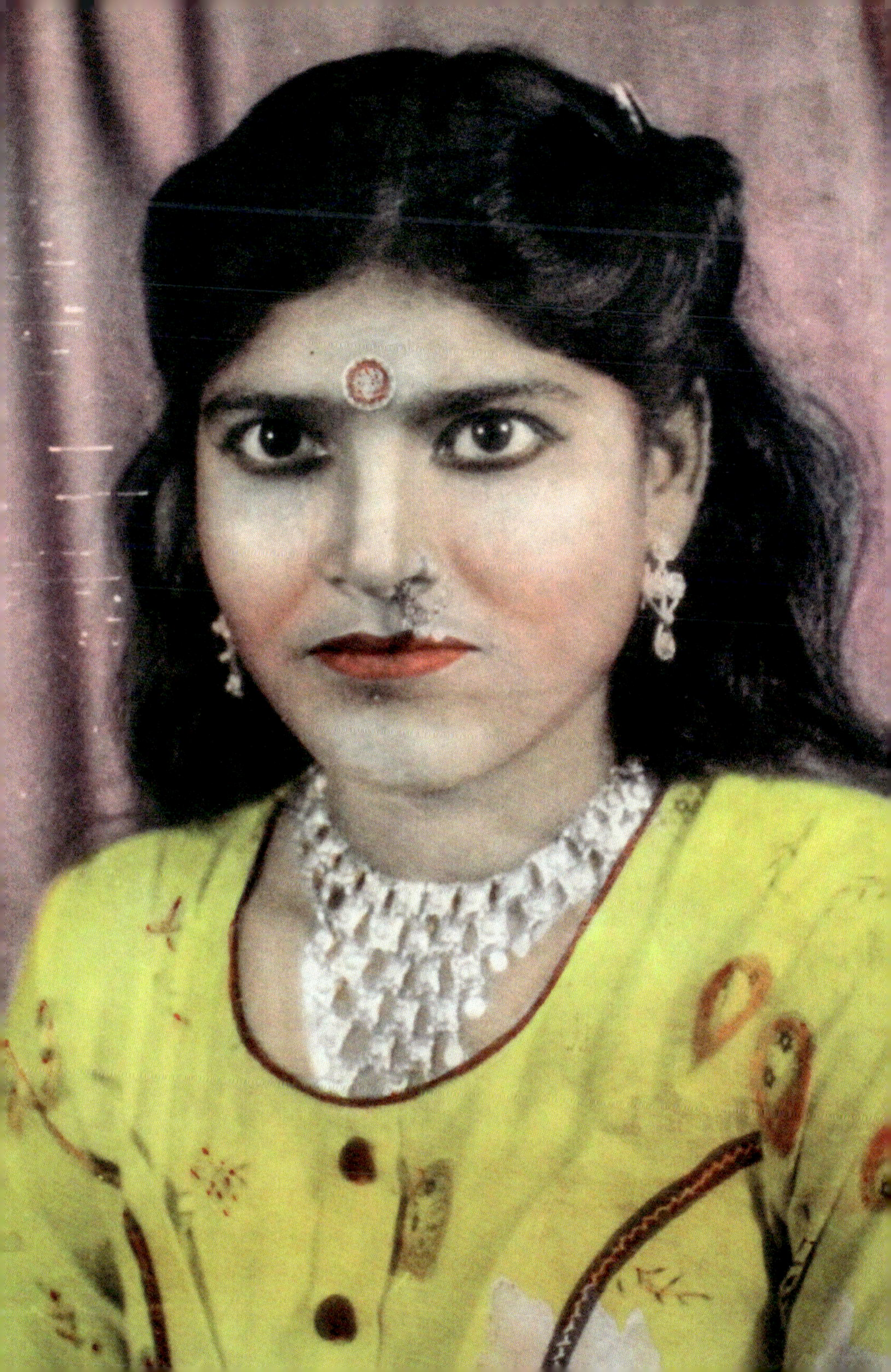

Hand-colouring practice piece by Tahir Usman, c.1980s.

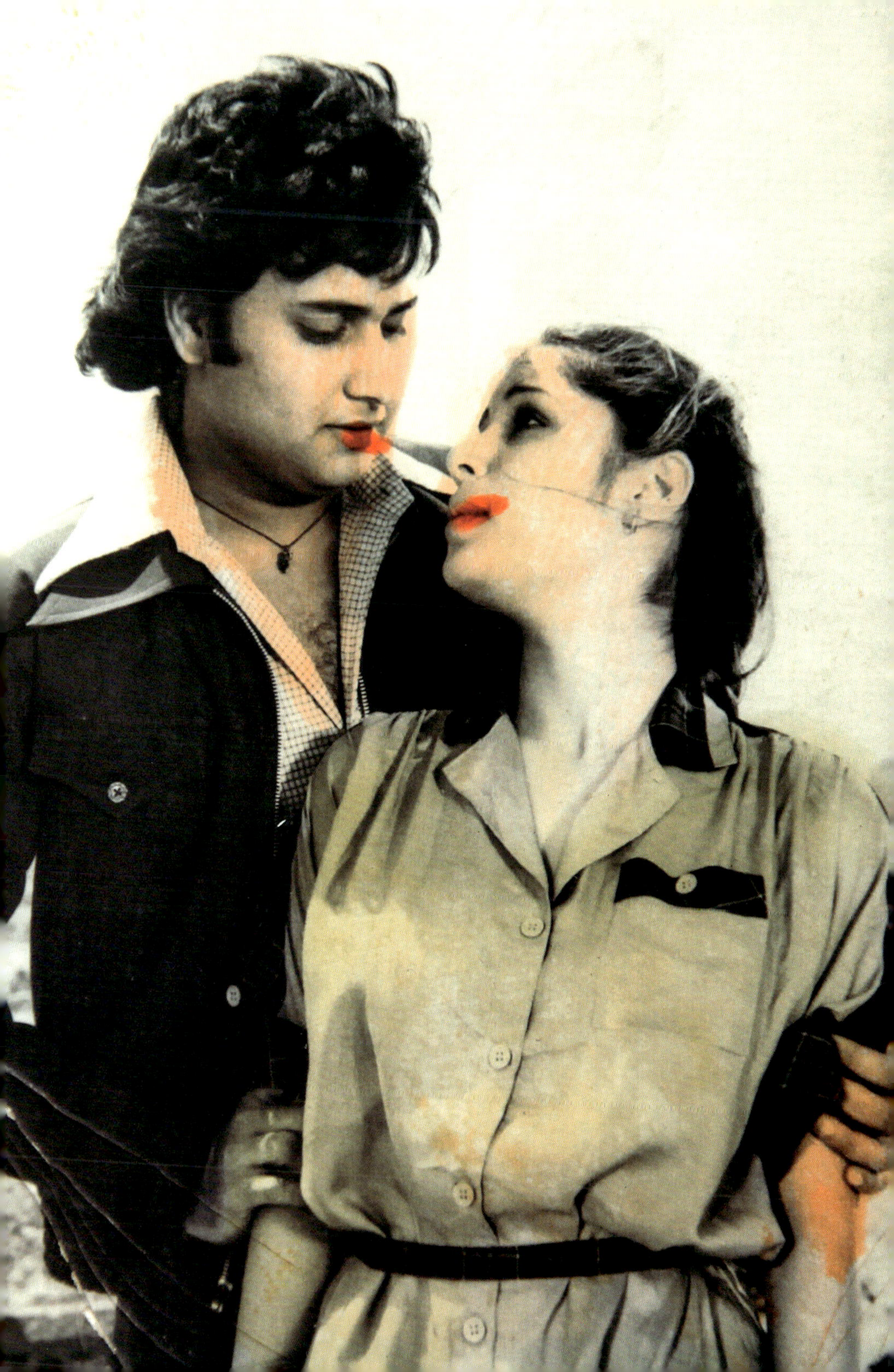

Opposite: "A man can only meet God through work in which he has lost himself," says Tahir Usman, a master hand-colourist, photographer and painter. Here, Tahir is hand-colouring a portrait in the back of his studio on Cinema Road in 2014.

Pages 156–159: Hand-coloured self-portraits by Tahir Usman from the 1980s to 1990s.

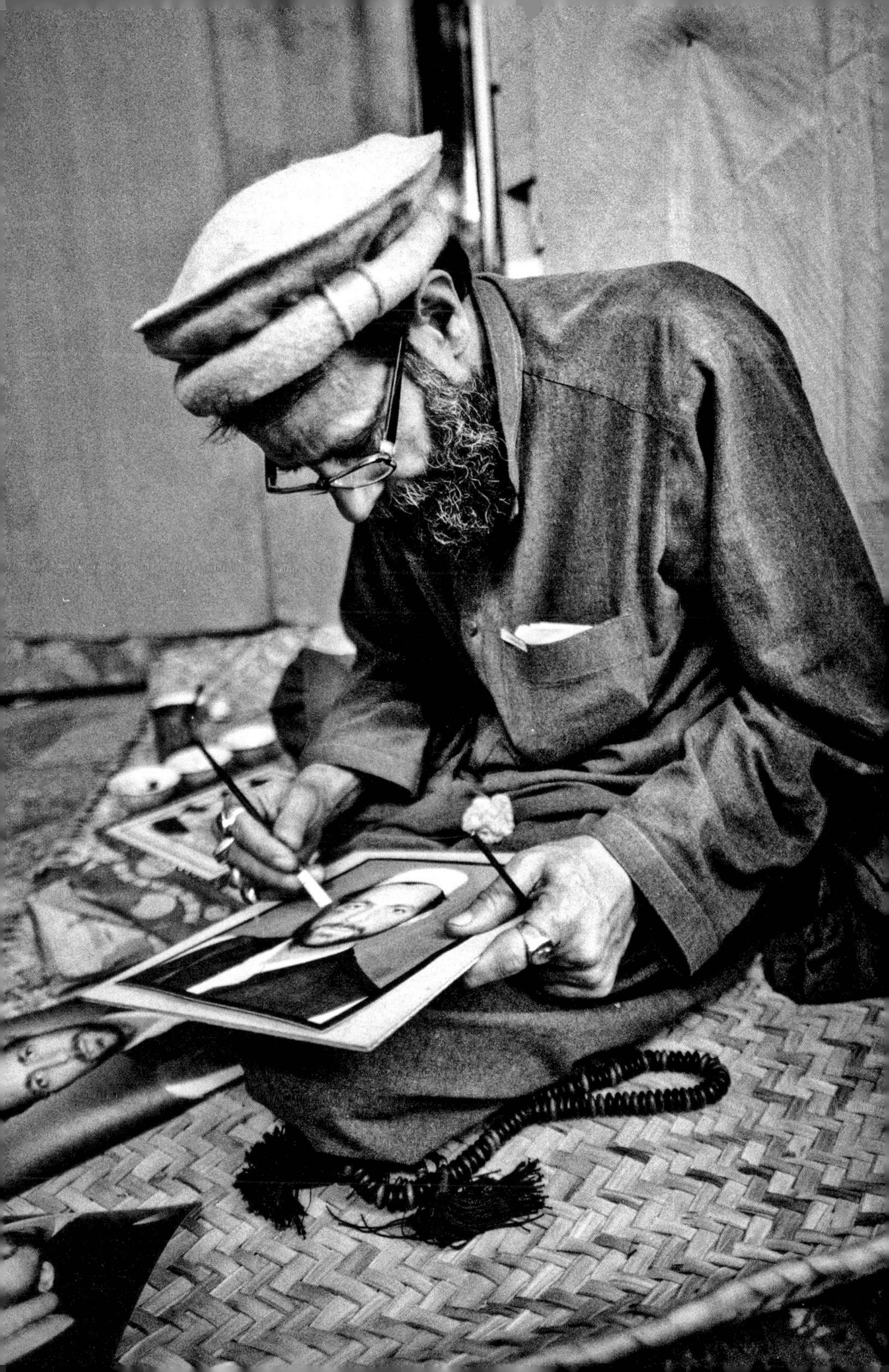

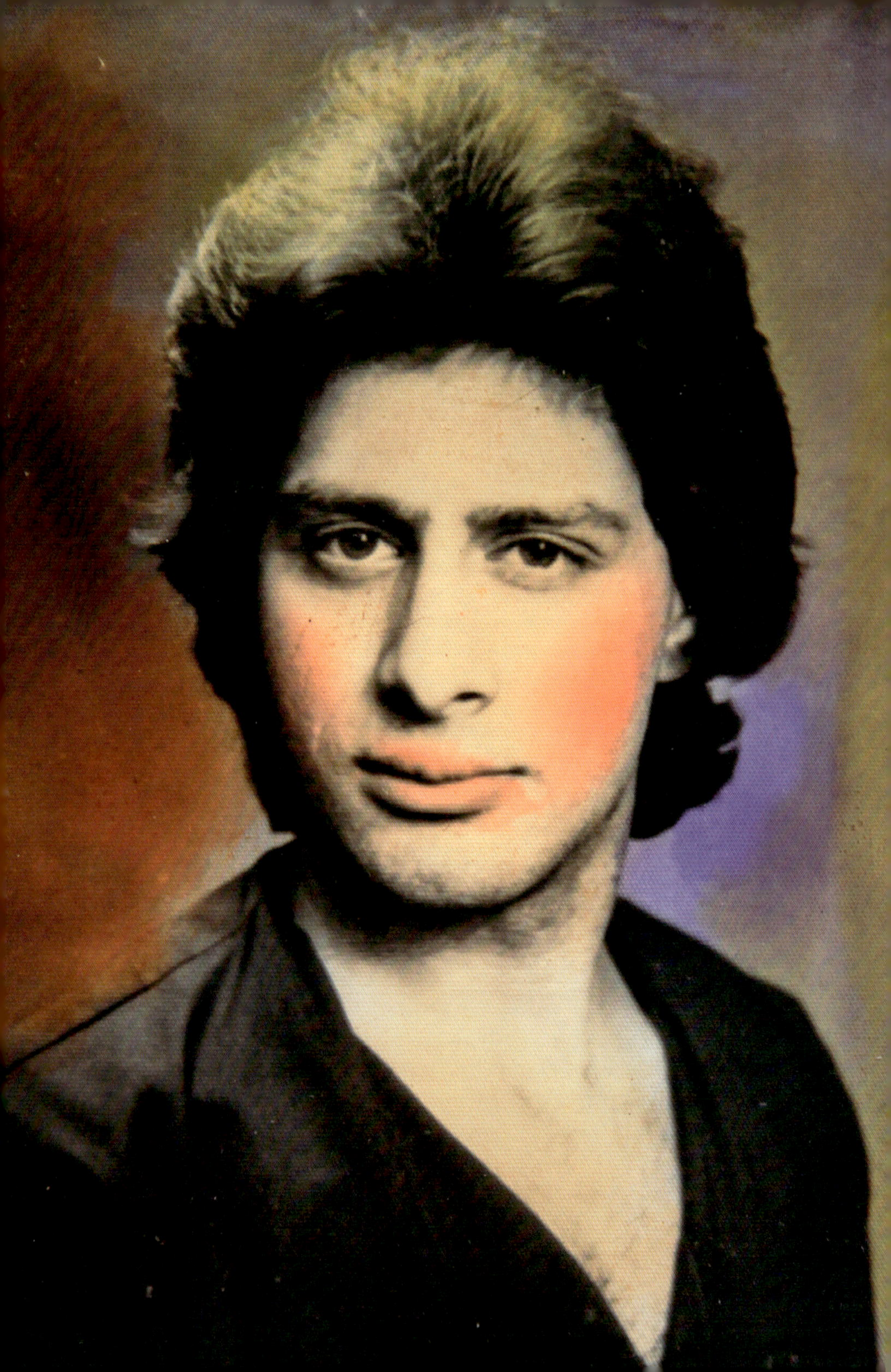

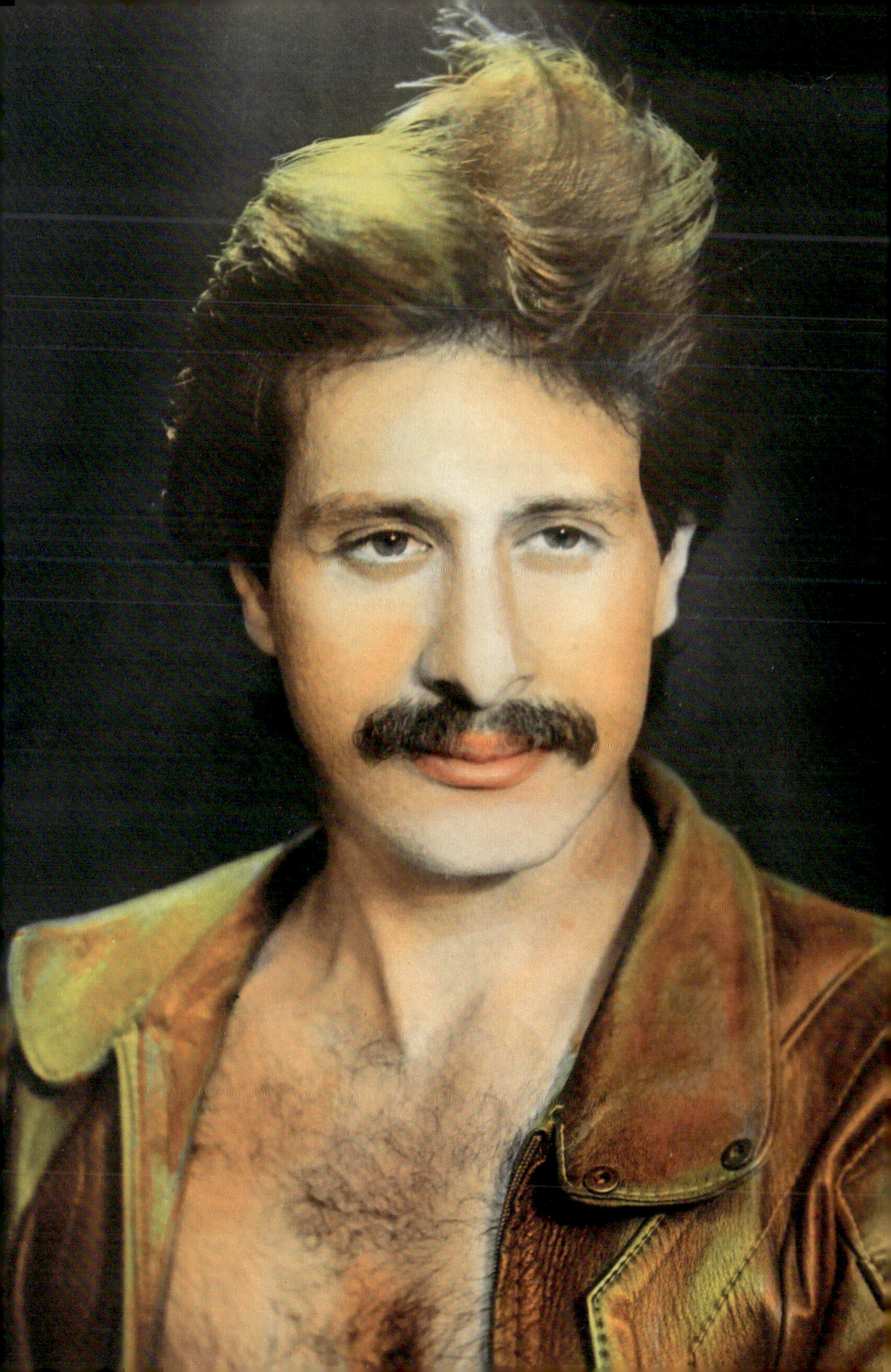

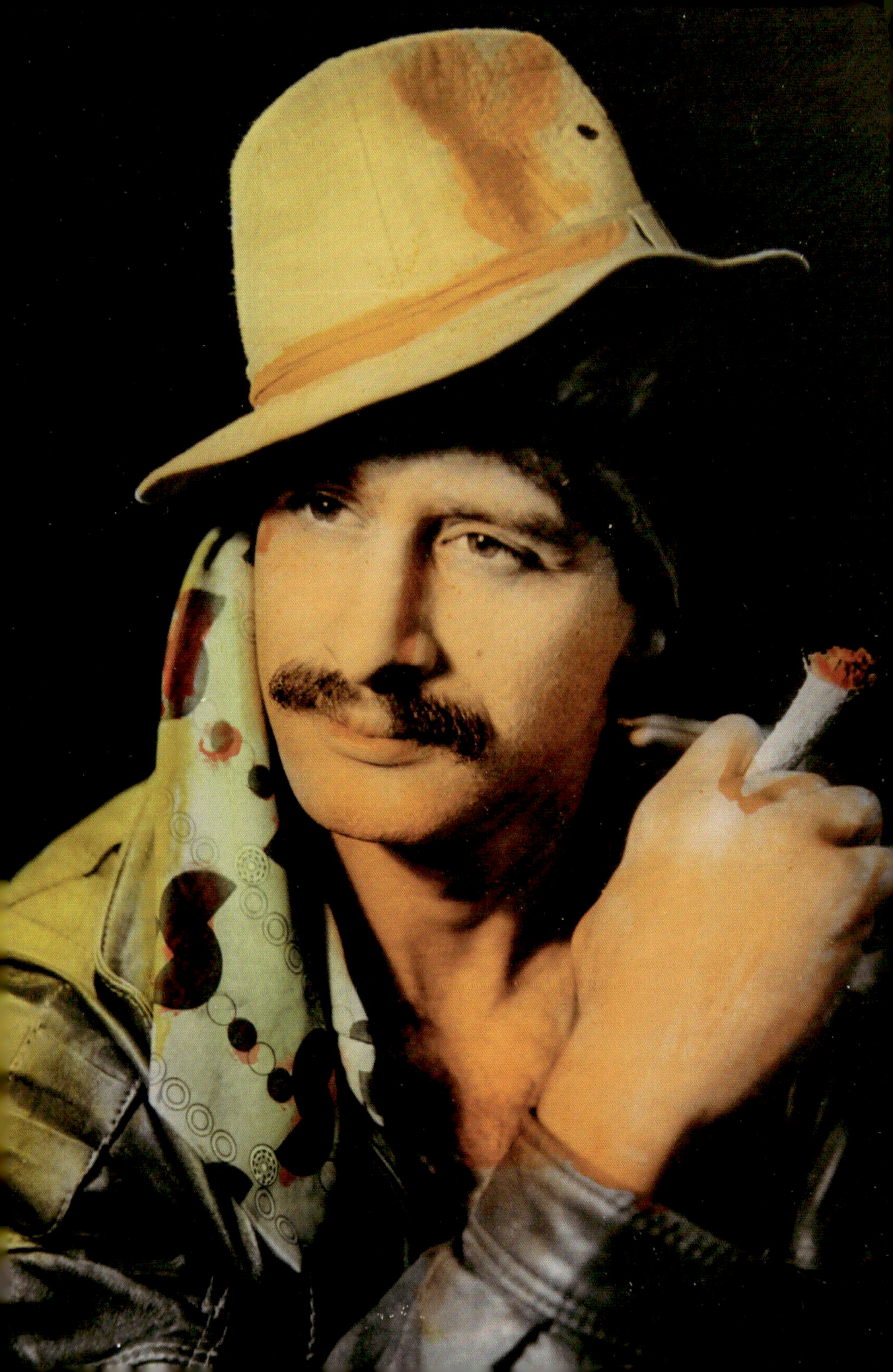

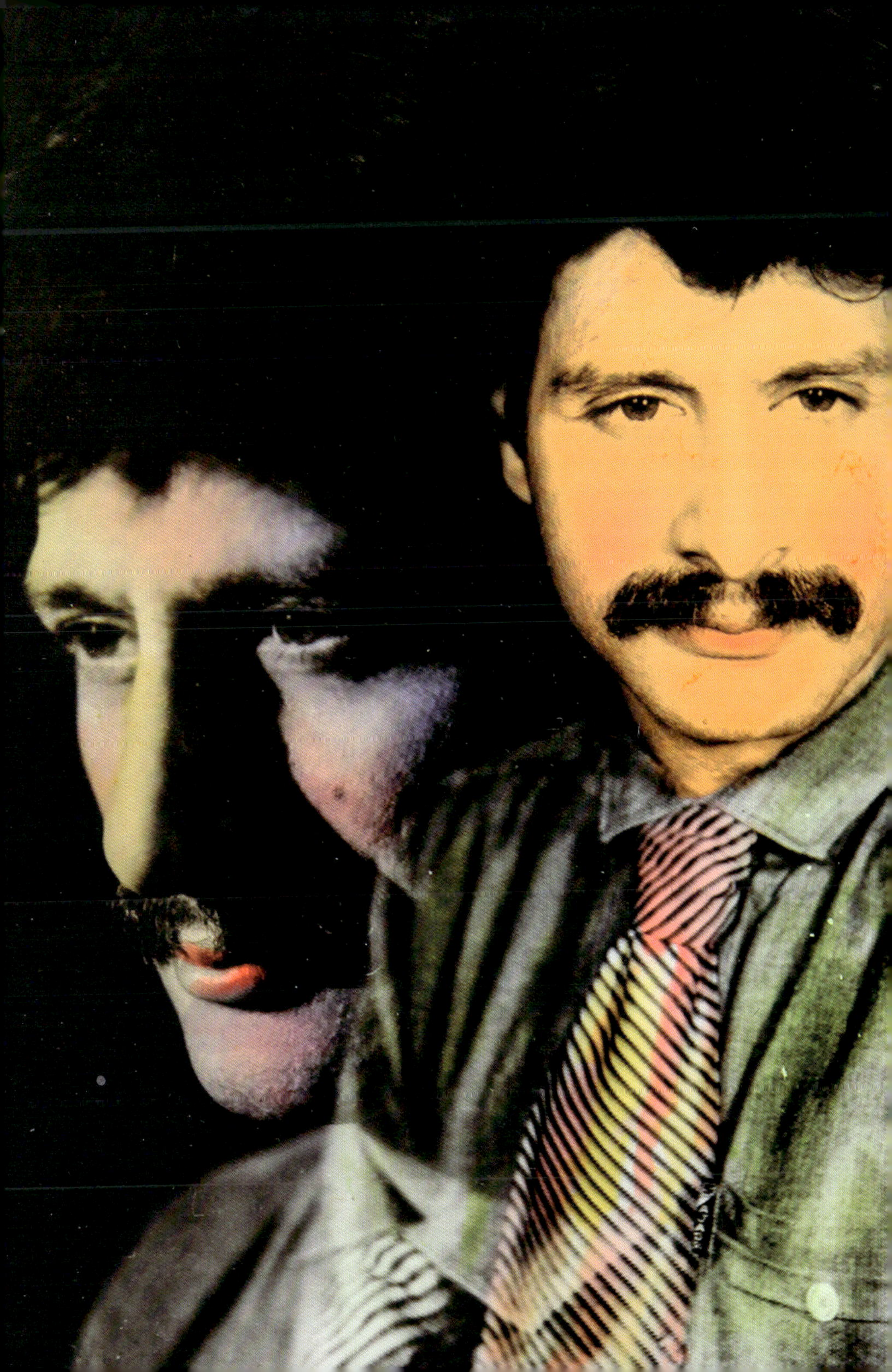

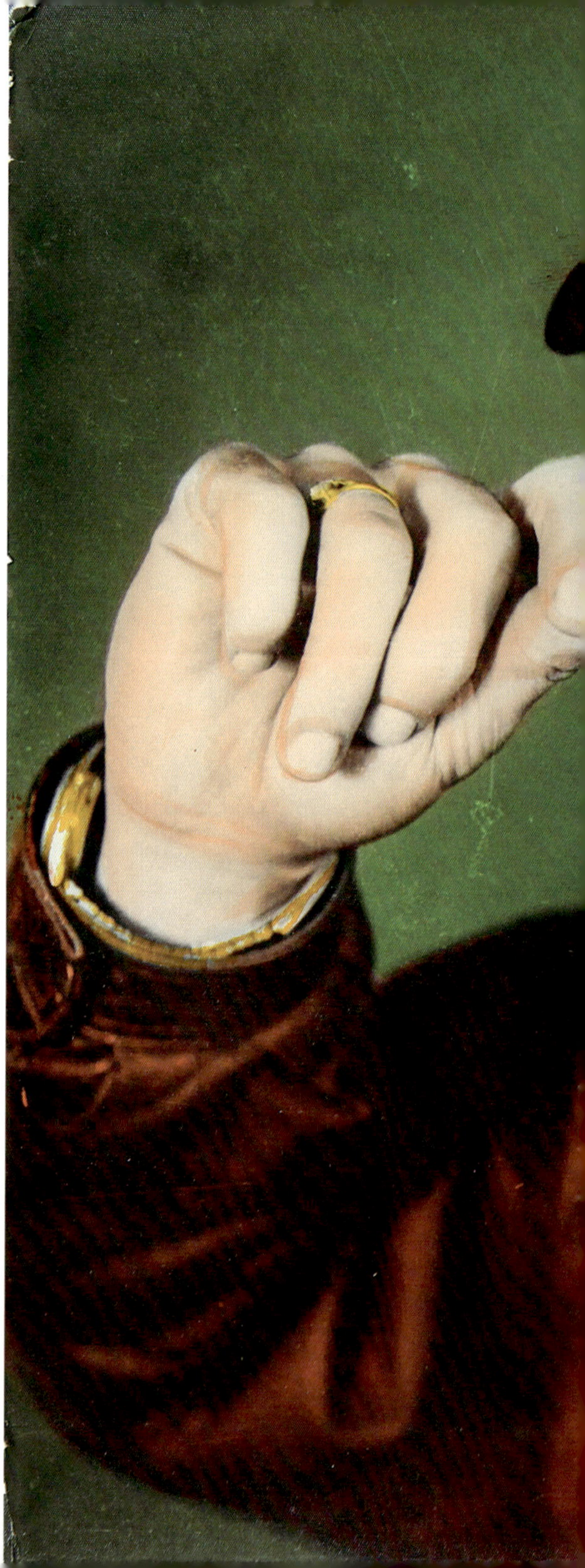

Opposite: Hand-coloured self-portrait by Tahir Usman, c.1980s.

Page 162: Hand-coloured portrait of Tahir's daughter by Tahir. *Page* 163: According to Tahir, when he was a baby a poisonous snake slid into his cot, coiling itself around his sleeping body. It left him unharmed, and without a fear of snakes.

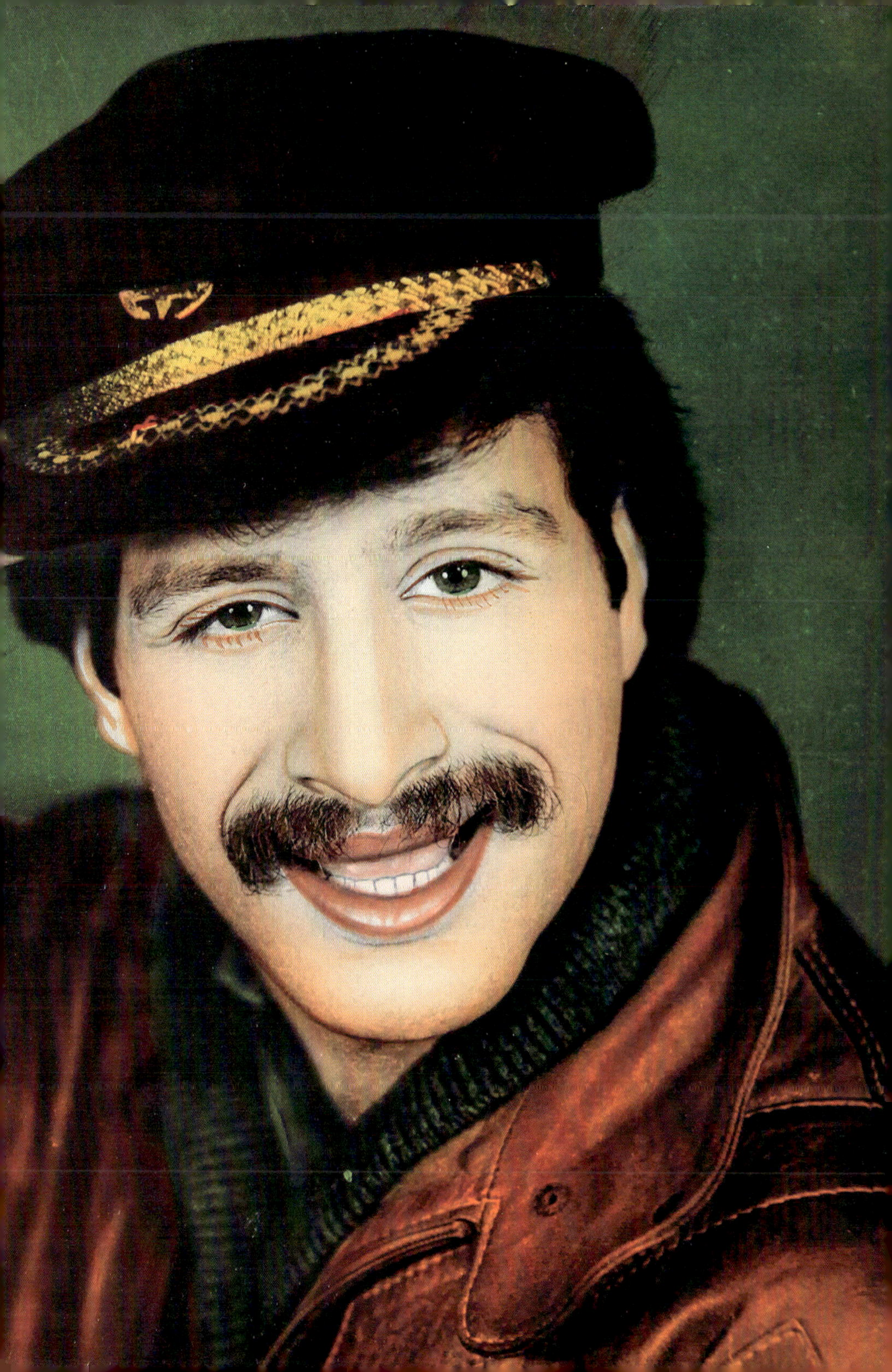

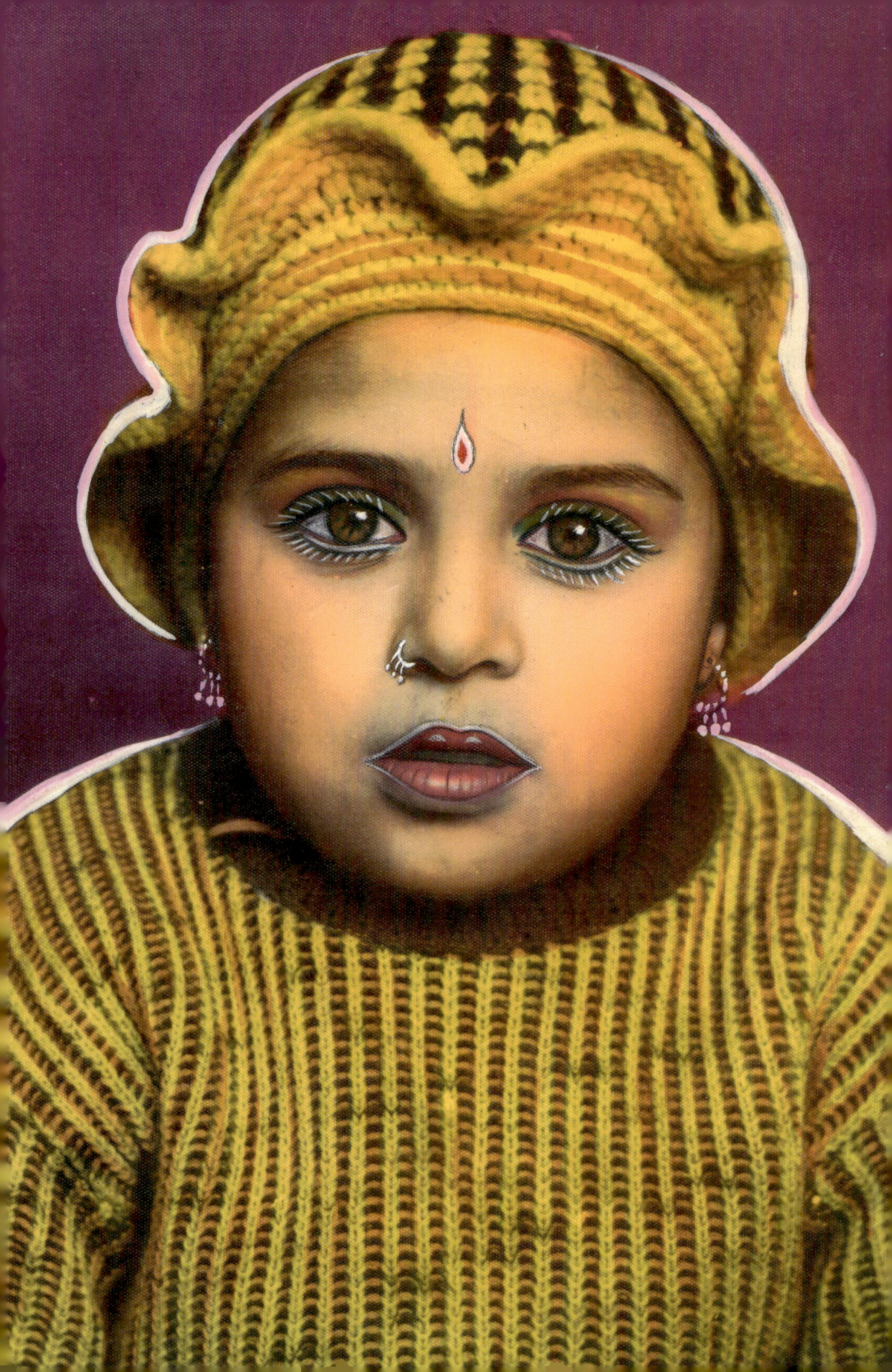

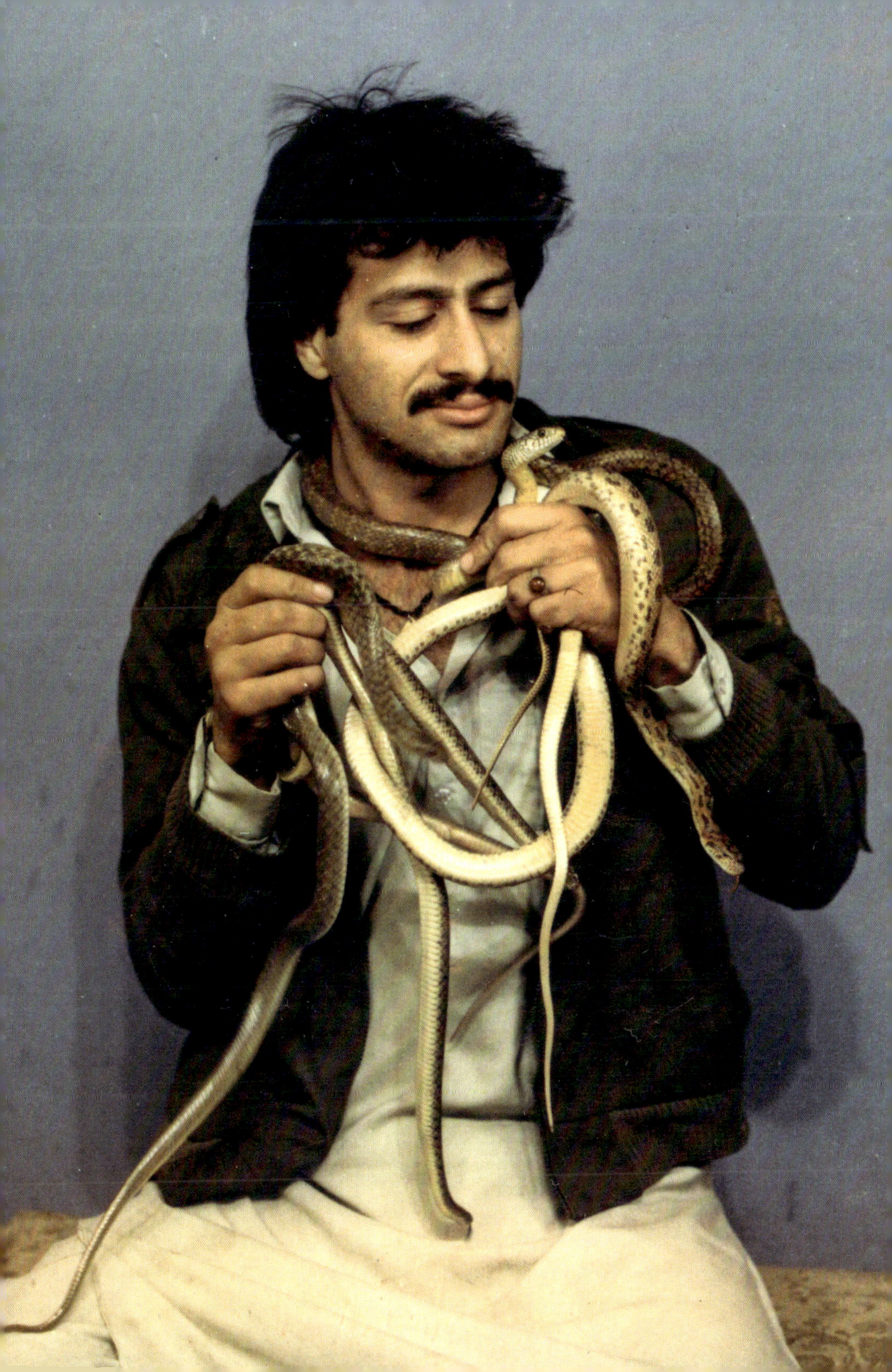

Opposite: Tahir Usman's latest self-portrait taken in 2012, which hangs in his studio on Cinema Road. Tahir used poster paint to dye his beard and eyebrows grey, to give an aged effect. In recent years Tahir, who has turned to the mystical teachings of Sufism, uses the paintbrush exclusively to paint episodes from the Koran, which stem, he says, from his dreams.

Pages 166 & 167: A playful take on the photomontage. Tahir cut his own hand-coloured portrait and that of a female model, possibly an actress, in small strips and placed them on a single piece of cardboard in alternative rows. He then created a frame in the same size as the strips to cover either the image of himself or the model, depending on which one or what the viewer wants to see.

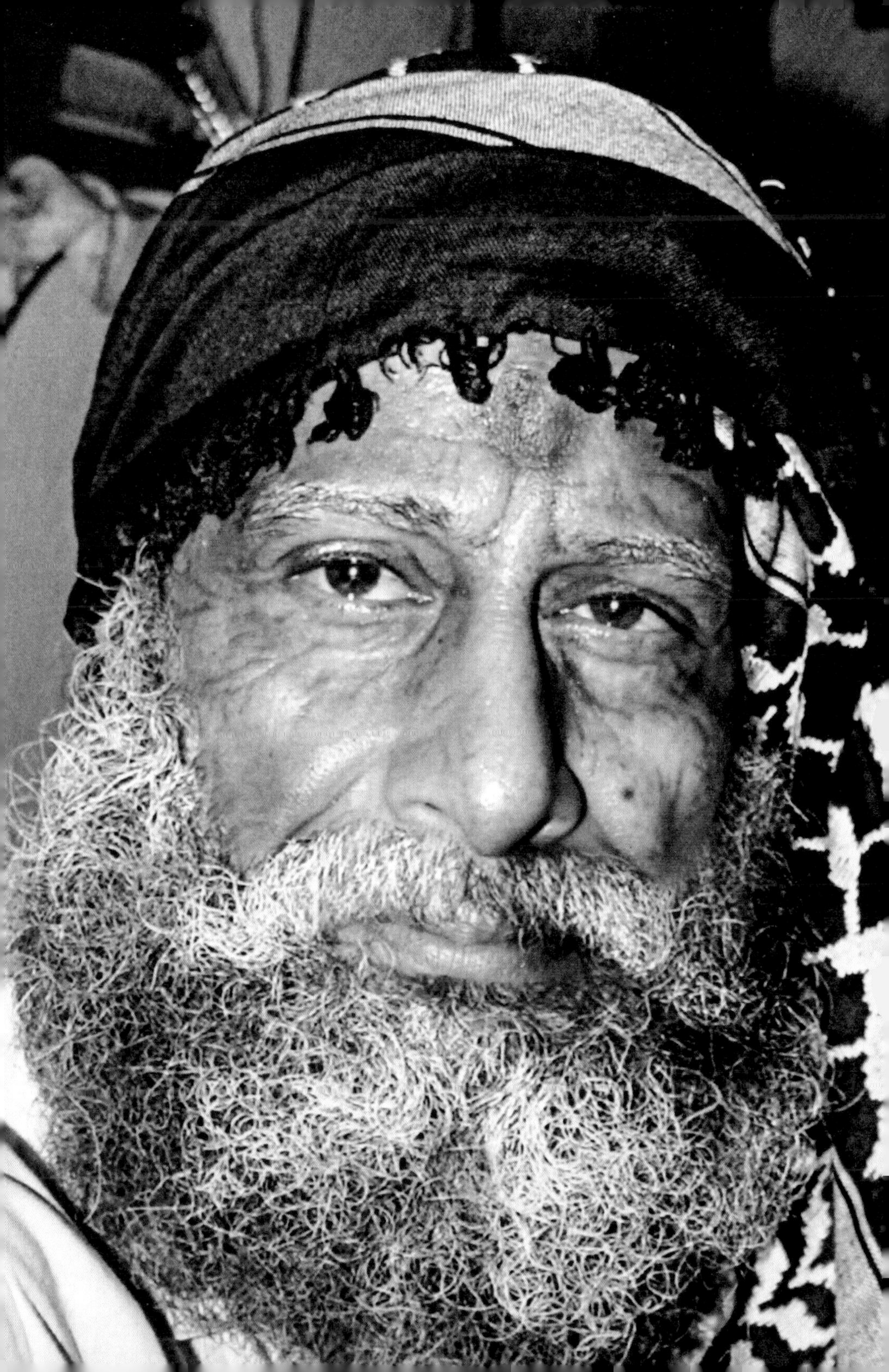

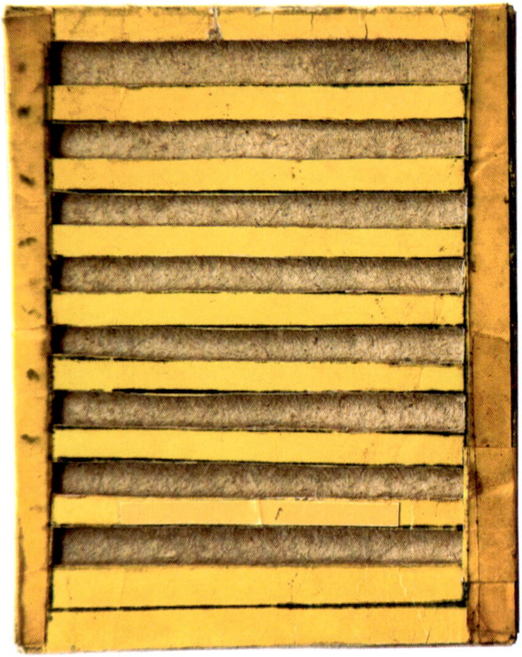

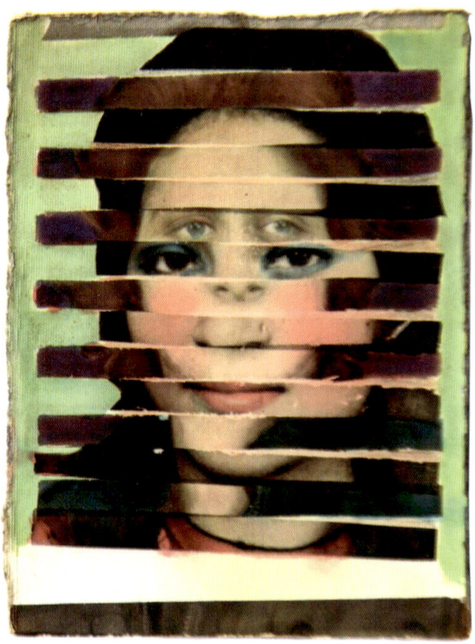

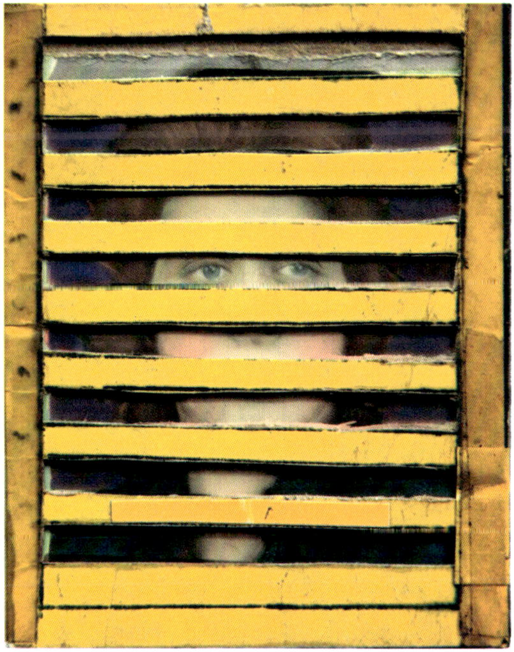

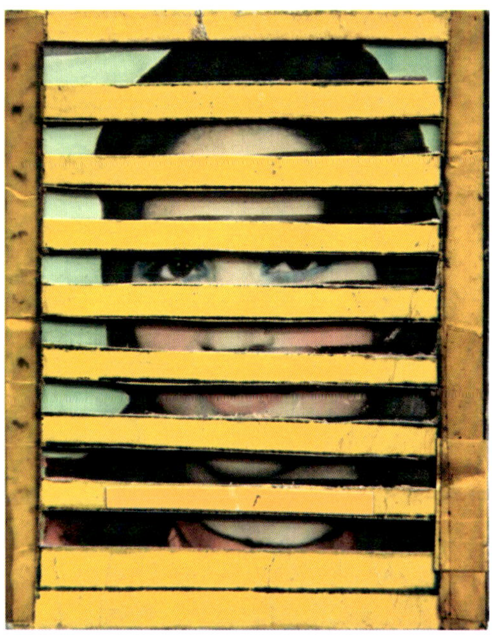

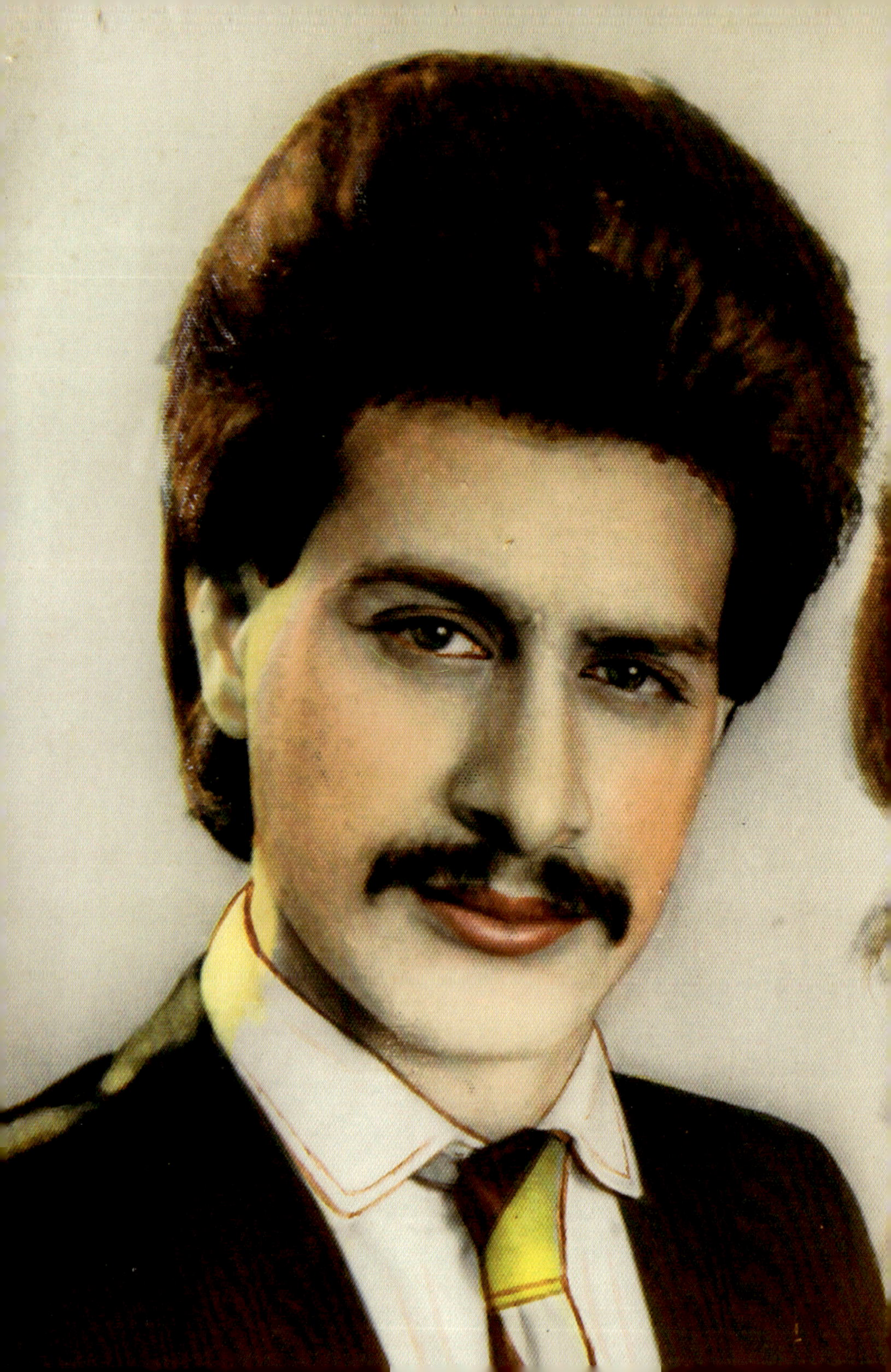

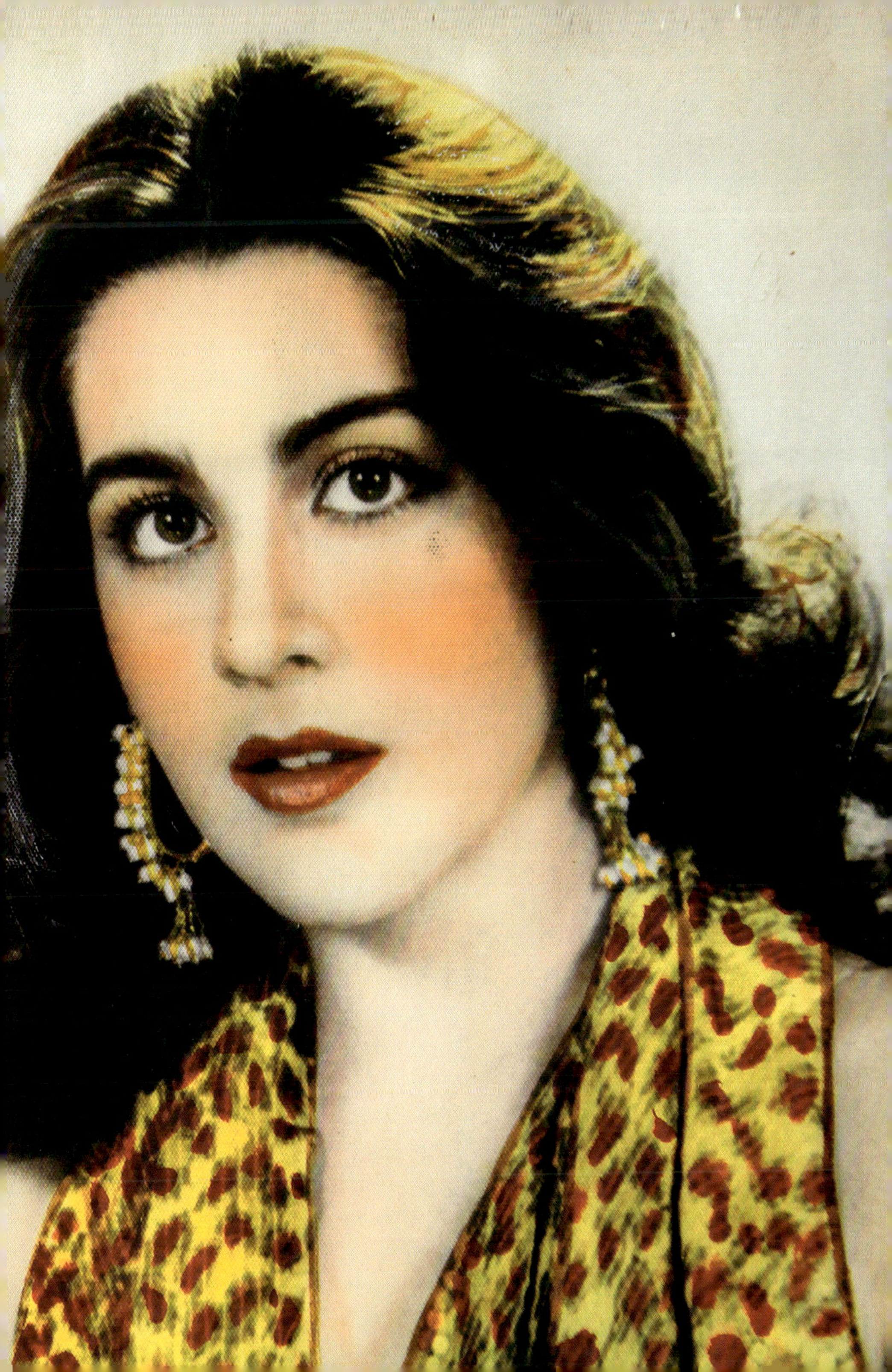

Preceding pages 168–169: Hand-coloured montage by Tahir Usman of himself with an Indian actress Amrita Singh.

Opposite: The grandmother of Tahir Usman. Requested by his mother to paint an enlarged portrait, Tahir divided his grandmother's image into sections to allot the correct proportions to the painting.

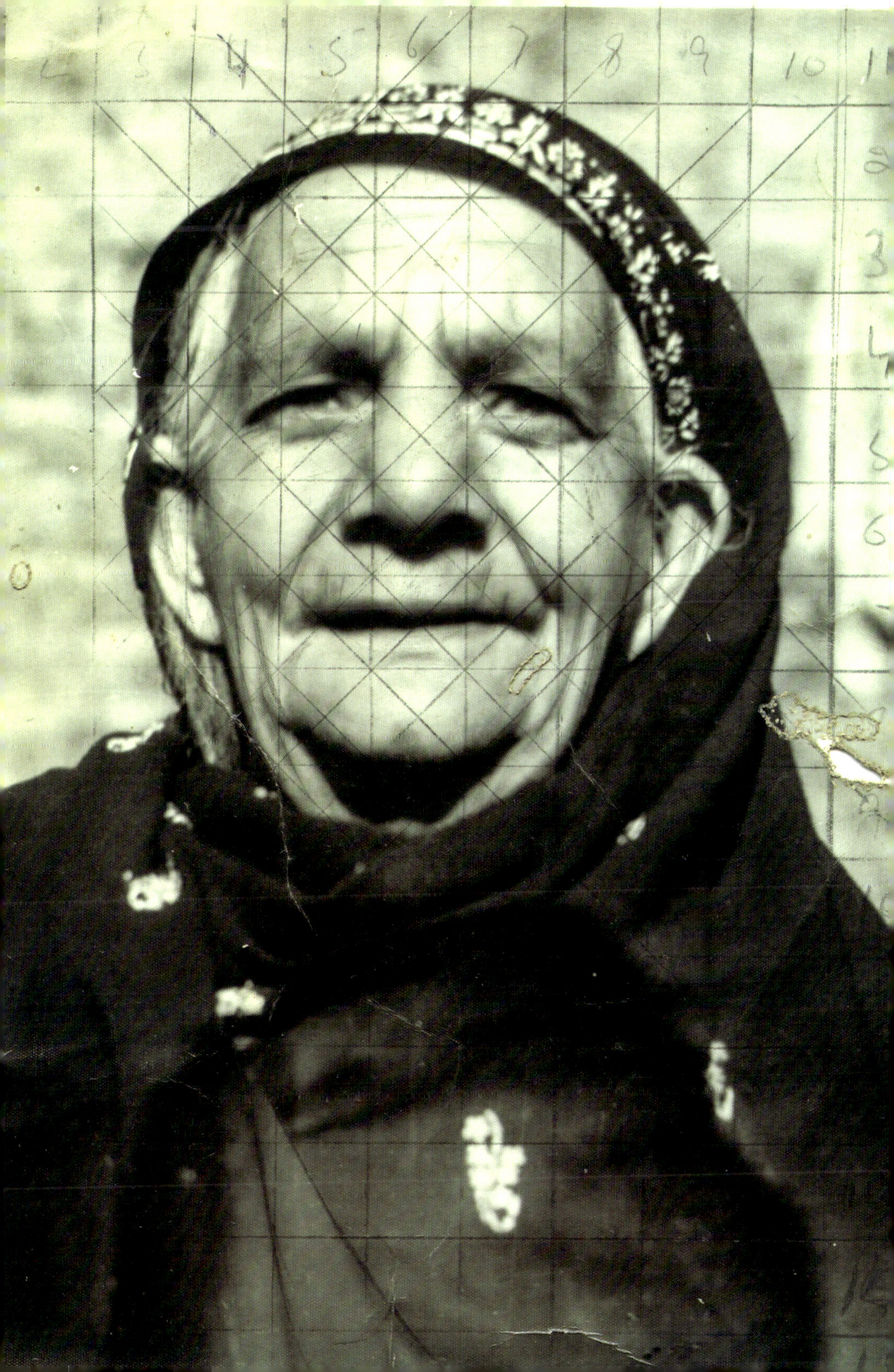

Half of a large format negative. The photographer cut off and disposed of the left side of this negative, showing the Pasthun client's wife, before gifting it to the authors. The segregation of mature females beyond the immediate family is a deeply-rooted tradition in Pasthun culture in the Peshawar region, and if transgressed may lead to violent confrontation. Peshawar, c.1970s–1990s.

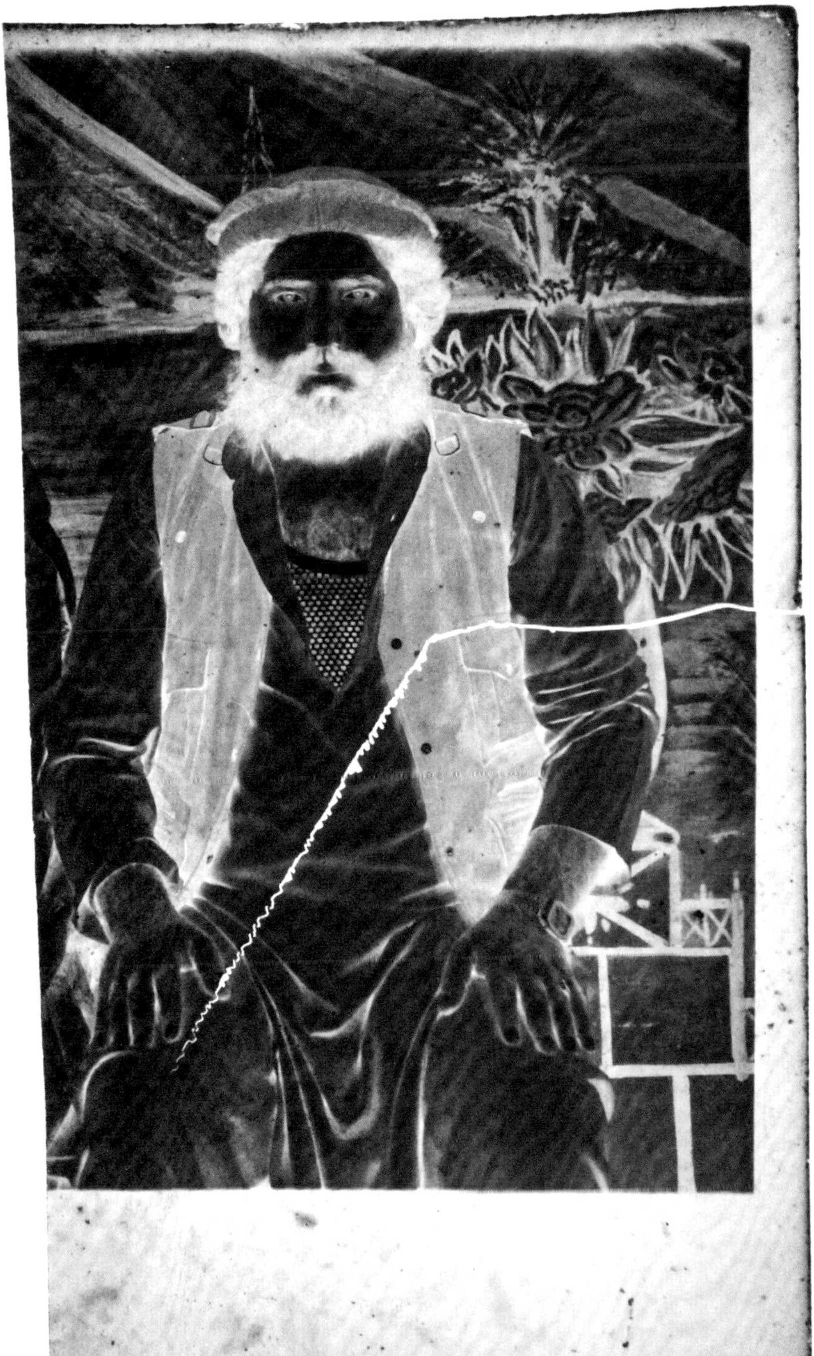

Hand-coloured photograph of former Pakistani Prime Minister Benazir Bhutto. Bhutto, who was assassinated in December 2007, was the Prime Minister of Pakistan from 1988–90 and from 1993–96. She was the eldest daughter of Zulfikar Ali Bhutto, also a former Pakistani Prime Minister and founder of the Pakistan Peoples Party. Tahir Usman, who hand-coloured this photograph, offers customers montages with Benazir Bhutto; and portraits of political leaders are commonly sold in Peshawari photo studios. As one photographer put it frankly: "Our leaders sell us [out], so we sell them." Royal Studio, c.1990s

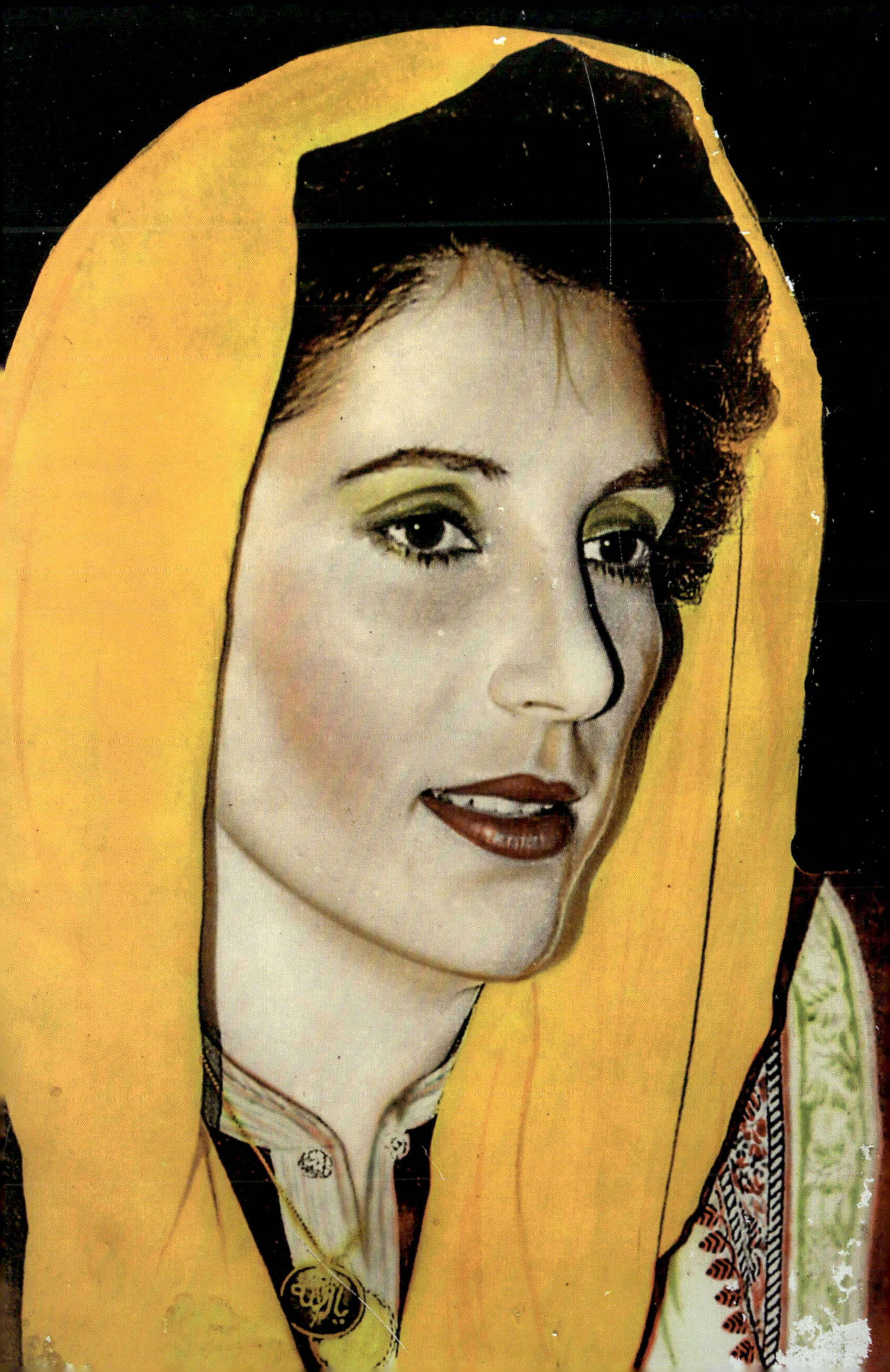

Hand-coloured photograph.
Hand-colouring by Tahir Usman. Royal Studio, c.1990s.

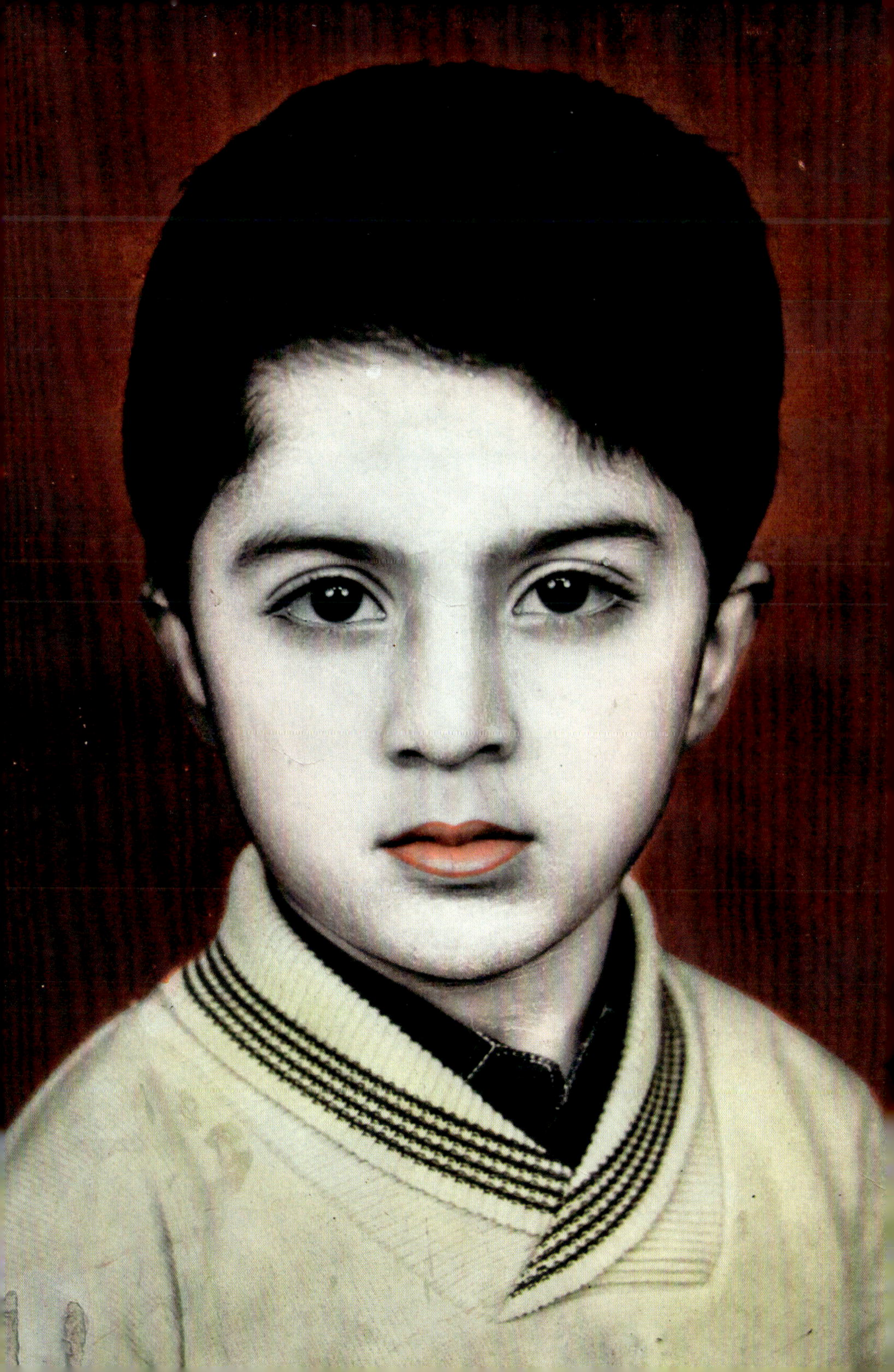

Hand-coloured photograph. Customers' heads were sometimes outlined by a nimbus so they stood out from the background. Hand-colouring by Tahir Usman's Royal Studio, c.1990s.

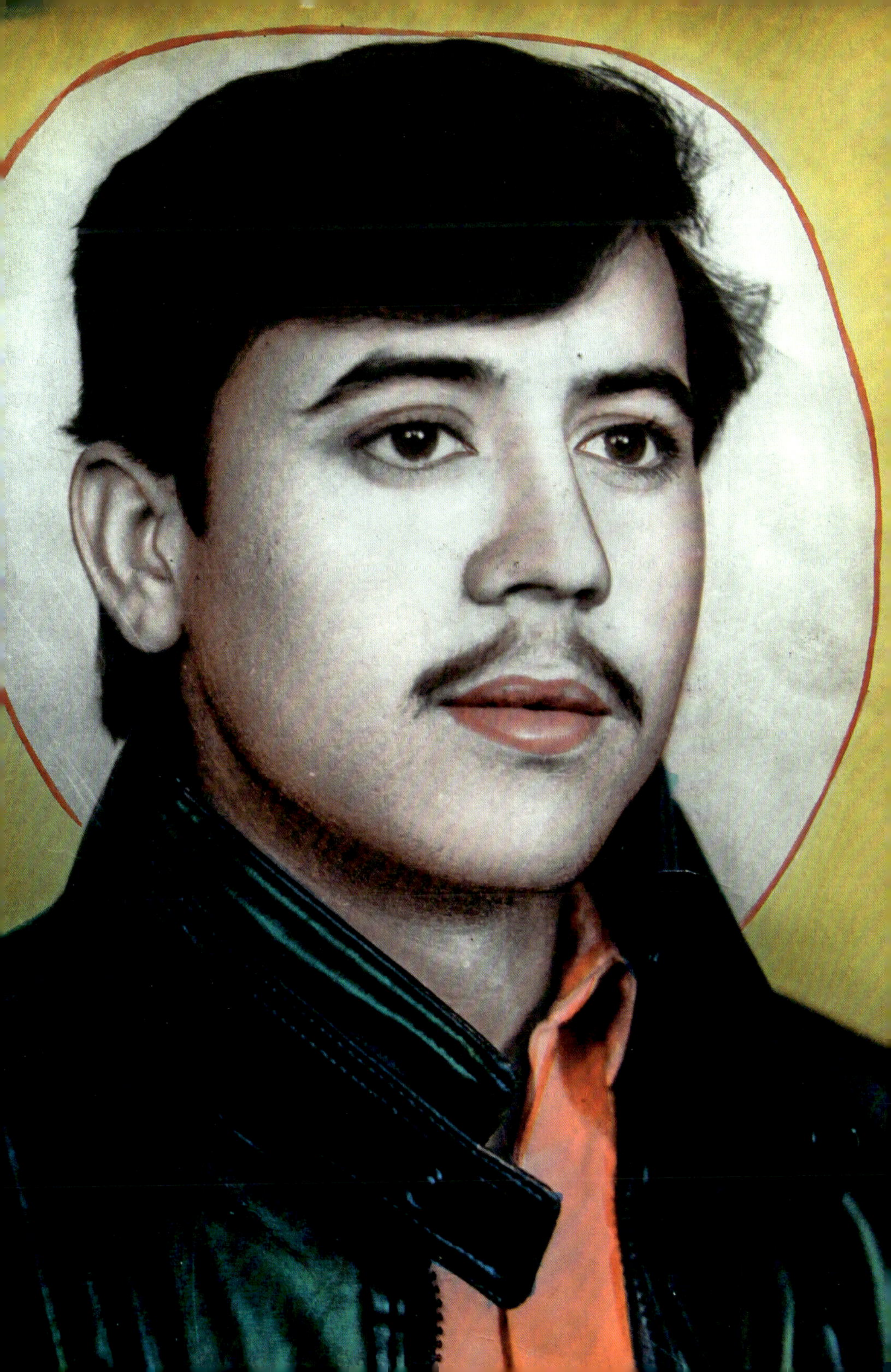

Hand-coloured photograph. Hand-colouring by Tahir Usman.
Royal Studio, c.1990s.

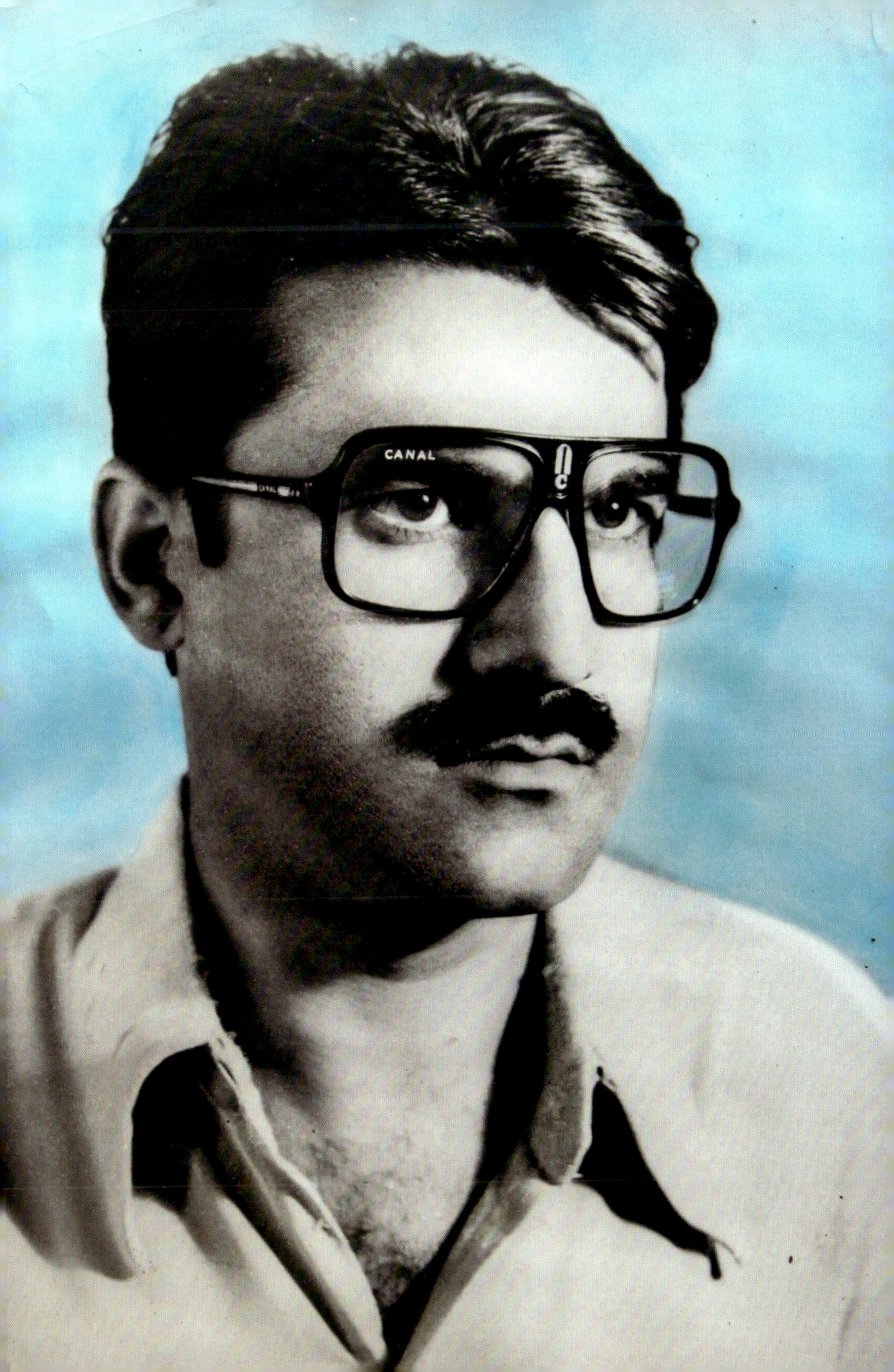
CANAL

Hand-coloured photograph. The hand-colourist, Tahir Usman, took into account the out-of-focus sections in the bottom right of the original photograph and painted the image accordingly. Royal Studio, c.1990s.

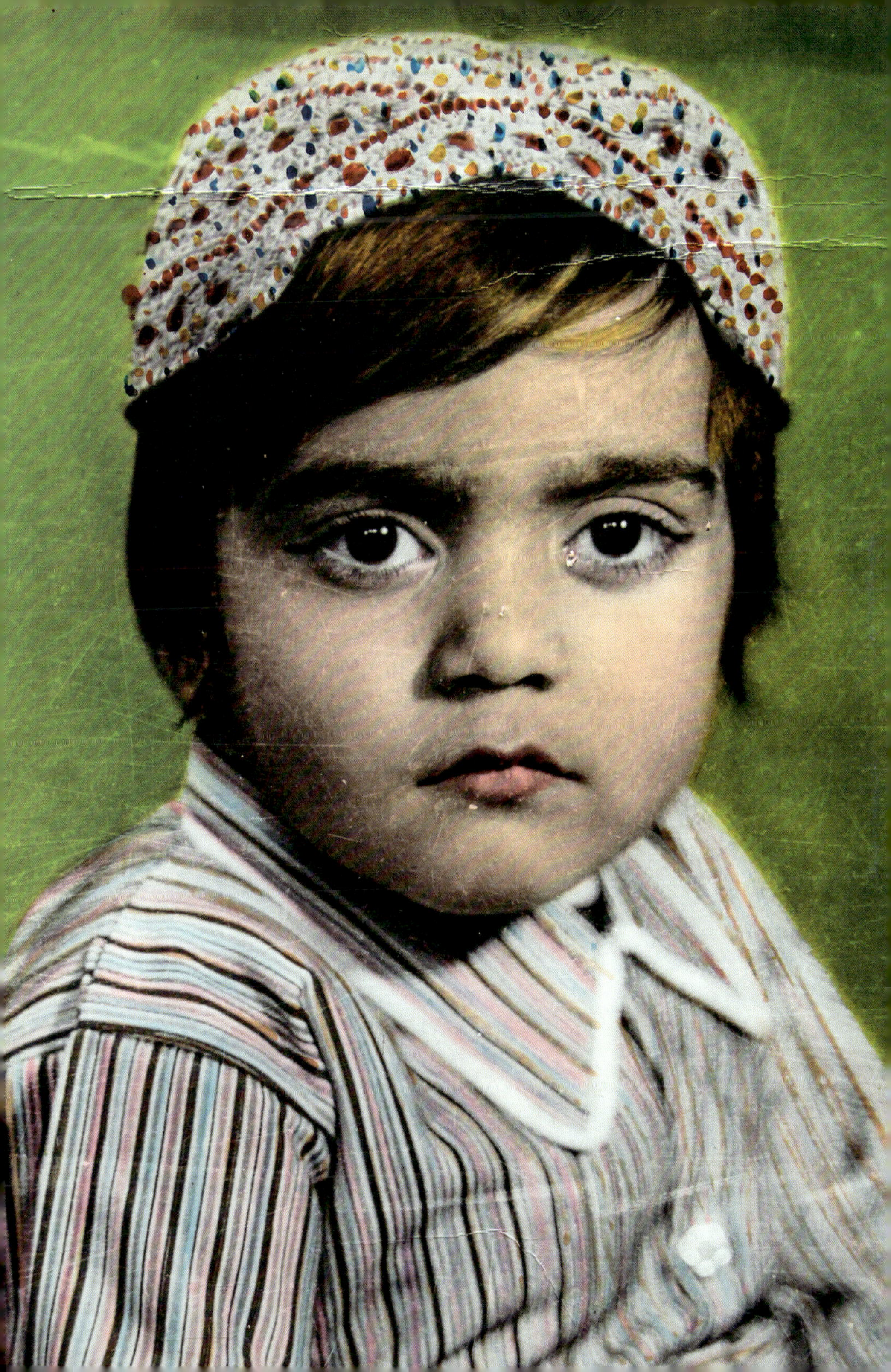

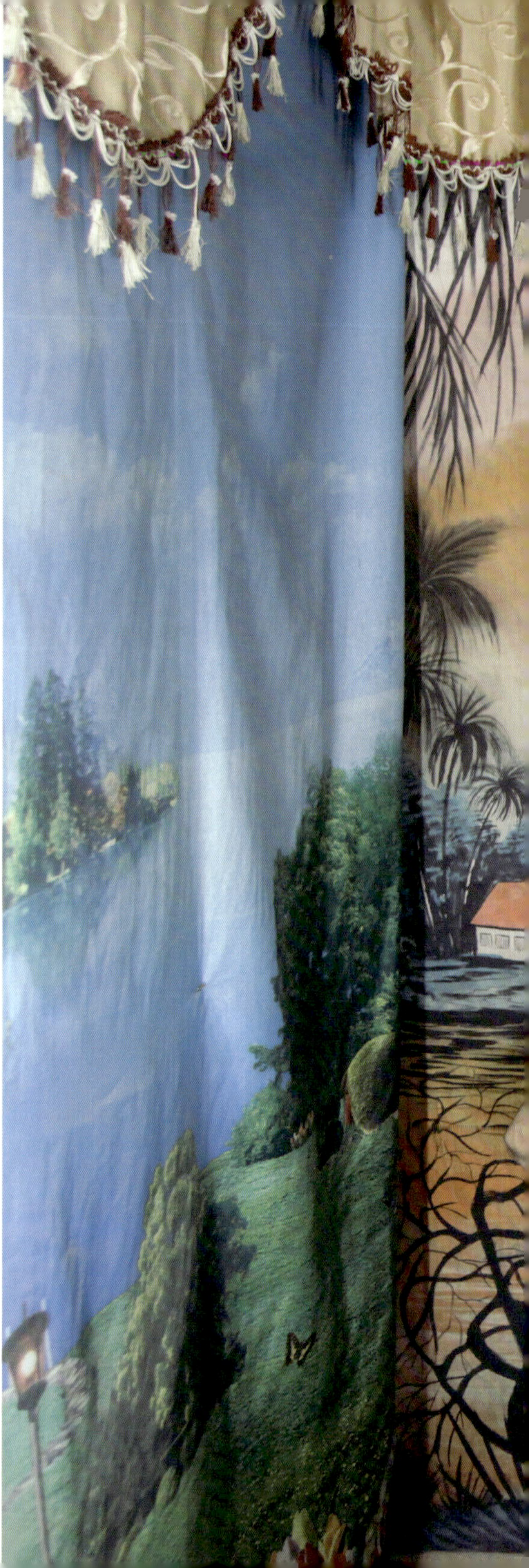

Opposite: Kamal from Abdul Majeed Photo Studio, with his sons, lives and works in the Afghan Colony, an area in Peshawar inhabited by migrants and refugees from Afghanistan since the 1980s. For many years he used a paper-negative minute camera to take instant portraits.

Pages 186–187: After querying Tahir Usman about paper-negative cameras in 2012, he was inspired to purchase one, and set up a shot of himself photographing a 'customer', his friend Nur Gul – just for fun; *Pages* 188–189: Tribesmen manning a roadblock against the police. Heavy and light munitions including replica Kalashnikovs are produced locally in the tribal areas. Photo by Naqash Studio proprietor, Muhammad Iqbal, from his former news photography days, 1995.

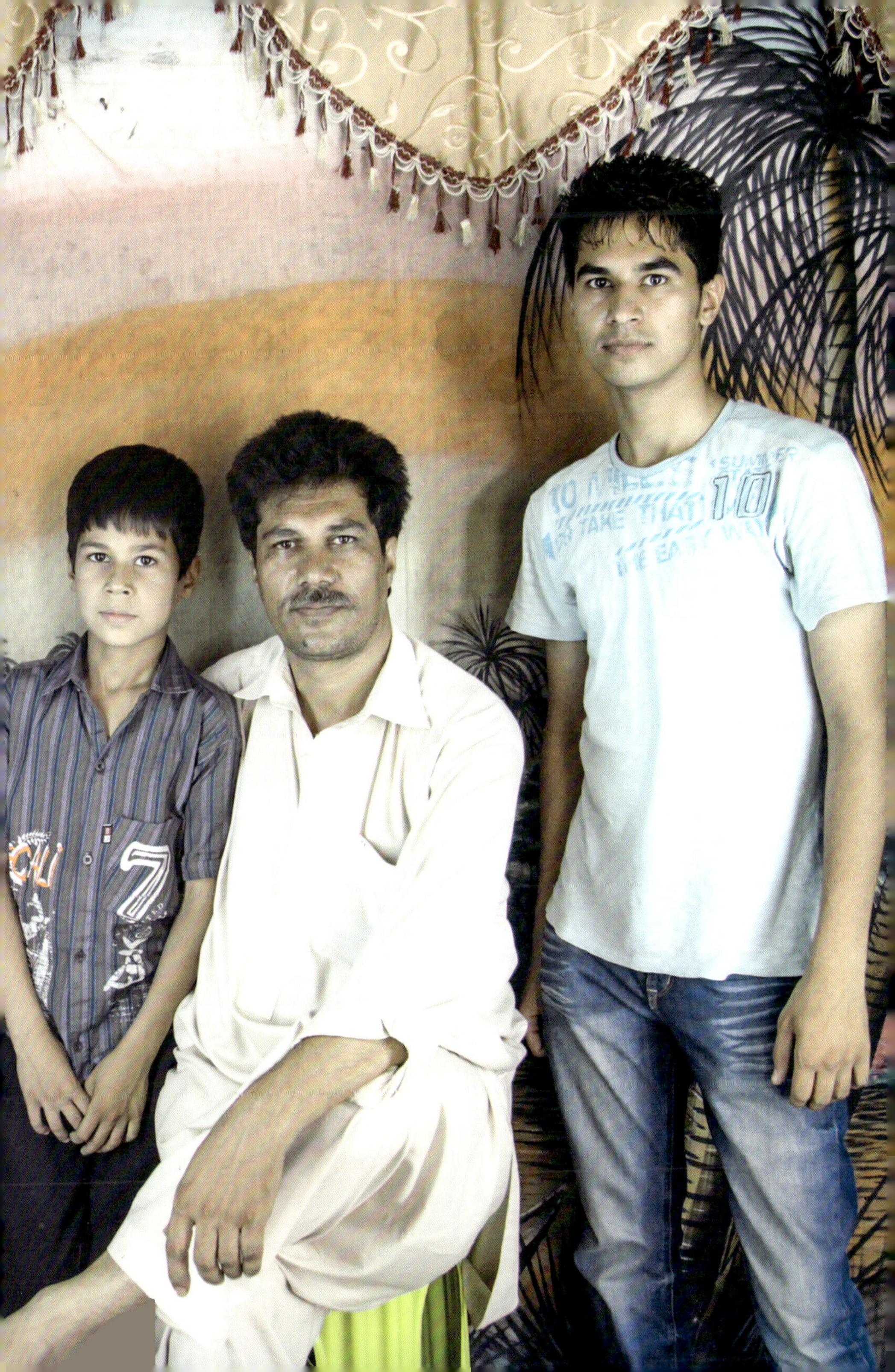
TAKE THAT
10

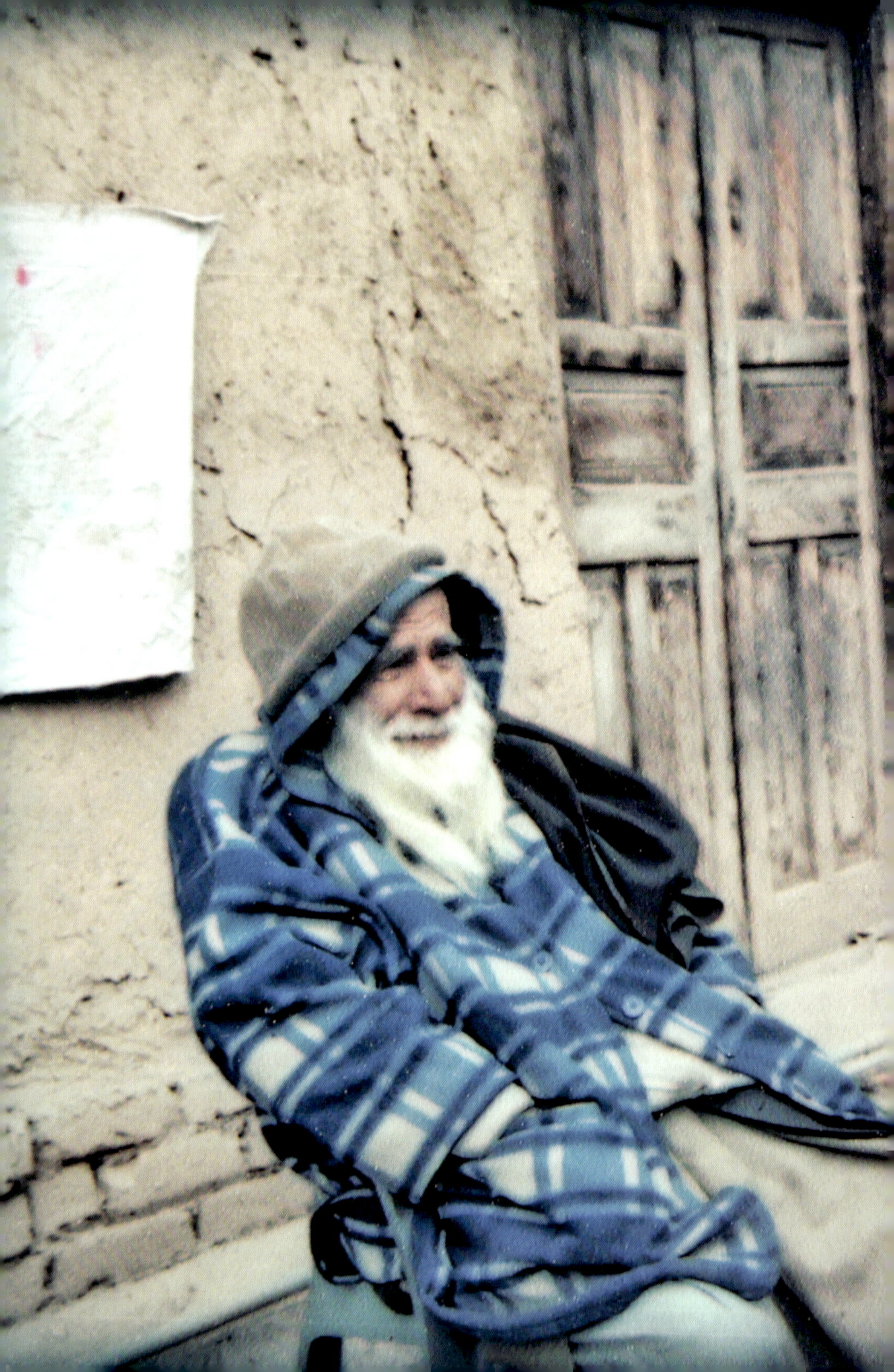

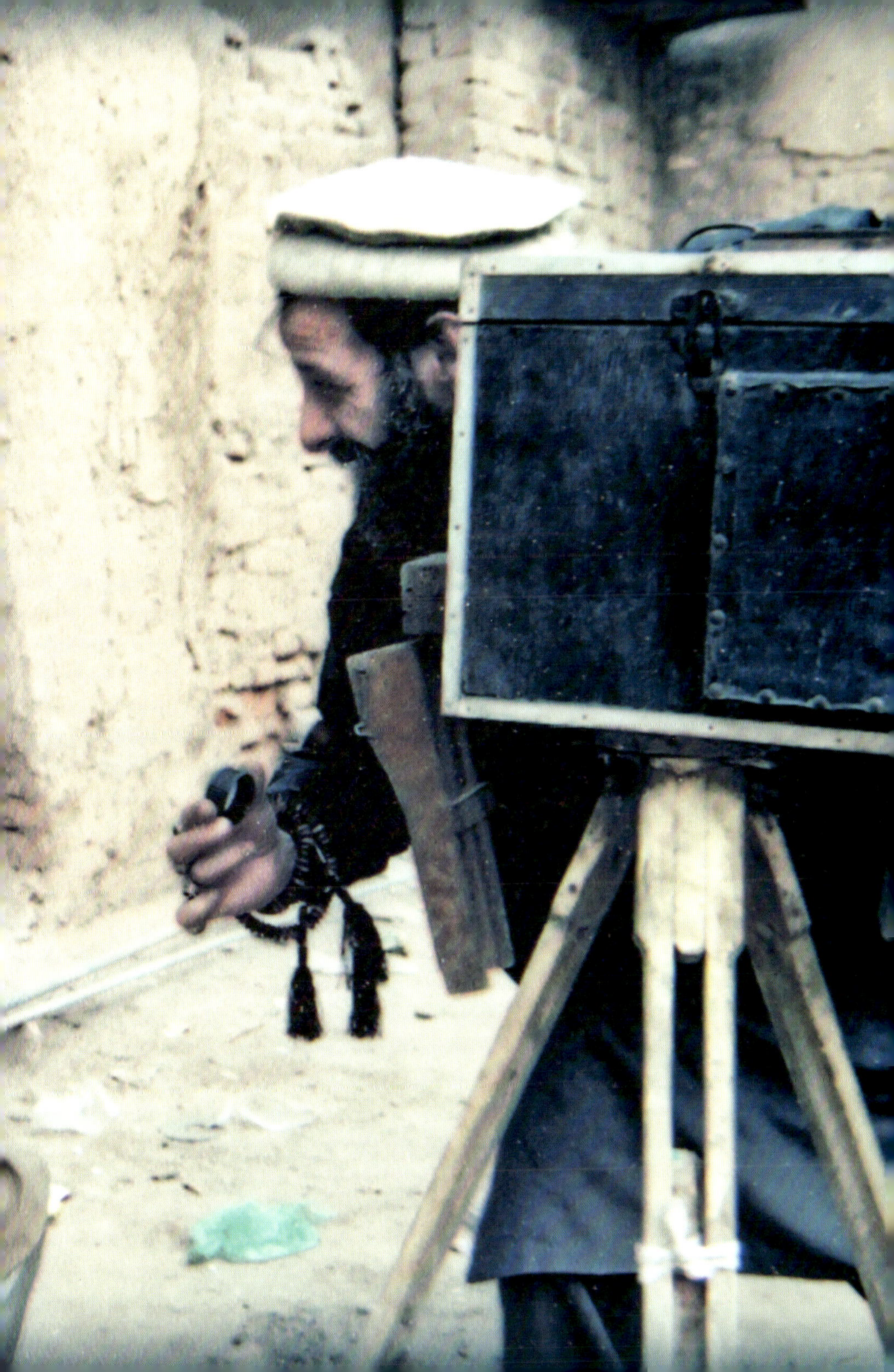

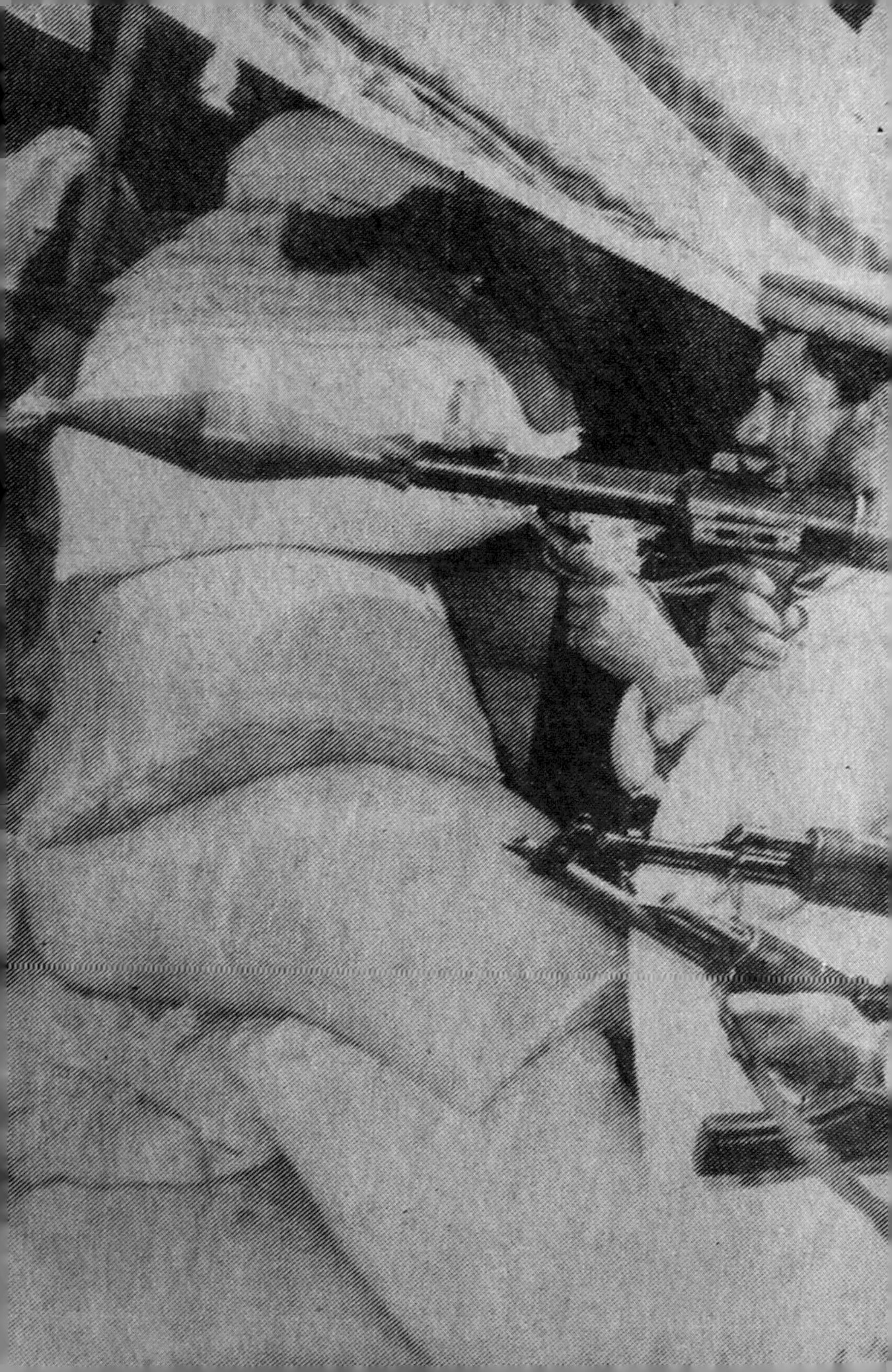

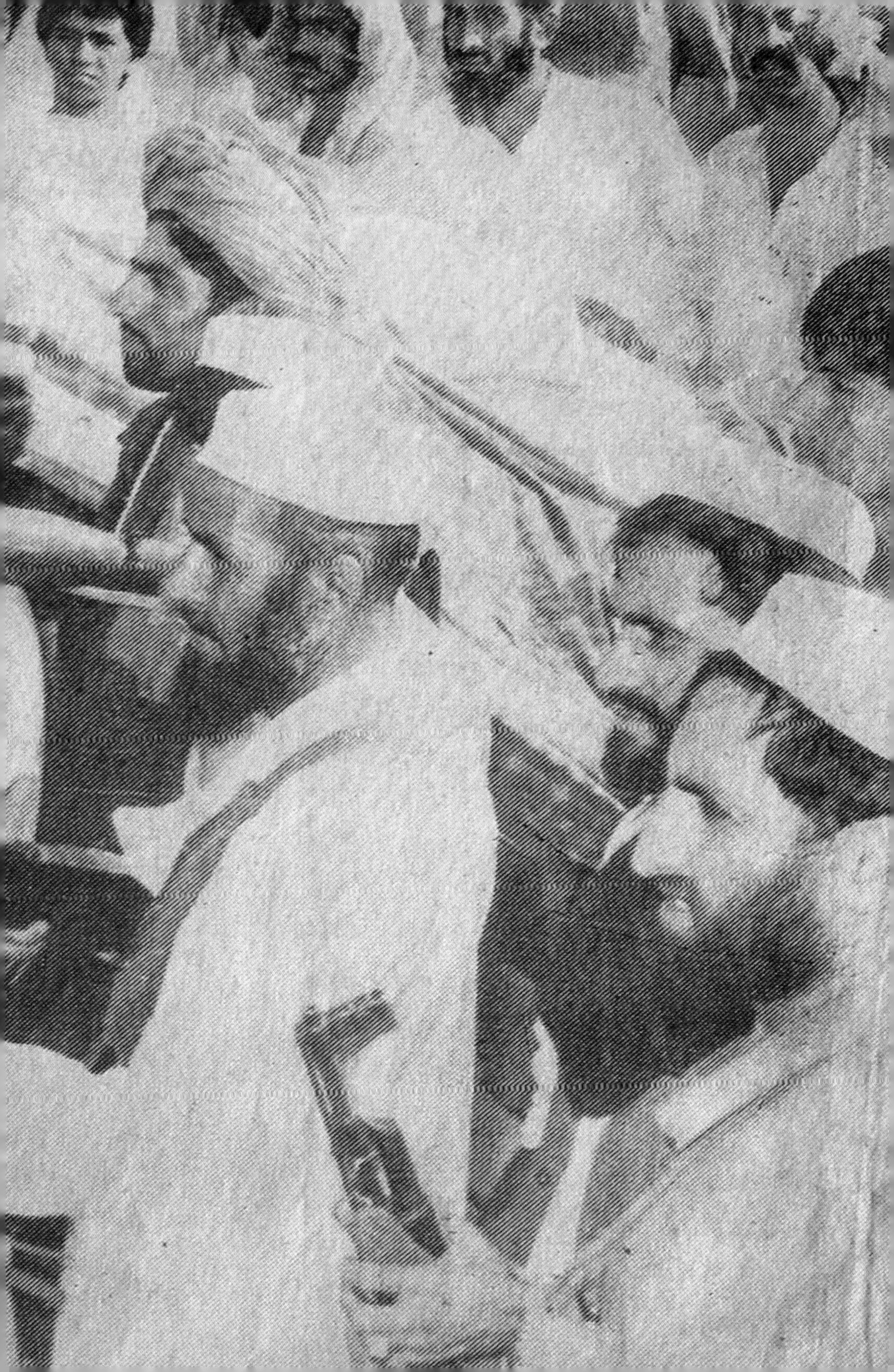

THE MUSLI

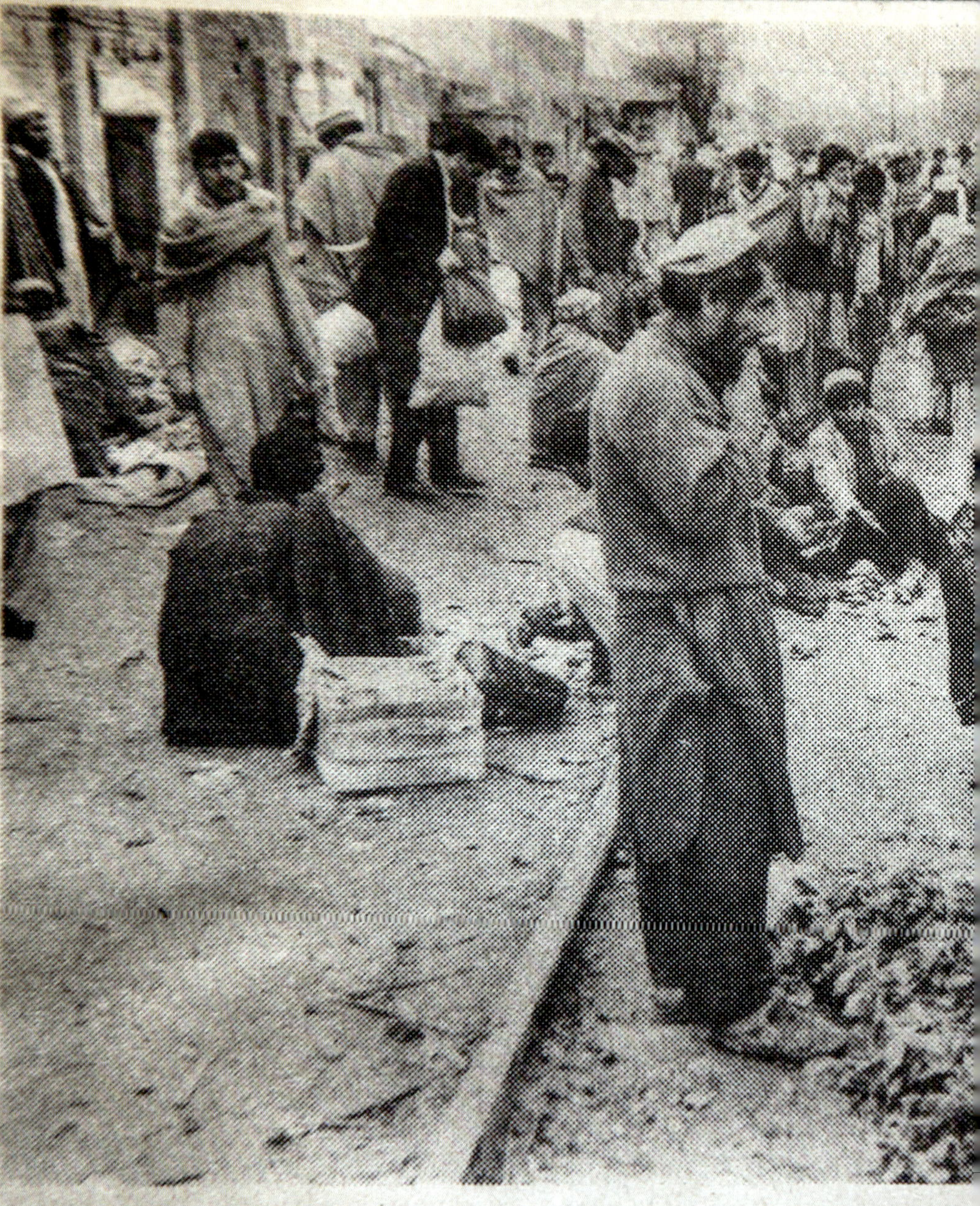

The railway track in Peshawar being used by v
The vendors disappear for a while when trai
tact.—Staff Photo by MOHAMMAD IQBAL

Thursday, December 21, 1995

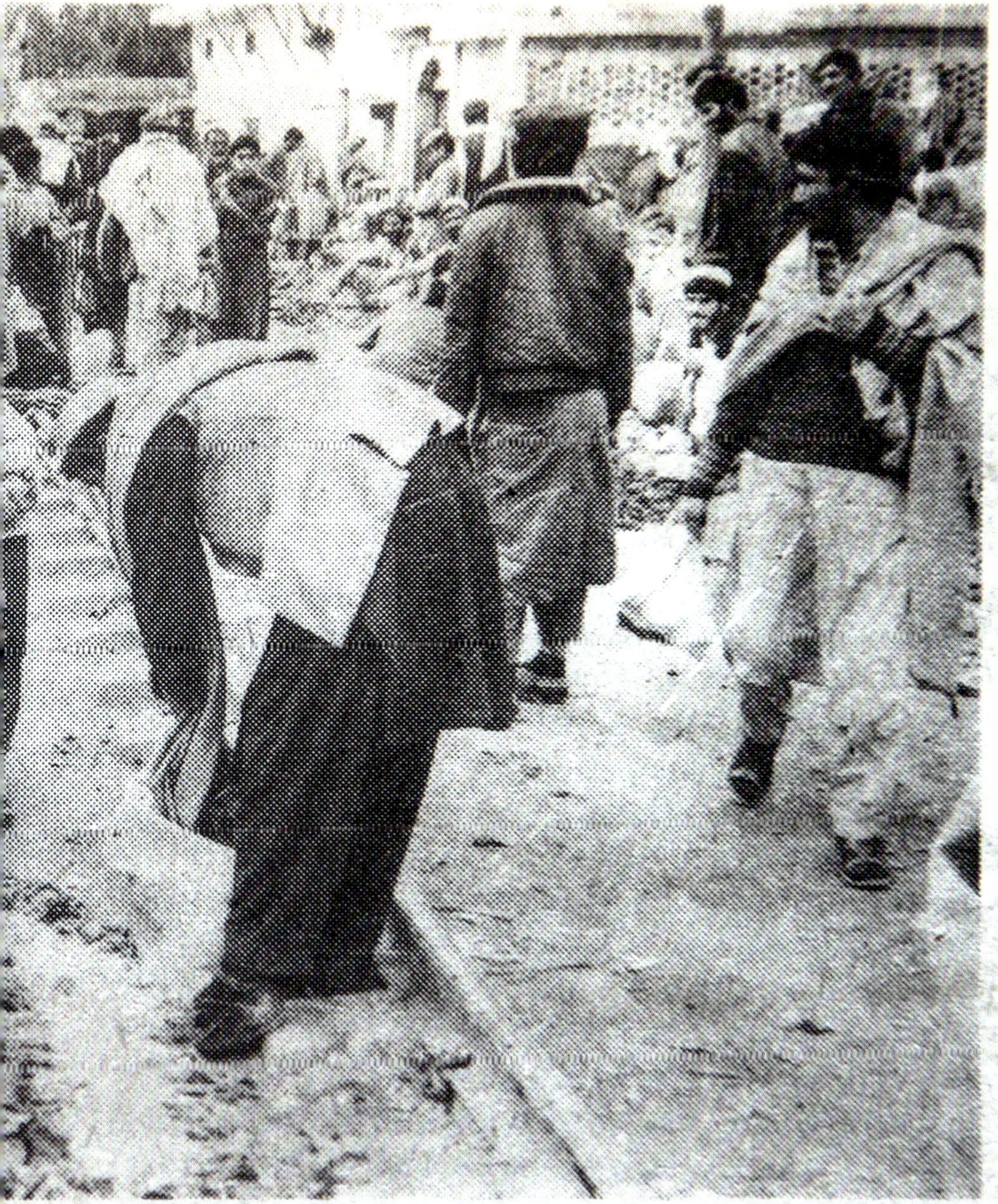

ors and vegetables sellers as market place.
arrive, leaving heaps of vegetable in-

Preceding pages 190–191: Newspaper photo by Muhammad Iqbal of Naqash Studio.

Opposite: Khalida, a young woman smoking heroin in Peshawar. With neighbouring Afghanistan being the largest centre of heroine production in the world, drug abuse in Pakistan is rampant. Newspaper photo by Muhammad Iqbal of Naqash Studio, 1995.

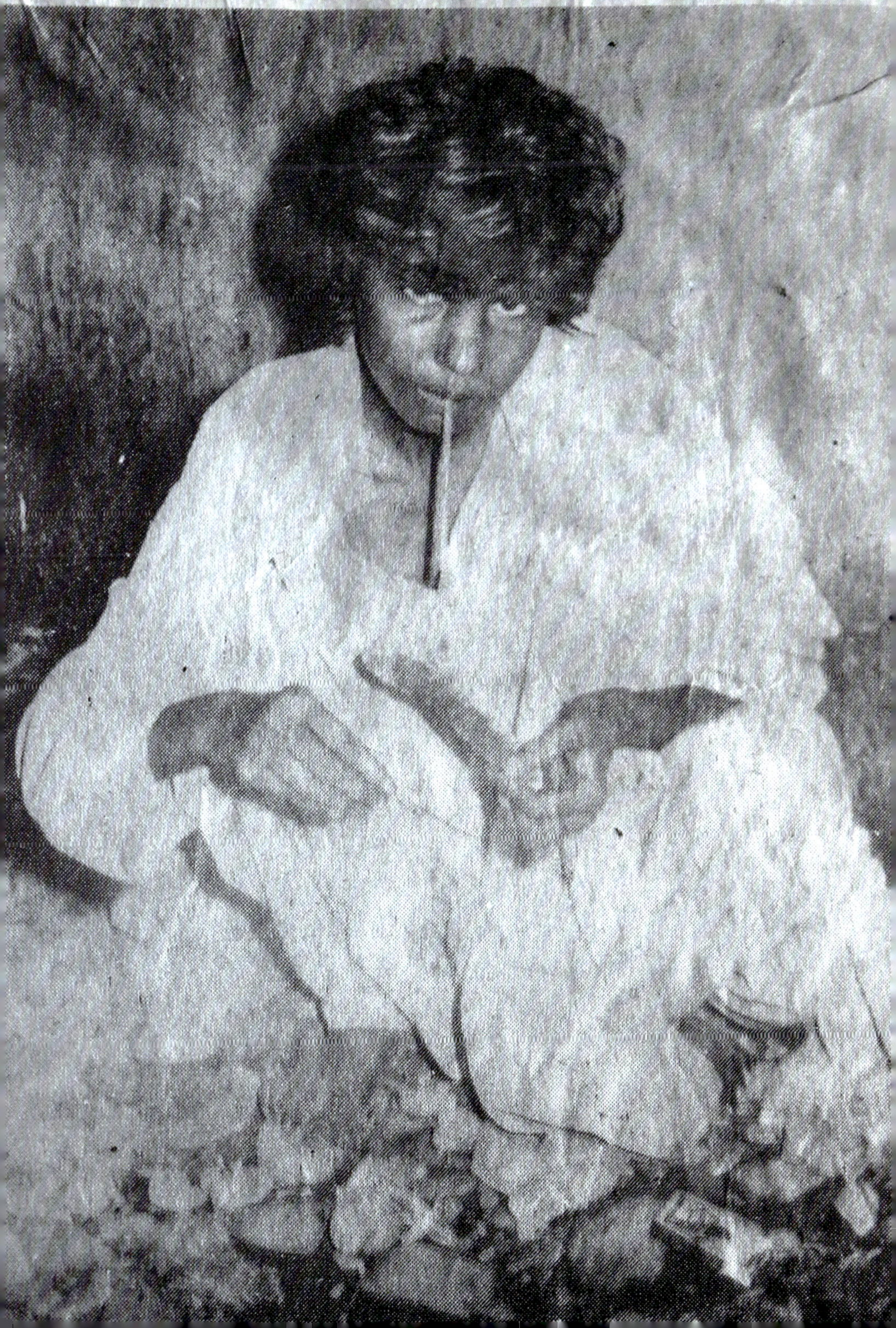

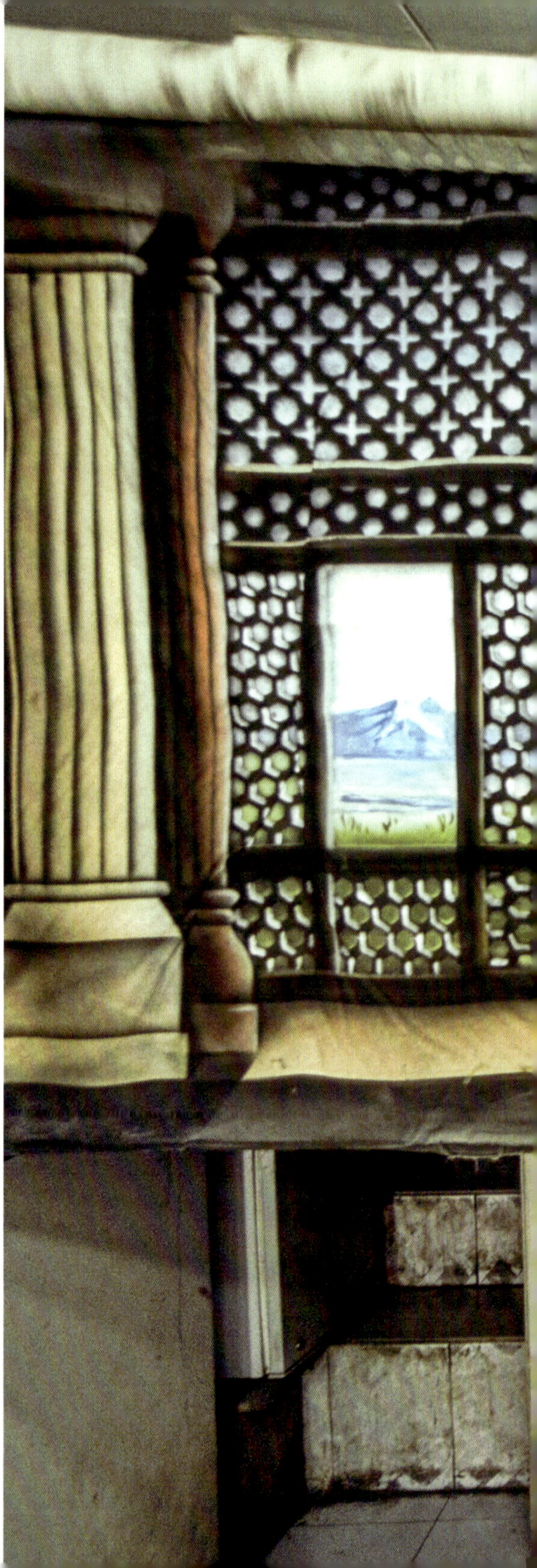

Opposite: Uncle Tony, born Fakhar Zaman Azer in pre-Partition India, is a prominent photographer living in Peshawar, and well connected with the artistic scene in the city and beyond. Besides cameras, he also collects hats on his annual global travels. Here, he is pictured preparing a backdrop for a photo shoot in his studio.

Pages 196–197: Buzkhashi, the heart-bounding national sport of Afghanistan was played by Afghans in the north-east of Pakistan in the 1980s and '90s. The aim is for players, mounted on horses, to deposit a dead goat in a goal; *Pages* 198–199: Woman and parrots, Hawaii; *Page* 200: American scholar and archivist Nancy Dupree (1927–2017). Resident in Kabul since the 1960s, she lived in Peshawar during much of the Afghan Civil War; *Page* 201: Studio model in India, where Uncle Tony occasionally hires female models; *Pages* 202–203: Womans' celebration at a Pakistani wedding. All photos by Uncle Tony, 1980s–2000s.

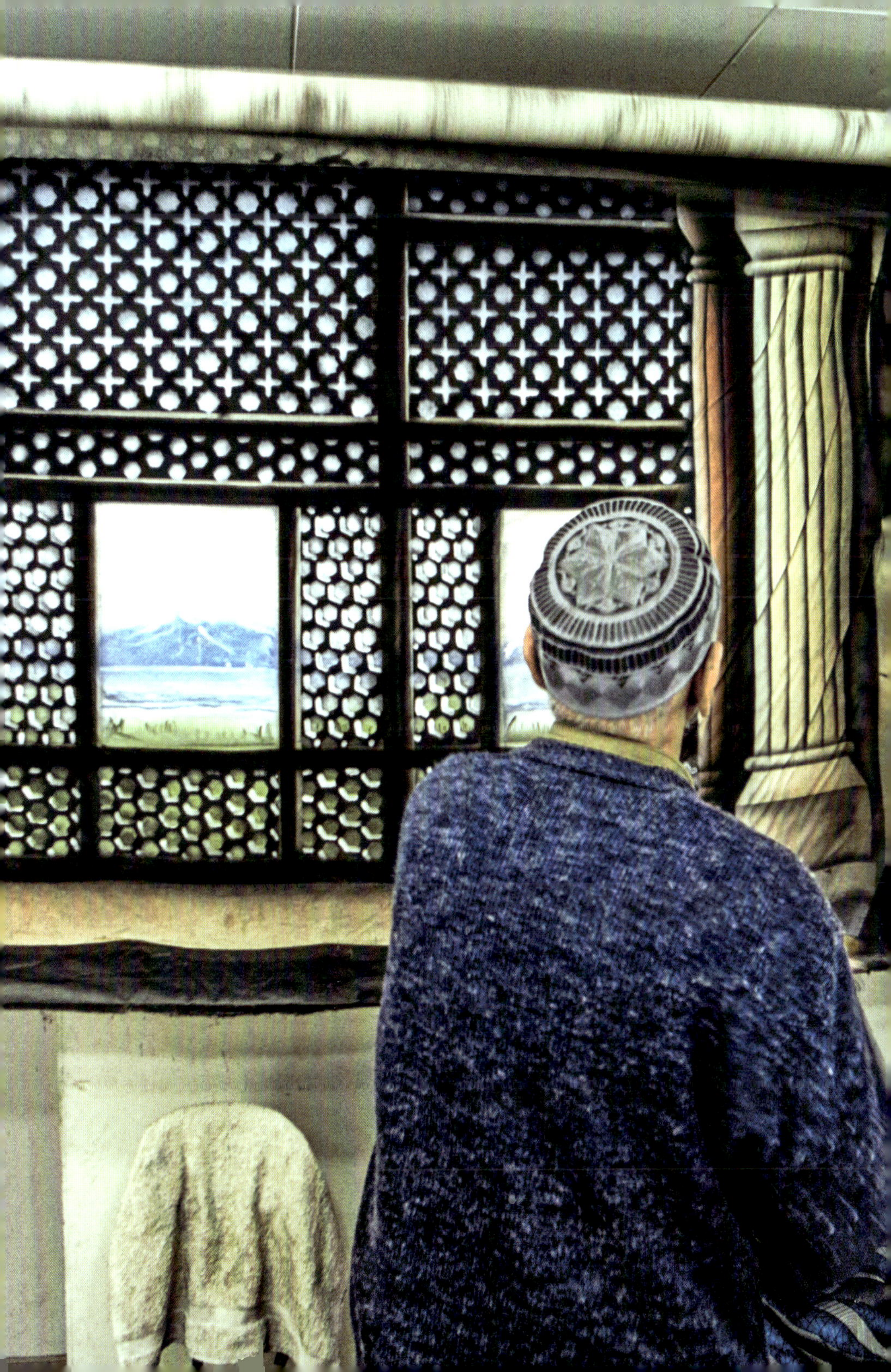

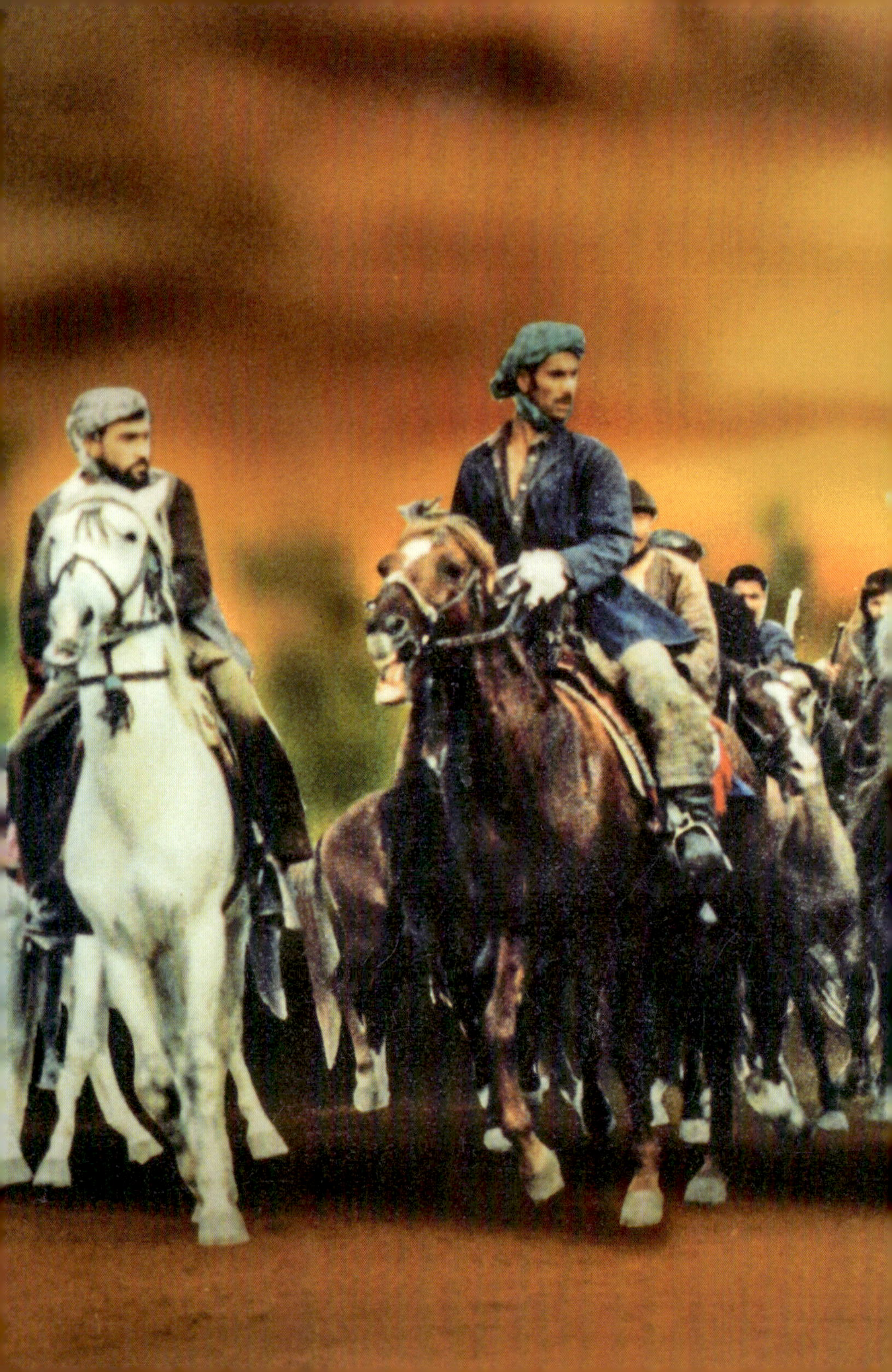

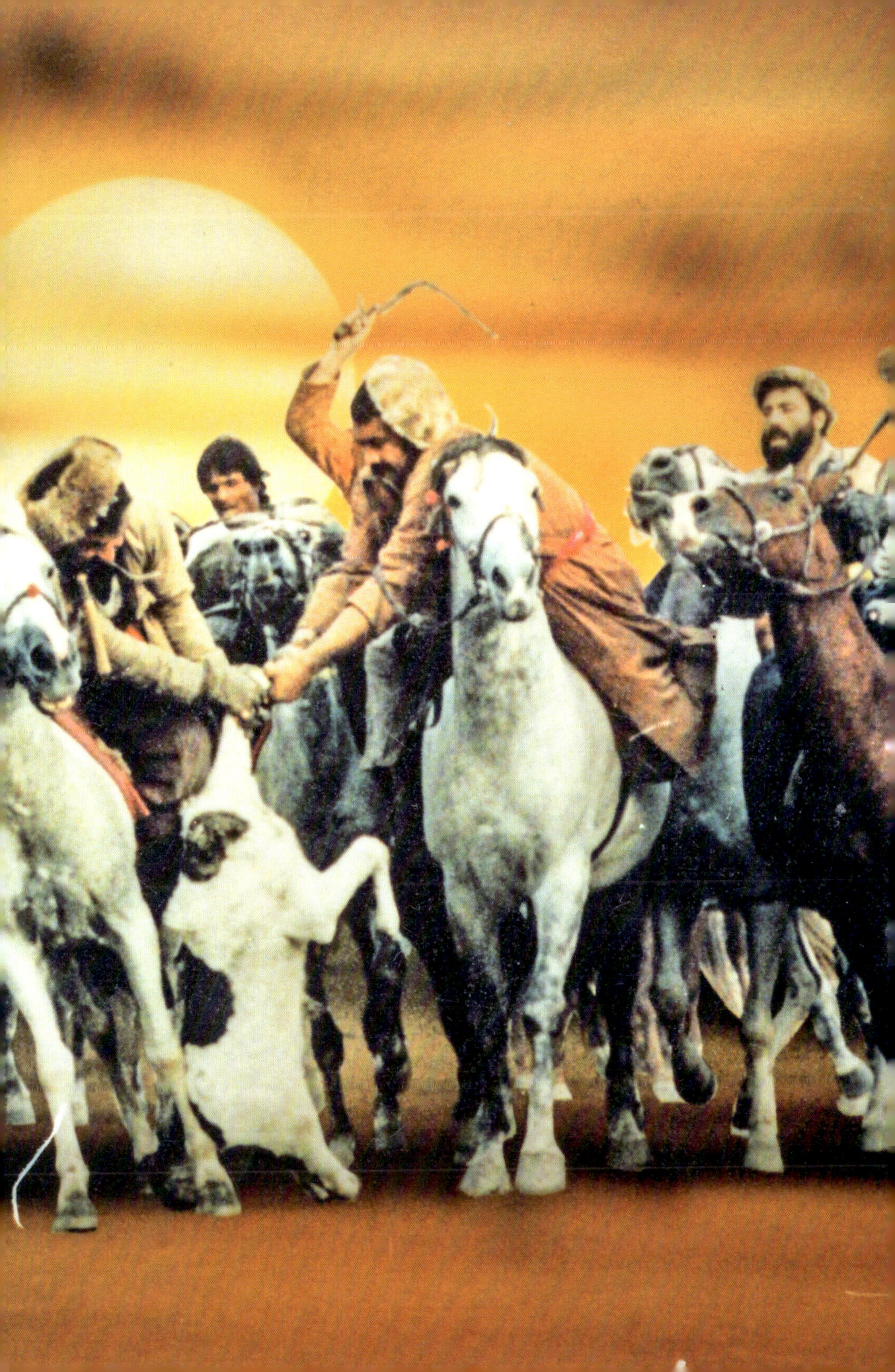

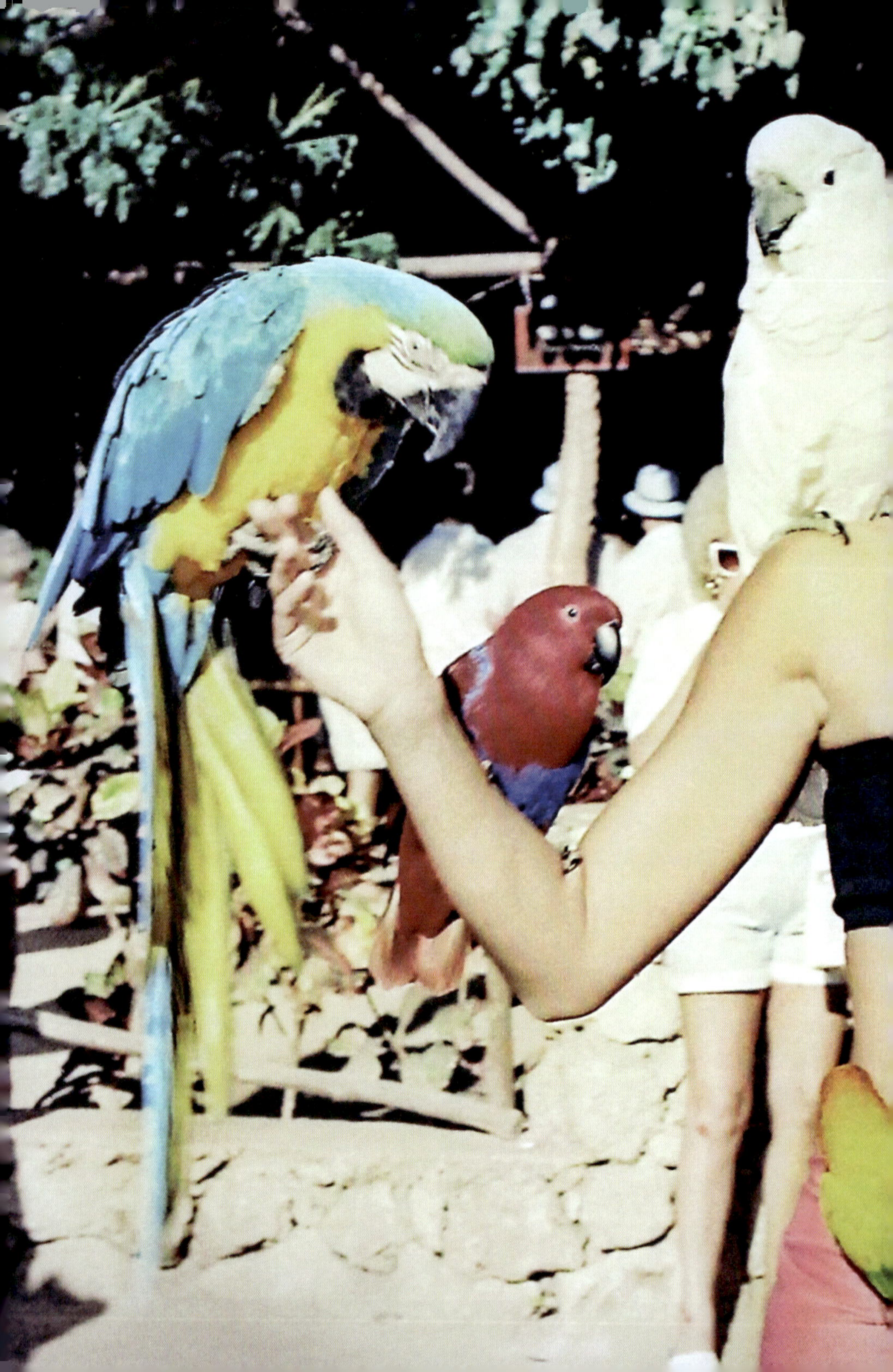

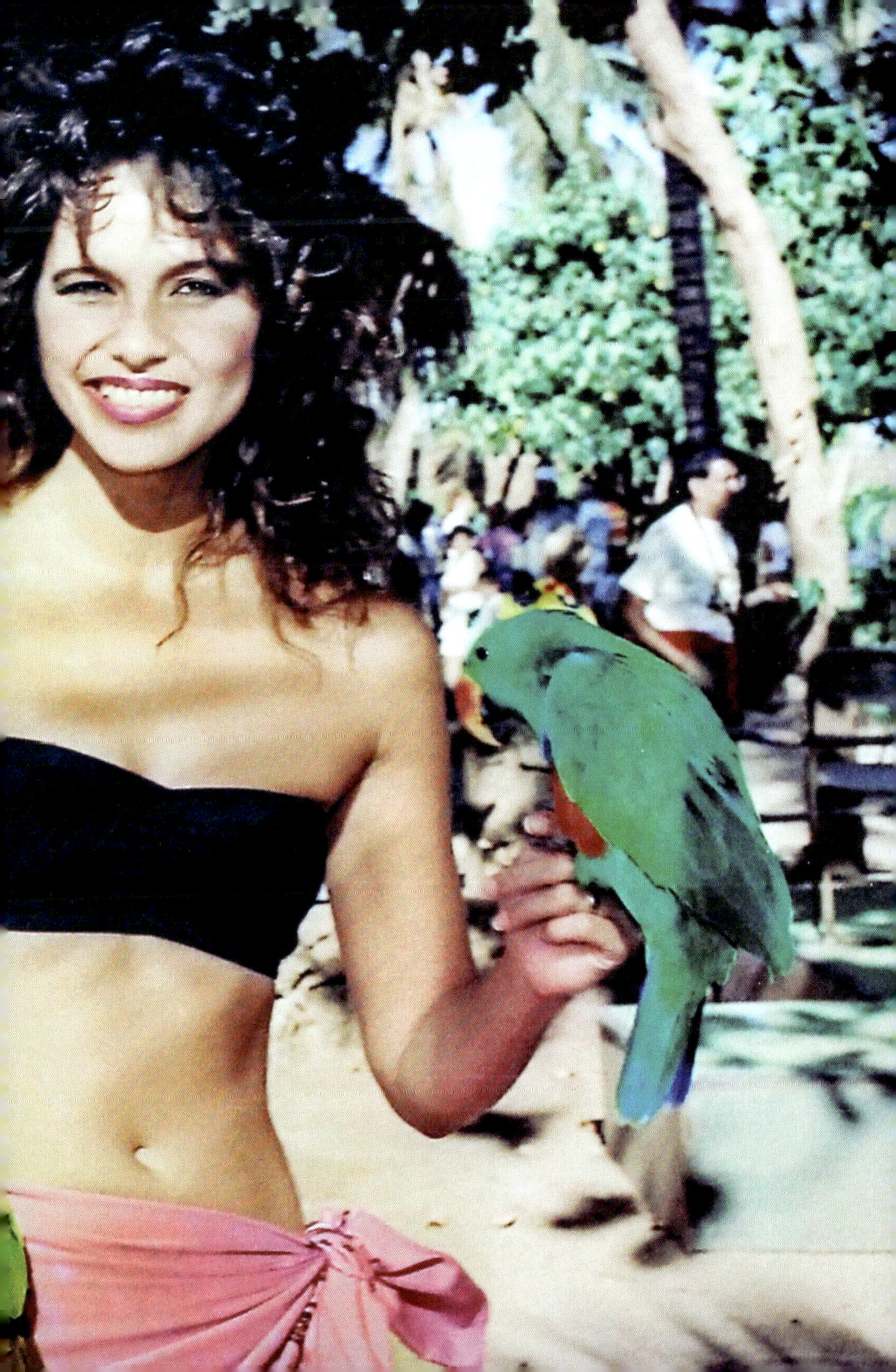

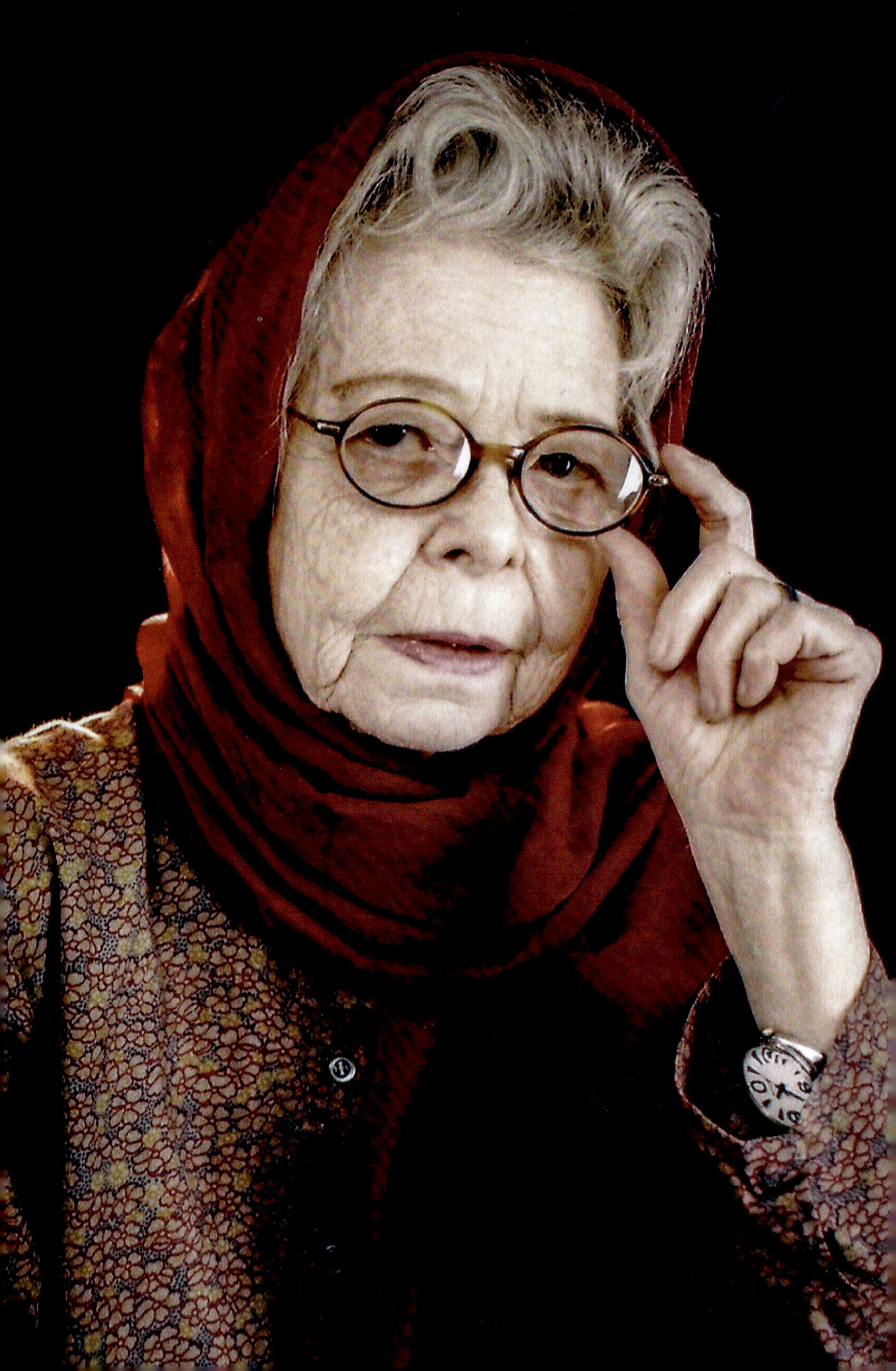

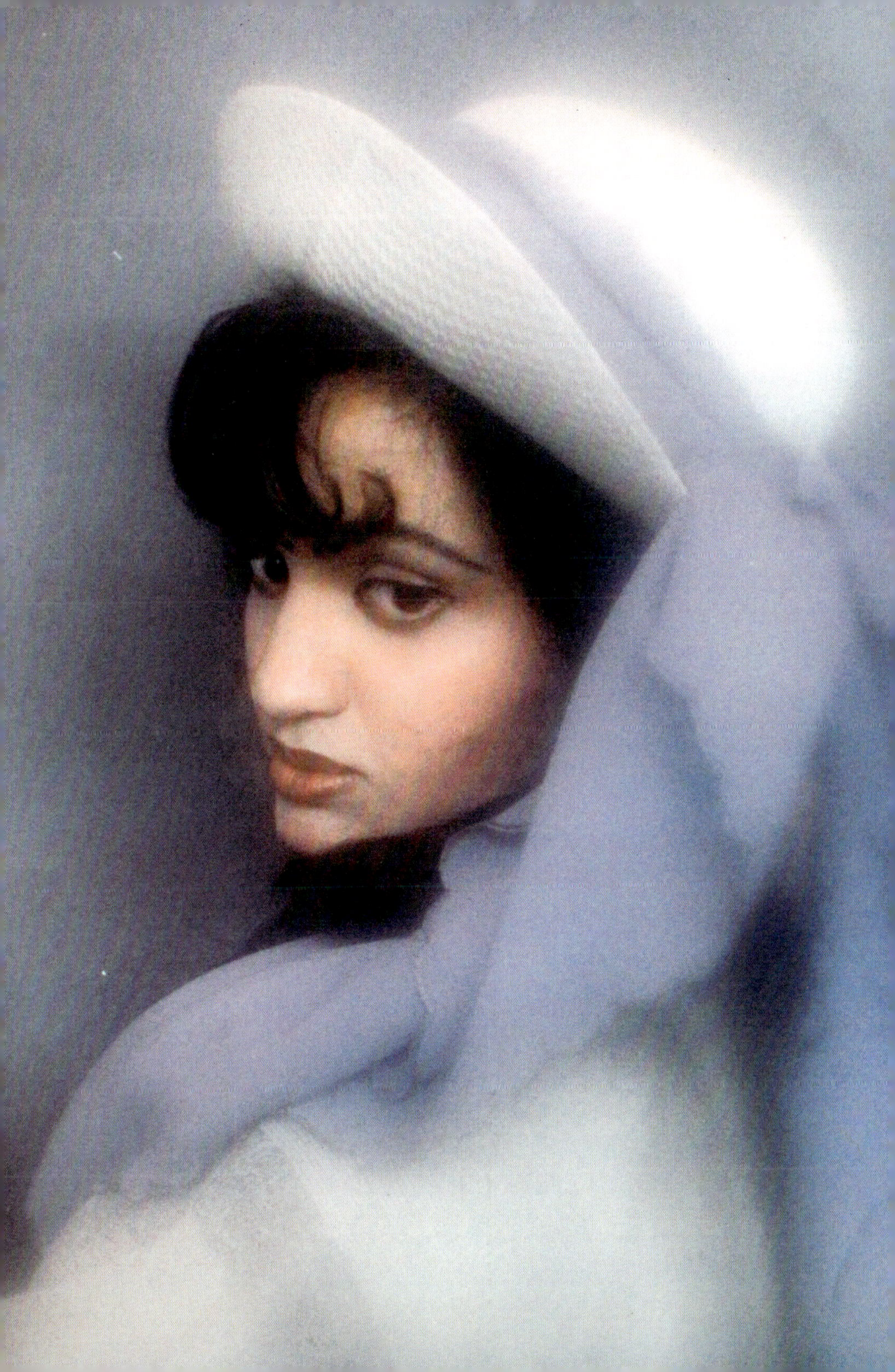

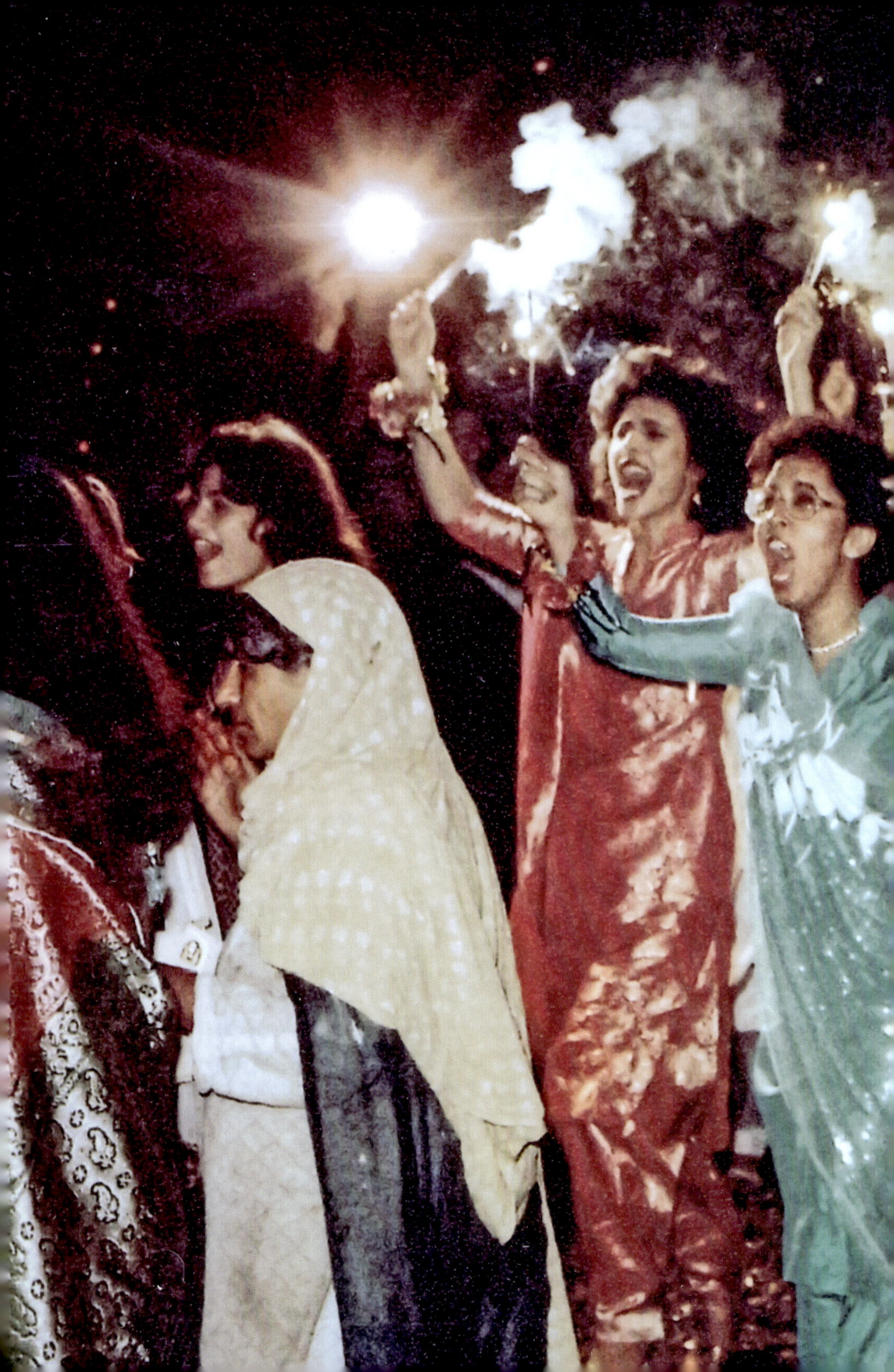

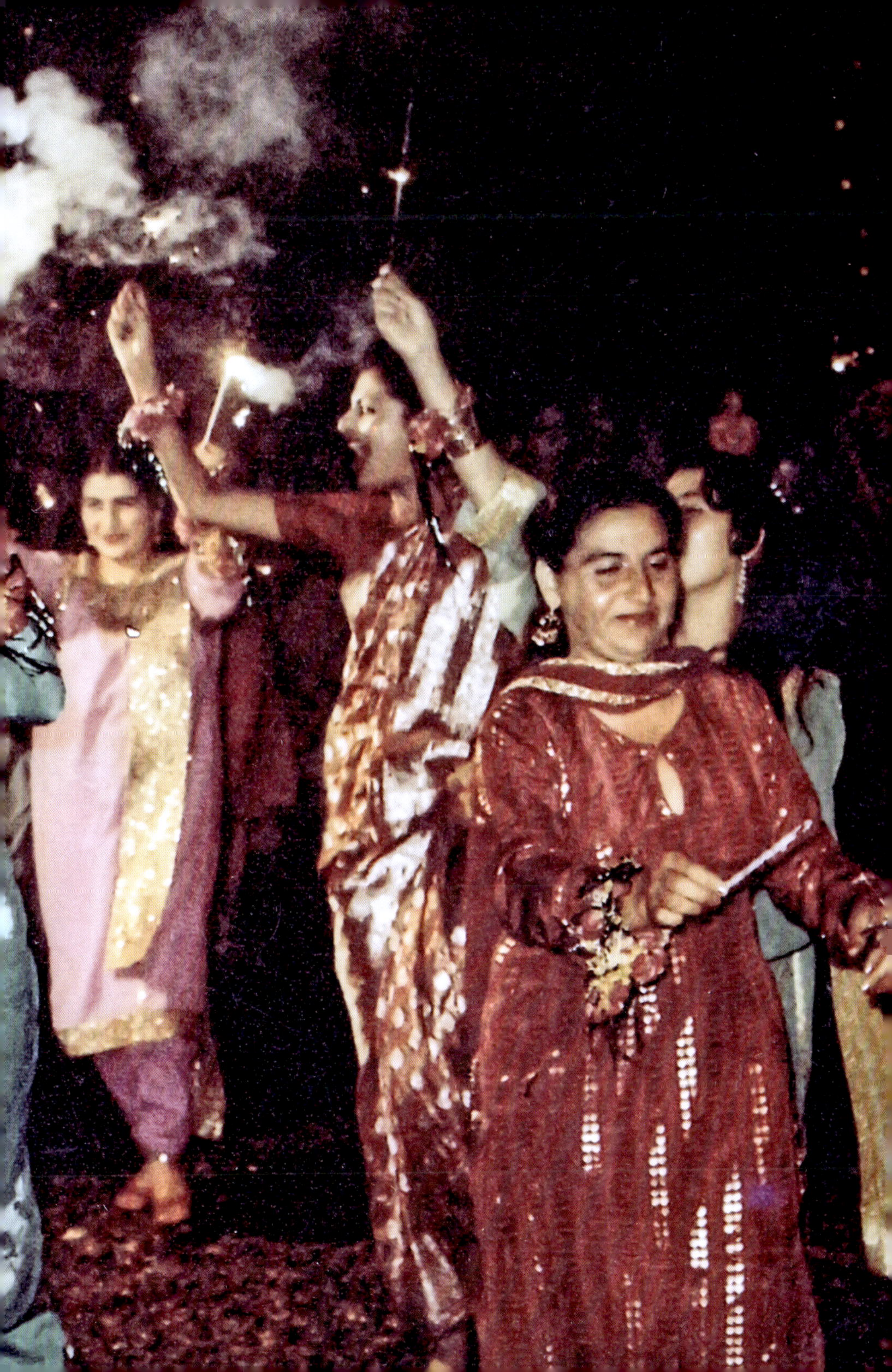

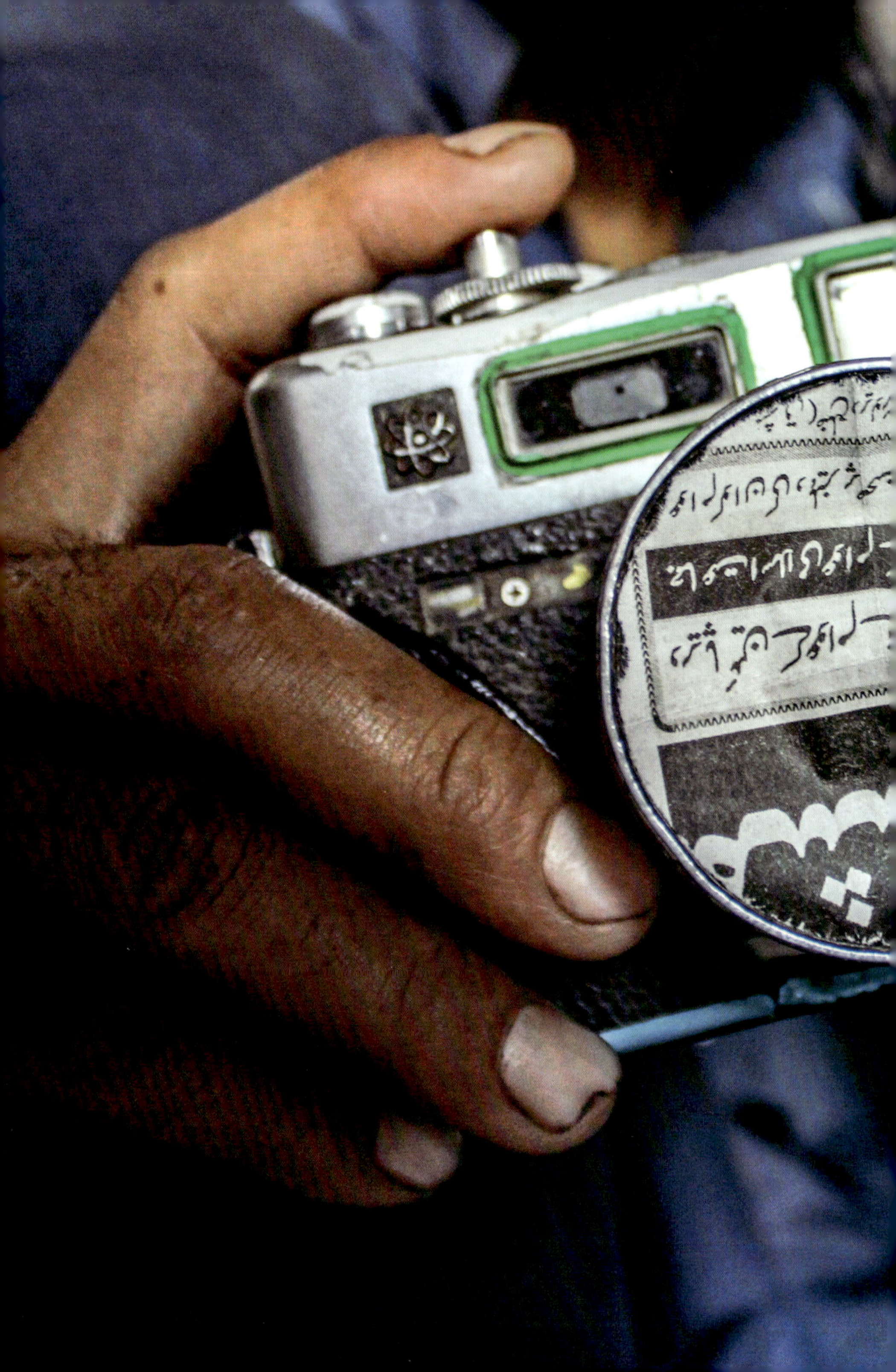

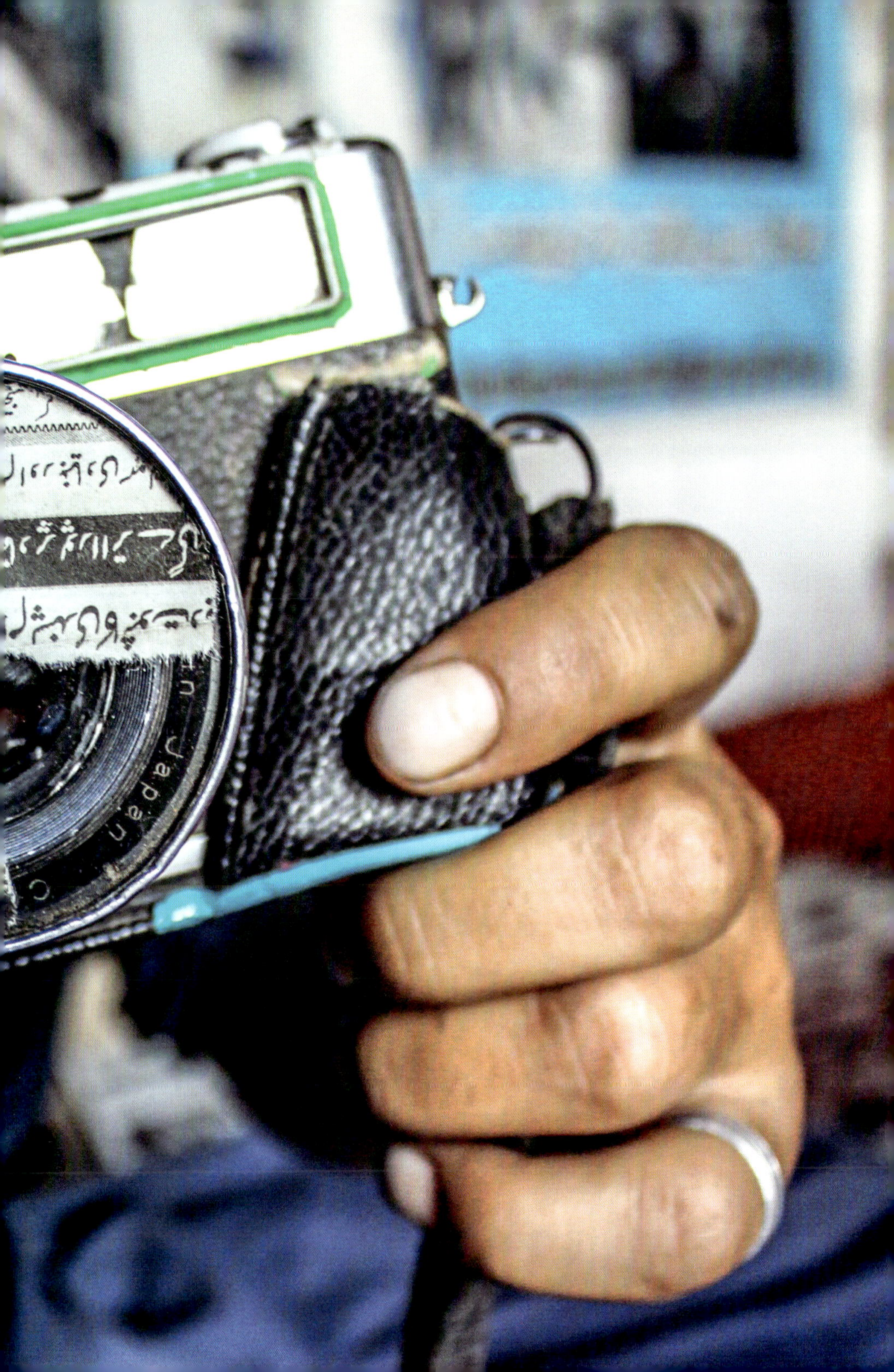
Japan

Preceding pages 204–205: Abdul Wali illustrating his analogue multiple-exposure technique.

Opposite: Abdul Wali is a travelling photographer who primarily works on foot around the Grand Trunk (GT) Road, a highway in the outskirts of Peshawar, as well as in the tribal areas (FATA), neighbouring Peshawar. He travels to Cinema Road in Peshawar city to print his photographs. Abdul travels to Cinema Road to print his photographs. Nowadays, Abdul only takes digital images but up until a few years ago he used film, double exposing his clients onto negatives and montaging them.

Pages 208 & 209: Double and multiple-exposure shots taken on film by Adul Wali, 1990s.

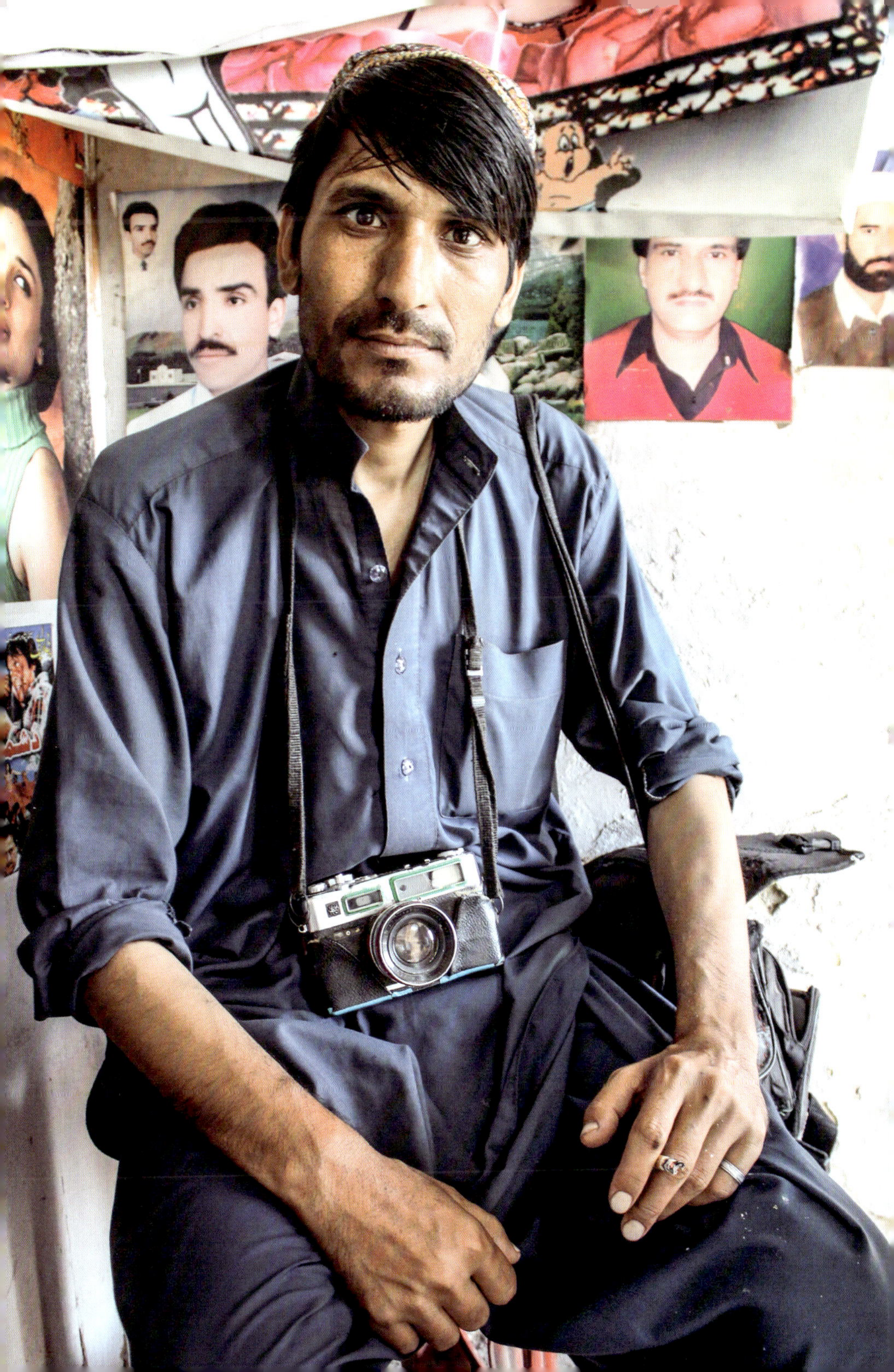

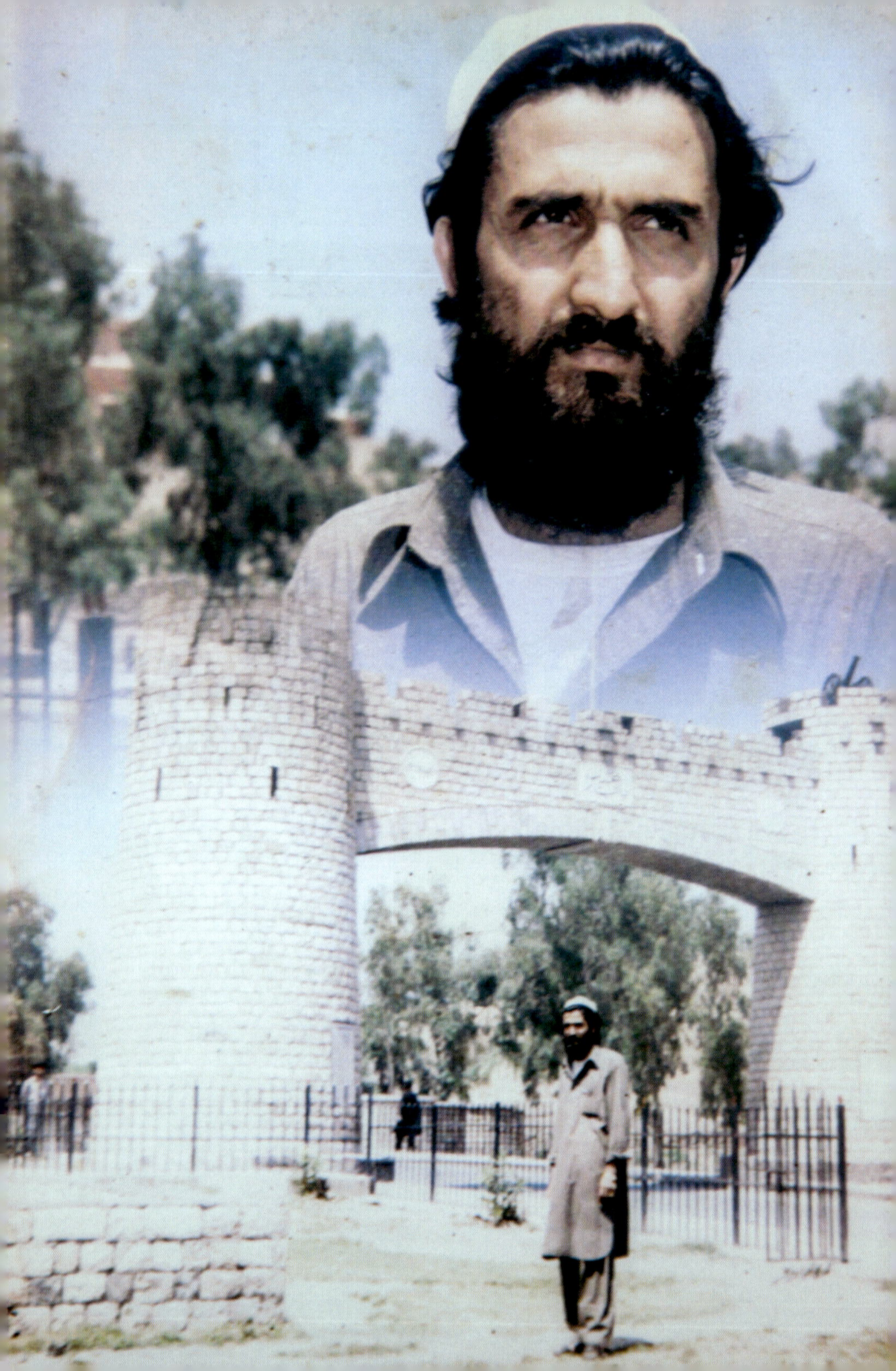

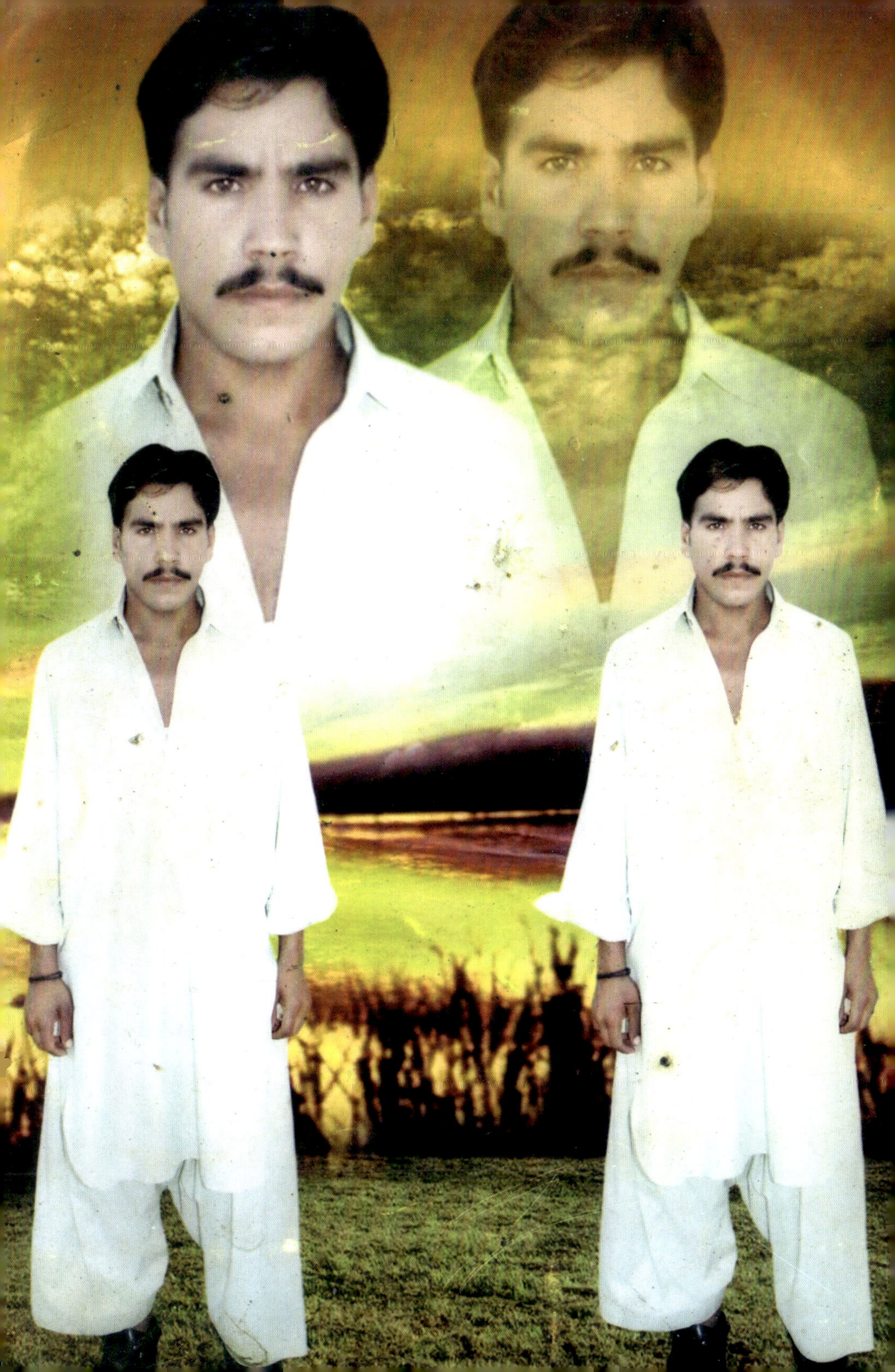

Opposite: Double-exposure taken on film by Adul Wali, 1990s.

Pages 212–213: The first stage in creating a photomontage of a client and a female entertainer, whose image will be overlaid on top of this photograph and reshot. Photo by Abdul Wali, 1990s; *Pages* 214–215: Head-on-hand photomontage, under construction. Photo by Abdul Wali, 1990s; *Pages* 216–217: Double-exposure by Abdul Wali, 1990s.

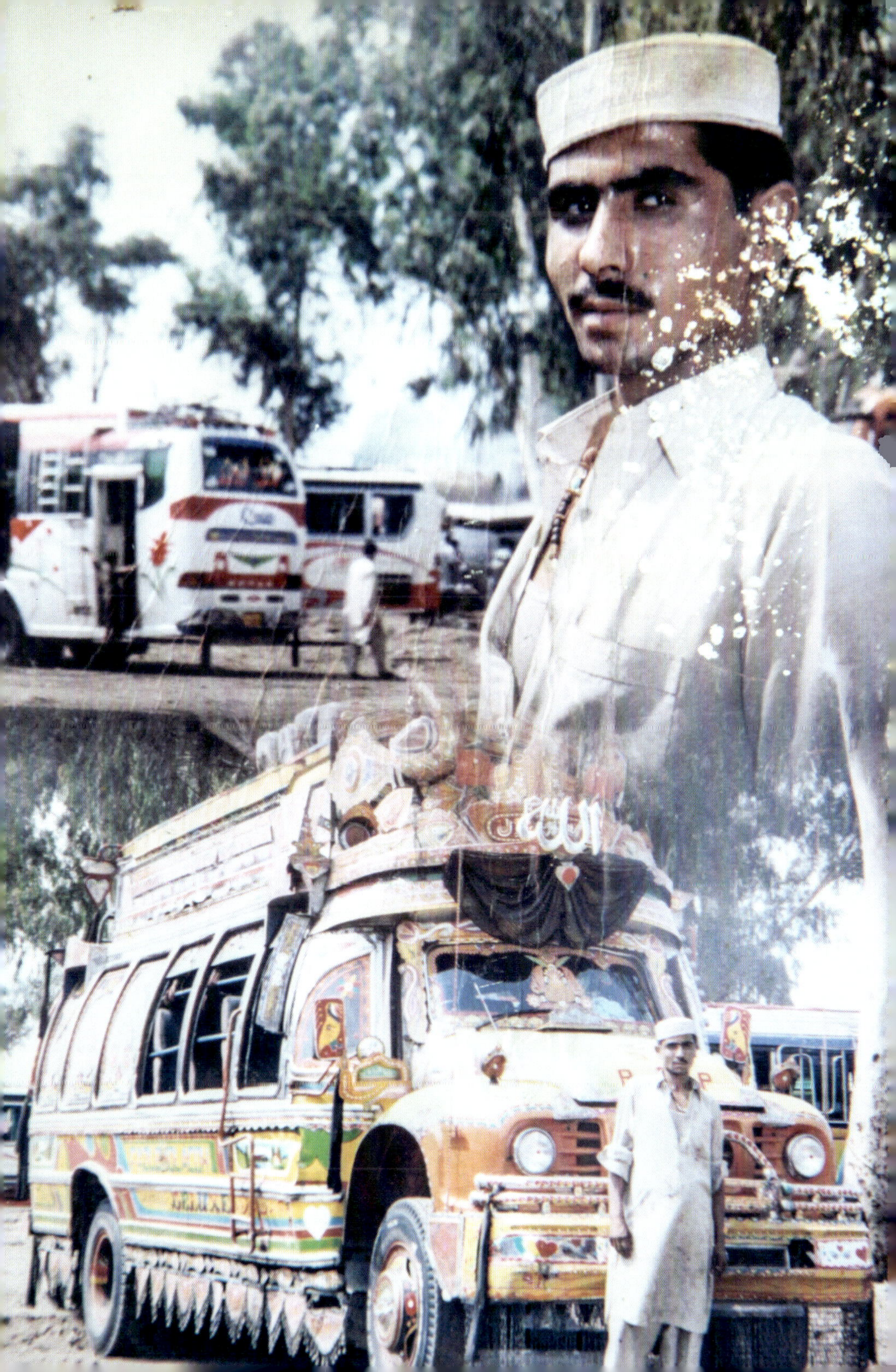

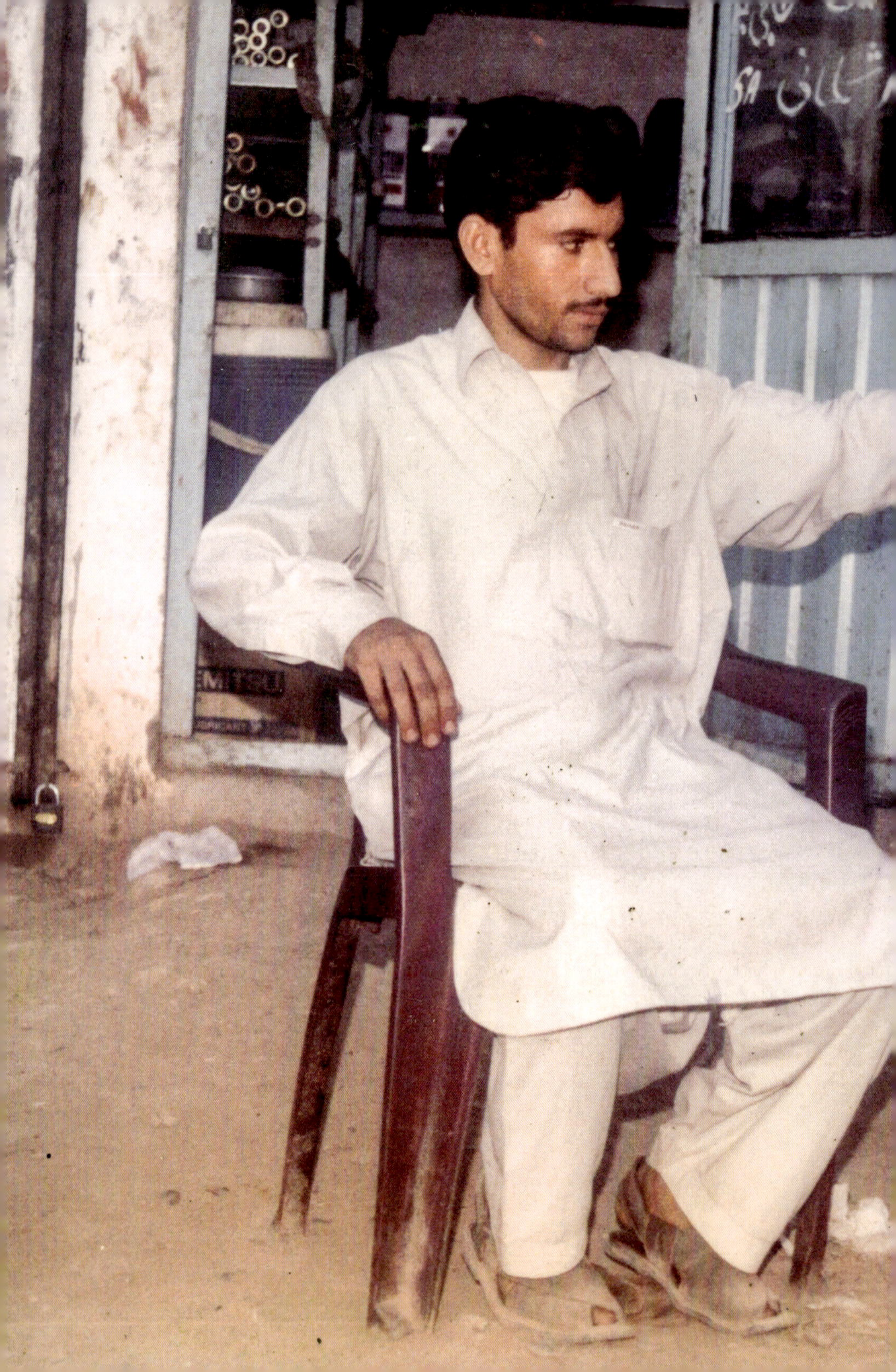

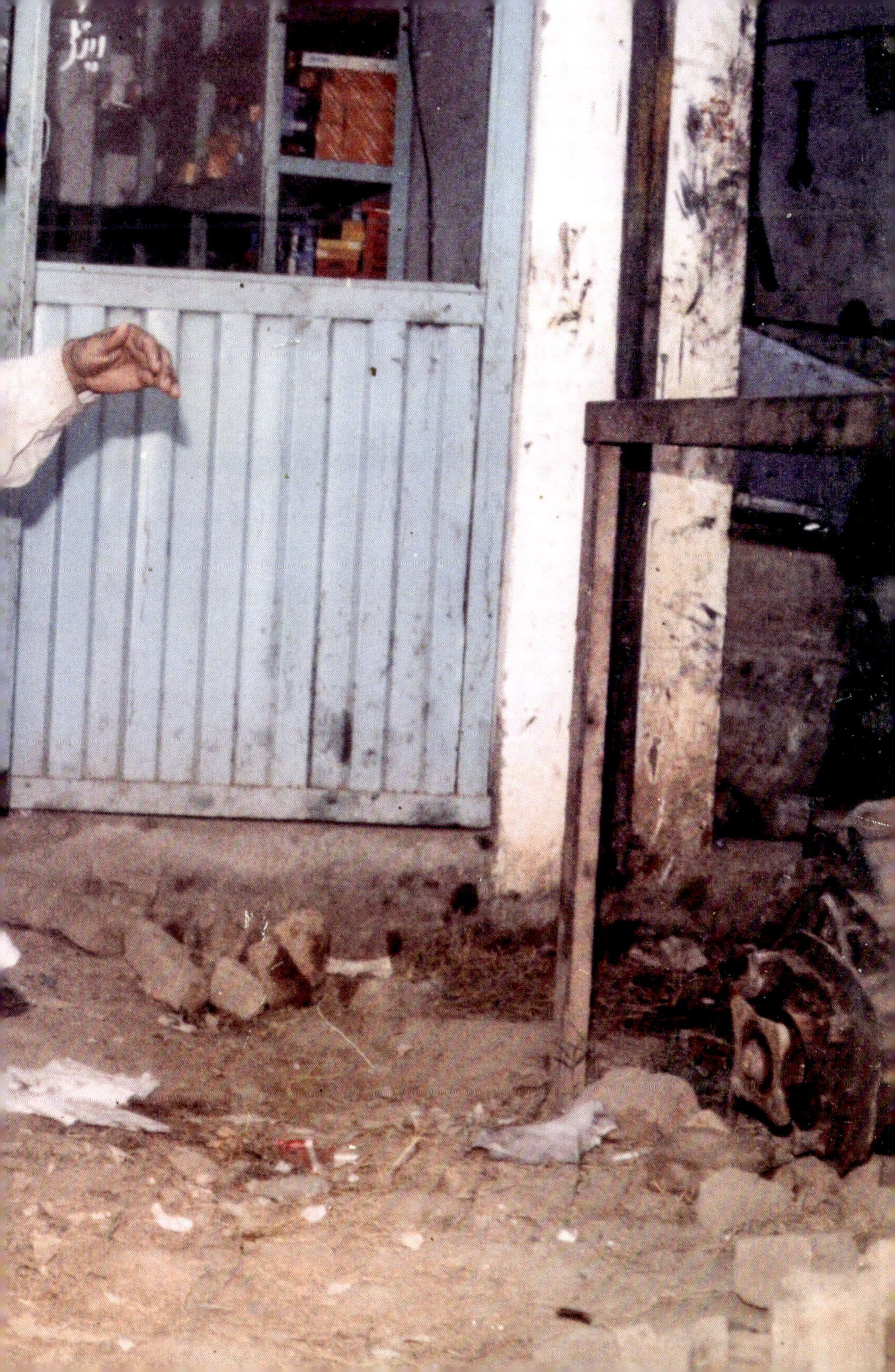

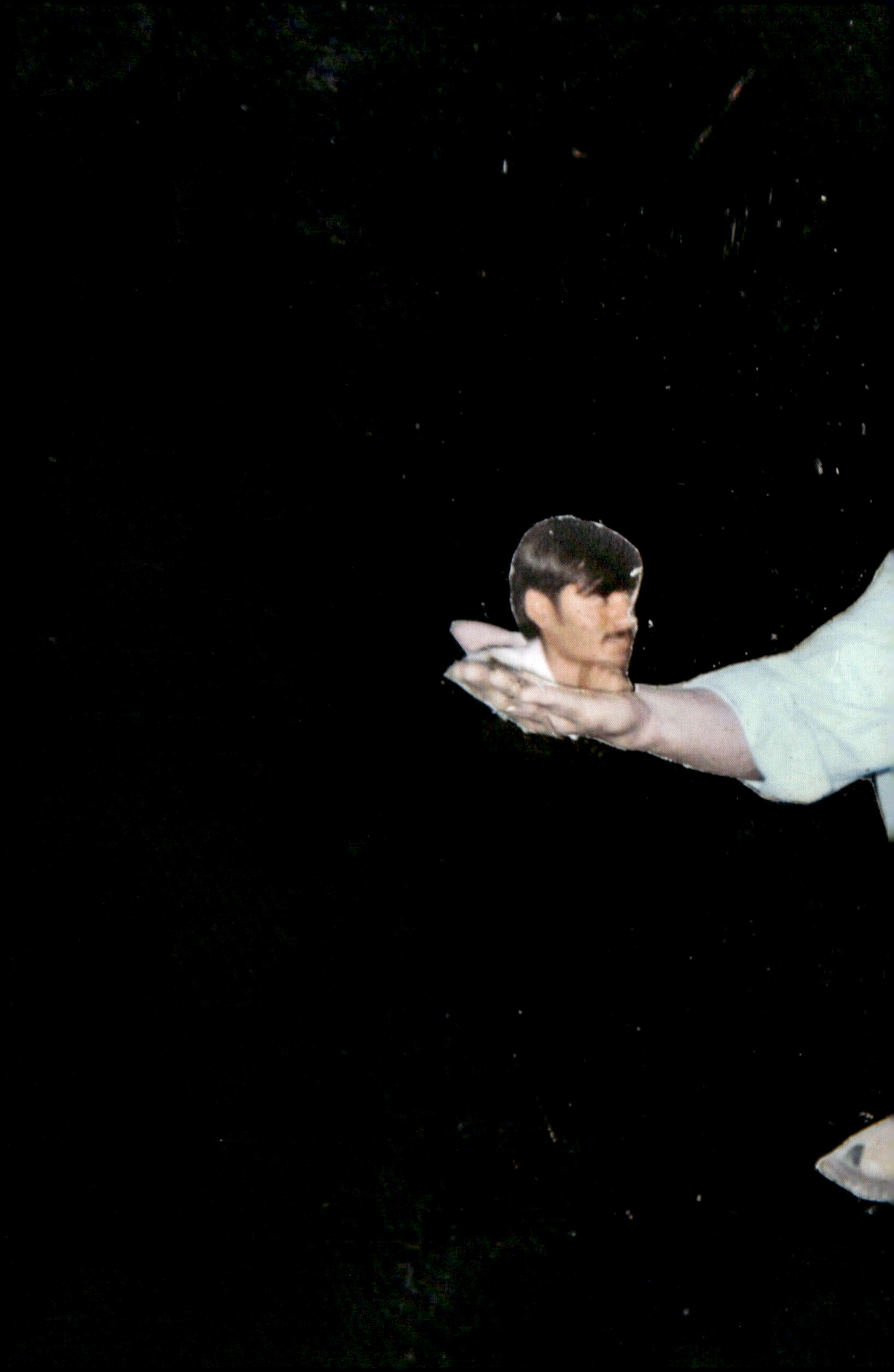

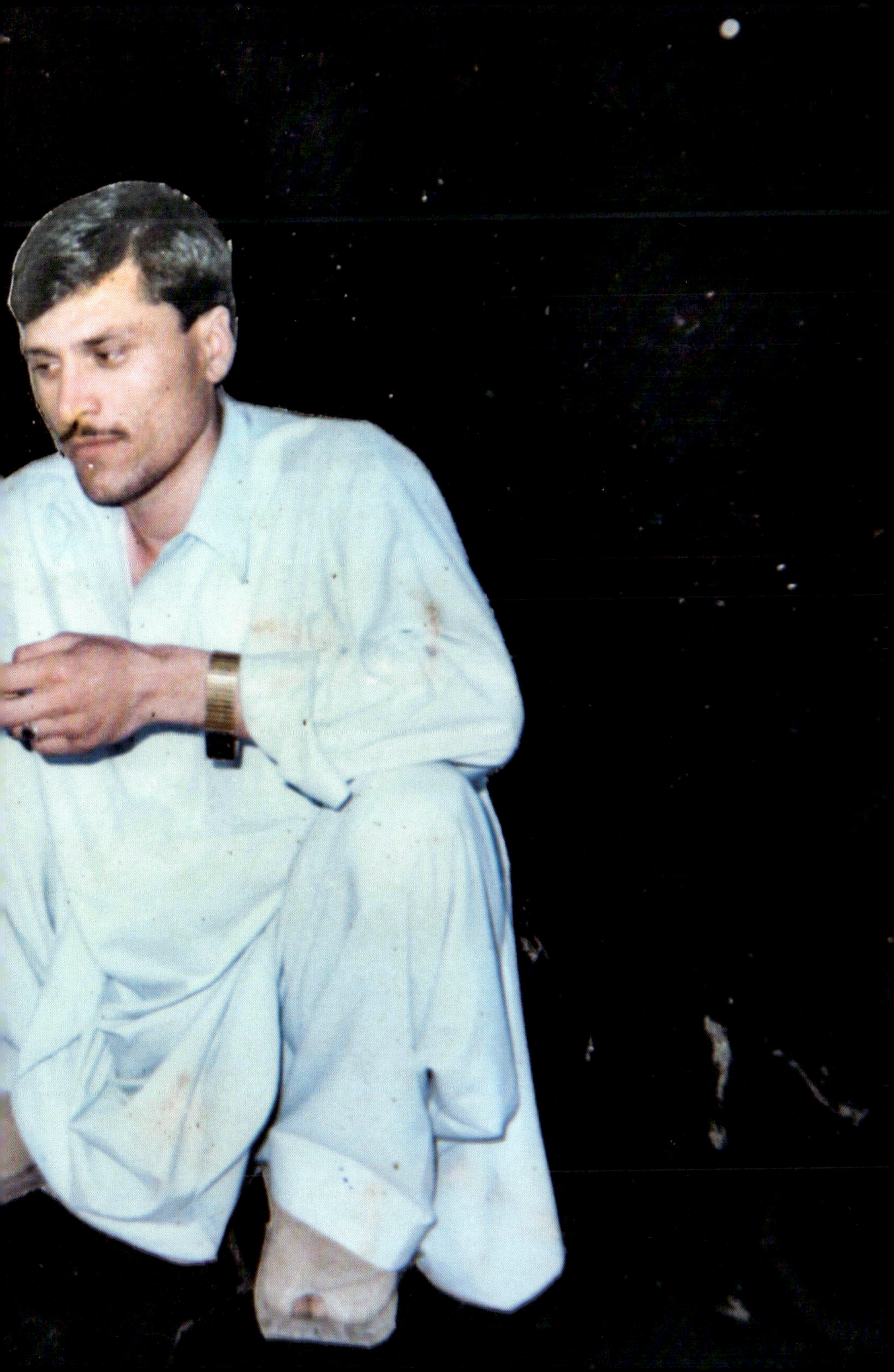

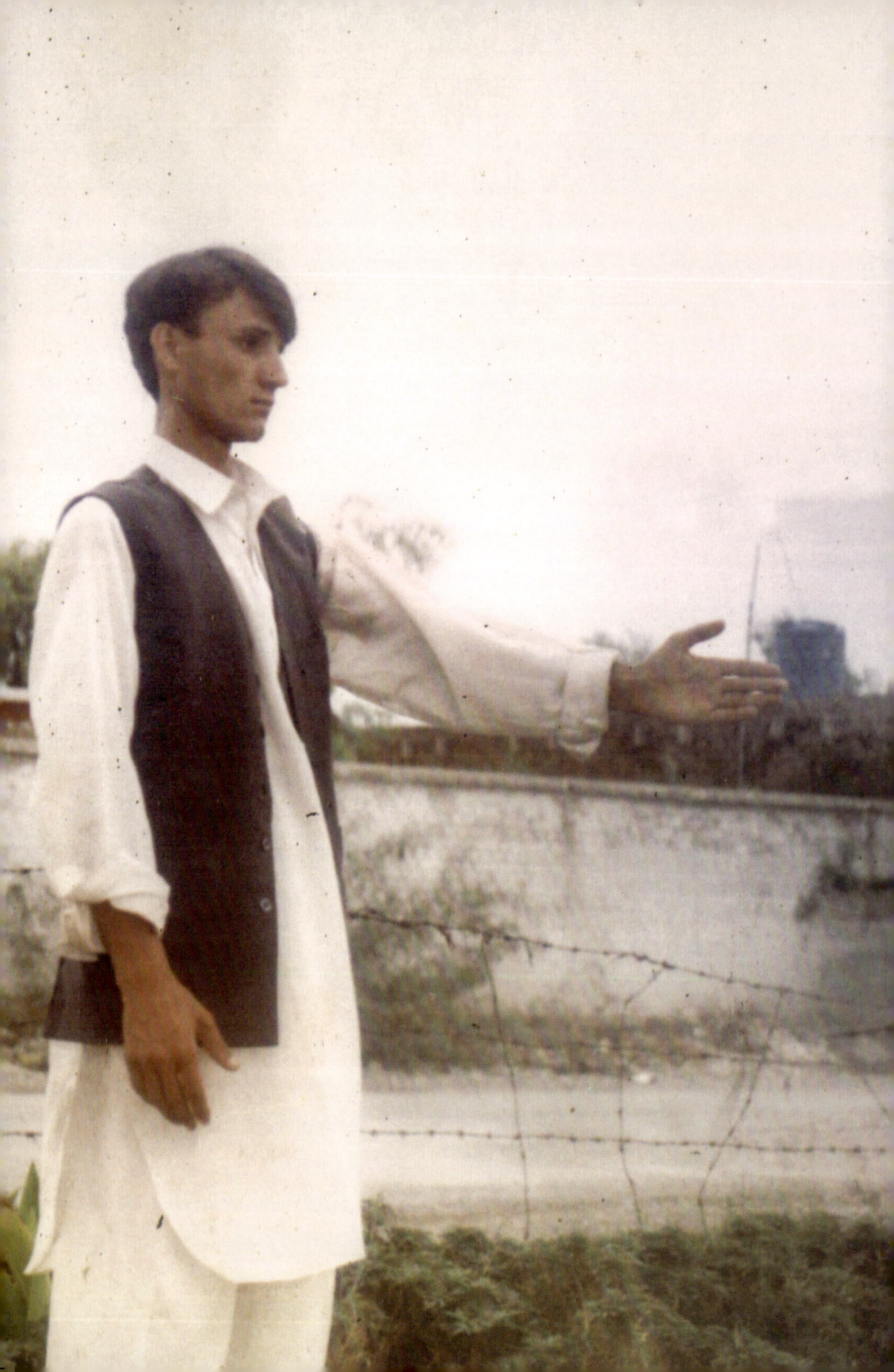

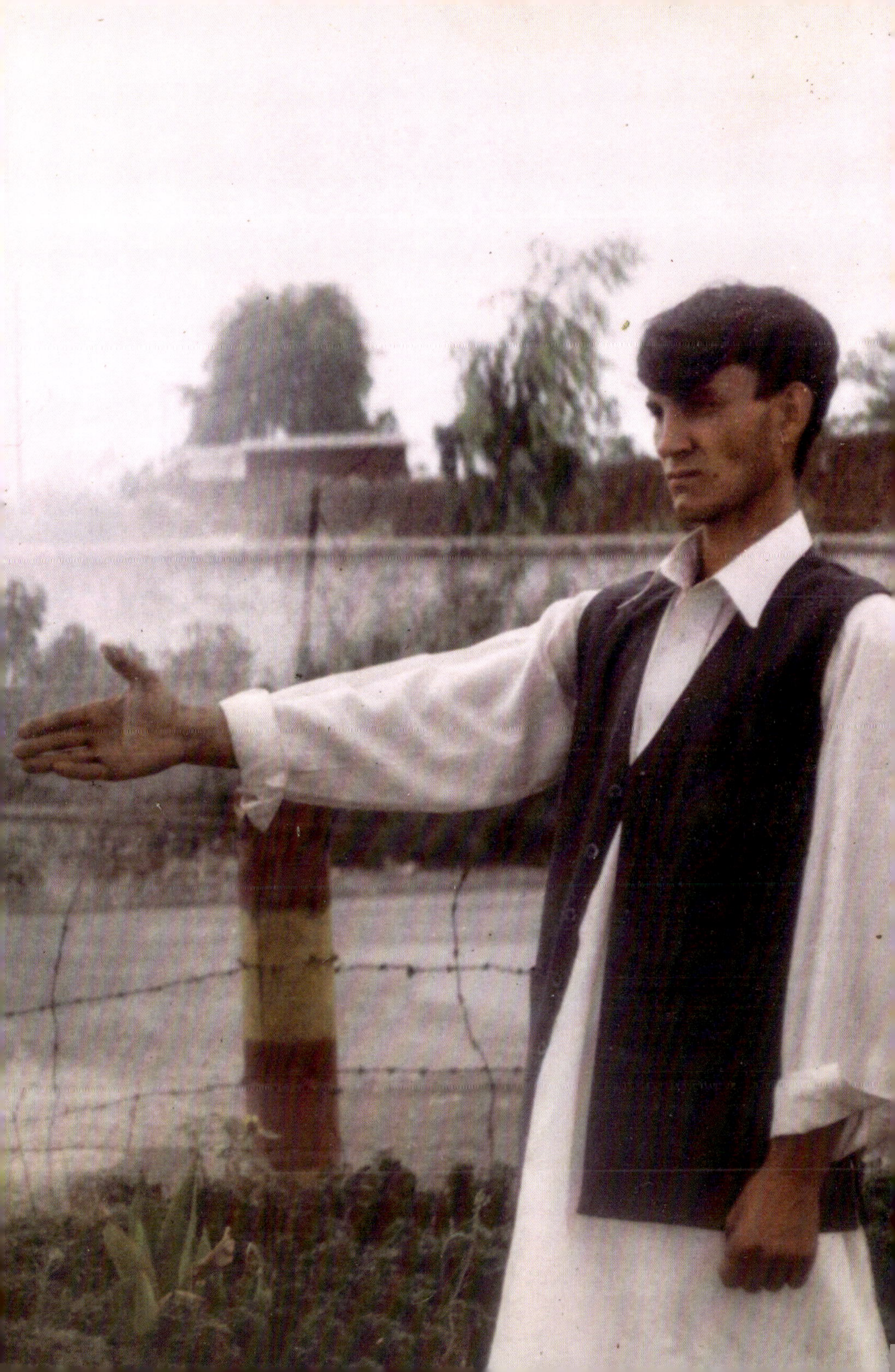

Opposite: Aziz Rehman Slonaar, a travelling photographer, cycles twice a week for about two hours from a village east of Peshawar to Cinema Road in order to print photos from his digital camera. The studio in Cinema Road adds the flower frames and enhances the images he brings. Digital photography, Aziz says, has made his life a lot easier and he would never go back to film. He usually has an air gun and flowers with him as props. Once the images are printed, he delivers them to the costumers in the countryside.

Pages 220–223: Digital photos by Aziz Rehman Slonaar. The decorative floral borders are added by Shama Studio on Cinema Road, 2014.

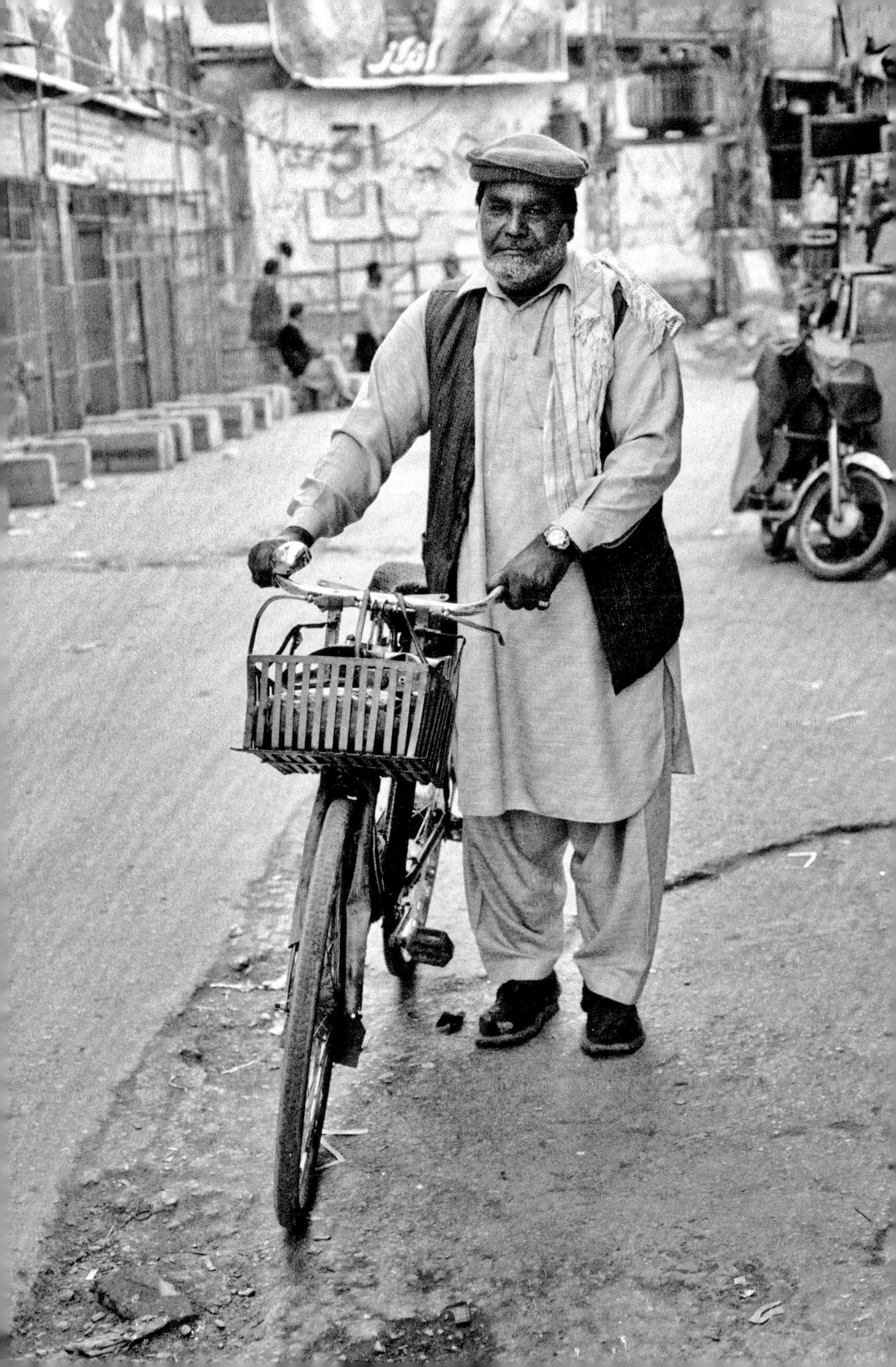

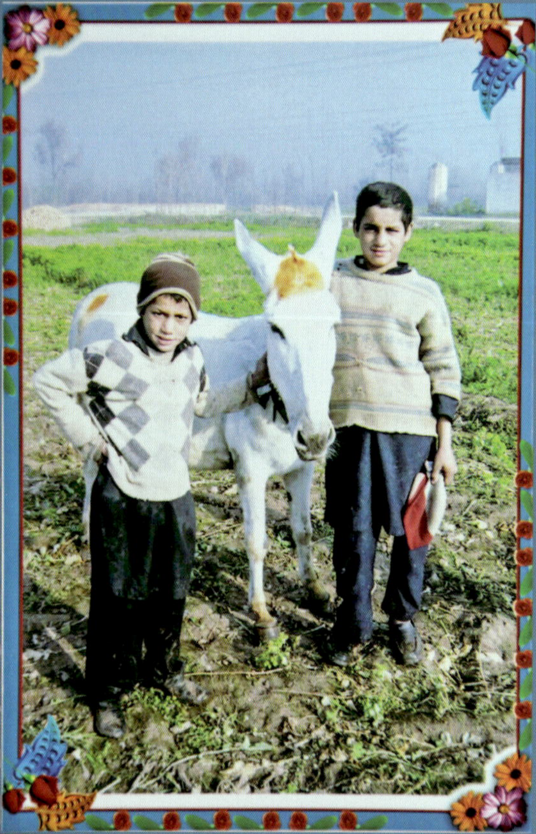
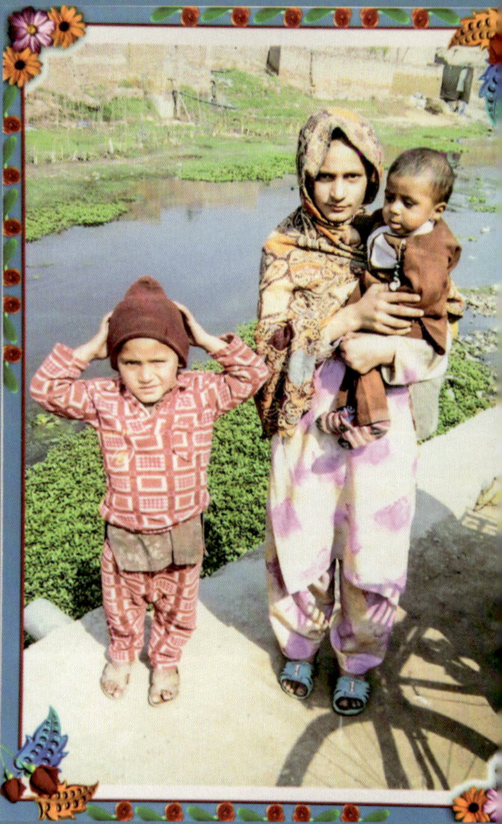
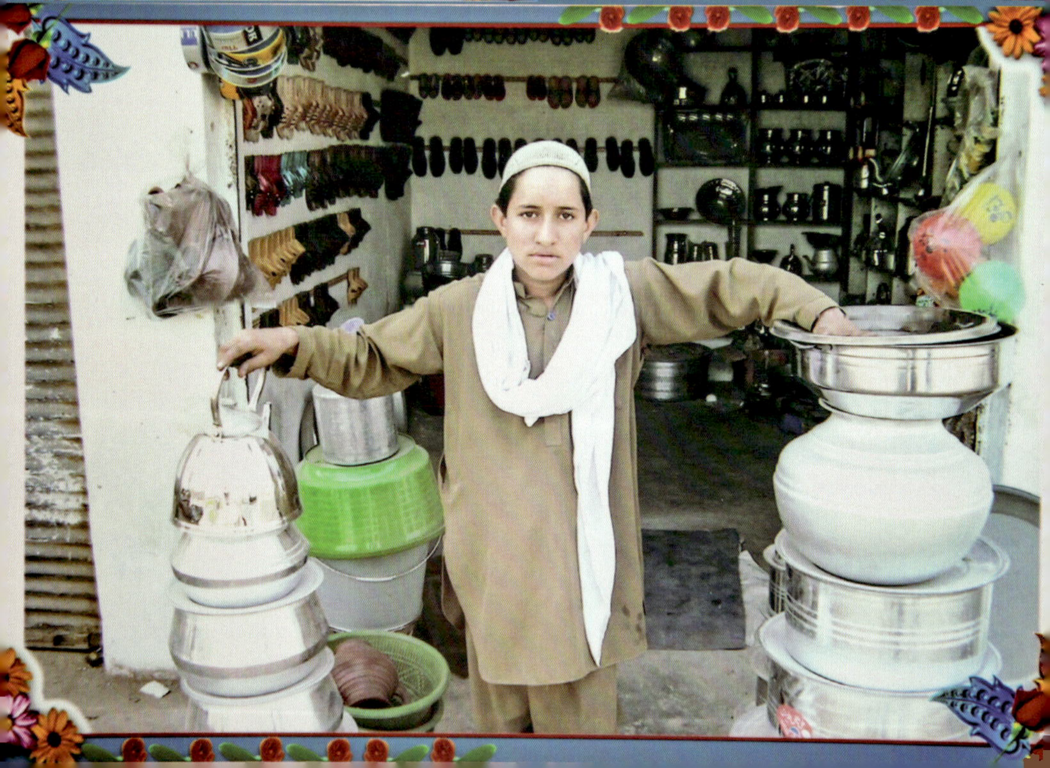

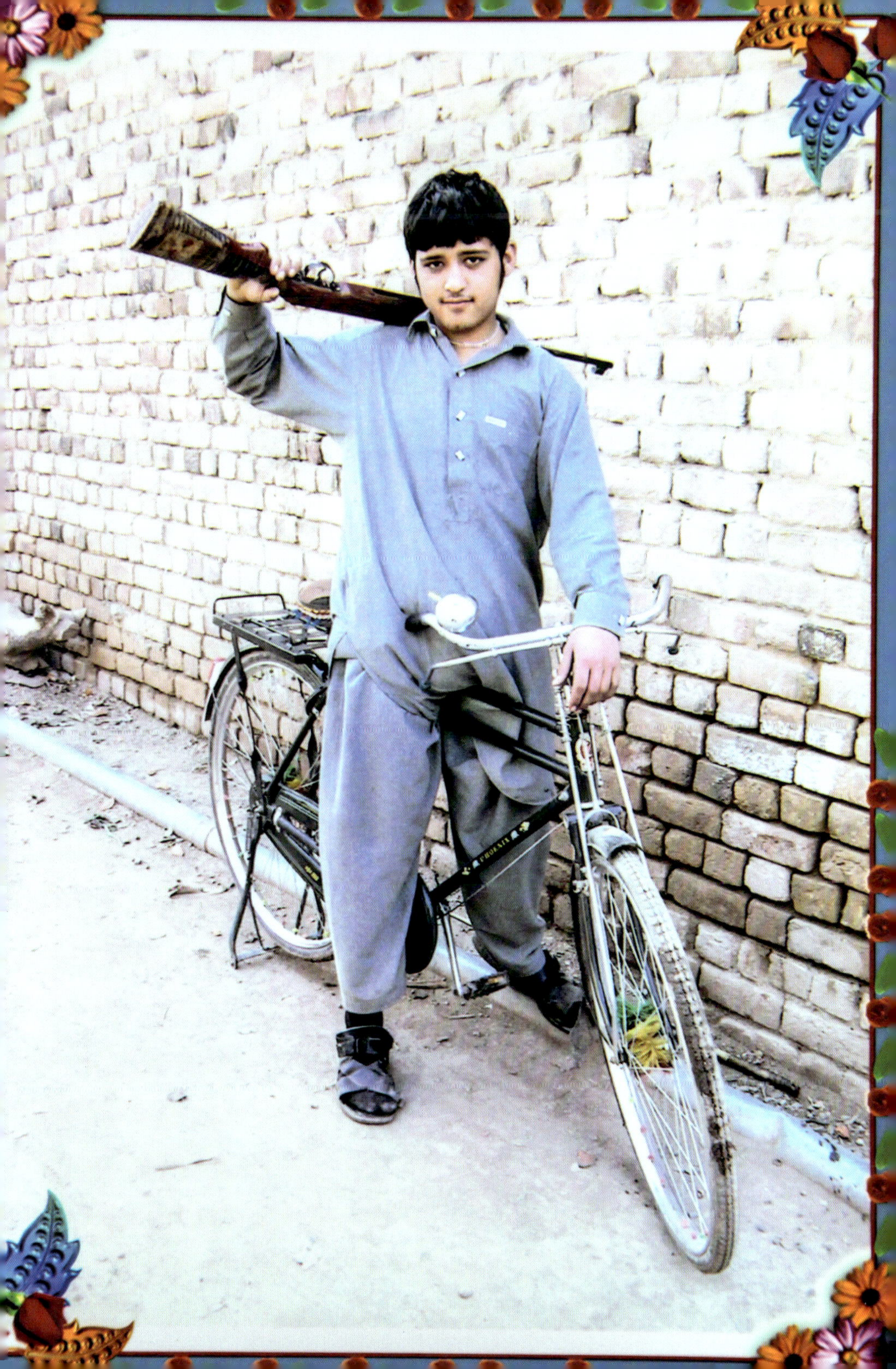

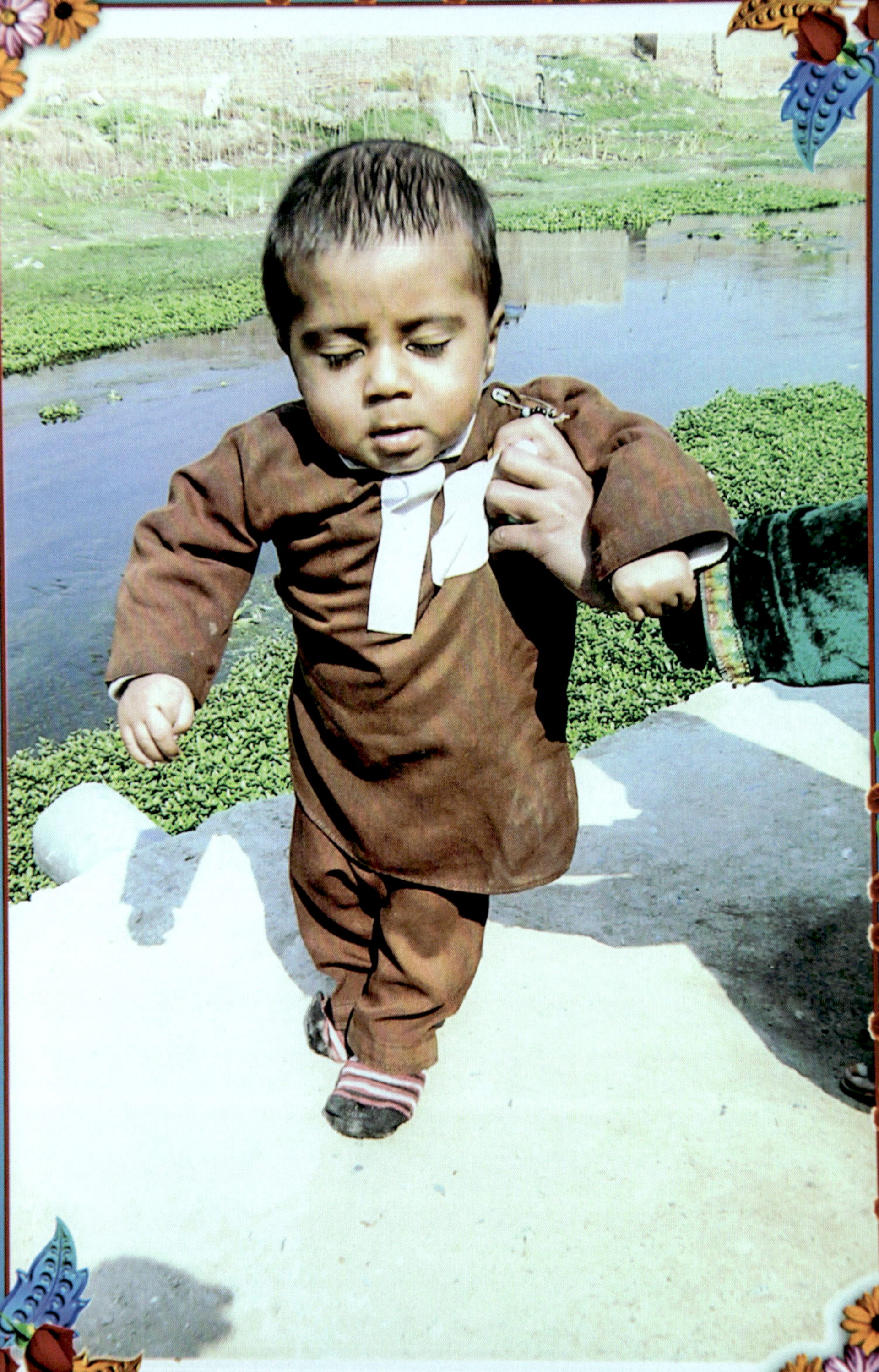

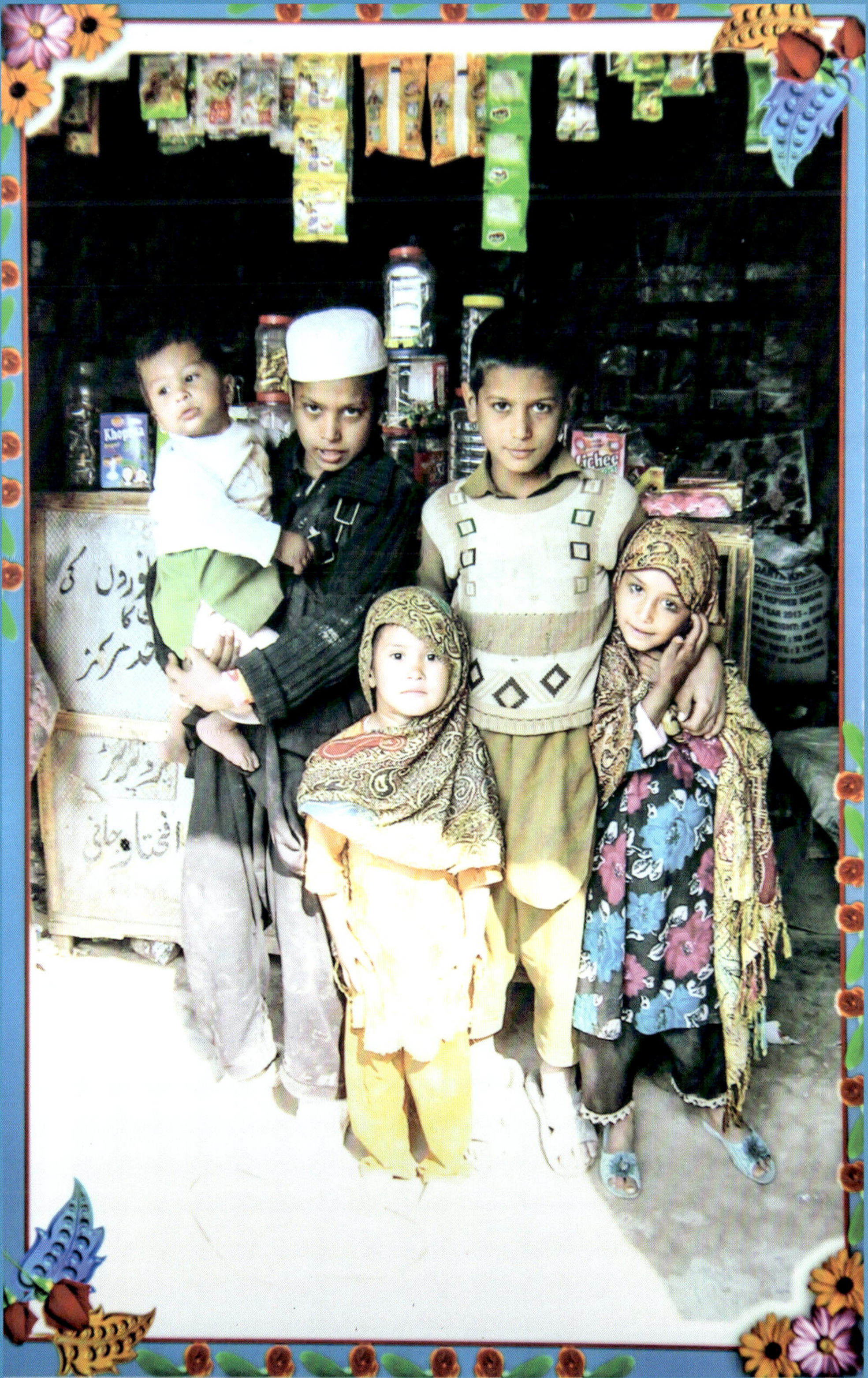

Fayaz Ahmad of Shama Studio on Cinema Road, the biggest printing and development laboratory on the road, is nephew of photographer Kala Khan (d.2013) who began his career as a paper-negative minute camera photographer on the road in the 1960s.

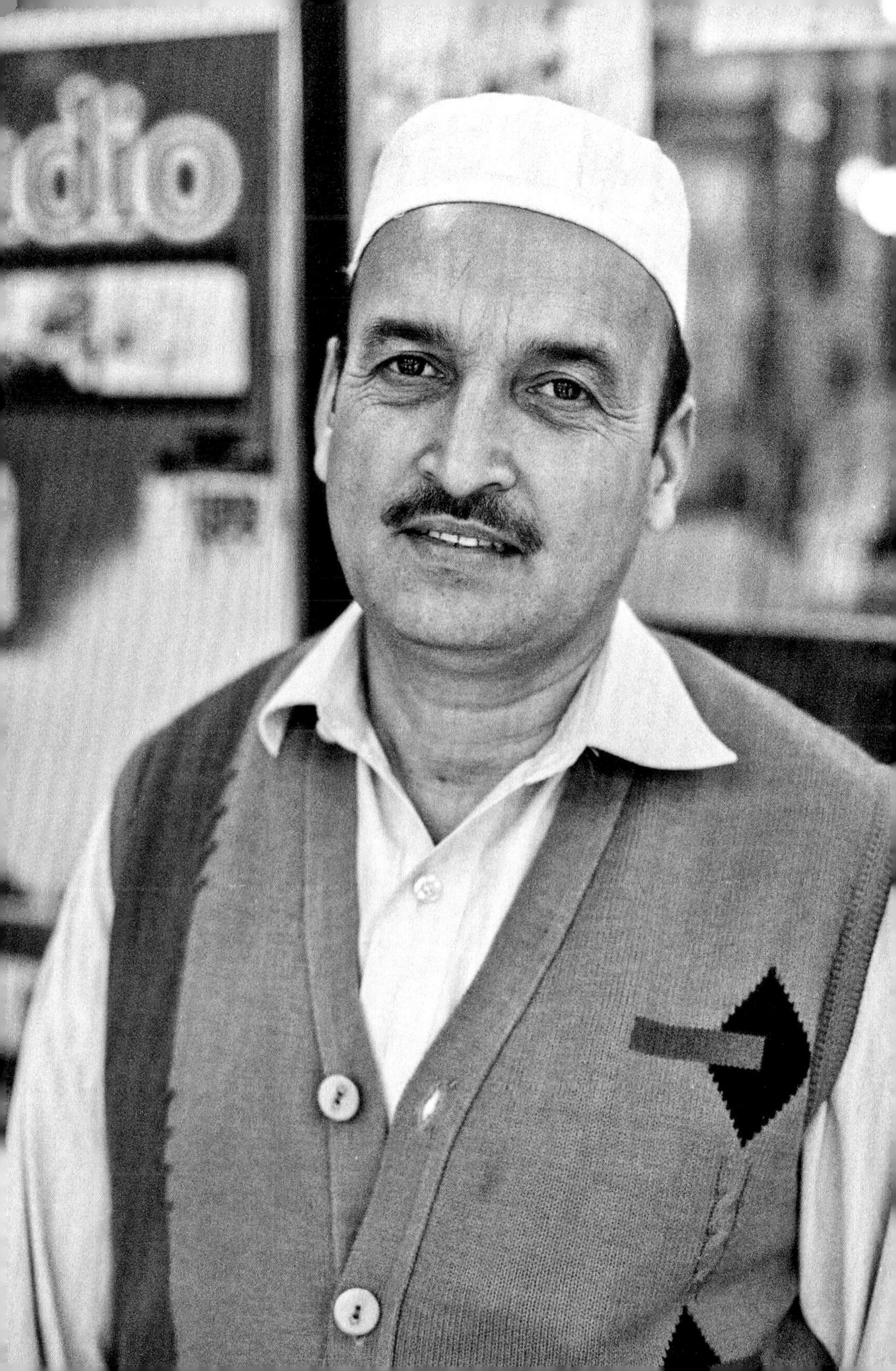

Opposite & pages 228–233: Hand-coloured photographs from the garrison town of Kohat, south of Peshawar, c.1985–1995.

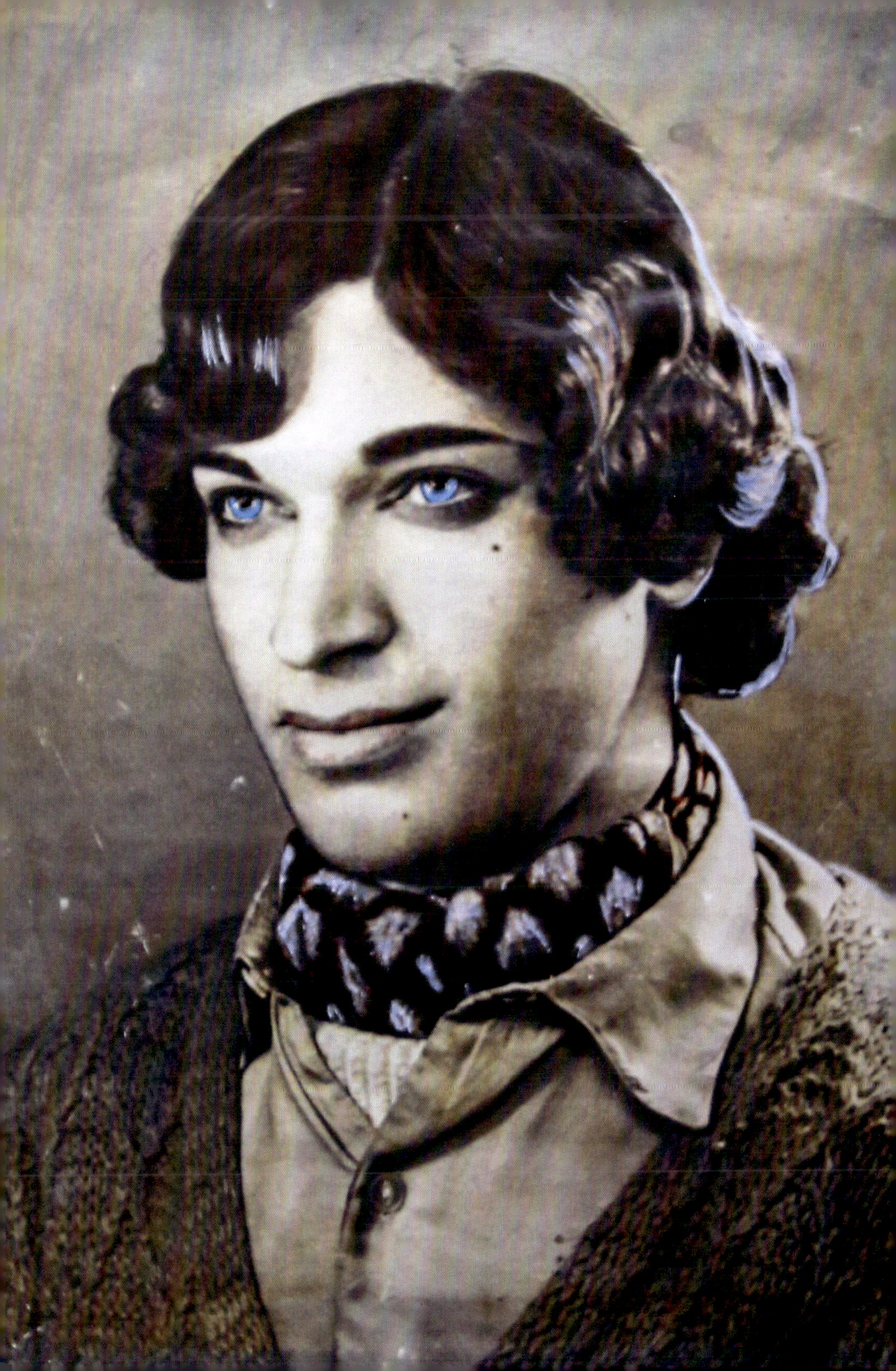

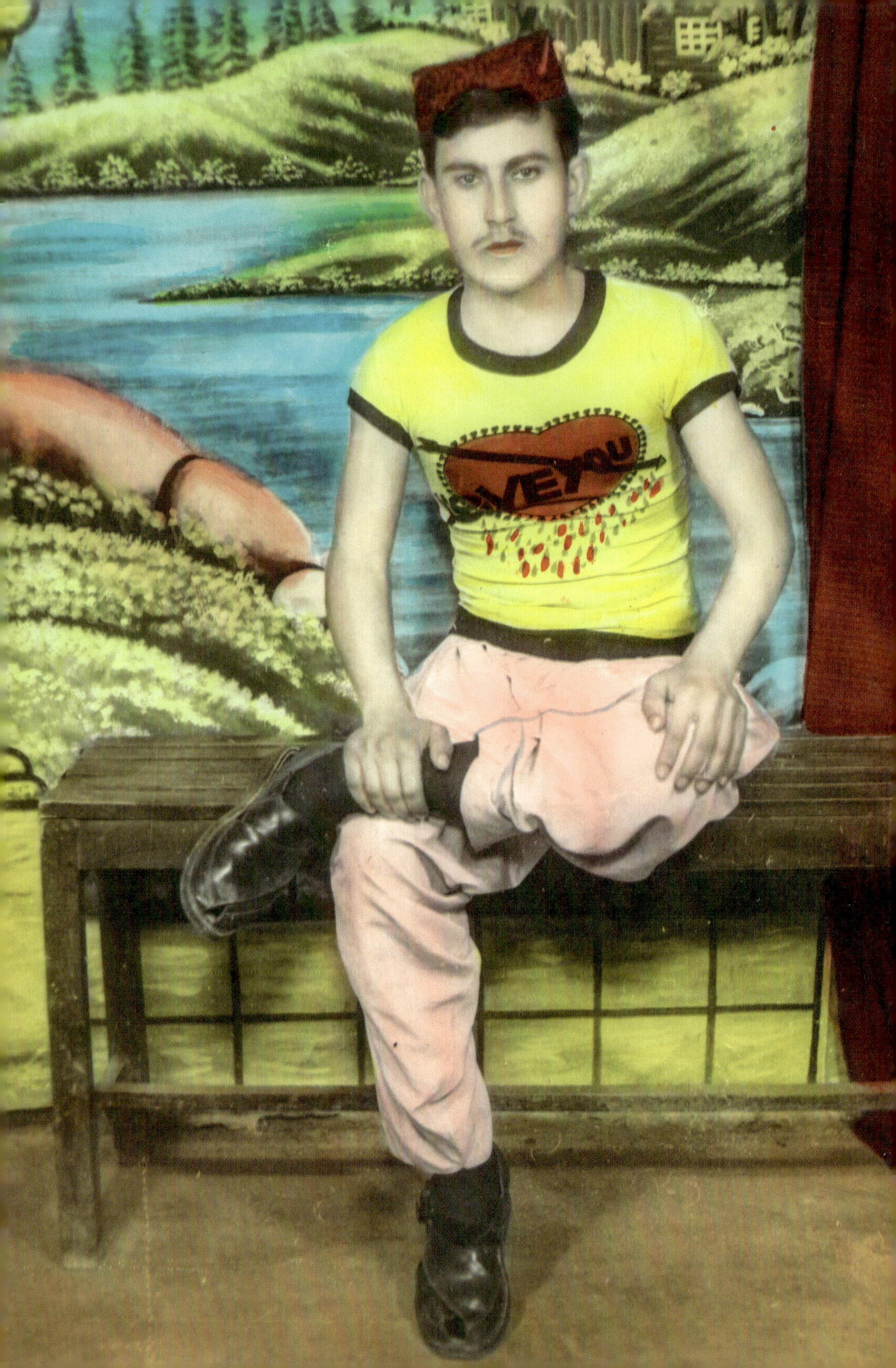

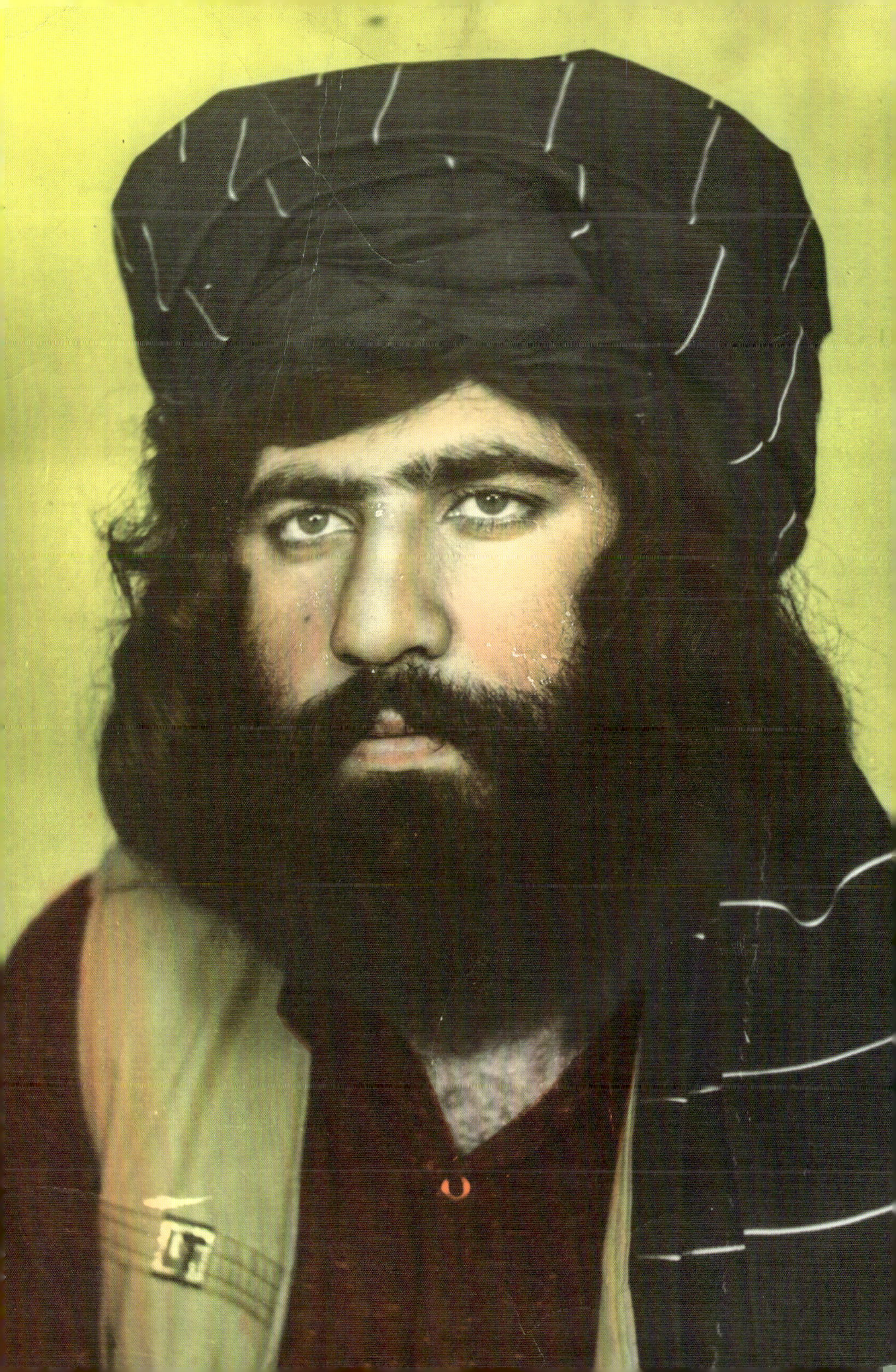

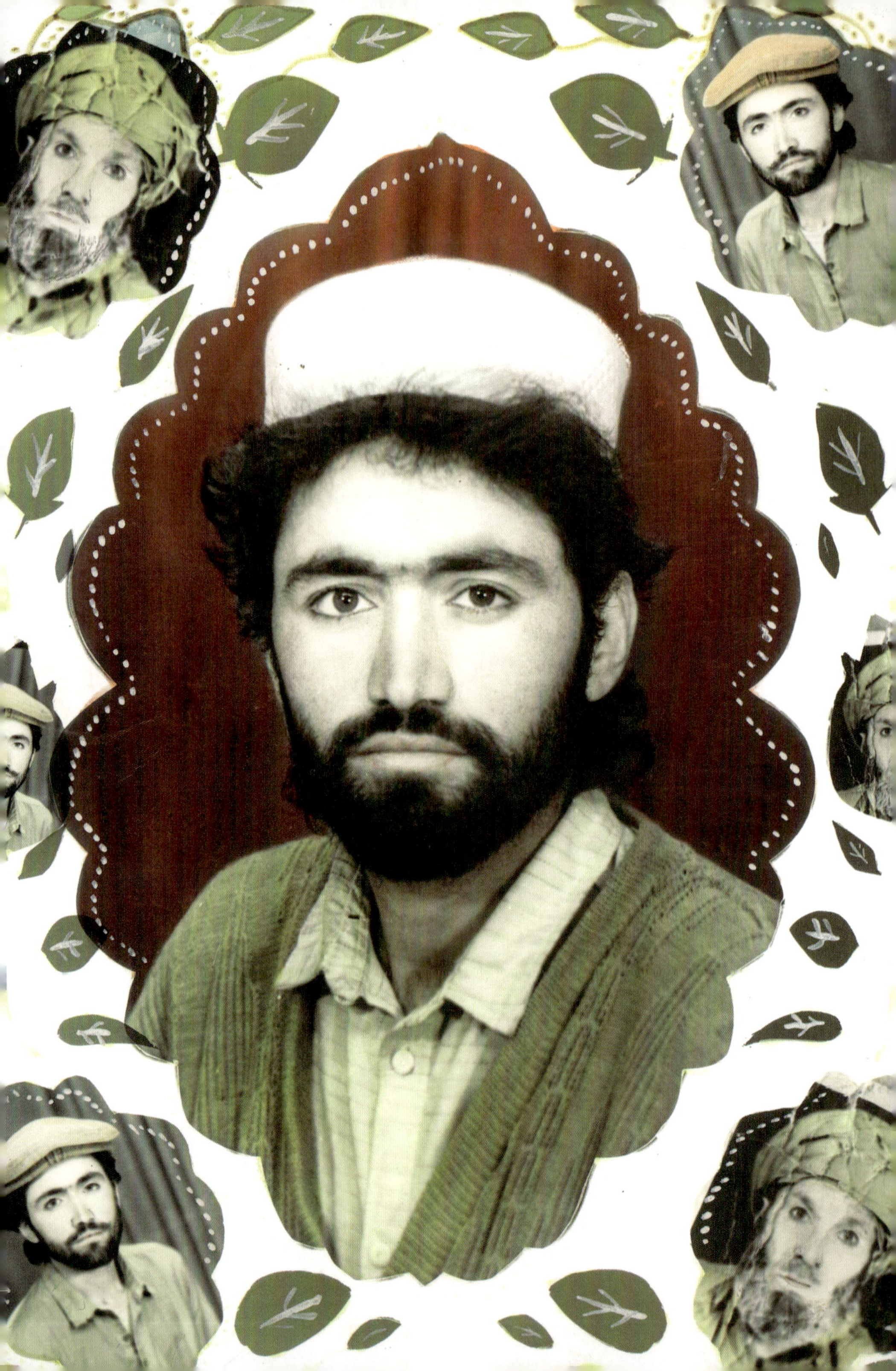

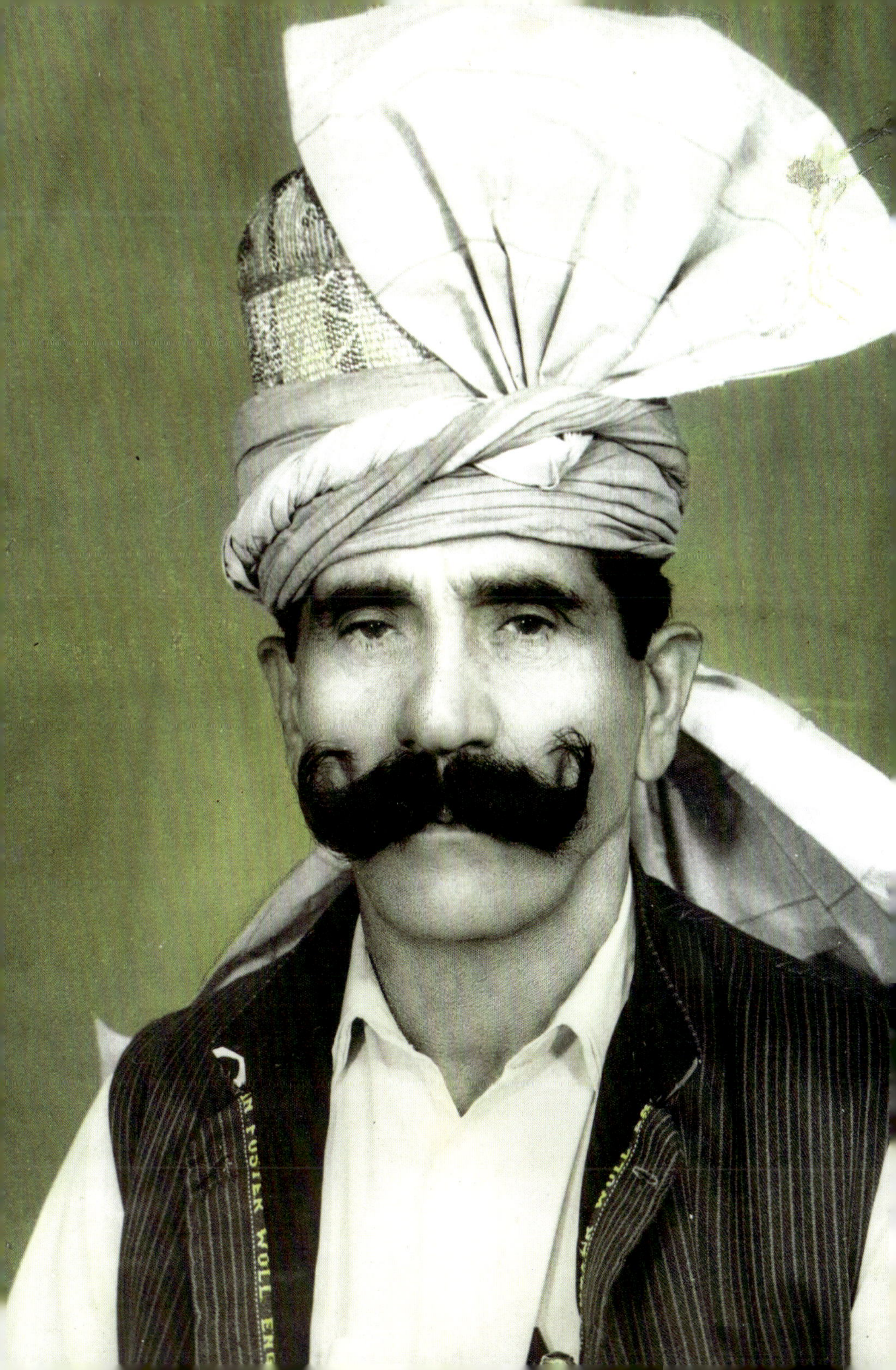

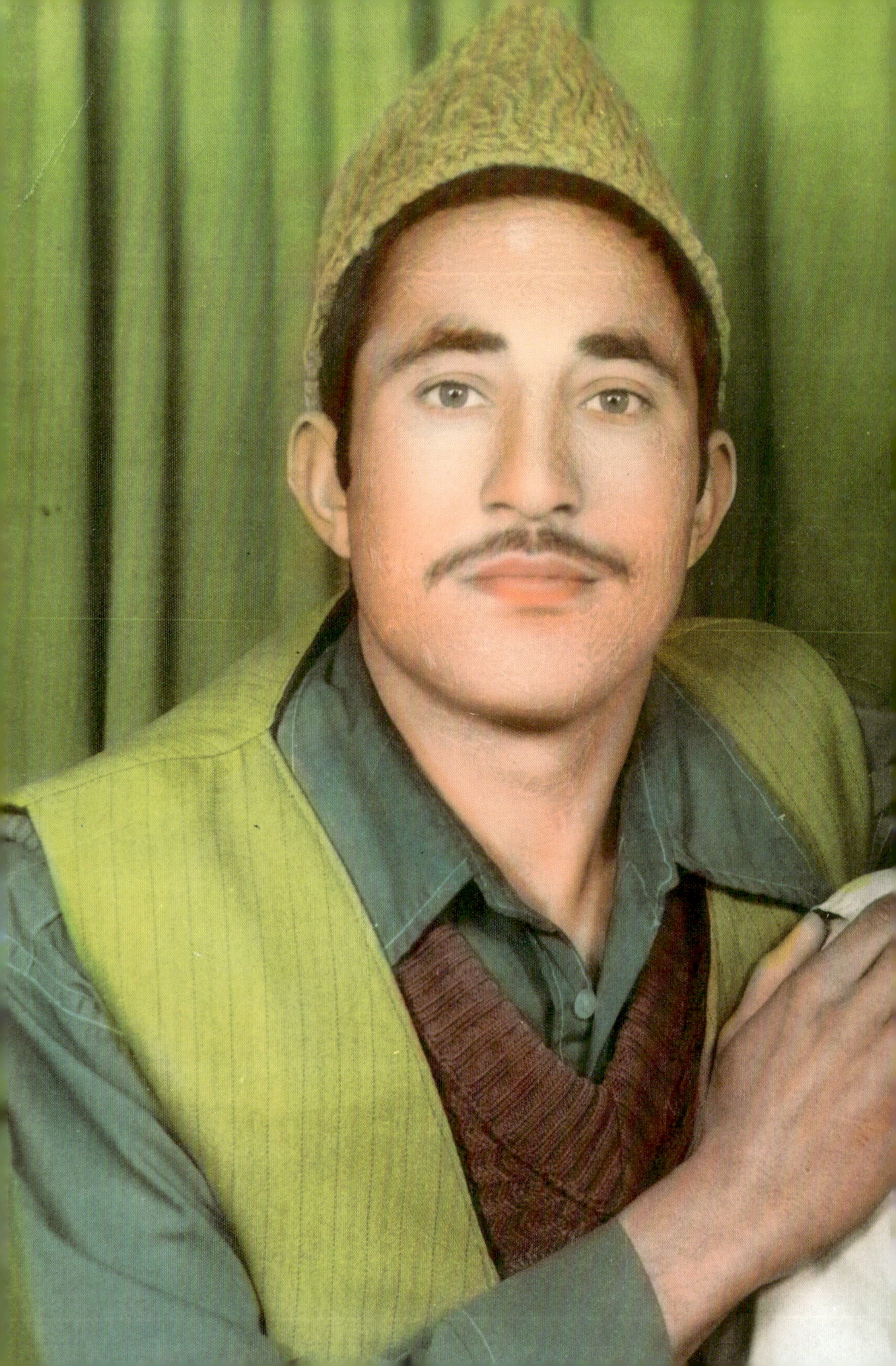

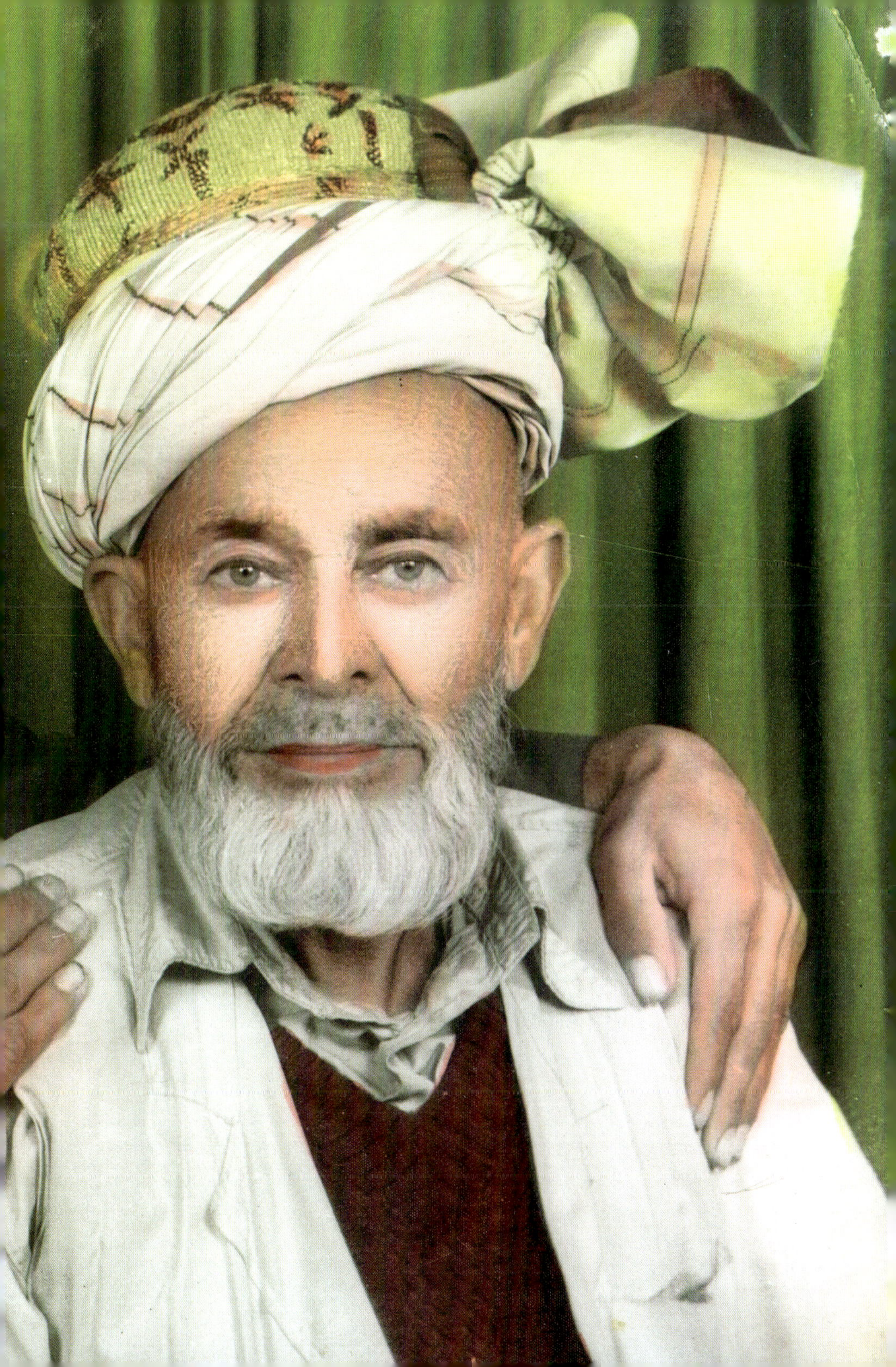

Notes

١ This essay is largely based on research conducted in Peshawar between 2012 and 2014, which included informal interviews, photo-shoots, and many cups of tea with dozens of local photographers, a number of whom were, and still are, senior practitioners who began working in the city shortly after Partition in 1947. Our research into the culture of Afghan photography, conducted in Afghanistan and Pakistan in 2011 and 2012, also contributed to the picture we paint here; *see*: Lukas Birk & Sean Foley, *Afghan Box Camera*, UK, Dewi Lewis, 2013. As does research by Sean Foley in India on paper-negative minute camera photography, between 2013 and 2017.

٢ Noor Muhammad Khan, *Some Time on the Frontier: A Pakistan Journal*, USA, self-published, 2009.

٣ Shahbaz Khan, a photographic materials supplier, whom we met in Herat in eastern Afghanistan in 2012, would make the lengthy journey from Herat via Kandahar to Jalalabad and onto Peshawar to buy stock; the Herat to Kabul road, which is infrastructurally much poorer than the route Shahbaz took, was also more insecure due to conflict in the area; *see*: http://www.afghanboxcamera.com/abcp_camera_materials.htm.

٤ With plans, as of 2017, to incorporate FATA into the Khyber Pakhtunkhwa, there are hopes that the situation may be stabilising; *see*: Raza, Syed Irfan, "Cabinet approves steps for FATA's merger with Khyber Pakhtunkhwa", *Dawn*, March 3rd 2017, accessed 6/9/17 at https://www.dawn.com/news/1318095.

٥ Chris Pinney, *The Coming of Photography in India*, UK, British Library, 2008.

٦ Omar Khan, *From Kashmir to Kabul: The photographs of John Burke and William Baker,1860 to 1900*, Munich / Ahmedebad, Prestel/Mapin, 2002.; also: John Burke & Simon Norfolk, *Burke + Norfolk: Photographs from the War in Afghanistan by John Burke & Simon Norfolk*, UK, Dewi Lewis, 2011.

٧ Photographer Edward Grazda, while on assignment in the 1980s to cover the war in neighbouring Afghanistan, purchased a catalogue from Umar Khan's studio in Peshawar, and kindly shared some images from the catalogue with the authors.

٨ Nancy Hatch Dupree, "The Archive of a Nation," *PIX: Afghanistan Special Issue: Renewal,* Vol. 12, October 2015, p.106–108; Boone, Jon, "A librarian's labour of love for Afghanistan", *Financial Times*, February 14th 2009, accessed 7/9/2017 at https://www.ft.com/content/45a7ebca-f712-11dd-8a1f-0000779fd2ac.

٩ "Tribute to a legend: Cinema Road to be renamed after Badir Munir." *The Express Tribune*, October 11th, 2013, accessed 6/9/2017 at https://tribune.com.pk/story/272931/tribute-to-a-legend-cinema-road-to-be-renamed-after-badar-munir/.

١٠ "Pashto singer Ghazala Javed shot dead." *Dawn*, June 19th 2012, accessed 6/9/2017 at https://www.dawn.com/news/727758. We were working in the city the same day; our research-assistant broke the news to us.

١١ "The downfall of cinema culture in Peshawar", *Frontier Post*, April 27th 2009, accessed 9/9/2017 at https://www.flickr.com/photos/noor-khan/3479273019/.

١٢ Yusufzai, Ashfaq, "New Pashto films woo people back to the cinema", *Dawn*, August 6th 2014, accessed 9/9/17 at https://www.dawn.com/news/1123629; *see also*: Ullah, Izar, "For Peshawar's movies buffs, all roads lead to Islamabad", *Dawn*, May 11th 2016, accessed 9/9/2017 at https://www.dawn.com/news/1257485.

١٣ In a similar vein, when the Pakistani Taliban took over the Swat District, only 250kms north of Peshawar, between 2007 and 2009, they closed all of the local cinemas, in addition to banning any other forms of entertainment which, they said, offended Islam. *See*: "Swat locals welcome cinema re-opening", *Dawn*, September 24th 2009, accessed 5/9/2017 at https://www.dawn.com/news/492329. For a broader discussion on the repercussions of the Taliban take-over of Swat, *see:* Anatol Lieven, *Pakistan: A Hard Country*, London: Penguin, 2013, p.462–476.

١٤ *See*: https://www.thenews.com.pk/archive/print/664620-10-killed,-65-injured-in-peshawar-cinema-blast, accessed 8/9/17.

١٥ *See*: https://tribune.com.pk/story/407544/blast-in-peshawar-cinema-injures-three-people/, accessed 8/9/17.

١٦ Bacha, Ali Hazrat, "Twin blast in Peshawar cinema claims four lives", *Dawn*, February 3rd 2014, accessed 8/9/17 at https://www.dawn.com/news/1084536.

١٧ Sherazi, Zahir Shah, "Three explosions hit Peshawar cinema; 13 killed", *Dawn*, February 11th 2014, accessed 9/9/2017 at https://www.dawn.com/news/1086328.

١٨ Bacha, Ali Hazrat, "Bomb attack in Peshawar claims five lives", *Dawn*, September 19th 2011, accessed 9/9/2017 at https://www.dawn.com/news/660225; *see also*: http://www.pakistanpressfoundation.org/pakistan-press-foundation-ppfreport-on-threatsviolence-against-musicians-attacks-on-music-shops-2000-2011/.

١٩ There also tends to be a relatively high turn-around in studio ownership on Cinema Road. One of the reasons, according to long-time Cinema Road photographer, Tahir Usman, is that landlords hike the rent once a studio is becoming successful. Ironically, of course, higher rents contribute to studios going out of business. Some notable old-time studios still survive, however, including Capri Studio and Famous Studio, both founded in the 1970s.

٢٠ From *Warrior's Portrait*, an unpublished text by Benjamin Gilmour, Australian director and writer. Gilmour made the feature-film length film, Son of a Lion (2007), filmed with local amateur actors on location in FATA, and wrote a book describing the experience: *Warrior Poets: Guns, Movie-making and the Wild West of Pakistan*, Australia, Murdoch Books, 2008. *See also*: Ebrahim Alkazai, Rahaab Allana, & Pramod Kumar K.G, *Painted Photographs: Coloured Portraiture in India, The Alkazi Collection of Photography*, Ahmedabad, Mapin, 2008, p.28–33.

٢١ *See*: Lukas Birk & Sean Foley, *Afghan Box Camera*, UK, Dewi Lewis, 2013; Chris Wroblewski, *Smudgers*, self-published, 2003; Ann Parker & Avon Neal, *Los Ambulantes: the Itinerant Photographers of Guatemala*, Cambridge, Ma.: MIT Press, 1982.

٢٢ An example of a hand-coloured and montaged minute camera portrait from Cinema Road in the 1980s of a customer superimposed alongside Pashtun actress Yasmeen Khan appears in our book on the culture of Afghan photography; *see*: Lukas Birk & Sean Foley, *Afghan Box Camera*, UK, Dewi Lewis, 2013, p.43.

٢٣ For a comparison of the Afghan and Indian paper-negative cameras; *see*: http://www.afghanboxcamera.com/abcp_photographers_muhammadiqbal.htm.

٢٤ The last working minute camera photography in Kabul, up to 2012, was Qalam Nabi who had a pitch in the city-centre; *see*: http://www.afghanboxcamera.com/abcp_photographers_qualamnabi.htm.

٢٥ Ahmad Shah Faqiri, a travelling bicycle photographer we met in Kabul in the summer of 2012, actually profited from phone-camera technology by offering customers the opportunity to print images from their mobile phones. Ahmad would download customer images onto his own mobile phone via the wireless transfer technology, *Bluetooth*, print them at a studio in the city, and return the prints to customers the same or next day; *see*: http://www.afghanboxcamera.com/abcp_about_photographyinafghanistan.htm.

٢٦ Rona Naseer Ahmad introduced colour photographic development to Kabul in the mid to late 1960s after training in the process at an AGFA laboratory in Germany; *see*: http://www.afghanboxcamera.com/abcp_about_photographyinafghanistan.htm.

٢٧ A Taliban decree in December 1996 ordered that: "To prevent idolatry: [...] pictures/portraits should be abolished." In practice, the decree was inconsistently implemented across the country, and did not entail an outright photographic ban; studios were not forced to shut and photographers mostly continued to take ID portraits unhindered, though, reportedly, at times, even this activity was prohibited. An English translation of the decree appears in Edward Grazda's book, *Afghanistan Diary: 1992–2000*, New York, Powerhouse Books, 2000.

٢٨ A number of studio photographers in Kabul also testified to this fact during our research in Afghanistan in 2011 and 2012. While in the southern Afghan city of Kandahar during Taliban rule, studios would send rolls of film across the border to the Pakistani city of Quetta for development; *see*: Varadarajan, Siddharth, "Inside the Taliban: Want to have fun? Enjoy the weather...", *Times of India*, March 25th 2001.

٢٩ Our translator, Kausar Hussain, made a case in point. One Eid some years ago, a friend of his hired a 35mm camera from a studio on Cinema Road, and took numerous photographs of himself and his friends as they enjoyed a day of leisure on the holiday. When his friend's grandfather saw the photographs he insisted they be burned, as photography is *haram*, and the grandson complied.

Authors' Acknowledgements

Aqeel Ahmad
Faraz Ahmad
Fayaz Ahmad
Ijaz Ahmad
Itizaz Ahmad
Mumtaz Ahmad
Sheraz Ahmad
Amjad Ali
Aziz Ali
Muhammad Aqeel
Malik Zahid Awan
Haji Allah Birdi
Daoud
Ghulam Farooq
Malik Umar Farooq
Tanveer Hussain
Ibrahim the jeweller
Imad
Ishfaq
Haji Muhammad Iqbal &
Muhammad Zubair (Capri Studio)
Muhammad Iqbal (Kamran Studio)
Muhammad Iqbal &
Aqub (Naqash Studio)
Kamal
Amir Khan
Shah Zahin
Muhammad Naeem
Javed
Zulfiqar Khan
Bishan Lal
Abdul Latif
Muhammad Naveen
Mansoor
Aslam Tahir Moghul
Omid
Haji Pervez
Abdul 'Gul' Rab
Abdul Rashid
Abdul Rehman
Hafeez-ur-Rehman
Aziz Rehman Slonaar
Uncle Tony a.k.a. Fakhar Zaman Aker
Izzat Ullah Haqyar
Malik Usman
Tahir Usman
Abdul Wali
Muhammad Wakeel
Muhammad Waseem
Syeed Ibrat Haidar Zaidi
Muhammad Ibrahim Zia
Shoaib Zia

With special thanks to our guides,
translators and guardians
Haji Kausar Hussain &
Prince Mahir Ullah Khan

Further thanks to
Benjamin Gilmour
Edward Grazda
Catherine James
Noor Muhammad Khan
Brendan O'Hanrahan
Timothy Prous (Archive of Modern Conflict)

and to Malik Khalid Awan who passed away
before this book was published.

Photographic Credits

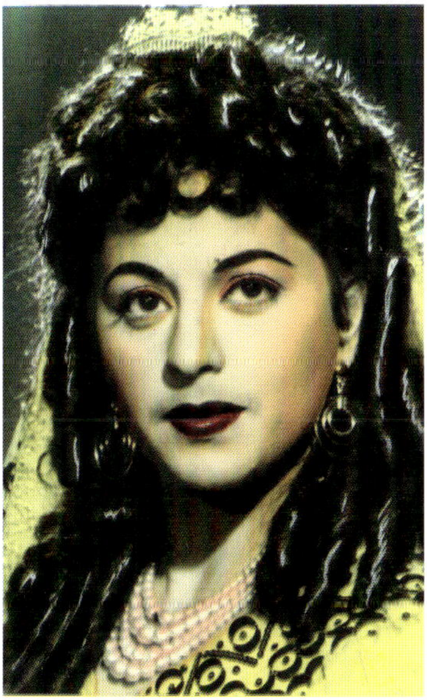

Portrait of an actress, hand-coloured by Tahir Usman.

Mumtaz Ahmad (Gul Sons studio), page 131
Lukas Birk, pages 58–59, 64–65, 78–79, 84–85, 91, 110–111, 113, 114–121, 134–135, 137–139, 151, 184–185, 194–196, 218, 225
Daoud (Welcome Studio), page 141
Ghulam Farooq (Famous Studio), pages 123, 142–143
Sean Foley, pages 145, 204–205, 207
Haji Muhammad Iqbal (Capri Studio), pages 124–129
Muhammad Iqbal (Kamran Studio), pages 95–103, 149
Muhammad Iqbal (Naqash Studio), pages 188–193
Javed (Javed Studio), pages 80, 81, 83
Abdul 'Gul' Rab (Zaidis Studio), pages 61, 62–63
Abdul Rashid (Jumbo Studio), page 71 (top left, bottom right)
Aziz Rehman Slonaar, pages 220–223
Uncle Tony a.k.a Fakhar Zaman Azer, pages 196–205
Tahir Usman (Tahir's Studio), pages 153, 155–183, 186–187, 234
Muhammad Wakeel (Jamilistan Studio), pages 2, 39–57, 66–67, 69, 73
Abdul Wali, pages 108, 109, 208–217
Muhammad Ibrahim Zia, pages 75, 77
Syeed Ibrat Haidar Zaidi (Evernew Studio), page 71 (top right, bottom left)

Images on pages 104–105, 227–233 are courtesy of author Benjamin Gilmour, www.benjamingilmour.com. The images are held in the collection of the Archive of Modern Conflict, London.

The following original images gathered by Birk & Foley are in the collection of the Archive of Modern Conflict, London; pages 93, 95–103, 149, 155–162, 165–169, 175, 177, 179, 180, 183, and The Alkazi Collection of Photography, New Delhi; pages 208–217, 220–223.

Title calligraphy: Sayed Masoom Shah

First published in India in 2018 by
Mapin Publishing Pvt. Ltd
706 Kaivanna, Panchvati, Ellisbridge
Ahmedabad 380006 INDIA
T: +91 79 40 228 228 • F: +91 79 40 228 201
E: mapin@mapinpub.com • www.mapinpub.com

in association with
PIX Publishing
E-68, Second Floor, Greater Kailash 3
New Delhi 110048, India

International Distribution
Worldwide (except North America and South Asia)
Prestel Publishing Ltd.
14–17 Wells Street
London W1T 3PD
T: +44 (0)20 7323 5004 • F: +44 (0)20 7323 0271
E: sales@prestel-uk.co.uk

North America
Antique Collectors' Club
T: +1 800 252 5231 • F: +1 413 529 0862
E: sales@antiquecc.com • www.accdistribution.com/us

South Asia
Mapin Publishing Pvt. Ltd

ISBN: 978-93-85360-46-6

Design: Sean Foley / Lukas Birk

Copy-editing: Rahaab Allana, Nandita Jaishankar
Proofreading: Neha Manke
Production: Gopal Limbad, Sukanya Baskar
Printed at Naveen Printers, New Delhi

Endpapers: Map of Pakistan and the surrounding region

PIX Publishing
www.enterpix.in

PIX has been a theme-based photography initiative since 2011, poised to investigate and archive expansive fields of contemporary photography and writing practices in India and South Asia. Focusing on a subcontinental zone that speaks to cross-cultural histories and traditions, over the last seven years, we have undertaken projects in Iran, Pakistan, Afghanistan, Nepal and Sri Lanka, and most recently, Myanmar, thereby engaging in a dialogue around photography with a transnational focus, and researching ways in which co-existing image-making practices are informed and evolve in relation to neighbouring regions.

With *Photo Peshawar*, we are pleased to announce an internationally distributed series through PIX Publishing, a new endeavour focusing on photography's little-known histories emanating from the same geographic region. We believe that all image-practices, and hence lens-based media too, communicate in culturally specific ways. At the same time, given that it is a universally accessed form, we are also keen to recalibrate traditional dichotomies within the field such as high or low – innovative and reproductive – with the inclusion of marginalised vernacular models – subcultures of the medium that have been crucial for the circulation and scrutiny of the image in the present.

In an age of simultaneity and synchronicity, the power of the photograph – or the moving image and the virtual – needs greater understanding and recognition in relation to all that is being swiftly transformed, and at times replaced – the analogue and the archive – in order to discover new lines of communication between past and present. PIX Publishing hopes to further investigate such circuits of exchange in the future.

Rahaab Allana
Founding Editor

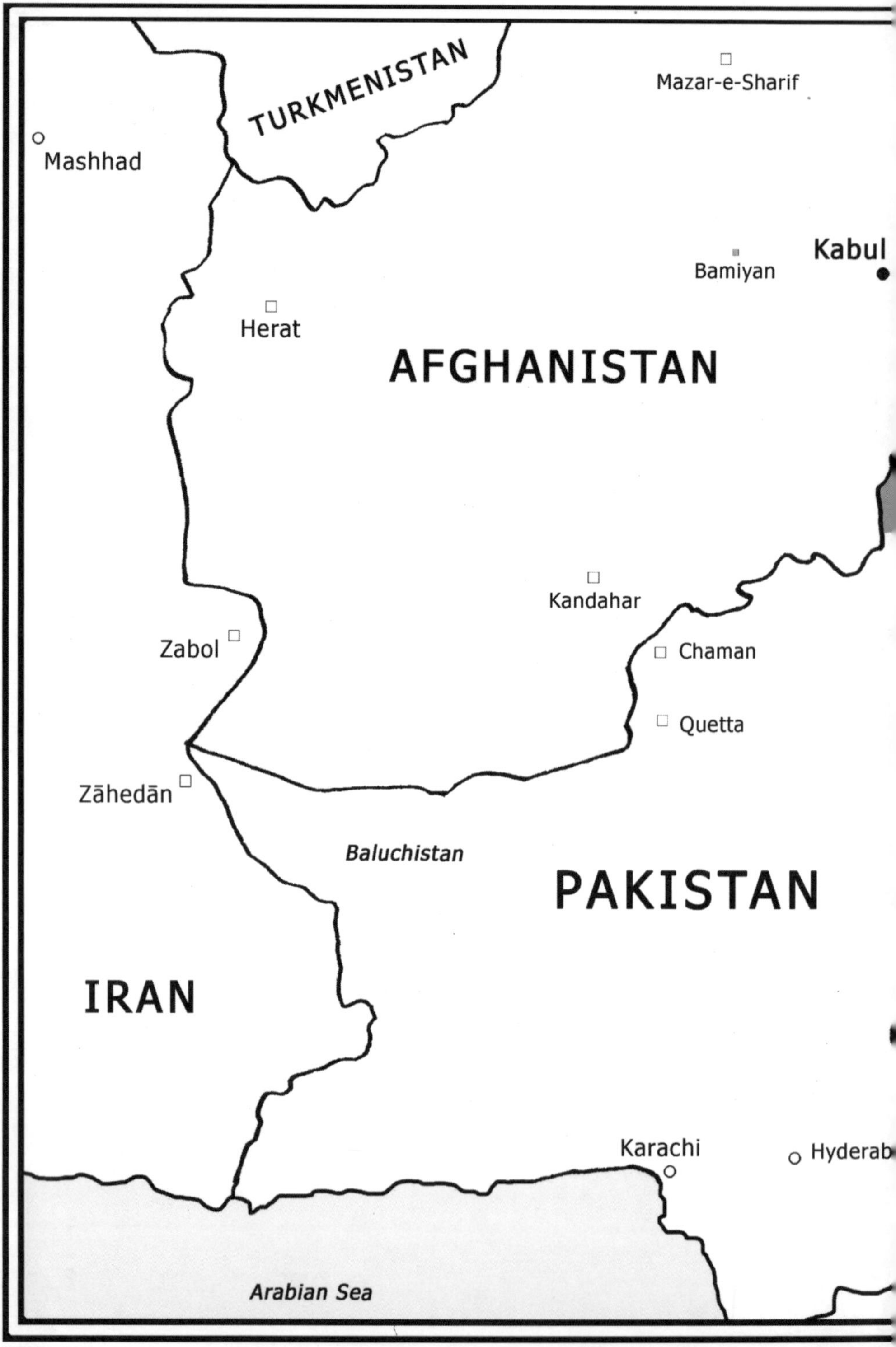
TURKMENISTAN
Mazar-e-Sharif
Mashhad
Kabul
Bamiyan
Herat
AFGHANISTAN
Kandahar
Zabol
Chaman
Quetta
Zāhedān
Baluchistan
PAKISTAN
IRAN
Karachi
Hyderab
Arabian Sea